STENGEL

His Life and Times

STENGEL

His Life and Times

ROBERT W. CREAMER

Thorndike Press • Thorndike, Maine

Library of Congress Cataloging in Publication Data:

Creamer, Robert W.
  Stengel: his life and times.

  Reprint. Originally published: New York: Simon and
Schuster, 1984.
  Includes index.
  1. Stengel, Casey.   2. Baseball — United States — Managers
— Biography.   3. New York Yankees (Baseball team) 4. Large type books
I. Title.   LT
[GV865.S8C73 1984b]   796.357'092'4 [B]   84-16469
ISBN 0-89621-569-5 (lg. print)   STE

Large Print edition available through arrangement with
Simon & Schuster, Inc.

Cover illustration by Charles Cowell.

For Martha and Jane
. . . and Jerry

CONTENTS

1 · *PRELUDE:*
Who Was Casey? What Was He?   11

2 · *FAMILY AND CHILDHOOD:*
One Very Dead Chicken   29

3 · *SCHOOL DAYS:*
"I'm Charley Stengel"   47

4 · *THE MINOR LEAGUES:*
A Coffin in Kankakee   69

5 · *MOVING ON UP:*
The Tabasco Kid's Advice   85

6 · *DEBUT IN BROOKLYN:*
Stengel the Phenom   102

7 · *SETTLING IN:*
The Good Days and the Bad   123

8 · *THE FEDERAL LEAGUE WAR:*
A Matter of Money   137

9 · UNCLE ROBBY:
Who Dropped the Grapefruit?   155

10 · THE 1916 PENNANT:
Casey Hits the Big One   180

11 · MOVING ON DOWN:
Farewell to Brooklyn   204

12 · AFTER THE WAR:
A Sparrow in His Hat   231

13 · THE LITTLE NAPOLEON:
McGraw of the Giants   248

14 · THE POLO GROUNDS:
Wake Up, Muscles!   264

15 · WINNING FOR McGRAW:
Casey Comes Through   274

16 · THE 1923 WORLD SERIES:
Stengel the Hero   298

17 · TO BOSTON AND POINTS WEST:
Mud Hen Glory   317

18 · THE 1930s:
"Is Brooklyn Still in the League?"   338

19 · DISCHARGED AGAIN:
Cheers for a Broken Leg   361

20 · COMEBACK:
Helping Out Jolly Cholly 376

21 · OAKLAND:
It's Nice to Have a Bridge Around 393

22 · THE 1949 YANKEES:
Biggest Thrill of All 407

23 · TAKING COMMAND:
It's Casey's Team Now 436

24 · GROWING YOUR OWN:
The "Instructual School" 447

25 · FIVE FLAGS AND MICKEY:
The One Disappointment 465

26 · BECOMING A LEGEND:
Stengel the Public Figure 487

27 · BILLY, PHIL AND ESTES:
"I Was No Doubt Discharged" 503

28 · SIGNS OF DISINTEGRATION:
The Long Yankee Slump 526

29 · THE LAST WORLD SERIES:
A Shortstop's Throat 539

30 · OUT AND IN:
Goodbye Yankees, Hello Mets 552

31 · *A WAY TO RETIRE:*
One Broken Hip   577

32 · *DO NOT GO GENTLE:*
Talking, Talking, Talking   595

33 · *CODA:*
The End of a Man   630

AUTHOR'S NOTE   636

1 PRELUDE: WHO WAS CASEY? WHAT WAS HE?

Casey Stengel naked was a sight to remember.

At seventy, holding court after a game for a retinue of sportswriters in his office off the New York Yankees' dressing room, he would in time begin to undress. He'd take off his uniform shirt and his spikes with the rubber heels, still making telling points in his heavy, gravelly, nonstop voice. He'd take off his uniform pants, pausing perhaps to gesture in his argument. He had a lot of gestures, little flips of the hand, pulling his forearm suddenly close to his chest, a curious way of raising his chin high, his mouth closed in a grim, serious line, his eyes half closed, as he listened to someone else. He'd go on undressing, taking off his long-sleeved baseball undershirt and his baseball stockings, taking off his underwear pants, taking off the athletic supporter he wore as though he too were going into ac-

11

tion on the ball field.

Then, naked except for slippers, he'd march out of his office and through the players' locker room, a towel hanging from one arm like a toga, looking for all the world like a Roman senator on his way to the baths. You felt that he was accompanied by a covey of courtiers as he trudged on (although it was usually only one or two last writers trying to get a clear answer), his head held high, the fierce nose canted toward a distant horizon, the diminished buttocks of age following sadly after. His long-torsoed, short-legged body had an old, dead, pale tone, gray hair on his chest and at the crotch blending with the pallor of his skin, like old snow after a few days of residual fallout. The ravages of time had pulled and tweaked the muscles of his arms and legs and trunk, leaving gullies and ravines and potholes. His right leg, broken in an accident in Boston years before, had a startling clifflike protuberance halfway down the shin, where the broken ends of the tibia had grown together unevenly in the healing.

He was a bizarre spectacle, this naked old man parading through a room full of hard-muscled young athletes, but Stengel never gave a sign that he recognized the incongruity. On the contrary, he was vain about his body, even as an old man, as he was vain about many things. He loved to pose for photographers, mugging extravagantly, twisting his leathery face into grotesque winks, wearing odd bits of clothing for props, doing almost anything the photographers wanted when he was in the mood to do it. And he was something special for them to photograph, with his craggy seamed face, jutting jaw, wide mobile mouth, huge hooked nose, amazingly blue eyes, great pendulous ears, long arms, crabbed stooped body.

On the field he was almost quaint in appearance, wearing his uniform knickers tucked in at the knee, the way knickers should be worn, the way they were worn in his youth before the fashion changed and ballplayers began to extend the legs of their baseball pants almost to their ankles. And Casey wore his dark-blue Yankee outer stockings full-length, showing the barest cuticle of white understocking just above the shoes, whereas his players pulled up the stirrups of the outer stockings to the stretching point, so that they seemed to be wearing white socks with just a narrow black clock up the sides to the bottom of the uniform pants.

Stengel wore good clothes off the field, even though his ungainly figure and leathery,

13

worn features tended to make his expensive suits look like something bought off the rack in a cheap men's store. He always looked rumpled in a baseball uniform, and when he put on street clothes he looked a little like the hired man decked out in his store-bought Sunday-go-to-meeting suit. Nonetheless, his clothes *were* expensive. He dyed his hair (he never admitted he did) in an effort to turn the encroaching whiteness to something closer to the blond-brown (mud-gutter blond, that shade used to be called) of his youth. In his seventies he still did push-ups on the floor of whatever hotel room he was staying in, and he was proud of the strength his tough old body retained. He'd grab your arm sometimes to hold your attention, and more often than not he'd give it a squeeze to emphasize an argument — or maybe just to hurt you a little, to make you wince or pull away, to remind you (or himself) of the strength he had when he was young. He had a cruel streak ("He's a funny guy," wrote his antagonist Dave Egan of the *Boston Record* in 1942, "always funny at somebody else's expense . . . always funny in his cruel and malicious way"), and he was not at all reluctant to enjoy another's discomfort. Some of his players hated him for that, but Stengel never seemed to mind their antipathy. He'd been around too long to be upset by transient dislikes.

Yet he had keen awareness of other people's dignity — those whose dignity, or right to dignity, he respected. During ceremonies before an old-timers' game in Yankee Stadium in 1954, when Stengel, then a relatively youthful sixty-four, was managing the Yankees, Connie Mack tottered onto the field to be introduced. Mack, ninety-two, had retired as manager of the Philadelphia Athletics only a few years before, after fifty consecutive seasons managing that team. It was a hot mid-summer day, and Stengel, not yet the perennial part of old-timers' doings that he would be in later years, was in the tangle of people in the Yankee dugout — old ballplayers, current ballplayers, officials, reporters, hangers-on. After Mack had been introduced and applauded, he was left alone, blinking up at the huge crowd as other old-timers were introduced, one by one. No one seemed to notice Mack except Stengel, who stirred restlessly in the dugout and then prodded an aide. "Get that old man out of the sun," he said. Gently, without fuss, Mr. Mack was led off the field and into the shade of the dugout, where Stengel sat talking quietly with him while the ceremonies droned on.

Casey respected history — baseball history — and Mack was part of it. He liked everything about the game of baseball, all its subtleties and complexities, and he particularly admired people in the game who knew what they were doing and why they were doing it. On that same old-timers' day, Stengel stood up in the dugout to watch the two-inning exhibition game played by the heroes of the past, looking out at the field over the broad backs of his young Yankee players, most of whom were sitting up on the dugout steps to watch. The players grew particularly attentive when Joe DiMaggio batted against Carl Hubbell. Hubbell, a superb left-handed pitcher for the New York Giants twenty years earlier, was in his fifties and had been out of the game a long time. DiMaggio, barely forty, had retired only two or three years before and was still strong and capable, the hero of the day for the roaring stadium crowd and for the current Yankees, too, many of whom had been his teammates. Hubbell had a 2–0 lead, but there were two men on base.

DiMaggio was greeted with tumultuous applause, and the crowd waited for him to hit one a long way for old times' sake. Hubbell, still as lean and trim as he had been in his playing days, his pitching motion as elegant as ever, kept throwing screwballs to DiMaggio, pitches that broke down and away from the batter. DiMaggio, waiting for a ball that he could pull toward the left-field seats, let them go by. The umpire called two of the pitches strikes and three of them balls. Hubbell threw again, same pitch, same spot. The umpire was in a dilemma. He didn't want to call DiMaggio out on strikes, but the big crowd didn't want Joe to walk either — they wanted to see him hit one. Before he could decide what to call the pitch, Mel Allen, the Yankee broadcaster who was handling the public address system during the old-timers' game, blithely called out, "Ball three!" again. The crowd cheered, because it meant Joe was still up. Hubbell threw another screwball to the same spot and another one, and Allen continued to call out "Ball three!" on each pitch.

The crowd was laughing, but in the Yankee dugout the players began grumbling. One of them called, "Come on, Hubbell! Put it over!" Behind him stood Stengel, his arms folded, an admiring little smile on his face as he watched Hubbell pitch. "You don't think he's gonna give him anything good to hit, do you?" he said.

The player looked around, startled. He

hadn't noticed what Casey had been appreciating, that Hubbell was as serious and gifted a practitioner of his craft as DiMaggio was of his, and that he was showing what *he* could do too. Finally he eased up, laid one through the middle, and DiMaggio lifted a long fly to left that reached the seats for a home run. Three runs scored. The fans were delighted. They had seen Joe D's graceful swing and they had seen him send a ball a long way.

Stengel was pleased too. He had been uneasy in his relationship with DiMaggio during the three seasons Joe was under him as a player, but that didn't matter now. What he had enjoyed was seeing a master craftsman demonstrate a fine point in the sometimes delicate art of baseball. Not many in the stadium that day savored what Hubbell had done before DiMaggio's homer but Stengel did.

He always saw a lot of things in baseball that others didn't. He was remarkably intelligent, although with little education beyond the minimum forced on him in grammar and high school and what he picked up during two semesters or so as a dental student when he was a young man. He had a prodigious memory, a startling ability to recall relevant detail. In baseball he had the kind of understanding of a situation that is often described as intuitive — immediate comprehension of a problem and its solution without recourse to orderly, reasoned analysis — but that is probably just rapid-fire, computer-speed deduction derived from long experience. The best chess players occasionally play this way, making moves they can't immediately explain or justify; Stengel did the same in baseball, although he would often go on to explain complex or simple moves in long-winded, roundabout lectures that amused and diverted his listeners without necessarily informing them.

His explanations did not necessarily convince anyone, not even baseball adepts. Al Lopez, one of the most intelligent and successful of big- league managers, played under Casey at Brooklyn and Boston in the 1930s, managed against him in the American League in the 1950s (and was the only manager to interrupt Casey's flow of pennants) and was his good friend. Yet Lopez once said, "I swear, I don't understand some of the things he does when he manages. I've tried to figure them out, but they just don't make sense." One of the more famous of such dubious moves occurred in the 1951 World Series between the Yankees and the New York Giants. In the final game of the Series the Yankees were leading 4–1 in the ninth inning. The strength of the Giants' batting order was up, and the first three men singled, loading the bases with nobody out. The Giants thus had the tying runs on base, the winning run at bat, and their two most powerful hitters, Monte Irvin and Bobby Thomson, both right-handed batters, coming to the plate. John Sain, a right-hander, had been pitching for the Yankees, but Stengel took him out after the Giants loaded the bases. Instead of following standard baseball theory by bringing in another right-hander to pitch to the right-handed Irvin and Thomson — there were three or four available to him, including the redoubtable Allie Reynolds, who had beaten the Giants soundly a couple of days earlier — Stengel stunned baseball people by calling on an undistinguished left-hander named Bob Kuzava, who had not previously appeared in the Series. The first batter, Irvin, flied deep to left off Kuzava, scoring the man from third and advancing the other runners to second and third. The second batter, Thomson, also flied to left, driving in another run and bringing the score to 4–3, with the tying run on second base. The third successive right-handed batter, a pinch hitter named Sal Yvars, who had batted .317 that year, hit a hard, sinking line drive to right field off Kuzava which was caught for the final out.

Stengel's tactic had worked — somehow. Three hard-hit balls, but the Giants had not been able to tie the score and the Yankees had won the game and the World Series. No one has ever been able to fully decipher Stengel's tortuous reasoning for bringing in Kuzava. Perhaps he had anticipated that the Giants' right-handed batters would be likely to hit fly balls that would be caught without too much trouble in the spacious Yankee Stadium outfield. But how could he be so sure that not one of those fly balls would go through for a double or a triple or reach the seats for a home run?

Besides, ground balls are what you want in a situation like that, grounders that will let your infielders come up with a double play while a run is scoring, grounders that, even if one did get through into the outfield for a base hit, would most likely score only one run, not the devastating three or four that a long hit might bring across. Stengel could point out that Kuzava had the best earned-run average on his staff that year and had excellent control, a desirable talent when the bases are full. But even so, a lefty? And, after all, he *did* give up three hard-hit balls.

Nonetheless — and this is where Al Lopez would shake his head in wonder — it worked. Kuzava *had* saved the game, the Giants had not caught up, and the Yankees had won the World Series.

The only fair conclusion is that Stengel *sensed* something deep in the information bank of the runaway computer that was his brain, some retrieval of data on what the Giants' right-handed batters had done or could do combined with what his left-hander had done or could do, tied in with the lovely spaciousness of the outfield in Yankee Stadium and the cushion of a three-run lead. *Whirr, bzzzz, click-click-click,* and Kuzava was the answer.

Baseball absorbed Stengel. It was his life, and if that sounds like a cliché it is still true. He was born in Kansas City, Missouri, in 1890 and died in Glendale, California, in 1975, and for most of the eighty-five years in between baseball mattered more to him than almost anything else. During his life he grew famous and came to know and talk with kings, presidents, generals, actors, writers. That was important to him — he *liked* being famous — but it was secondary to baseball. Baseball was the thread his life hung on. "He doesn't talk about anything else," his wife said. "He doesn't think about anything else. He has only one life, and that's baseball. That way he's happy, and I'm happy for him."

John McGraw liked horseracing and gambling. Babe Ruth golfed, bowled, hunted, ate, drank and chased women. Ted Williams was almost as fascinated by the intricacies of fishing as he was by hitting. Reggie Jackson likes the glitter of the social ramble. George Brett talks earnestly of settling down on a ranch someday. Stengel said, "I don't play cards, I don't play golf, and I don't go to the picture show. All that's left is baseball."

He did like to drink and had the reputation of absorbing large amounts of liquor (bourbon, usually) without adverse effect. One night during a World Series in Los Angeles a sportswriter taking a shortcut down a flight of service stairs in a hotel was stunned to find Stengel on the bare cement floor of a landing, his shoulders and head leaning against the wall, his eyes closed. "I thought he was dead," the writer said. He shook Casey, and Stengel aroused himself, mumbled something, shook off the offer of assistance and made his way stiffly and awkwardly on up the staircase to his room. "I thought he was sick," the writer said. "I felt bad. I couldn't help but think he was getting close to the end." The next morning the writer, not feeling too perky himself, made his way downstairs for coffee and there was Stengel at a table, eating breakfast, waving his hands and talking, apparently as sound as ever.

Some of his friends insist that his drinking was exaggerated. "He drank to be sociable," Lopez claimed. "It was his way of staying up all night," Lee MacPhail said. "While other people were drinking, he was talking."

He was always talking and performing. During a game, when he came out of the dugout to talk to his pitcher or argue with an umpire, the crowd sat up and paid attention. When he spoke — at banquets or luncheons or just sitting around a table — he performed with his body as well as with his mouth, making his odd little gestures, lifting his head this way and that. His speeches rambled incredibly, sliding from one subject to another in midsentence as one thought led him to another. "Casey babbles in front of an audience," a writer once claimed, "because he gets flustered. He's afraid to stop, so he says anything that comes into his head." Another newspaperman said, "If somebody talks as though he's crazy, there are only two possible explanations. Either he *is* crazy, or he's putting on an act. No one ever accused Stengel of being crazy."

Much of the attention he received focused on him as Stengel the Clown. He was a very funny man, a quick-witted wisecracker, a physical comic, a natural mime who could wonderfully mimic other people. And his restless energy and exuberant spirits led him into one amusing scrape after another. "There was never a day around Casey that I didn't laugh," said his old Brooklyn teammate Zack Wheat.

Yet he was always serious about the game of baseball, about how it should be played, and particularly about his role as manager. Red Smith wrote, "It is erroneous and unjust to conceive of Casey Stengel merely as a clown. He is something else entirely — a competitor who always had fun competing, a fighter with a gift of laughter."

He could be clear and even concise when he had to be. Red Barber said that when he switched from the Dodgers to become a Yankee broadcaster after the 1953 season, he had to learn a lot in a hurry about his new ball club. Early in spring training he approached Casey and asked him if he could spare some time someday to go over his players. Stengel understood at once that Barber wanted to be briefed on the particular talents and on-field idiosyncrasies of the various Yankee players, things that would help the broadcaster as he did the play-by-play of a game. "Sure," he said. "Let's do it right now." The two sat together on a bench, and Casey took a small printed roster of the team from a back pocket. "He went down the list man by man in detail," Barber said. "There was no double-talk, none at all. In thirty minutes he gave me a detailed, analytical report on every last man on his roster. It was remarkable. And all season long, everything he told me about every man held up."

On the other hand, sometimes when he tried to explain something precisely, his efforts to enhance his listeners' knowledge would get hopelessly tangled. There was a pronounced stream-of-consciousness effect in his monologues, one thing reminding him of another *ad infinitum*, although he usually tried, sometimes with hilarious success, to get back to the starting subject at the very end of his answer. If you had a general idea of what he was talking about — John McGraw's theories of baserunning, say, or Mickey Mantle's speed — it wasn't always that hard to follow him, but at times he could be very confusing. He would switch from point A to related point B and on to remotely connected point C without bothering to explain the reasons for the sudden switches, and it was easy to get lost. At a baseball dinner early in 1954, talking about the rings members of the winning team in the World Series receive, he said, "That ring don't cost so much. I got four or five rings and don't know whether I'm going to wear five of them when I go out. Unless you're broke, the ring is the best thing you can get which money comes in handy all the time. If a player don't shoot he can go and play against us which is all right in the first place too. The situation is for five years and they still haven't found the end of it, the other guys. They say the owners are rich, so what? We must have the umpires, not the same ones. It's the money the Yankees got. On the ball club you can't write it all down. You do it. So they say it's the lively ball and the damn bunting. . . . What about the shortstop Rizzuto who got nothing but daughters but throws out the left-handed hitters in the double play?"

Casey could be wildly amusing, but there was burning ambition in him too. He enjoyed being funny, but he wanted to be recognized for his accomplishments, which were many. He faced a lot of problems in his life, and he coped with them. "I'm a man that's been up

27

and down," he told Harry Paxton, when Paxton was working with him on the autobiography Casey published in 1961. He never gave in. He kept coming back. And always in baseball.

2 FAMILY AND CHILDHOOD: ONE VERY DEAD CHICKEN

Casey Stengel's boyhood in Kansas City was one of sustained happiness, filled with adventure and accomplishment and a kind of aggressive, reckless joy. It may be a bit of a stretch to drag Mark Twain in here, but that other son of Missouri was only fifty-four when Stengel was born, and Casey would be twenty and a professional ballplayer before Twain died, so they were in a sense contemporaries. Life in Missouri had changed drastically in the half century between Twain's birth on the state's eastern edge and Stengel's on its western. When Twain was born in 1835, Missouri was a frontier state, one of the smallest in population of the twenty-four then in the Union. By the time Stengel was born in 1890, the state had grown tremendously and had become one of the most important in the country (fifth in population among the forty-three that comprised the United States when

Casey was born). Yet there were strong similarities between Twain's day and his. Despite the spreading network of railroads, the presence of electricity, the growth of factories, the proliferation of towns, Missouri was still largely open, with plenty of land, plenty of fields, plenty of big yards around the houses in the towns, empty places to play in and explore even in the heart of a city. Sam Clemens and Charley Stengel were both products of a young, brash, confident, expanding society; both were younger brothers who were stronger, more energetic, more talented and more accomplished than their older siblings, for whom they had a tolerant, almost paternal, affection.

Twain and Stengel each went a long way in the world, achieved fame and fortune far from home, died half a continent away from Missouri, and yet each retained to the death the assured, confident, sometimes outrageous but always at-home-in-the-world personality they had acquired in their Missouri boyhoods. They found vigorous life all around them as they were growing up — colorful people, memorable places, lively language — and they grabbed hold with both hands and never let go: "The place where I am is the place where I ought to be." Both consciously played a public role, but neither could be called a poseur. Both were thought of primarily as purveyors of humor, yet both were intensely serious about their work, and both had a hard, almost brutal streak of reality in their makeup, coupled with a sarcastic cutting contempt for people who didn't measure up, those whom Twain called jackasses and Stengel road apples.

Stengel's background was middle-class, Middle West, classic middle-American. His ancestors came to the United States in the middle of the nineteenth century in the first great wave of immigration from northern Europe. Political turbulence — 1848 was a year of unrest and rebellion throughout Europe — and the threat of obligatory military service were probably among the reasons why Casey's German great-grandfather decided to pay attention to the sales pitch of the agents for railroad and steamship companies who regularly roamed Europe drumming up trade. In any case, in 1850 he took his wife and four children from their home in Bavaria, in southern Germany, and made the long journey across the Atlantic to the new world. They landed in New York City, took a train upstate to stay for a time with relatives near Utica, New York, soon moved on and by

1855 were settled on a farm near Rock Island in northwestern Illinois, not far from the Mississippi River.

Karl Stengel, Casey's grandfather, who was only twelve or thirteen when his family left Germany, reached the age of twenty-one in 1859 and, his name now Americanized to Charles, married the daughter of a neighboring family of German immigrants. A year later he fathered a son, named Louis, who was to be Casey's father. When Louis was four, Charles Stengel died of tuberculosis at the age of twenty-six, and a few years later his widow married another German-immigrant farmer named Charles Wolff, Casey's step-grandfather.

Meanwhile, harsh economic conditions in Ireland, most dramatically evident in the potato famine of the 1840s, prompted people named Jordan and Dillon, among thousands of others, to leave Ireland and follow a similar route across the Atlantic and out to the Midwest — to Davenport, Iowa, just north of Rock Island on the other side of the Mississippi, which in one of its great meandering curves flows almost due west at this point. A disenchantment with the land that had failed them at home led most Irish immigrants to abandon all ideas of farming and to settle in the cities. A few moved on restlessly, beyond the major cities, many getting ahead of the priests, so that, as Thomas Beer wrote in his book *The Mauve Decade*, "families named O'Donnell, Connor and Delahanty are now discovered drowsing in Protestant pews."

A cluster of Irish, mostly tradesmen, settled in Davenport around 1850. Because they did not have to learn a new language, the English-speaking Irish moved quickly to positions of importance in the rapidly growing world of new immigrants. John B. Jordan became a merchant and a successful businessman in Davenport and married the sister of John F. Dillon, a prominent lawyer who served as counsel for the railroads and later became a judge, first on the Iowa supreme court and later on the U.S. Circuit Court of Appeals in St. Louis. The Jordans had several children, among them a daughter Jennie, who was born in Davenport in 1861.

With people pouring into the vanishing frontier and the towns growing in importance, Charles Wolff, over on the Illinois side of the river, decided to leave farming and move into Rock Island. His stepson Louis must have welcomed the change, for family tradition says that when he lived on the farm he had to walk eight miles back and forth to

attend grade school. Wolff opened a gun-
smith shop down near the riverfront, not far
from a wharf where the ferry docked that
plied the Mississippi between Rock Island
and Davenport. Trains crossed the river over
a bridge, but the ferry was the usual form of
local transportation back and forth, and social
intercourse between the towns was common.
As the years passed, Louis Stengel met and
courted Jennie Jordan. Jennie's family was
better established and more prosperous than
the Wolff-Stengel family, and Louis undoubtedly felt pressured by a need to keep up
with the Jordans. Possibly egged on a bit by
them, maybe even helped by their influence,
he applied for and got a job as an agent with
the Joseph Stiebel Insurance Company in
Kansas City, Missouri. Landing that job was
apparently the catalyst for the wedding, because after Louis, twenty-six, and Jennie,
twenty-five, were married at the beginning of
1886 they moved to Kansas City and settled
there, three hundred miles southwest of the
Rock IslandDavenport ferry.

Near the end of 1886 their first child, a girl
they named Louise, was born, and a year
later a son they named Grant. Their third and
last child, a boy two and a half years younger
than Grant, was born on July 30, 1890, and

was named Charles Dillon Stengel — Charles for both his paternal grandfather and step-grandfather, Dillon for his maternal grand-mother's maiden name, not to mention Uncle John Dillon, the judge. The new baby was called Charley by the family, then and always.

Kansas City was only about fifty years old when Charley Stengel was born. It had formally changed its name from "city of Kansas" to Kansas City only a year earlier. In the previous quarter century it had grown from a frontier jumping-off point to the Wild West into a reasonably modern community. Most of its streets were still unpaved in 1890 and there were great swatches of open ground, but trolley-car lines laced the city together and trains from the east and west, north and south, rolled in and out of town day and night. Kansas City was the distribution center for a rich agricultural area, with the emphasis on livestock, and manufacturing and business in general were becoming important. It was a metropolis, although it retained strong overtones of small-town living.

Louis Stengel was not a sensational success as an insurance agent, but the family survived and got along comfortably. Rents were low, and while the family moved several times during Charley's boyhood they always seemed to end up in a roomy house with a big yard. In looking back at those days Stengel would occasionally refer to a "rich boy" or "rich people," but when he was a boy differences in wealth and position were not factors of great importance. Certain streets, such as Independence Avenue, had big homes, but for the most part the same neighborhoods embraced people of different economic levels. "There'd be poor people who didn't have anything," Stengel said, "others who had a little, others who had everything." His father made enough to get by, and there was no sense of deprivation. They had a warm, pleasant family life. Louis Stengel had a farm boy's appreciation of food, and he spent a good part of his modest income making sure that he and his family ate well. He'd do a lot of the family food buying, going to this market and that one, appraising the vegetables and fruit and meat with a farmer's eye, buying the best he could find. He liked fresh fish from local streams and ponds, and in the winter, following the wisdom of the time, which held that you needed fresh beef in cold weather, he'd buy steak. Steak was not a particularly expensive item in the meat-packing center that Kansas City was, and the family had it comparatively often. Louis also kept hens in the backyard for fresh eggs and an occasional chicken dinner (more of a treat then than beef), and he often kept a cow in an adjacent lot for fresh milk and butter and for the few extra dollars he'd make selling surplus milk.

Louis was an amiable, easygoing man, not very ambitious, with great affection for his family and not much interest in imposing strict discipline. There was no strong family feeling for religion, for instance. Jennie's religious heritage was Catholic and the Stengels' was Lutheran, but in Kansas City Charley went to St. Mark's Episcopal Church for a while, at least while they lived in the neighborhood. In short, while Stengel's background was not *non*religious, the family was not intense about church allegiance.

Young Charley resembled his father physically ("He was built strong, something like myself," Stengel recalled, "and he had large ears, which I do"), but his lively, energetic mother probably had greater influence on him. As her youngest child he was her obvious favorite, and you remember that Freud said a confident man is one who is secure in the knowledge of his mother's love. For another, while he was built like his father, he looked like his mother. A photograph of Jennie Stengel as a young woman bears a strong resemblance to her famous son, even to fairly prominent ears peeking through the mass of curls about her head. Lest you jump to the conclusion that Stengel's mother was a bizarre-looking woman (she looked like *Casey?*) you should know that in his youth Stengel was a handsome, fine-looking man. She was friendly and gregarious and loved having her children bring their friends home to play. "The best thing I had," Stengel said, "was that the family allowed everybody to come to our home. My mother always liked everyone in the neighborhood, and they could all come and use our yard."

Jennie was also a skilled and generous cook, one who did things like making her own preserves, her own ketchup, her own soups. She baked remarkable lemon pies, although lemons were relatively scarce commodities in Kansas City. "We liked everything my mother cooked," said Stengel. "She put out the best meals in the neighborhood." In his old age he rhapsodized over her mashed potatoes ("We'd push mashed potato on the plate, drown it in gravy, and put a big hunk of steak on top"), and was moved to lecture on the nutritional value of gravy:

"Nowadays people say, don't eat gravy, it's bad for you, but I've been taking gravy all my life." The obvious moral was, "I'm still here, but a lot of people who didn't eat gravy aren't."

Stengel's closest friend as he grew up was his older brother, Grant. Charley was precociously big for his age, with a broad chest and thick arms and legs, whereas Grant was lithe and slender. As a result there was little difference in size despite the two-and-a-half-year difference in age, and they played together constantly. They played cowboys and Indians and cops and robbers, alone or with other children. Their particular heroes were the outlaw James brothers, Jesse and Frank, who grew up not far from Kansas City, and the equally infamous Younger gang. They played hide and seek. They played tag. They played baseball. They played shinny, a primitive form of field hockey in which they used rough sticks to hit a crushed can that served as the puck. Stengel said it resembled the game of hurling, which he saw for the first time in 1924, when he visited Ireland.

They roller-skated on flagstone sidewalks on simple skates they clamped to their shoes. Such skates were not free-rolling affairs but stiffly moving devices in which the wheel bearing turned directly on the axle. To lubricate the cumbersome wheels, Charley and Grant and their friends would lie down between the trolley tracks when the cars weren't coming, poke a stick down through a slit in the surface and scoop grease from the underground cables that were used to pull the trolley cars along.

They rode other kids' bicycles and had at least one bicycle of their own — a tandem that their father gave them one Christmas, possibly because he couldn't afford a bike for each of them. The tandem led to furious arguments as to who had to ride in back (the boy in front got to do the steering). They raised pigeons, trained their dog, Sport, to climb ladders and do other tricks, shot the air rifles their Grandfather Wolff sent them at Christmas, and in winter ice-skated or went sledding *en masse* with other kids (a new sled at Christmas was a glamorous event), or made ice slides, or had snowball fights. Some of their exploits sound like adventures out of old-time comic strips. Fifteen or twenty boys would build a snow fort along one of the busier streets and wait for a horse-drawn wagon to come by. Often the teamster would have a clay pipe clenched between his teeth as he handled the reins. The kids would fire snowballs at the teamster, trying at first to knock the pipe out of his mouth, then just throwing at him and the wagon for the hell of it. If their aim was bad and the snowballs missed, the teamster would seldom do more than curse a little. But if he was hit, more often than not he'd stop his team, hop off the wagon and angrily chase the boys. "We usually got away," Stengel remembered, "but once in a while they'd catch one or two of us and beat us up."

Stengel belonged for a time to the Brotherhood of St. Andrew, a boys' society at St. Mark's Church, which held its meetings on Wednesday nights. The director of the group was a man named McKinnon, who wore a high silk hat to church. Even though the boys got along with McKinnon, and knew his son John, who later played baseball with Stengel at Central High School, when it snowed they would lay an ambush for him after the meeting was over, waiting in hiding outside the church hall until Mr. McKinnon left the building to walk home. They'd throw snowballs at him, trying to hit the silk hat. *Just* like the comic strips.

"Mischievous" is what they called rambunctious kids in those days. A genuine juvenile delinquent would have been called a bad boy, an opprobrious term. Charley and Grant never got to that stage, but they did manage to get into, or cause, a fair amount of turmoil. When they were very small and the family was on one of its periodic trips to visit the grandparents (the mother's folks in Davenport, the father's across the river in Rock Island), Grant, always amiable, was pulling four-year-old Charley in a little wagon along some trolley tracks in Rock Island. As they passed a ground-level ditch filled with water, the wagon tipped and Charley fell in. Grant, who couldn't swim, could do nothing, but a man passing by saw what had happened and pulled Charley out. The Rock Island paper reported that "little Charles Stengel was saved from drowning," the first time Casey's name ever appeared in print.

He got in trouble over in Davenport, too. He liked to hang around with his Grandfather Jordan, who was retired. Grandpa chewed tobacco, and Charley would pretend to chew and spit, too. Grandpa also had close-cropped hair, whereas Charley had a full head of long blond curls. When Charley said to Grandpa, "I want hair like yours," Grandpa gave him some money and sent him to a nearby barber shop. When he came home with his head shorn, his mother screamed in anguish, and so did his aunt and his grandmother, and all hell broke loose. The ladies scolded Charley and berated Grandpa when they discovered that he was responsible, and they went down to the barbershop and gathered locks of the boy's hair from the floor. His mother kept the blond ringlets in an envelope for years.

One Christmas, Grandpa Wolff sent Grant and Charley toy pistols, blank pistols armed only with powder held in by wadding. For some reason, possibly to see what kind of noise or flash would result, Charley decided one day to pick the wad out of the charge. He broke the pistol open, but as he poked at the wad something happened, the pistol went off, and the unrestrained wad buried itself in the palm of the boy's hand. Too scared to tell anyone, he said nothing for a few days until the hand became infected and was swollen to twice its normal size. His mother noticed it, found out what had happened and in a great state of concern took him to a doctor. Blood poisoning was a real and present danger in those pre-antibiotic days. After examining the wound, the doctor pressed the boy's fingers back, flattening the palm, and the pressure forced the wad to pop out. The doctor cleaned and bandaged the wound, and in a short time the hand was as good as new.

Along with teetering on the edge of physical disaster, Charley and Grant did other things that got them into trouble. They tried, occasionally with success, to lure other people's pigeons into their loft, justifying such kidnapping on the dubious grounds that others swiped their birds in the same way. Sometimes their father would give them a few pennies as a bonus if they could coax extra milk from the cow, which gave the family more milk to sell. The boys discovered that they could augment their income by lacing the milk with water from the rain barrel. It worked fine until customers began to complain about the thinness of the milk. Mr. Stengel argued that the milk couldn't be thin, that it came from an excellent Jersey cow, but then he discovered what his young racketeers were doing and for once in his life lost his temper with his sons.

He never caught on to another trick they pulled. The father had become interested in cockfighting and had bought a few birds that he entered in fights at a cockpit near Independence, just east of Kansas City. One cock turned out to be a capable battler. Charley and Grant had heard their father boast about the bird's exploits, but they were too small to go with him to see it fight. So they decided to stage a fight at home in their own chicken coop. They took the fighting cock from its cage and put it in the pen with the domestic hens and roosters. Quite a battle ensued, with the result an upset. The domestic chickens ganged up on the fighting cock and killed it. When Mr. Stengel came home that night and found his champion dead, he was distressed and confused. He was astonished that it had been killed by amiable barnyard fowl, but, more than that, he could not understand how it could have escaped from its cage and made its way over the high fence around the chicken coop. Charley and Grant were all innocence — *they* didn't know what had happened. Maybe the cock had broken open the cage door, they said, and maybe it had made a big flying leap over the fence to get at the chickens. Their father couldn't completely accept that explanation, but he didn't seriously challenge them about it.

Along with other kids, Grant and Charley had a sort of continuing war with grown-ups. There was a nine-o'clock curfew for kids in Kansas City, and just before nine boys would be sprinting down streets to get home before the cops saw them. The police were the boys' natural enemy, although they seem to have been more benevolent than harsh. When Charley and his brother and a couple of other kids were caught swiping an ice-cream freezer from the back porch of a house in which a big party was going on, the cop who nabbed them merely confiscated the ice cream, took their names and sent them home; he reported the crime to the principal of the school the boys went to, and the principal ordered them to make a public apology. That was fairly serious, because their parents learned about it then.

3 SCHOOL DAYS: "I'M CHARLEY STENGEL"

Grade school was painful for Charley Stengel, sometimes literally so. The principal of his grammar school would whip misbehaving students with a thin wooden switch, or sometimes, Casey claimed, with a slender rubber hose. Parents didn't object — children were supposed to do what their teachers told them to do — but Stengel's memory of it was not warm, nostalgic, condescending, or forgiving. "You remember the names of the schoolteachers that had little love for you," he said, adding that the principal's name was Mrs. Buchanan.

He was no student, and he had the added handicap of being left-handed in a right-handed world. His first-grade teacher made him write with his right hand. He never became proficient at it and he put much of the onus for his lackadaisical work in school on his inability to write swiftly and smoothly.

"Anything you can't do well and don't enjoy, you generally fall behind in," he observed. The subject of handwriting also served as inspiration for a display of Stengelian logic. "I know many people right now," he told Harry Paxton, "intellectual men that can dictate a letter amazing and be outstanding people to stand up and give you a line of conversation and wonderful English, when they sign their name you can't read it. I don't blame Mrs. Kennedy for making me change over. When I got into baseball I thought it was a great thing that she made me write right-handed because I became a good fielder after being an awkward kid because I could use my right hand better. I stayed left-handed in throwing and hitting but in catching the ball I naturally had to use my right hand, and because of my penmanship I was more agile with my right hand than any person who had stayed left-handed in everything. So that helped me more as a ballplayer than writing ever would."

The dominant bully at school was a boy five years older than Stengel named Ivan Olson, known as Ivy. Ivy Olson was the toughest kid in school, despite his odd name. "They let him be the boss," Stengel recalled, "because he *was* the boss." One of the games the boys played was a reverse type of tug o' war. Instead of having two teams at either end of a rope, pulling, these teams lined up ropeless along a wooden fence and pushed. Olson ran the game. If he felt a boy wasn't pushing hard enough, he'd pull him out of the line and shove another into his place. "If it was you he was replacing," Stengel said, "you wouldn't say no, because he threw you around. He was the strongest boy in the school." Olson was also a baseball player, a fine one who began playing professional ball when Charley Stengel was still in school. They were to meet again later.

The playground was thus a kind of prison. Away from school was where the fun was. Charley and Grant were always doing something, like trying to earn a little money so that they could buy ice cream or candy or go downtown to see a vaudeville show at one of the local theaters. They'd ride downtown on the trolley, sometimes avoiding paying the fare by an adroit but time-consuming technique in which they'd retreat before the conductor as he advanced through the car collecting fares and then drop off the rear of the car and wait for the next trolley, on which they'd do the same thing, thus slowly working their way downtown. Charley and Grant loved vaudeville. Stengel always dismissed suggestions that vaudeville inspired in him a secret ambition to go onstage — he just liked watching it, he said — although it seems obvious that in observing the actors and comedians he picked up some of the gestures and mannerisms and show-biz tricks that surfaced during his impromptu performances later on. During hard times Charley and Grant used the money they earned to help out at home. At other times they'd be paid at home for doing extra chores, such as carrying into the cellar huge orders of coal and firewood that had been delivered to the yard. Now and then Charley earned a few cents fetching drinking water for laborers working on construction jobs. On Sundays he earned twenty-five cents for pumping the organ at St. Mark's Church. He delivered flowers for a florist for a couple of years, and once worked for a patent-medicine company, filling bottles with the magic elixir and carefully pasting labels on the bottles.

In between times he played, and much of what he played, at least from March to September, was baseball. Football was basically a college game, which boys occasionally played in season on side lawns or in high school, although not with anything approaching the organization and quasi-religious fervor the game is wrapped in today. Basketball, which had been invented only a decade or so earlier, was popular but was ordinarily played for only a couple of months in midwinter. Boxing and wrestling and track were followed with interest, but they were not common athletic interests, nor were golf and tennis, which were strictly upper-class pastimes.

But baseball! It had been growing steadily in popularity since before the Civil War. Vacant lots and open fields were its province. The smooth, geometric infields etched into manicured grass were still in the future. You could tell a baseball field by the deep paths cut into the rough grass where countless players had run from home to first base to second base to third base and back to home again. The site of home plate could be determined by the two shallow pits worn on either side of the plate by the feet of batters digging into the earth to get a better purchase. After rainstorms the pits at home plate and the grooved base paths were usually filled with water, and they'd remain muddy after the rest of the field had dried out.

There were always places to play. Houses generally were not built very close together, and some had huge yards. It was not unusual to play in side lots where people kept cows.

Baseballs were hard to come by and were kept forever, rips and tears in the seams repaired by friction tape until the ball was a heavy round black lump. Bats were kept in repair, too, split handles tacked together and strengthened with tape. A glove was a treasure, although they were flat little leather things, barely larger than a man's hand. Spiked shoes and uniforms were nonexistent until a boy grew older and managed to catch on with a club or school team.

The game was the thing, not the field or the equipment, and boys played it hour after hour, day after day, through the spring and summer months, sometimes with full nine-man teams but just as often with two, three, four, five on a side. Grant Stengel probably introduced his little brother to the game in the mid 1890s, and by 1900, when Charley was ten, they were both first-rate players. Their father was not a baseball player — he liked hunting and fishing, a farm boy's pastimes — but he enjoyed having his sons play the game, and whenever he had time to spare, usually on a Sunday, he'd go watch them. He was a little taken aback one day when he heard his younger son let loose a stream of profanity, but after calling him down for it at home he put the blame on the older boys who must have taught

Charley the rough words.

Grant, despite his light build, was an out-standing baseball player, very fast and well coordinated. "He had five or six strong points in baseball," Casey recalled. "He was skinny — he claimed that was because I got most of the food at home — and he wasn't a slugger, but he could hit, and he could place the ball, and he very seldom struck out. He could run like a deer and he was very sharp and bright on the bases. He was a good fielder and an accurate thrower. He had what was wanted in baseball in those days before the lively ball."

Grant was able to get a game almost anywhere (to "get a game" a boy hung around while teams were being selected, imploring, "Lemme play! Come on, gimme a game!"). In the practical, unsentimental way children handle such things, good players were picked and weaker players weren't. Grant was good. Since he almost always had Charley with him — his father made him take his younger brother along — he'd insist that Charley play, too. Because Grant was so good the others would reluctantly accept the kid brother as well. As Charley grew older and more skillful, there was no problem, and the Stengel brothers became a matched set. Grant usually played shortstop, Charley second base or third base. "It didn't matter none that I was left-handed," Stengel said. "Nobody seemed to notice or care, as long as you could hit."

And Charley, a left-handed batter, could hit. He wasn't as fast or as graceful as Grant, but he was pretty good. He described himself as a workhorse who had to fight his way and play extra hard to do well. But he was a powerfully built youngster who could throw hard, and was often called upon to pitch. When he did, he and Grant would sometimes try to work a hidden-ball trick they had developed. They'd look through the potato bin at home and select a round potato about the size of a baseball. Before the game, Grant would tuck the potato inside his shirt. If there was a base runner on second at a crucial point in the game, Charley would throw the ball to Grant in an ostensible attempt to pick the runner off. He'd get back to the base safely, and Grant would turn and apparently throw the baseball back to Charley. But he'd toss the potato instead. No one would notice the difference because by that time the one baseball used in the game, which would be kept in action for nine innings unless it got lost or its cover fell off, would be scuffed and brown with dirt. Charley would dawdle on the mound, looking in at the next batter, the runner would take a lead off second, and Grant would sidle over and suddenly tag him out.

The play worked fine a couple of times on their home field, but when they were playing a game on the Parade, a big open park area that was a considerable distance from their neighborhood, the trick backfired; the opposition was morally outraged, a brawl developed, and the Stengel brothers had to run all the way home. It was one of the few times Charley ran away from a fight. He was tough as a kid (as he was as a man), and he was not averse to mixing it with a rival. Before a game played at the East End ball park at 15th and Kansas avenues, he bet the rival pitcher thirty cents that he'd get more strikeouts. Stengel fanned nineteen of his opponents to win the bet handily, but when it came time to collect, the stakeholder had disappeared. Charley was furious at being done out of his money, and he grabbed a bat and began to threaten the other team with it, demanding his thirty cents. His rage was so evident that his opponents dug in their pockets and made up the pot. After he began playing professional ball, Stengel was described as "petulant, perhaps truculent, maybe even bellicose." He himself said, "I was always too aggressive. I made too much trouble."

By the time Grant was fourteen and Charley barely twelve, they were playing on teams with sixteen- and eighteen-year-olds. "I wasn't as good as Grant," Stengel said, "but he'd get me on those teams." One of the first formal teams Grant got Charley a game with was the nine that played for the Armour Packing Company. They also played for the Parisian Cloak Company, a clothing store owned by a man named Siggy Harzfeld. Charley played weekend ball for Parisian Cloak all through high school, but at that period Grant suffered a damaging injury that ruined his baseball career. Coming back from a game in a suburb called Dobson, the players were fooling around on the horse-drawn surrey they were riding in, and Grant fell off. He caught his foot between a wheel and its brake shoe, and his heel was badly torn. It took six months for it to heal, and after that one leg was weaker than the other, and Grant never regained his old speed and dash. "He no doubt would have advanced to the big leagues if he hadn't had that accident," Casey said. "He was a better ballplayer than I was."

Turning from baseball, Grant worked with his father on a horse-drawn water-sprinkler wagon that his father operated, a device that sprayed water to keep the dust down on the dirt streets of the city. The insurance company he worked for had owned the sprinkler, and Mr. Stengel had been assigned to run it. In time he took over the operation — which he named the Kansas City Improved Street Sprinkling Company — and it became his main source of income. Unfortunately, it was a dying business, the market for laying dust shrinking as more and more roads were paved, and by 1915 or so it had become more or less moribund.

But a decade earlier it was still a going concern, and Grant began to work with his father. He loved the job, loved working with horses, loved guiding the unwieldy sprinkler around the city. Grant had an amiable outlook on life. He was never hungry for money, never burning with ambition to get ahead. As his brother said, "Grant had a great disposition, but he never had any ideas on high finance." Grant didn't care too much about anything except to live the way he wanted to. He took care of the sprinkler horses well and trained them to follow him and to do what he wanted. Charley would sometimes ride along with him on the wagon and laugh when Grant would deftly manipulate the sprinkler to squirt water toward an unsuspecting friend passing by or at a pretty girl. In later years

Grant drove a taxi for a living. Mr. Stengel once said to Casey, "If I hadn't put that boy on the water wagon, he'd have gone through high school and college." But, as Casey pointed out, Grant wanted to work only where it was fun for him to work.

Charley finished grammar school in January 1906, when he was fifteen and a half years old. By this time he was generally known as Dutch Stengel, a nickname he had picked up a few years earlier. Dutch was a common nickname for anyone with a German last name in those ethnically conscious days, and Stengel had been tagged with it by a boy he didn't know too well in whose yard he was kicking a football back and forth. By the time he reached high school he was called Dutch by just about everyone but his family. A woman named Fern Zwilling, telling Maury Allen about those days, recalled going to a high school basketball game with Stengel's sister, Louise. When Stengel came over to them after the game he introduced himself by saying, "Hello. I'm Charley Stengel." That impressed her, because she had never heard him referred to as anything but Dutch.

Dutch graduated from Garfield Grammar School on January 27 and immediately entered Central High School. At the Garfield graduation ceremonies he had been acutely embarrassed when he was called upon to sing the popular refrain "School days, school days, good old golden rule days." He struggled through it, to the glee of his male classmates, who pretended all sorts of distress as he sang, including the need to throw up. At Central High he became an outstanding athlete, but that was about all he was interested in. He didn't study much. He was amused by the students who were diligently studying Shakespeare and would mock them (he must have collected a few shards of knowledge in the classroom) by striking a pose and greeting them with, "Ye gods, men! And how are you today?" One of the Shakespeare students was William Powell, the actor who became lastingly famous in the 1930s for his performances in the Thin Man films. Stengel said Powell also played basketball — he remembered his sharp elbows. Dutch himself was able to pass English, a compulsory subject, through the kindly assistance of a teacher named A.F. Smith, who liked sports, liked Dutch Stengel and carried him through. Stengel appreciated what Smith had done; he never forgot the name of this teacher who did love him a little.

He was at home in the rough-and-tumble

world of sports but ill at ease elsewhere. He liked girls (he once borrowed Grant's shoes to wear on a date, disregarding the fact that his feet were considerably larger than his older brother's; trying to pull them on he ripped the tongue off one shoe, incurring a rare outburst of anger from the easygoing Grant), but he dropped the practice of taking them to affairs at Central High after he and a date were greeted with loud cheers and raucous whistles from his bachelor friends. He did much of his socializing thereafter through the medium of his sister, Louise, taking Louise *and* a girl out for ice cream. But he did enjoy dancing, went at it vigorously, and once won five silver dollars in a dancing contest.

He was shy and awkward before large audiences, perhaps because of his experience singing "School Days." In 1909, during his last year in high school, he was the star of the Central High basketball team that won the city championship. At a school assembly the principal, Mr. I.I. Cammack, asked him to come up and accept the championship trophy on behalf of the team, but he blushed and refused to. Afterward, Mr. Cammack called him into his office and said, "Dutch, I'm surprised at you. It hurt me that you wouldn't get up and accept that award for the school."

Dutch said nothing.

Basketball was a static, low-scoring game in those days, with muscles more important than height. There was a lot of passing and not much shooting, and Stengel was good (all of 22 baskets in 17 games one season). Fern Zwilling remembered him looking over at the stands whenever he made a basket. He was hot-tempered, too. When a rival grabbed the back of his shirt to hold him when the lone official was not looking, Stengel reacted angrily, shoving the opponent away and taking a swing at him.

In his junior year at Central, the school organized a football team, and Stengel joined it. His five-foot-eight-inch, 170-pound build made him one of the stronger men on the squad, and he became fullback and was elected team captain. The game they played had no forward pass and very little mobility; it was a grinding, plunge-into-the-middle-of-the-line battle, with short gains and very little scoring. The players did not use helmets. It was a rough sport, and Dutch Stengel was good at it, too. The school played some of its games against club teams, and one of those games, against a club from Kansas City, Kansas, on the other side of the Missouri River, degenerated into an only slightly regulated brawl. During that season one Central High player was kicked in the head and badly injured, and the school dropped the sport again and did not field another team for years.

Baseball continued to be Stengel's favorite activity. From the time he had been a small boy he returned to it every spring when the ground was still wet and the air chilly, and he'd play it practically every day until the weather turned cold again in the autumn. Everyone did. It's difficult now to appreciate the extraordinary hold that baseball had on the country at that time. It wasn't called the national pastime by some promotion-minded flak from the Baseball Commissioner's office; it *was* the national pastime. Every city had dozens and dozens of teams, and on Saturdays and Sundays and holidays there were ball games everywhere. Men would play ball at picnics for kegs of beer. There were sandlot teams and school teams and semiprofessional teams and minor-league teams everywhere. College baseball was big-time, with huge crowds going to stadiums to see games between, for example, Yale and Harvard. The best players — Cap Anson and Dan Brouthers in the 1880s, Ed Delahanty and Amos Rusie in the 1890s, Honus Wagner and Nap Lajoie in the 1900s — were famous.

Yet most attention was paid to local teams and local heroes. There was no television and no radio and not much photography, so if you wanted to *see* baseball you went to watch a game nearby. In the spring, big-league teams barnstorming their way back from training camps to their home cities would play games in the smaller cities and towns, and during the season crack semipro clubs would play here and there, sometimes traveling considerable distances for games. There were minor-league teams relatively free of major-league control all over the country, and a good ballplayer who was not of major-league quality could have a long career in the minors.

Stengel began to earn money playing baseball when he was still in high school and still technically an amateur. Parisian Cloak had been using him more and more as a pitcher, and Dutch decided that he ought to be paid. He asked for $3 a game. Siggy Harzfeld countered with an offer of $1.50. Stengel grew stubborn and said he wouldn't pitch for that, and Harzfeld gave in and paid the youngster the $3 he asked for. In 1955 after the Philadelphia Athletics' franchise had been transferred to Kansas City, when the Yankees came into the city to play for the first time, Edna Stengel was presented with a bottle of fine perfume by the Harzfelds, along with a note recalling that Siggy had been Casey's first employer on the diamond.

In the summer of 1907, Stengel and several of his friends rode the train out to western Kansas to earn money in the wheat fields. They got jobs, but when the harvest petered out they were a long way from home without as much money as they had anticipated having. They wandered east, looking for more work and sleeping under the stars in order to save the money they would have had to pay for rooms. In Park, Kansas, 300 miles west of Kansas City, a sheriff found them sleeping under trees. He arranged for them to get something to eat and then sent them on the road toward home.

Stengel and his friends were used to sneaking rides on trains. They'd go the thirty-five or forty miles from Kansas City to Lawrence, Kansas, to see a University of Kansas football game or a track meet, ducking conductors out and back. Once Casey hid by riding on top of a car, but the smoke and cinders from the locomotive forced him to come down and conceal himself between two cars. Just as the train was slowing for a stop he lost his grip and fell, but the train was going so slowly that he was able to roll away to safety.

But western Kansas was a lot farther than Lawrence, and getting home from their wheat-farming jaunt was difficult. By the time they got to Council Grove, still more than a hundred miles from home, they were broke and hungry. Some local people in Council Grove mentioned that there was going to be a baseball game there that day, and when it was learned that Stengel and a couple of the others were high school players from Kansas City they were pressed into service. The game went into extra innings, and Dutch batted in the winning run. The admiring townspeople fed them, put them up for the night and took up a collection to help them on their way home in the morning.

Stengel's reputation as a ballplayer was growing. A year after the trip to the wheat fields he made another journey west, this time with the Kansas City Red Sox, a slick semipro team (Casey always said "sem-eye pro"). A Central High student named Ira Bidwell had organized the tour, spending the spring writing letters and setting up a schedule. The team went as far west as Utah, playing local teams practically every day, but substituting basketball games in local YMCAs when it rained. The star of the Red Sox was a right-handed pitcher named Claude Hendrix from Olathe, Kansas, a few miles south of Kansas City. Hendrix, a little older than Stengel, followed Ivy Olson into professional ball a year or so later. He, too, would meet Stengel again.

The barnstorming trip with the Red Sox was Stengel's first introduction to the sometimes carefree, somewhat rowdy life of a professional, playing ball every day, chasing around for something to do at night. In 1908 much of their entertainment lay in horseplay, the callow humor that is still evident among baseball players and other athletes. In Stengel's time it was heavy with such subtleties as dumping buckets of water on unsuspecting people, putting snakes in teammates' beds, and so on. Dutch Stengel ate it up. The travel and the fun were major compensations for the players, who were paid only $1 a day, along with rooms and meals.

Despite this more overt venture into play-for-pay baseball, Stengel was back pitching for Central High again in the spring of 1909, his last year. He was the unquestioned star of the team. The school yearbook, *The Centralian,* said, "The baseball team this year was strong in almost every way, with the feature the hurling of Stengel." At the state high school tournament in Columbia, Missouri, he pitched a fifteen-inning 7–6 thriller over Joplin that gave Central the championship.

It is typical of the tricks that memory can play, notably on baseball people who have seen or played in thousands of games, that Stengel thought for years that he had pitched a 1–0 game in the championship showdown with Joplin, and it was only when he was working on his autobiography and looked up the game to verify the facts that he discovered thirteen runs had been scored in it instead of just one. The shutout game had been earlier.

But he did win it, and he was a hero, the best player on the best high school team in the state. He went off again with the semipro Red Sox that summer, playing games as far east as St. Louis and out west again up into Wyoming and back. He was finishing his fourth year in high school that fall (he was a midyear student) when the local minor-league team, the Kansas City Blues, came after him. The Blues were in the American Association, the highest level of minor-league ball, just one step below the majors. In January 1910, Dutch completed four years in high school but lacked sufficient credits to graduate. He decided to chuck school and go with the Blues.

Because he was only nineteen, he needed

parental approval. Breezily, he approached his father, contract in hand, and said, "Here, Pop, sign this, will you?"

"What is it?"

"It's a contract to play ball with the Blues. You have to sign it because I'm under twenty-one."

"What about school?"

"Ah, I'm finished with school. The Blues will pay me $135 a month."

That was a lot of money for a boy of nineteen. Men married and raised families on less. Laborers worked for $7 to $10 a week. A messenger boy or an office boy might make $5. A skilled telegraph operator, a really good job in those days, might make $20 to $25. You could rent a house for $35 a month. A salary of $135 a month, even if it was only for the summer months when the season was on, was a startling amount of money for a young kid to earn.

"So I put down my paper and signed," Louis Stengel said. "You never could change that boy's mind anyway."

4

THE MINOR LEAGUES: A COFFIN IN KANKAKEE

Thus, in the early spring of 1910, Charley Stengel became a bona fide professional ballplayer, a rookie pitcher with Kansas City, only one step below the major leagues. Before going to join the Blues at their training camp, Charley had a chat with a neighbor, a man who lived across the street from the Stengels and came over to talk to him. The neighbor was Charles Nichols. Although he was past forty, most people called him Kid, a nickname he had picked up twenty years earlier when he began pitching for Boston in the National League. Boston won five pennants in seven years with Nichols pitching for them — he won thirty or more games in each of those pennant-winning seasons — and he was easily the peer of his more famous contemporaries Cy Young and Amos Rusie. Nichols' career ended early. He and Young started in the National League the same season, but Nichols left the majors ten years before Young did (although he came back later for a couple of seasons). When Stengel talked with him in 1910 he had won more games — 362 — than any other National League pitcher, and in the more than seventy years since, only three other National Leaguers, Christy Mathewson, Grover Cleveland Alexander and Warren Spahn, have surpassed him. (Of Young's 511 victories, only 325 were in the National League.)

Nichols told Stengel, "I understand you get in a lot of trouble and in a lot of arguments. Now I want to tell you something. Don't be arguing all the time. Listen to your manager. Or if you have an old player teaching you, listen to him. Never say, 'I won't do that.' Always listen. If you're not going to do what he says, don't tell him so. Let it go in one ear, and let it roll around in there for a month, and then if it isn't any good let it go out the other ear. But if it *is* good, memorize it and keep it. You do that and you'll learn something, and you'll keep out of a lot of trouble."

Stengel let *that* advice go in one ear, and if he didn't always pay attention to it he kept it rolling around in there, because half a century later he still remembered it. In his first

season he put Nichols' advice to good use —
at least the part about listening to older players — but he didn't always follow the Kid's
ukase about not arguing.

The Kansas City Blues trained at Excelsior
Springs, about twentyfive miles outside Kansas City. Professional baseball then was very
different from what it is today. There had
been professional ball since just after the Civil
War, which had ended forty-five years earlier. In the 1870s, various teams came together in a loose organization, and in 1876 the
more formal National League was established. The number of franchises in the
league fluctuated wildly the first few years,
and in the 1880s the National was challenged
by a second major league called the American
Association (a name later applied to the minor
league that Kansas City was part of in 1910).
In 1890, the year Stengel was born, most of
the top major-league players rebelled and
formed the "Players League," which lasted
only one season. By 1892 the American Association had died, too, and the National
League held a monopoly for several years. In
1901 another rival league, the American, was
formed, but the owners worked out an
armistice and by 1903 major-league baseball
had settled into a monolithic structure of six-

teen teams that continued without change for more than half a century. In the early decades of the century, none of these teams owned minor-league farm clubs, as we know the term, although a few big-league club owners also owned one or two minor-league teams on the side. For the most part the minor-leaguers operated autonomously, augmenting income earned at the gate with money received through the sale of promising players to big-league teams. Under baseball's "National Agreement," big-league clubs had the right to "draft" a certain number of players from the minors, paying a standard fee for each such drafted player.

Sometimes a big-league club would sign a player and then assign him to a minor-league club, with the right to reobtain the player at a later date. The higher minor-league clubs, like Kansas City, operated in much the same way with teams in the lesser minor leagues. The minor leagues were "classified": Originally, the top leagues were Class A and the lowest leagues Class C, but in time the differences between the leagues became more refined until at one point they ranged from AAA through AA and A all the way down to D. A team like the Kansas City Blues, with which Stengel had signed, was not just a nursery for developing young players for the majors. Selling players to the majors was important, but the minor-league owners were primarily interested in winning games and attracting crowds, just as the big-league teams were. Minor-league teams back then tried to obtain the best players they could, regardless of age, and teams in the high minors were filled with veteran players down from the majors, men whose skills were no longer up to big-league standards but who were still fine, capable ballplayers. Some of them played in the minors for years after ending their big-league careers. Kid Nichols, for instance, had won forty-eight games for the Blues after coming back down from Boston.

New young players like Stengel were therefore in the minority, and when he reported to Excelsior Springs he didn't get much chance to show what he could do. The Blues were too busy getting into shape. When they went into Kansas City one day to play a preseason exhibition game with the Boston Red Sox, Stengel was the bottom man on the roster. Boston drew a big crowd for its game with the Blues, mostly because Smokey Joe Wood was pitching for them. Wood, born in Kansas City, a year or two before Stengel, was precociously expert as a pitcher. He joined Boston in 1908 and in 1909, when Stengel was pitching for Central High, Wood won eleven games for the Red Sox, including four shutouts. He was a coming star and a hero to Kansas City people, and everybody came to the game to see him pitch, but Stengel, the rookie, did not even get into the game. Worse, he was given the embarrassing job before the game of carrying the team's water bucket onto the field. His raucous high school friends humiliated him by chanting, "Water boy! Water boy!"

Things didn't get better after the Blues returned to Excelsior Springs to resume training. Manager Danny Shay let Stengel pitch in a couple of games, but the youngster was hit hard. The straight fastball and the nickel curve that had worked so well in high school were meat on the platter for the veteran professionals he went up against. Shay could see nothing to indicate that Stengel would ever make it as a pitcher, but he liked the way the boy swung a bat and decided to try him at another position. Because Stengel was a left-handed thrower, Shay obviously couldn't make him a catcher, or play him at second, short or third, and he was too short to play first base. That left the outfield, where Stengel had never played. His inadequacies were glaring. He could handle routine fly balls, and he threw well when he returned the ball to the infield, but on long drives over his head he was helpless. He tried to backpedal the way infielders often do, but floundered. Shay said caustically, "With that big ass of yours, it's no wonder you can't move under the ball." Stengel also had trouble with balls bouncing off the outfield fences — in high-school baseball, played on huge open fields, there had been no fences — and Shay kept yelling at him.

"Play the angles! Play the angles!" he'd cry.

"If you want somebody to play the angles," the frustrated rookie replied, "why don't you hire a pool player?"

"You ought to be a pool player," the manager said. "You've got a head as hard as a billiard ball."

Billiard Ball Stengel, he was called for the next several days.

But he could hit, and he could throw, and he could run pretty fast, and Shay didn't give up on him. When the club left on a brief exhibition-game tour, he left Stengel behind with two veteran players, Patsy Flaherty and William (Spike) Shannon, both in their thirties and both former major-leaguers. Shannon was an outfielder who had played for John McGraw's Giants for a couple of years, and Flaherty was a pitcher. Flaherty would hit fungoes to the outfield, and Stengel would chase them. Shannon would stand in the outfield — or, sometimes, sit in a chair in the outfield — and tell Stengel what he was doing wrong. They did this by the hour, and after a while the youngster began to catch on to the finer points of outfielding. He worked hard, and some of the lessons hurt, literally. To break the tedium of outfield practice, the old-timers would sometimes let the rookie bat for a while, with Flaherty pitching and Shannon shagging the balls. At one point, after repeatedly using a big windup before throwing the ball, Flaherty quick-pitched, suddenly throwing without resorting to a windup, a practice now illegal but at that time within baseball law. The pitch not only took Stengel by surprise, it hit him in the chest and knocked him down. He got up angrily, but the old pitcher said calmly, "Kid, I just wanted to give you a lesson. Never take your eye off the ball."

When the club returned from its trip, manager Shay was encouraged by Stengel's improvement, but he and the club's owner, Patsy Tebeau, agreed that the boy was not yet ready to play for the Blues. They arranged to send him on an option agreement to Kankakee, Illinois, in the Class C Northern Association. This was a comedown for Stengel, but he packed his cardboard suitcase and rode a train across Missouri and Illinois to Kankakee, about fifty miles south of Chicago.

In Kankakee he took a room in a hotel at $1 a day but soon moved to a rooming house where he got room *and* board for $4 a week. The food was filling, but he also bought meal tickets at McBroom's Restaurant, where for $3.50 he could get a coupon worth $5 in food. Each time he ate at McBroom's the cost of the food he ate was punched out on the ticket. He also got to know some local people and was sometimes invited to dinner. He had a few dates with local girls, the dates usually consisting of sitting on a front porch talking.

On the ball field his play was adequate but not outstanding. Back in Excelsior Springs, Patsy Flaherty had told him to keep doing what he and Shannon had taught him. "And I want you to learn how to slide," Flaherty said. "Practice sliding."

"I'll have to do that next spring," Stengel said. "I won't have time anymore this year."

"The hell with that," Flaherty said. "You'll

have time. You practice sliding, you hear me?"

Stengel made friends with two players his age, cousins from Tennessee named Willard Scheetz and Bill McTigue, both pitchers. Scheetz never made it to the major leagues, but McTigue did, briefly. The three would go out to the ball park early and work out together. They'd hit fly balls to each other, giving Stengel practice in catching them and the two pitchers the extra running time all pitchers feel they need to build up endurance on the mound. Whenever there were lulls when Stengel was in the outfield — if the ball was being hit to the other man, for instance, or if a throw to the one hitting the ball got away for a moment — he would practice sliding. He'd toss his glove fifteen or twenty feet away, sprint toward it, and slide as though he were going into a base. He did this repeatedly, even during regular practice sessions with the team, and it drew some caustic comment, particularly from an older player named Gilligan. Across the way from the ballpark was the Kankakee State Hospital, a mental institution. One day Gilligan said, "Stengel is one guy who won't be playing here next year." A teammate, surprised, said, "Yeah? Where's he going?" Gilligan pointed to the insane asylum and said, "Over there."

Stengel heard Gilligan's comment, and the remark festered. In a game some time later a short fly ball began falling just beyond the infield. Stengel came running in for it from center field, while Gilligan raced back from his position at second base. Stengel, determined to catch the ball, didn't see Gilligan until the last moment and then, in trying to avert a collision, accidentally stepped on the second baseman's foot and spiked him. Gilligan had to leave the game and was unable to play for several days. That was a serious matter, because the Kankakee club — the entire eight-team Northern Association, for that matter — was in financial trouble, and there wasn't enough money to carry an injured player very long. Thus, Gilligan's job was in jeopardy. He blamed Stengel.

The Kankakee team was owned by local people, among them a mortician named Hickey, who acted as the treasurer of the club. The players were paid at Hickey's funeral parlor, and they used it as a mailing address where letters would be held for them when they were out of town on a road trip. A day or so after the spiking incident Stengel went around to Hickey's to pick up his mail and ran into Gilligan and another player, a catcher named Boyle. Gilligan began to be-rate Stengel, declaring that he had called for the ball and that Stengel should have heard him. Gilligan said the club was trying to get another second baseman, and he said Stengel was trying to get him fired. Stengel's temper rose. The accident had been as much Gilligan's fault as his, he said. An outfielder isn't supposed to give up and let a fly ball drop in. He called Gilligan "duck nose," an unflattering reference to the other player's long, flared, scoop-snoot nose. Gilligan swung at him, Stengel swung back, and in the melee he fell against an empty coffin standing on display in the office and knocked it over. Hickey came rushing in. He blamed Stengel for the row — after all, Gilligan and Boyle had been talking peacefully before Stengel appeared — and ordered him out of the place. "Don't you come in and get your mail here anymore, either," he said.

Despite such distractions, Stengel's performance at Kankakee wasn't bad. He batted only .251, but another left-handed-hitting outfielder on the team, twenty-two-year-old Bobby Veach from Kentucky, batted only .221, and Veach later played twelve years for the Detroit Tigers in the same outfield with Ty Cobb. Stengel had fifty-one hits in 203 at bats, including one home run, and he stole sixteen bases.

Then, in July, the Northern Association collapsed. The league, which had seven teams in Illinois (Kankakee, Clinton, Decatur, Elgin, Freeport, Jacksonville and Joliet) and one in Iowa (Muscatine), had had trouble all season. Around the end of May the Decatur franchise was switched to Taylorville, Illinois, and then a few days later back to Decatur. Late in June, Joliet's team was transferred to Sterling, Illinois. A little later the Clinton club just gave up and bowed out of the league, and so did Freeport. The surviving clubs reorganized into a six-team league, but on July 11, Elgin folded and so did Kankakee. A week later the remaining four gave up the ghost, and the Northern Association was abandoned.

Stengel was out of a job. Moreover, when Kankakee went out of business it owed him half a month's salary, or $67.50, which he never received. (As a matter of fact he did receive it, but not until 1956, a short time after he had made a joking reference to his unpaid salary in Kankakee during a talk he made in Kansas City when the Yankees were playing there. A Kankakee bank presented Casey with a check for $483.05, representing the $67.50 plus modest interest since 1910. Stengel in turn gave the check to the Kankakee Little League.)

But in 1910 in lieu of salary he took his Kankakee uniform with him when he left. Before he could go back home, Kansas City reassigned his contract to a team in Shelbyville, Kentucky, in the six-team Class D Blue Grass League. Class D was another step down for Stengel, and to aggravate matters Shelbyville was in last place and it too was in a lot of trouble. Stengel played there only a month or so before the franchise was awarded to J. W. Fitzgerald and Preston Wells of Maysville, Kentucky, who paid $500 for it, plus $100 to pay an overdue league "assessment." They immediately moved the team to Maysville, a town on the Ohio River with a long tradition of fine baseball. In the spring of 1895, for instance, a Maysville team starring a Kentucky boy named Dan McGann (who was born, it is interesting to note, in Shelbyville) beat the Cincinnati Reds twice in three games; McGann went on to play in the major leagues for thirteen years with such teams as the Baltimore Orioles and the New York Giants.

After the somewhat disenchanting experience in Kankakee and Shelbyville, Maysville turned out to be fun for Stengel. He played there only a little more than three weeks before the Blue Grass season ended, and the team did not rise out of last place (it finished with a pretty bad 37-85 record), but having a team in organized ball meant a lot to Maysville, and the townspeople rallied round the ballplayers. Merchants put up prizes for the players to vie for. In a game against Frankfort on Friday, September 2, a week after the new club arrived in town, Stengel hit a ball "way out toward the sand dunes," made it all the way around the bases and won a box of candy and a "Duplex safety-razor outfit" for hitting the first home run of the season by a Maysville (not a Shelbyville) player. His feat was saluted in the *Maysville Bulletin* with a one-word headline: STENGEL. The copy referred to him as "Maysville's hard-hitting little batter and nifty center fielder." Three days later in a Labor Day doubleheader against Richmond he hit another home run, and this time won himself a $3 hat. He is also said to have caught a fly ball in one ball park by running into a small stream that flowed past the far reaches of the outfield and catching the ball with water flowing around his ankles.

Casey made good friends in Maysville, among them a twelve-year-old boy named Robert Willocks, who liked to hang around the Central Hotel, where the ballplayers lived. Casey told the boy, "You meet me here at one o'clock every day and I'll take you out to the park with me." Stengel would give him his spikes and his glove to carry. They'd board a streetcar and ride out to the ball park. There, Casey would walk past the gatekeeper, winking as he went by, and his young friend would get in free.

But if Stengel had a good time in Maysville, his performance fell off in the Blue Grass League, even though it was a lower classification than the Northern. He batted only .221 in Kentucky, and his average for all of 1910 — in 128 games at Kankakee, Shelbyville, and Maysville — was .236, not terribly impressive. But he did display power at the bat, and when he got home to Kansas City, the Blues put him on their roster for the last few games of the season. Playing before the home folks as a professional, Dutch Stengel got to bat three times as a pinch hitter and had one base hit — a .333 average, if you're scoring.

5 MOVING ON UP: THE TABASCO KID'S ADVICE

It had been a hectic, sobering but generally exhilarating year for Charley Stengel, now twenty years old. He settled in at home to take it easy for a while, until his father asked him what he was going to do now. Charley looked surprised. He hadn't planned on doing anything much. His father said in no uncertain terms that no son of his was going to sit around all winter doing nothing. Charley said, well, he had been talking to one of his friends from the old semipro Red Sox days, a boy named Billy Brummage, and Brummage had mentioned that he was going to study dentistry at Western Dental College in Kansas City. Charley thought he'd like to try that, too. Although he hadn't graduated from Central High, he had enough credits to enter the dental college, and he had enough money saved from his baseball salary to pay the tuition.

Stengel studied dentistry that fall and winter, working at it earnestly. Western was a respected school, not the fly-by-night mail-order outfit some legends about Stengel make it out to be, and if Casey had not made it as a ballplayer he almost certainly would have been a dentist. Some of the stories he told about his dental training were laced with hyperbole, most of them linked to the assumed impossibility of a dentist's being left-handed. The difficulties the left-handed Stengel had using right-handed dental equipment were the core of most of his stories, although there are, of course, many left-handed dentists. The courses he took included an anatomy lab where the students dissected mouths and jaws of cadavers. This led to the usual medical-school humor. Stengel said, "This was a serious business, naturally, but once in a while fellas would fool around with those bodies when nobody was looking, and the first thing you knew you'd find an extra thumb in your pocket." Naturally, Stengel became the class clown, the one who would stick a cigar in the corner of a corpse's mouth, the one who would lie down on an empty slab with a sheet over him and then rise slowly, moaning. He was also one who would "fool around with those bodies." When he stopped on his way home from class one day to see his close friend Harold Lederman (whom he would introduce to sportswriters in later years by saying, "This is my Jewish friend from Kansas City and he can sell you a ring cheap"), he shook hands with Lederman and left a cold finger in the palm of his hand. Also, Stengel had discovered in his baseball travels something called "cow's itch," a powder that irritated the skin. He'd palm some and then clap a man jovially on the back of the neck, or playfully pinch his cheek, then surreptitiously watch with friends who were in the know when the man would start rubbing his neck or scratching his face.

During the winter Stengel kept in touch with the Blues, who told him they'd look at him again in spring training but that in 1911 he'd be playing the outfield for Aurora, a town thirty-five miles west of Chicago, in the Class C Wisconsin-Illinois League. Aurora was run by Al Tebeau, a brother of Patsy Tebeau, the Kansas City owner. It wasn't much of a step up, although the fact that the Blues were still interested in him was encouraging. But the $135 a month that had seemed so impressive a year earlier didn't look very big now. Baseball salaries ended with the season, and what with losing half a month's pay at

Kankakee, his income from baseball in 1910 had come to less than $700. He said he wanted $200 a month this time. Al Tebeau told him he might be able to raise him to $150 a month, but no more. Stengel replied that he would come down to $175, but anything less than that and he'd stay in dental school. Tebeau and his brother discussed the salary dispute, and the upshot was that Stengel got the $175. It was his second argument over baseball pay (the first was with Siggy Harzfeld) and his second success. Later on in his career he had frequent disputes about salary. An old friend said, "I don't think it was just the money. I think Casey enjoyed arguing with the owners and getting his own way."

Stengel reported to Aurora and had a terrific season. He led the league in batting with a .352 average and had the most base hits and the most stolen bases. He also got into what could have been serious trouble. He had a running argument one day during a game in Rockford, Illinois, with an umpire named Arundel, who twice called him out on strikes early in the game. Stengel, feeling his oats as one of the big hitters in the league, took loud exception to the umpire's strike calls. When he was called out on strikes a third time and complained again, the umpire laughed at him and said, "You're out, big shot." Fuming, Stengel walked back toward the bench, still carping at the umpire over his shoulder. Noticing that Arundel had crouched over to watch the first pitch to the next batter, Stengel tiptoed quickly back to the plate and whacked the umpire across the behind with his bat. The Rockford crowd booed, the Rockford manager said Stengel ought to be thrown out of the game, Arundel agreed, arguments broke out all over the place, and the upshot was that Rockford was awarded the game on forfeit. Stengel was called before league president Charles Morral and got away with a fine, although he could have been suspended for the rest of the season.

Maybe it was his personality that saved him. Despite his truculence and belligerence, Stengel had undeniable charm, and people liked him. He had a natural talent for getting into trouble, but people took the time to help him out of it. He began losing a lot of money playing poker with his teammates, and Al Tebeau took him aside. Tebeau owned a bar and a gambling joint as well as the ball club. "Listen," he told Stengel, "I'm a gambler. That's my business. Now, you look to me like you can go on up to the big leagues. You've got the ability, and you work hard.

But if you want to be a big-leaguer, you better quit playing poker. If you don't you're going to be broke every payday, because you sure can't play cards."

One day that summer of 1911 a traveling man named Larry Sutton paused in Chicago to check train schedules. Sutton's job was to wander around the country, watching base-ball games and recommending players to his employer, Charles Ebbets of the Brooklyn Dodgers. Such scouts became common in later years, but at that time there were only a few of them. Most major-league teams learned about promising players by reading about them or by word of mouth. Old friends or former players would tip a team to a likely prospect.

But a few years before, the astute John Mc-Graw, manager of the New York Giants, had hired Dick Kinsella to travel around and look for players. Kinsella, described as "a portly, peripatetic man in a derby hat," turned up some first-rate prospects for McGraw, who rapidly established himself as the premier manager in baseball. Other clubs hired scouts, and after the 1908 season Ebbets, principal owner of the Dodgers, followed suit. He was particularly aware of Kinsella's accomplishments, because the Giants were the Brooklyn club's great rivals. Ebbets ran into Larry Sutton at baseball's winter meetings in New York that December and took an instant liking to him. Sutton, from upstate New York, had been a printer's devil before he became a minor-league umpire. He took to the road for Ebbets and scored a signal success in 1909, his first year of scouting for the Dodgers. He advised Ebbets to buy a young outfielder named Zack Wheat from Mobile, although Wheat had batted only .245 there.

"What can I do with a fellow who hits only .245?" Ebbets demanded.

"You put him in your outfield," Sutton replied. "That's where he plays."

"But .245?"

"I don't care what he batted," Sutton said. "This fellow is a ballplayer."

Ebbets dutifully purchased Wheat and brought him up to Brooklyn late in 1909. Wheat batted .303 in twenty-six games and the next spring told Bill Dahlen, the Brooklyn manager, "I had malaria in Mobile, but it doesn't bother me now. I think I'll hit all right up here." He did. He was the Dodgers' left fielder for seventeen seasons, won the batting title in 1918, had a lifetime average of .317, and was elected to the Hall of Fame in 1959.

Sutton also came up with a first baseman named Jake Daubert, who won back-to-back batting championships for Brooklyn in 1913 and 1914 and had a lifetime average of .303 for fifteen seasons in the majors. And Otto Miller, a big, powerfully built catcher who was with Brooklyn for thirteen seasons and played in two World Series. And several others, including Charles Dillon Stengel.

Sutton spent most of his time watching clubs in the higher minor leagues, but he had read about Stengel's hitting, knew that Aurora was playing at home and found it was only an hour or so from Chicago. It wouldn't take too much time to hop on an interurban car and go and look. He did, and he was impressed by Stengel and by a left-handed pitcher named Len Madden. When Ebbets prepared a list of the minor-league players he intended to go after at the annual draft meeting in Cincinnati in August of that year, he followed Sutton's recommendation and bought Stengel and Madden. That was significant, because they were the only Class C players on Ebbets' lengthy list, the others all being in higher classifications.

Madden was eventually sold to the Chicago Cubs — drafting players was partly an exercise in entrepreneurship, buying here, selling there — but Stengel was assigned to play the following year for Toronto in the International League, which was on the same level as the American Association, one step below the majors. Then Brooklyn changed its mind and decided to send Stengel instead to Montgomery, Alabama, in the less demanding Southern Association, a step lower.

Stengel, gratified by his performance at Aurora and pleased that he had been noticed and drafted by a major-league team, nonetheless returned to his studies at Western Dental that fall. Even though his absences to play ball meant that he had fallen behind the other members of his class, who were to graduate after that school year, he appeared in the formal photograph of the graduating class of 1912 and had a school photograph taken of himself in a stiff collar and a dark suit, his blond hair smoothed down and neatly parted. How serious he was about remaining with dentistry is hard to determine. He may have been thinking of using his continued attendance at school as a level in salary discussions, as he had a year earlier.

It didn't work this time. When he received his contract to play at Montgomery he was chagrined to discover that it was for only $150 a month, or $25 less than he had made for playing in Aurora. He summarily rejected the contract and told the Brooklyn club he'd quit baseball and stay in dental school before he'd accept it. Ebbets, busy with financial problems related to a brand-new ball park he was building, was of no mind to pay much attention to a minor-league holdout, but he *had* paid $500 for the boy's contract, so Old Scout Sutton (as he was usually called) wandered out to Kansas City and soft-soaped his twenty-one-year-old find. He urged Stengel to accept the $150 and report to Montgomery. He pointed out that in the five months of a minor-league season a $25-a-month cut added up to only $125, and $125 wasn't that much. It couldn't keep you alive. Stengel would be dumb to quit baseball over a little sum like $125. On the other hand, if he accepted the contract and played well at Montgomery, the chances were good that he'd move up to the big leagues with Brooklyn in a year or two, and there he'd make a really big salary.

Sutton's circuitous logic appealed to Stengel, whose elastic mind often worked in the same way, linking odd little reasons together to show the good sense of something that at first glance seemed pointless. "I knew he was right," Stengel said. "I was still a long way from finishing dental school, and I knew I couldn't get a job in Kansas City for $150 a month."

Again withdrawing from Western Dental in good order, assured of his right to return as a student the following autumn, he reported to the Montgomery team at its training camp in Pensacola, Florida. His manager was a former major-league outfielder named Johnny Dobbs, but Stengel paid more attention to an old shortstop named Norman Elberfeld, known in baseball as the Tabasco Kid, or, more commonly, just Kid. Elberfeld was even older than Dobbs; he had spent thirteen seasons in the majors and had managed the New York Highlanders (later to be called the Yankees) for part of a season. He was a smallish man, about five feet seven, peppery and pugnacious. There was a fierce rivalry between Montgomery, managed by Dobbs, and Atlanta, managed by a fellow named Dolan, and feud-minded Southerners referred to games between the clubs as battles between the McDobbs Clan and the McDolans. In Atlanta, the Montgomery players rode from their hotel to the ball park in an open horse-drawn stage. When Atlanta fans saw them passing they would jeer and hoot, and occasionally some would run close to the wagon as though to spit or let loose a particularly cutting epithet. Elberfeld would sit on the side step of the wagon holding a bat in his hands, and whenever people came too close he'd threaten to whack them with the bat.

Elberfeld took a liking to Stengel and told the twenty-one-year-old outfielder, "Listen, if you want to get to the big leagues, watch me." He taught Stengel the niceties of the hit-and-run, showed him how to bat a ball behind the runner and how to coordinate his efforts at bat with a base runner so that he could poke a ground ball through the spot vacated by an infielder moving over to cover the base the runner was heading for. Elberfeld showed Stengel how to stand close to the plate at bat so that he could get himself hit with a pitched ball when it was especially desirable to get to first base, and how to defray suspicion that you'd gotten yourself hit on purpose by throwing your bat angrily toward the mound and moving threateningly toward the pitcher, shouting and cursing.

Stengel was an apt student, but sometimes he didn't learn as well as Elberfeld wanted him to. The old shortstop liked to work a play when he was at bat and the swift-running Stengel was on second base. He'd have Stengel break toward third base on the pitch, which would prompt the shortstop to move toward second base and the third baseman toward third, each anticipating a throw and a possible rundown with the rash young base runner caught between bases. Elberfeld, who had great bat control, would poke a simple ground ball to the left side, and neither the third baseman nor the shortstop could get back into position in time to field it, which meant that Stengel would reach third easily and sometimes be able to keep going all the way to home plate. Now and then the play would backfire. Elberfeld wouldn't be able to hit a grounder and instead would hit a pop fly or a soft line drive. He had cautioned his pupil to be alert to such a possibility, but Stengel, vain about his baserunning, his eyes set on reaching third, would run blindly and be easily doubled off second. This happened a couple of times, to Elberfeld's considerable annoyance. When it happened a third time — Stengel running full tilt toward third while an infielder was settling under an Elberfeld pop-up — the Tabasco Kid raced down the third-base line, waving his bat and screaming. The startled young Stengel put on the brakes, wheeled, and sprinted back toward second base, too late to avoid being doubled off, but away from the cursing Elberfeld anyway.

When he was still in spring training with Montgomery, Stengel one day noticed a metal cover half hidden in the lush grass of the outfield. Always curious, he opened the cover and found that it concealed a shallow hole containing water pipes and valves and enough space to hide a crouching man. Glancing around and realizing no one was watching, he ducked into the hole and closed the lid, holding it open just wide enough so that he could keep an eye on what was going on elsewhere around the field. Someone hit a high lazy fly ball in his direction, and when everyone looked toward the outfield Stengel got his desired effect: No one could imagine where he had gone. Then he climbed out of his hiding place, holding the metal cover over his head. He planned to hold the cover like a shield and let the ball bounce off it before he caught it, but it was too heavy to maneuver easily and at the last moment he had to drop it and grab the ball one-handed.

A scout for the Washington Senators named Mike Kahoe heard about that and when he was asked his opinion of Stengel as a major-league prospect said, "Well, he handles the bat well, and he can run and field and throw. He's a dandy ballplayer, but it's all from the neck down." His reputation for eccentricity was growing. A lot of people enjoyed his fooling, but not everyone. "Being a clown wasn't safe in the minors," Stengel said. "Some of them bush-league managers could hit you with a bat at fifty feet."

But he batted .290 with Montgomery and led all outfielders in the league in assists. He had developed in three seasons from a raw, unschooled greenhorn into a skilled, competent professional. Brooklyn was well aware of his progress, and in August, a month before the end of the Southern Association season, it announced that it would exercise its option and reclaim Stengel's contract. He was ordered to report to the Brooklyn club as soon as the Southern Association season ended in mid-September.

Montgomery's last game was on Sunday, September 15. Elberfeld took charge of Stengel's departure. He made him buy a new suit. Stengel protested, saying that he was saving his money for dental school. Elberfeld said, "You're going to the big leagues. You're not gonna be a dentist." He told Stengel he had to dress right if he were going to be a big-leaguer, and Stengel reluctantly bought a new suit. Then Elberfeld told him he had to get rid of the cardboard suitcase he'd been using and buy a decent leather one. Stengel protested again, but Elberfeld said, "If you get caught in a hard rain with that cardboard suitcase all that you'll have left will be the handle." Stengel thought the old suitcase would see him through the few weeks of the season still remaining. Elberfeld said no, and made Stengel buy a new bag.

Elberfeld also set up a farewell dinner for the departing hero and made Stengel buy the wine for it. Stengel, pinching his $150-a-month salary, disliked spending all that money, but Elberfeld's insistence that he do things right made him understand the meaning of "big league." Casey went first-class the rest of his life, and he insisted that his players understand the reasoning: "If you're a big-leaguer, act like a big-leaguer."

That also meant you should be treated as a big-leaguer. In 1953, Red Barber, long the broadcaster of Brooklyn Dodger games, refused to do the telecast of the World Series between the Dodgers and the Yankees that year unless the sponsor would let him negotiate for better payment than the $200 a game he had been paid a year earlier. The sponsor told him he could take it or leave it. When Walter O'Malley, the Dodger owner, failed to support Barber in the dispute, Barber left both the World Series broadcast and the

Dodgers. He moved to the Yankees the next season, but during that 1953 Series he was without a job. After the Yankees won the final game of the Series, Barber made his way through the crowd in the dressing room to congratulate Stengel. Casey was surrounded by reporters in the usual mob scene when Barber put out his hand and said, "Congratulations, Casey." Stengel raised his eyebrows, grabbed Barber's hand and said, "Let me congratulate *you!* I want to tell you, a major-league job is worth major-league money!"

The Tabasco Kid sent his protégé to the big leagues in style, a style he'd never forget.

6 DEBUT IN BROOKLYN: STENGEL THE PHENOM

Most of the stories about Stengel's debut in the major leagues, including his own (which varied from time to time, as any good improvising performer's will), picture him as a young innocent arriving in the big city, too scared to venture far from his hotel on his first night in Manhattan, and the next morning finding his way out to the ball park in distant Brooklyn like a nervous explorer pushing his way into an uncharted jungle. The raw busher finally shows up at the clubhouse, is tempted into a crap game with some veteran players, loses his money and is caught with the dice by his new manager, who asks him gruffly, "What are you, kid, a gambler or a ballplayer?" The abashed rookie mumbles, "A ballplayer," and the manager growls, "Well, then, get out on the field where you belong." And so on.

There are undoubtedly elements of truth in

this, but in September 1912, Charley Stengel was far too sophisticated a traveler to be fazed by a new city, even New York. He had been playing baseball in far-flung parts of the country for five years, and he was used to finding his way around. He had known for a month that Brooklyn had exercised its option on him and that he'd be going north to join that club as soon as the Southern Association season was over. He surely had discussed New York with his mentor Elberfeld, as well as with other ex-major-leaguers, and he must have learned at least the rudiments of handling the big city. He had written his family with the good news, and Stengel himself said that his Uncle Charley Jordan of Davenport, another traveling man, was in New York to welcome him.

Uncle Charley may have been in town, but he did not meet his nephew at Pennsylvania Station when the train that had carried him on the last leg of his long overnight journey from Montgomery arrived in New York early in the afternoon of Monday, September 16. There was a ball game in Brooklyn that afternoon and Stengel did not go to a hotel from the station but, carrying his new suitcase, went directly out to Washington Park, the Dodgers' ancient ball field, where he reported to the front office. Ebbets was not there, but his adult son, recovering from an appendectomy, was. He looked up inquiringly at the stocky, blond young man with the suitcase.

"Yes?" he said.

"I'm Stengel," the man said. Young Ebbets looked confused. "From Montgomery," the newcomer added.

"Oh," said Ebbets. *"Oh!"* He was surprised. The club had not expected its new recruit to arrive so promptly. The Southern Association season had ended only the day before. "Much obliged to meet you," he said. They shook hands. It was nearly three o'clock and the game between Brooklyn and Pittsburgh would be starting at three-thirty, the usual starting time in those days.

"Well," said young Ebbets. "Do you want to put a uniform on and go out and meet the players?"

To Ebbets' surprise, Stengel said, "No. I've been traveling all night and all day, and I'm dead tired."

"All right," Ebbets said. "Do you want to stay and watch the game?"

"Yes," Stengel said. "I'd like to look the big fellows over, and then break in tomorrow. I know some of them already. I know Zack

Wheat. He comes from Kansas City, and that's my hometown." He looked at his suitcase. "Can somebody keep an eye on my duds?"

Young Ebbets showed him where to put his suitcase, and they went out to the grandstand to watch the game. Pittsburgh, managed by Fred Clarke, was one of the best teams in the league. The Pirates had finished first, second or third in twelve of the past thirteen seasons, or since Honus Wagner, their incomparable shortstop, had joined the club in 1900. Brooklyn, on the other hand, had not finished higher than fifth in ten years and was seventh again in 1912.

It was a dreary team, but the elder Ebbets, who had joined the club as a $75-a-month clerk in 1883 and had worked his way into principal ownership, was trying to revive it, hoping to lift it back toward the glory it had experienced during his early years with the team. Brooklyn had won pennants in 1889 and 1890, had slipped back during the '90s, when the team acquired the nickname Trolley Dodgers (given to all residents of Brooklyn because of the multiplicity of streetcar lines in that tangled city), but returned to the heights at the end of the decade with pennants in 1899 and 1900, after the outstanding manager Ned Hanlon had switched from Baltimore to Brooklyn and had brought a nucleus of players from his famous Old Orioles with him. The team also took on a new nickname then, for there was a well-known troupe of vaudeville gymnasts called Hanlon's Superbas, and the sportswriters were quick to tack that name onto Hanlon's ball club. "Superbas" persisted as an alternate name for the Dodgers for the next fifteen years. The Superbas prospered under Hanlon for a while, but then the gloom of perennial defeat descended, Hanlon left and Brooklyn found itself muddling along year after year — fifth, sixth, eighth, fifth, seventh, sixth, sixth, seventh, seventh. The team Stengel joined less than three weeks before the end of the 1912 season had a record of fifty victories and eighty-five defeats, a .370 percentage that was considerably below their unadmirable pace of a year earlier.

But Ebbets was *trying*. Left fielder Wheat and first baseman Daubert, who had been discovered three years earlier by Sutton, were proving themselves two of the best players in the league. Miller, another Sutton find, had taken over the principal catching duties from the incredibly weak-hitting Bill Bergen (who in eleven big-league seasons had lifted his bat batting average into the .200s only once). A crack second baseman named George Cutshaw, plucked from the Pacific Coast League in the same draft that gave the Dodgers Stengel, had strengthened the infield. Enos Kirkpatrick, a highly praised minorleague third baseman, had just been brought up from Newark, and another rookie, Bob Fisher, was at shortstop. A retread major-leaguer named Herbie Moran was in right field.

Ebbets was even building a new ball park on land he had acquired "on the outskirts of Flatbush" in an area rather pungently known as Pigtown. He had put more than half a million dollars into the new park. Construction had begun the previous March, and with appropriate ceremonies — including the reading of a letter from President Taft and a wire from Admiral Peary, hero of the North Pole — the cornerstone was laid on July 6, 1912. Plans were made to have the grand opening at the end of August on the anniversary of the Revolutionary War battle of Long Island, but someone discovered belatedly that the National League schedule had the Brooklyn team out of town that day, so the date was reset for September 5. Construction delays made that impossible, too, and the opening was postponed further to October 3, when the team would begin a season-ending series with the Giants. It soon became obvious that the park wouldn't be ready then, either, and soon after Stengel arrived in Brooklyn the Grand Opening was finally put off until the beginning of the 1913 season.

Meanwhile, Ebbets found himself in an uneasy financial condition because of the steady outflow of cash to build the new park. Near the end of August, after gaining complete ownership of the club by buying out a silent partner, he sold half his interest to Edward J. and Stephen W. McKeever for $500,000. The McKeever brothers had made a fortune in the construction business and were a powerful force in Brooklyn politics. Ebbets was made president of the reorganized club, with Ed McKeever as vice-president. The McKeevers kept an eye on the business side of the operation, but let Ebbets have a free hand in running the baseball end.

Thus, when Stengel arrived at Washington Park that Monday, he found a franchise that felt it was on the way up ("Baseball is in its infancy," Ebbets had said). There was new blood in the ownership, new cash, a new ball park on the way, new players coming in. A year earlier, at the draft meeting in Cincinnati at which Ebbets had picked Stengel on Larry

Sutton's recommendation, he had "put in drafts" for thirty-one minor-league players. This meant he had presented checks (or drafts) ahead of time to cover the cost of each player he wanted. Then a selection process took place, since some players were wanted by more than one club, and the prepayment for the ones he didn't get was returned.

Ebbets was called "lucky" after the 1911 draft because he got sixteen of the thirty-one players he had put drafts in for. He paid $13,500 in all for the sixteen players — at $1,000 each for Class AA and Class A players, $750 each for the Class B players, and $500 each for Class C players (Stengel and his teammate Madden). Ebbets also spent another $20,000 or so for the direct purchase of other minor-leaguers, so that in all he spent in the neighborhood of $35,000 for new players, a really substantial sum for the day.

Yet with Stengel watching that Monday afternoon, the Superbas lost their eighty-sixth game of the season. The second-place Pirates, led by Wagner, scored in the first inning and won 2–1, their twelfth straight victory in a futile pursuit of the Giants, who were on their way to a second straight pennant. Relieved by what he had seen, feeling, "I can play as good as these guys," Stengel retrieved his suitcase after the game, went back to Manhattan to the Longacre Hotel on 47th Street, and had dinner with his uncle. The next day, Tuesday, September 17, was a pleasant, sunny day with the temperature in the seventies. Stengel went out to the ball park early, refreshed by a long night's sleep. Wheat took him around to meet the players, introducing him as Charley Stengel from Kansas City.

He put on his first major-league uniform and went to the outfield to shag flies before the game. He was pleasantly surprised and perhaps a bit apprehensive when manager Bill Dahlen told him he was playing center field and batting second. He took the place of Hub Northern, another player in his first full season with Brooklyn. Northern was batting better than .280 but supposedly wasn't feeling well that day. In all likelihood Dahlen just wanted to get a fast look at his newest prospect. He had done the same thing with Kirkpatrick when Enos joined the club late in August, immediately putting him at third base in place of Carlisle (Red) Smith, a solid ballplayer. Whatever Dahlen's reason, there was Charley Stengel in Brooklyn's starting lineup.

Before the game began he went over to say hello to Pittsburgh's starting pitcher, who was warming up in front of the grandstand. The Pirate pitcher was Claude Hendrix, the big right-hander who had been Stengel's teammate four years earlier on the semipro Kansas City Red Sox. Hendrix was in his second season with Pittsburgh and was having a great year (he finished with twenty-three victories and nine defeats). Pitching for the Superbas was George (Nap) Rucker, Brooklyn's one genuine star — Daubert and Wheat had not yet fully established themselves. Rucker was a powerfully built left-hander whose career record — 135 wins and 136 defeats in ten seasons, all with Brooklyn — does little to reflect the esteem in which he was held by his contemporaries. His best years were with a second-rate ball club, and he lost an inconsolable number of 1–0, 2–1, 3–2 games. But he threw the ball very hard, and he was one of the most admired pitchers of his time.

The Pirates took a 1–0 lead in the first inning when Wagner hit a long, run-scoring double to left field. Stengel would say in later years that Wagner hit the ball over his head in center, and sometimes would add that even though he played him much deeper the next time he batted, Wagner hit the ball over his head again. But Casey told that same story about the first time he played the outfield against Babe Ruth, a few years later. Wagner's double to left was his only hit that day.

When Brooklyn came to bat in the first inning, trailing 1–0, Moran led off with a base on balls. Stengel, in his first major-league at bat, slapped a single to center, and Moran eventually scored on a hit by Wheat to tie the game. In the second inning Stengel came to bat again, this time with men on first and second. To the joy of the small crowd, the new rookie singled a second time to put Brooklyn ahead, 2–1.

The Pirates scored again, so did the Superbas, and so did the Pirates, so that when Stengel came to bat for the third time, in the fourth inning, the score was again tied, this time at 3–3. Again there were runners on first and second, but this time there were two out. He slammed his third straight hit off Hendrix to drive in another run and put his club back into the lead. A moment later the prize rookie stole second base. "The crowd was busy applauding the young man all afternoon," said one newspaper the next day.

When Stengel batted for the fourth time the Dodgers had opened a 6–3 lead, Hendrix had been routed, and there was a new Pirate pitcher named Jack Ferry. Stengel singled off him, too, and again stole second base. When he came to bat for the last time in the eighth inning he was greeted with uproarious applause. The Pirate pitcher now, their fourth of the afternoon, was a rookie left-hander named Sherry Smith. With the game safely in hand, 7–3, the mischievous Stengel, who was not ordinarily a switch-hitter, moved around and batted right-handed against Smith. He drew a base on balls and stole second again.

What a day! Stengel had been the key instrument in breaking the Pirates' twelve-game winning streak. He had four hits and a walk in five appearances at the plate, a perfect day that sent the sportswriters digging into their memories and the sparse record books of the era for comparisons. Some recalled that Clarke, the Pirate manager, had had five hits in five at bats when he broke in back in 1894, but the only other debut that came to mind was that of another Brooklyn outfielder named Talbot Percy Dalton, better known as Jack, who a day or so after he joined the club in 1910 had gotten four straight hits off Christy Mathewson. Dalton tailed off badly after that and by 1911 was back in the minors, a fact some of the sportswriters recalled, while others lavished praise on young Stengel ("The pet of the populace . . . the fair-haired youth," one writer called him). They had time to lavish praise, because it rained Wednesday afternoon, the day after the rookie's debut, and with the game washed out they didn't have much else to write about but Stengel's remarkable performance.

Sometime soon after he joined the Dodgers, maybe that rainy Wednesday with the players idling around the clubhouse, Stengel sat in on a poker game, despite Al Tebeau's admonition in Aurora two years earlier. He lost steadily, hand after hand. When at last he turned over winning cards, one of the other players said genially, "About time you took a pot, Kansas City." Like soldiers, ballplayers are quick to give each other nicknames, and a favorite is — or used to be — to call a man after his state or hometown. The voluble Stengel talked so much about Kansas City that it quickly became a part of his identity. While he was generally known as Charley that first season or so in Brooklyn, or occasionally Dutch, and, rarely, Jake (after an old-time outfielder named Jake Stenzel), he was called Kansas City or K.C., too. At about the same time, DeWitt Hopper, the actor, was making a big hit on the vaudeville circuit reciting Ernest Thayer's poem "Casey at the Bat." In time, whenever Stengel struck out, especially

114

with men on base, derisive comments would arise: "Hey, there's Casey at the bat again! Atta boy, Casey!" By the end of his first full season he was Casey to most of his teammates, and by 1914 the fans and the press were using the nickname, too.

It was still raining on Thursday, a fine drizzle that persisted through much of the afternoon, but Brooklyn played anyway, squeezing in a doubleheader with the Chicago Cubs, another of the traditional powers in the National League. This was the team of Tinker to Evers to Chance, although Chance, the Chicago manager known as "the Peerless Leader," had stopped playing first base and was about to be fired as manager, even though he had won four pennants and finished second twice in the previous six seasons. Chance had gone back to Chicago to discuss his situation, and Joe Tinker was serving as acting manager. He and Johnny Evers had never gotten along, even though they had played side by side for years, and between games they got into an argument in the Cub dugout. Tinker took a swing at Evers and other players had to pull them apart. Among the reporters watching this from the press box that afternoon was a tall, taciturn writer for the *Chicago Examiner* named Ring

Lardner. Quite a cast for a rookie's second day.

Jimmy Archer, the Cubs' marvelous fielding catcher, cocked a look at Stengel the first time the rookie came to bat. Archer was famous for his arm, and he took delight in throwing out overambitious runners who tried to steal on him.

"So you're Stengel, hey?" said Archer.

"Yeah, I'm Stengel," the rookie answered.

"I see you broke in pretty good."

"Yeah, pretty good."

"Well, when you get on there, let's see you run."

"Not today, Mr. Archer," Stengel said. "I know you."

And there were no Stengel stolen bases in the three games he played against the Cubs that day and the next. He did have a run-in with the terrible-tempered Johnny Evers when he slid hard into second on a force play. Evers was never particularly genial, and the run-in with Tinker had made his fuse burn shorter than usual. Stengel slid hard, and Evers turned on him angrily.

"You fresh busher," he yelled. "You come into me like that again, and I'll stick this ball down your throat. If you ever cut me, you'll never play another game in the big leagues."

Stengel said, "That's the way I slid in the bushes, and that's the way I'll slide up here."

There wasn't much more to it than that, but Stengel said, "For a while there, I didn't get along very good with Johnny Evers." Yet Casey didn't see Evers after that series of games until the next spring, after Tinker left Chicago to manage the Cincinnati Reds and Evers was given the job as Chicago's new manager, succeeding Chance. The first time Brooklyn and Chicago met, several of the Brooklyn players went over and shook hands with Evers, congratulating him, but Stengel hung back. Evers saw him and said, pleasantly enough, "Aren't you going to congratulate me, Stengel?" Casey, smiling, stepped forward and shook his hand. "Sure, John," he said, "I just didn't think you were talking to me."

Against the Cubs in that doubleheader in 1912, Stengel had three more hits and two walks, which meant that in his first three games as a big-leaguer he had seven hits in eleven at bats and a .636 batting average. The *Brooklyn Eagle* ran his photograph over a caption calling him "New Superba Phenom." The Phenom slowed down on Friday, going hitless against the Cubs, but on Saturday against the Cardinals before a big crowd he hit a tremendous homer over the right-field fence, said to be the longest ball hit in Brooklyn all season, and he had two other hits as the Superbas won 12–0. On Monday (there was no major-league ball on Sunday in New York State at the time) he came to bat with the bases loaded and singled to drive in two runs, and later hit a sacrifice fly to drive in another.

That completed one full week of play for him in Brooklyn, and he was hitting .478, with eleven hits in twenty-three at bats and nine runs batted in. It rained the next two days, but then he went against the Phillies and Grover Cleveland Alexander, who pitched a no-hitter into the eighth inning before finally giving up two safe blows; one was a scratch hit but the other was a clean single by Charley Stengel. Stengel also got the only base on balls that Alexander yielded. The next day he batted in the first run of a 3–1 Brooklyn victory over Philadelphia and later scored the third run almost all by himself; he reached first on a walk, sped to second on a short passed ball, stole third and scored on a sacrifice fly. Thomas Rice, the *Brooklyn Eagle's* sports editor, tying in Stengel's phenomenal debut with kids going back to school for the fall term, wrote: "Now that the schools are open and the bright young idea is beginning to exercise itself with profound essays on that great question, 'Whither are we drifting?,' let us suggest something more practical. Everybody knows that Brooklyn is in seventh place and drifting more or less toward eighth, but there's another question that the young idea might wrestle with while not cogitating on how much more it knows than its ma and pa, or pondering upon the vicious brutality involved in trying to make youngsters reasonably polite and wellmannered. The question is: how long is Stengel going to keep up the fast pace, and is he the real thing?"

Stengel's pace cooled — he had only one hit in his next twelve at bats — but he had made it. He was a big-leaguer, part of the team. He felt at home. He was having fun. When the Superbas went over to New Jersey on a Sunday near the end of the season to play an exhibition game with Newark of the International League, Stengel had a memorable day. The Newark pitcher, Eddie Dent, who had once played for Brooklyn, shut out his old team with two hits, but Stengel had one of them. Before the game there were some on-field festivities to amuse the fans, including the pursuit of a greased pig. Most of the play ers were not interested in that, but Stengel, no longer shy, was one of half a dozen who volunteered to be contestants, and he won $10 by catching the animal and wrestling it to the ground. He smelled so bad afterward from the grease and the pig that his teammates wouldn't let him sit on the bench with them but made him stand off to the side by himself. After the game he and Wheat and a pitcher named Frank Allen went to a restaurant in Newark that ballplayers regularly patronized. The proprietor recognized Wheat and treated the table to champagne. Stengel reciprocated by buying more champagne with his newly won $10, and when it came time to go back to Brooklyn, he and Allen were well sloshed. The rocking motion of the train back to New York was too much for them, and they began to feel woozy. Wheat had to hustle them out to a vestibule between cars, where they both got sick.

Stengel's hitting picked up again toward the end of the year, and when the Giants came to Brooklyn to close out the season he got on base seven times in thirteen plate appearances against McGraw's pennant-winning pitchers. These were the last big-league games ever played in old Washington Park, and Ebbets planned a touching farewell to the

the arena on its last day, a mild, lovely autumn afternoon. He arranged for the Twenty-second Regiment Band to play "Auld Lang Syne" after the final out, as the flag was lowered from the flagpole for the last time. Ebbets assumed the crowd would stand and sing along with the band as the flag came down, but the fans did what they always did. They filed out hurriedly and ran for seats on the trolleys.

Stengel hung around for a few days, getting three hits in an exhibition game the Brooklyn players played against a semipro team the day after the season ended, going to the Polo Grounds to watch Joe Wood and the Red Sox beat the Giants in the first game of the World Series, and then headed back home to Kansas City, already something of a folk hero. The Dodgers had played markedly better after he joined the team, before losing two out of three to the Giants as the season ended. Stengel batted .316, most of it established early. In his last ten games he had had only six hits in thirty-one at bats, a .191 average, but no one seemed aware of that. His sensational opening splurge and the fact that he had batted over .300 were what remained in baseball people's minds. Nor did many people bother to compare his batting record against right-handed pitchers with that against left-handers, although it was worth noting. In the twelve games he played in which right-handers started against Brooklyn, Stengel had thirteen hits in thirty-seven at bats, including a home run and a double, for a .351 average, with eleven runs batted in. In the five games he played in which lefthanders started, he had five singles in twenty at bats for a .250 average, with only two runs batted in.

But Bill Dahlen, the Brooklyn manager, had noticed the discrepancy in performance, and the seeds of platooning were planted.

7 SETTLING IN:
THE GOOD DAYS AND THE BAD

Stengel went home to Kansas City feeling splendid, an authentic major-leaguer, a hero. He ran into a casual acquaintance, a man he hadn't met since he was a boy, who said, "I see your brother is playing in the big leagues."

"That's not my brother," said Stengel proudly. "That's myself."

He played in a few exhibition games, including one in which he failed markedly against the renowned Walter Johnson of the Washington Senators, the major-league strikeout king. Stengel fanned four straight times against the hard-throwing Johnson — who pitched a 1–0 shutout and struck out twenty batters — and was accused by a reporter of failing in the clutch, since the man batting ahead of Casey was one of the few on Stengel's team to get on base against Walter.

The bloom came further off the rose when

he received his 1913 contract from the Dodgers. He had made $900 playing for Montgomery and Brooklyn in 1912, six months of baseball activity at $150 a month. Now he recalled Larry Sutton's counsel, when he accepted the $150-a-month rate after having made $175 at Aurora a season earlier, that if he made good at Montgomery and got to the big leagues he'd be in for real money. The Brooklyn contract called for considerably less than what Stengel considered real money; the precise figure is lost in time, but it was probably $250 a month, or $1,500 for the season. Stengel returned the contract unsigned and asked for more. Ebbets upped the ante, probably to $300 a month, or $ 1,800, but Stengel wanted more than that. Ebbets said no, and Stengel, a rookie with only three weeks of major-league experience, held out all winter. Ebbets finally yielded. Not until March 3, 1913, just as spring training was starting, did Stengel come to terms, probably for $350 a month or $2,100 a year. He wired his acceptance from Kansas City and took a train to Augusta, Georgia, where Brooklyn was training. Only twenty-two, he was the last member of the team to sign that spring, although there was no threat this time that he would quit baseball. He had given up dentistry. "I didn't go back to school," he told Maury Allen, "because I had a different job I liked better."

In Augusta, to his disappointment, he found that he did not have a lock on the center-field job he thought he had won the previous September. Another of Old Scout Sutton's discoveries was in camp, a pintsize outfielder from Boston named Leo Callahan, praised by Sutton as "another Willie Keeler." Manager Dahlen said that Callahan and Stengel were so evenly matched that he was "up a stump" trying to pick between them. That might have been a ploy on Dahlen's part to bring the cocky kid from Kansas City down a peg or two. One reporter wrote that Stengel "isn't keen for workouts and sidesteps them at every opportunity," referring to the tedious drills and exercises the players went through during the first few days of training. Even though there were no practice sessions scheduled for Sunday (the ball park was near a cemetery, and playing ball on the Sabbath would have run against the moral feelings of the community), Dahlen called out to Dan Comerford, the clubhouse man, to be sure to get out to the park early Sunday to get things ready. When Comerford started to protest, Dahlen told him *sotto voce*, "Never mind.

That was just for Stengel's benefit."

Stengel and Callahan both appeared in the few games the Dodgers were able to play that spring, for the weather was terrible, rain falling day after day. Stengel, listed on the Superba roster as five feet eight and a half inches tall, was only a couple of inches bigger than Callahan, but he outweighed him by thirty pounds. At 175 he was one of the heavier and more muscular men on the club, and one of the most energetic, despite his aversion to exercise. When the rain kept the Superbas from playing baseball, he, Daubert, Wheat, Kirkpatrick, and Smith formed a basketball team and played nine games against local teams. The reporter who had noted his distaste for workouts wrote, "Get him into a regular game and he fights every inch of the way, keeping up a line of chatter that puts pep in the team. For a player with only a few weeks in the big show Stengel has more nerve than many veterans. He ought to stick."

Casey got to know Ty Cobb that spring. The Detroit Tiger star was holding out himself, and he'd drive over from his Georgia home to the Dodger camp each day to work out. After one training session he couldn't get his big car started, and after cranking it and kicking it and "cursing blue" for two hours finally took a trolley into town and sent a mechanic out to fix it. Stengel also got chummy with Comerford, the clubhouse man, and Frank Kelley, the chief "rubber" or trainer, who boasted that he had once rubbed down Bob Fitzsimmons, the former world heavyweight boxing champion. Comerford and Kelley were the camp comedians, and Stengel enjoyed their rough, crude humor. One Saturday night Stengel was sitting with Comerford on the porch of the hotel, idling away the evening, when Comerford called over a black cab driver who was in front of the hotel in hopes of picking up a fare.

"Hey, boy," Comerford said, "come here." He told the driver that he was a doctor and that Stengel was his assistant. "We have to go out to the colored cemetery to pick up a dead body for some medical experiments. Can you come by about midnight and take us out there?"

The driver apparently had been through similar hazing before.

"No, sir," he said, "I can't go out to no cemetery that time of night."

"What's the matter?" Comerford said. "You're not afraid, are you? You're not afraid of a live nigger. A dead one won't hurt you."

"That's all right," the driver said, "but you

know we might get catched, and I don't like that county jail."

"Well, we have to go out there," Comerford said. "We'll pay you a hundred dollars. Don't you want to earn a hundred dollars?"

"Sure," the driver said.

"All right," Comerford said. "Be here at midnight."

According to the story, the driver showed up at midnight, or at least the comedians assumed with glee that he had. Comerford and Stengel, enjoying the rich joke, had long since gone to bed. Such were the humor and mores of the times.

On the field Stengel was aggressive, even pushy. Jake Daubert, known as Gentleman Jake because of his meticulous dress and dapper appearance, was standing off to one side talking to a reporter during batting practice one day. Suddenly he stiffened and said, "Watch Stengel try to grab my turn at bat." The young outfielder was standing near the cage with a bat in his hand. "He'll do it, nit," said Daubert ("nit," meaning "not," was a common usage then). He waited, watching, still talking to the reporter. When Herbie Moran finished his swings, Stengel popped into the cage, and Daubert raced toward the plate, yelling, "Hey, Stengel, get out of there!

It's my turn." Unabashed, the imperturbable Stengel yielded to the team captain, saying, "Oh, I thought you were in the clubhouse getting your nails manicured."

Stengel did not distinguish himself in spring training. He suffered a slight muscle pull a few days after arriving in camp that slowed him down, and he didn't do much in Augusta. Not until the team was on its way north toward Brooklyn and opening day did he begin to look good. He hit the team's first home run of the year in Richmond, Virginia, on April 1, and he had a triple the next day. Excitement was building. The new ball park, named Ebbets Field, was completed and waiting for the team to get home. The newly planted grass had not yet taken hold, and there was a controversy about the scoreboard (Harry Stevens, the concessionaire who had introduced scorecards to baseball, objected strenuously to the new scoreboards in both Ebbets Field and the Polo Grounds because he felt they'd hurt his sales), but fans were invited to an open house to inspect the new stadium.

On Saturday, April 5, a few days before the beginning of the season, Ebbets Field was formally opened with an exhibition game between the Dodgers and the New York Yankees. There were more than 25,000 people in the stadium, an enormous crowd in that day, and they filled the park an hour and a half before the game began. Ed McKeever's wife marched out to the center-field flagpole with the players and raised the American flag. Ebbets' daughter Genevieve threw out the first ball. Stengel, first up for Brooklyn, was the first Dodger ever to come to bat in Ebbets Field. He grounded out, but in the fifth inning he hit a hard line drive to left center field that landed safely and scooted along. Harry Wolter, the Yankee center fielder, angled back to his right in an effort to cut the ball off, but just as he reached down for it he inadvertently kicked it and sent it toward the outfield fence. Stengel raced around the bases and scored and was credited with a home run, the first ever hit in Ebbets Field. The Dodgers won 3–2, and the crowd was overjoyed; their young hero was back.

The regular season began a few days later, and the Dodgers lost the opener in Ebbets Field 1–0 to the Phillies, Stengel getting no hits in four at bats. He stayed in that slump for two weeks and was batting only .136, when his magic bat came alive again. He had a double one day, two hits the next, two more hits the day after that, including Brooklyn's first triple of the season. The Giants came to Brooklyn for their first game ever in Ebbets Field, and Stengel won the game with a two-run homer in the seventh inning, the first regular-season home run ever hit there. That happened on a Saturday, before a big crowd, and was in all the Sunday papers the next day.

Little Callahan, who was still with the club, was forgotten. Stengel got two hits off Christy Mathewson in the next game, and had three for four the day after that and drove in the winning run again. He also hit a double off the Bull Durham advertising sign in right field to win $50 and a supply of free ice (a welcome prize in the era before refrigerators and freezers). Everyone was talking about him again. He batted safely in eleven straight games, and had at least two hits every day in the last five games of that streak. His batting average climbed to .352. The papers were ecstatic: "Charley Stengel, who whizzed dizzily across the Superba horizon in 1912, added to his laurels yesterday." His fielding was praised: "He ate up five flies in a half gale." He was called a "center fielder extraordinaire." Fans all over Brooklyn were keeping daily track of his soaring batting average. Dr. William Felter, principal of Girls High in Brooklyn, said he was trying to interest his charges in mathematics by having them figure out Stengel's batting average each day. In fact, on Friday, May 2, Dr. Felter and a party of girls from the high school came to Ebbets Field to watch Stengel play.

And that day the bubble burst. He came to bat four times but made no hits, and his batting streak ended. Worse, he made a grievous bonehead play in the outfield. With the score tied 1–1 in the ninth inning and enemy players on first and second, with one out, Stengel suddenly began racing in from his position in center field toward second base. Perhaps he thought a pickoff play was on at second, but the batter swung and hit the ball to center field. It would have been a simple out if Stengel had been in position, but it went over his head and rolled toward the fence with the young hero in desperate, embarrassed pursuit. Three runs scored, and the Superbas went down to a stunning, humiliating defeat.

That seemed to take some of the starch out of Stengel. He continued to hit, but more modestly, and his batting average slid slowly down into the low .300s and, by the end of June, into the .290s. Yet the Dodgers were playing better ball than in previous seasons — they were second for a time in May — and by the end of June were still a respectable fourth.

That euphoric state ended abruptly on July 4 when Brooklyn lost both games of a holiday doubleheader to the Giants and Stengel sprained his ankle sliding into second base. With Stengel on the bench the Dodgers lost ten games in a row and fell far behind. Casey was out for eighteen days before Dahlen put him up to pinch-hit with the bases loaded on July 22. He hit a grounder to third that forced Wheat at home plate, and he hurt his ankle again running to first. He fell halfway down the line; he got up and stumbled safely across the bag but had to leave for a pinch runner. He was out of action for another week before getting back into the starting lineup at the end of July, but his ankle wasn't right and he played poorly.

The team kept losing and he wasn't hitting much, so on August 19 Dahlen brought Bill Collins, a right-handed batter, up from Newark and put him in Stengel's place in center. This happened during a road trip through the "western" cities of Cincinnati, St. Louis, Chicago, and Pittsburgh, and came at a most inopportune time for Casey. His father had come from Kansas City to Chicago to see his boy play ball and was stunned to find him sitting on the bench. Casey turned his father's discomfort into a laugh-provoking anecdote later on, but at the time it was a painful moment for both father and son. Stengel eventually returned to the lineup, but for a time Dahlen continued to use Collins in Stengel's place against left-handed pitchers. The Dodgers played terribly through July and August, winning only eighteen games while losing more than forty and dropping toward last place. Stengel hurt his shoulder and had trouble throwing, and the crowd began booing him whenever he came to bat.

In September, however, he reestablished his hold on center field when Collins stopped hitting and, perhaps coincidentally, the club picked up a little. It finished the season in sixth place, a little improvement over 1912, although not much. Stengel's injury had hurt the team badly, and both Wheat and Daubert missed games. Worst of all, Rucker, who had bursitis in his shoulder, was no longer the pitcher he had been.

Still, the team *looked* better. Wheat, unquestionably the best player on the club, had proved himself a consistent, dangerous line-drive hitter and an excellent outfielder. Cutshaw had the best range of any second baseman in the league and was superb on the double play. Stengel's high regard in later years for second basemen who could make a double play stemmed from his appreciation of what Cutshaw could do. Red Smith, who had reclaimed third base, was a good hitter and a fine fielder, although for some reason the Brooklyn front office had scant regard for him and traded him away less than a year later. Miller was a dependable catcher. Daubert at first base was one of the stars of the league — he hit .350 in 1913 to win the batting championship — although he wasn't nearly as good as his reputation made him out to be. He was given the "Chalmers Award" (a new Chalmers automobile) for being the outstanding player in the National League, although in retrospect it's obvious that Gavvy Cravath, the hard-hitting outfielder of the Phillies, was a far more valuable player. Cravath hit .341 to Daubert's .350, batted in 128 runs to Jake's 52 and scored 78 runs to the Brooklyn star's 76. And the Phillies finished second, compared to Brooklyn's sixth. Daubert's reputation reflected baseball thinking: His high batting averages year after year dazzled people. He *looked* good at bat, and he looked good in the field. He had quick hands, could bunt amazingly well, and very seldom made an error. But he had little power at bat and little range in the field. No one noticed. He was Brooklyn's captain, and its star.

As for the rest of the team, the shortstop, Bob Fisher, wasn't much good, and the pitching, with Rucker not himself, was unimpressive. The outfield, aside from Wheat, was still questionable. Herbie Moran, the five-foot-five-inch regular right fielder, had no power at all, Stengel had been disappointing after his injury (his final average was only .272), and the newcomers, first Callahan and then Collins, had fizzled.

8 THE FEDERAL LEAGUE WAR: A MATTER OF MONEY

After the season Daubert led a contingent of Dodgers, including Stengel, on a barnstorming trip through the South and on to Cuba. The players earned $600 each on the trip, with Daubert getting an extra $1,000 for handling all the details. Back in Brooklyn, Ebbets faced a lot of problems, one of them Dahlen, who was a favorite of the owner's but had been a disappointment as manager. And news had been bubbling for a year or more about a new "Federal League," a major league independent of organized baseball that now seemed certain to begin operations in 1914. Ebbets and the other major-league owners knew that the Federals would be raiding their rosters for players and that they had to be prepared to pay higher salaries to keep their charges from jumping to the new league.

In November, Ebbets dropped the ax on

Dahlen and surprised everyone by announcing that the new manager was Wilbert Robinson, a fat, pleasantly profane fifty-year-old who had been a star catcher on the old Baltimore Orioles of the 1890s. After running a restaurant for several years in Baltimore he had become a coach on the Giants under John McGraw, who had been his teammate on the Orioles. The genial Robinson and the hot-tempered McGraw had had a serious falling-out late in the 1913 season despite their long-standing friendship. Robinson, coaching at first base, misread one of McGraw's complicated signals and sent base runner Fred Snodgrass down to second on an attempted steal. Robinson thought it was odd that McGraw wanted Snodgrass to go, because the player had an injured leg and could not run well, but the autocratic McGraw's word was law, and Robinson knew better than to question it. Snodgrass was thrown out. After the inning McGraw demanded to know why Robby, as he was usually called, had sent Snodgrass down.

"You gave me the sign," Robinson said.

"Like hell I did," McGraw replied.

That night, at dinner, they renewed the argument. One thing led to another, and McGraw, who had a short fuse, declared,

"You're through on the Giants!"

If it hadn't been for Ebbets it's likely the fuss would have blown over. Robinson continued on the coaching lines for the rest of the season and through the 1913 World Series (when Snodgrass, still hampered by injury, was on base only once and did not attempt to steal). But there are few secrets in baseball, and when Ebbets heard about the dispute he realized it would be a coup for Brooklyn to steal McGraw's right-hand man away from him. He talked to Robinson, who liked the idea of becoming a manager, and he was hired. McGraw reacted badly, and he and Robinson were antagonists from then on, which didn't hurt the Dodger-Giant rivalry.

So Robinson came to the Dodgers and immediately endeared himself to Brooklyn. At a luncheon Ebbets gave in his honor a few days after he was hired, Robby poked fun at his own girth, saying that when he first went out to the baselines to coach for the Giants a fan had shouted to McGraw, "Hey, Mac, what time does the balloon go up?" He voiced approval of the lunch, saying, "I'm in sympathy with the Ebbets idea of having something to eat whenever an excuse can be found. I haven't been feasting on oysters and wild duck all these years in Baltimore for nothing." He praised Bill Dahlen, the manager he was replacing, blaming the team's poor finish in 1913 on injuries. He called Rucker, Brooklyn's pet, the best pitcher in the league but said he wanted more pitchers to give Nap the help he deserved. He said he thought there might be too many left-handed batters on the club (Wheat, Daubert, Stengel, and Moran were left-handed) and hoped he might get some right-handed-hitting outfielders to alternate with Stengel and Moran. He gave the impression of being a decent, pleasant man who knew baseball, knew what he was doing and knew what the Dodgers needed. After the luncheon an admiring Steve McKeever said, "Takes hold like a bullpup, don't he?"

Robinson and Ebbets sat down and talked about the team. Robby wanted a good shortstop, and in mid-December Ebbets made the startling announcement that he had obtained Joe Tinker for $25,000, a stunning amount of money, and two unimportant players. Included in the $25,000 was a $10,000 bonus to be paid to Tinker when he signed his Brooklyn contract.

Dodger fans were ecstatic. After Honus Wagner, Tinker was the best shortstop in the league — or had been. Brooklyn talked animatedly about the great infield the team would have now, with Daubert, Cutshaw, Tinker and Smith. Optimism ran wild. A vastly improved finish was a cinch, everyone felt, and Ed McKeever went so far as to say, "Looks like the pennant now."

Something was wrong, however. Despite the announcement that Tinker was coming to Brooklyn, he didn't. He hadn't said he would. He didn't sign a contract. He seemed to be differing with Ebbets on terms. One report said that Tinker wanted a big salary on top of that $10,000 bonus. Then another report began circulating that he was dickering with the "outlaw" Federal League. Ebbets hadn't sent contracts out to his players yet despite the Federal League threat because he wanted to get the Tinker thing settled first.

Late in December it was rumored that Otto Miller was "flirting" with the Feds. Then, just before the end of the year, the bad news came. Tinker would not be coming to Brooklyn after all. He had jumped to the Federal League, signing a lucrative contract to manage the Fed team in Chicago. The new league announced its formal organization, and the war was on. Pat Ragan, one of Brooklyn's starting pitchers, said he had received an offer and was threatening to jump. Bill Fischer, a reserve catcher, said flatly that he expected to sign with the Feds, and so did Enos Kirk-patrick, the erstwhile rookie sensation (not all of Old Scout Sutton's finds panned out).

There was more disturbing news early in 1914. Tinker, as manager of the Chicago Feds, had gone to Kansas City, where he pulled off a tremendous coup by signing Pittsburgh's Claude Hendrix. Apparently he also talked to Stengel, because rumors began that Casey was going to sign with the Federal League's Kansas City franchise. Stengel would be a big drawing card in his home-town. The *Brooklyn Eagle* wired Casey, asking him about the rumors. He wired back, "HAVE BEEN MADE FLATTERING OFFERS, BUT TO DATE CAN'T NAME CLUBS." The *Eagle* ran a story with a big headline saying, "STENGEL LATEST SUPERBA TO FLIRT WITH FEDERAL LEAGUE."

Now everyone was concerned about the Federal threat. Brooklyn fans recalled with relief that Daubert had signed a three-year contract the previous year, which meant he was safe for two more seasons. But players like Stengel, whose contract had expired, were bound to Brooklyn only by the lifetime option of the reserve clause, which was recognized only by clubs within the framework of organized baseball. The Federal League did not respect its restrictions. Daubert then created a sensation by revealing that he had been talking to the Feds anyway and would consider jumping if the money was right. Ebbets came down on Daubert like a ton of bricks, reminding him that he was under binding contract to Brooklyn. Daubert backed off in a hurry, saying he had only been "joshing," but his wife innocently told an inquiring newspaperman that Jake had been offered $10,000 a year and had been on the verge of signing with the Federals before Ebbets spoke to him.

Other players around the league began jumping: Russ Ford, the Yankee pitcher; Bill McKechnie, a Yankee infielder; Danny Murphy of the Athletics; Davy Jones, the old Detroit Tiger star; Artie (Circus Solly) Hofman of the Cubs; Bob Groom of Washington; Jack Quinn of the Braves. The powerful Philadelphia Phillies, who had finished second in 1913, were particularly hard hit. They lost two of their best starting pitchers, Tom Seaton, who won twenty-seven games in 1913, and Ad Brennan, who won fourteen, as well as their catcher, Bill Killefer, their shortstop, Mickey Doolin, and their second baseman, Otto Knabe.

Ebbets was getting nervous. He had that

big new ball park, and he needed spectators in it. He heard that the Federals were planning to put a team in Brooklyn, which meant Federal League competition right in town. Hurriedly, he began to court his own players. He hopped on a train and traveled around the country to talk to his men directly. He didn't cut corners. He offered generous salaries and long-term deals. By mid-January, to his and Brooklyn's great relief, the signed contracts began to come in. Wheat accepted a three-year contract. So did Rucker. Miller signed for three years, Pat Ragan for three, Cutshaw for two. In Kansas City, Ebbets offered Stengel $4,000, almost double his 1913 salary, and for three years. Casey liked the money but, with his eye on the future, not the long-term agreement. He felt that if he had not been injured he'd have been in a much stronger bargaining position. If he could keep his batting average above that glamorous .300 mark next season . . . He signed, but for only one year.

Ebbets said later, with considerable pride, "I have assumed the burden of the biggest payroll I have ever been called upon to meet. The Federal League wanted my stars — well, so did I. That meant I had to outbid them, and I assure you those fellows certainly did boost their figures. But I met them. I didn't let one of my good players get away."

Late in January, safely signed, Casey left Kansas City and went down to Oxford, Mississippi, at the invitation of William Driver, who had been his baseball coach at Central High and was now coaching baseball (and all other sports) at the University of Mississippi. Casey's shoulder was better, but he wanted to work on his throwing before reporting to spring training, and he could do that at Mississippi. He also helped Driver coach the baseball team, his first experience in directing other players. The Ole Miss team was good — it won the state championship later that spring by defeating Millsaps College 5–3 — but in a game in Baton Rouge against Louisiana State University, the LSU players batted around against George (Sawney) Culley, even though Culley was a left-hander and it was generally accepted that LSU couldn't hit lefties. Stengel, who had accompanied the team on its trip, decided that someone was stealing Mississippi's signals, and he suspected the umpire, a former LSU player. The one umpire working a game would call the pitches from behind the mound when men were on base, which would give him a perfect view of the catcher. Stengel suggested that Ole Miss quietly change its signals. When the next LSU batter confidently stepped into the pitch to swing at what he had been advised would be a curveball he was hit with a fastball. That cooled off the signal-stealing.

Casey enjoyed his six weeks at Ole Miss, visiting fraternity houses, telling stories, being interviewed by the college paper, the *Daily Mississippian.* "Tell 'em I'm single yet," he suggested to the reporter who did the story. At the end of February he left for Augusta to join the Dodgers, now often called Robinson's Robins by the sportswriters, who sometimes referred to the portly manager as the Round Robin. Casey was full of stories about campus life at Mississippi, and some of his teammates began calling him "Professor."

Kid Elberfeld was with Brooklyn as a coach and reserve infielder (almost forty, the aging Kid got into eighteen games for Brooklyn that season), and the presence of his old mentor, combined with his recent coaching experience at Mississippi, filled Casey with tutorial zeal. More and more frequently he expressed his ideas on how the game should be played. He told Wheat, for example, that Zack ought to stand with his feet closer together when he batted so that he could get a faster start running toward first base.

Robinson had some ideas of his own, one of which had to do with switching Stengel from center field to right. Moran, the right fielder in 1913, had gone to Cincinnati in the abortive Tinker deal, and Robinson had a new outfielder in camp named Joe Riggert, a veteran minor-leaguer who had played a few games for the Red Sox in 1911. Riggert, a right-handed batter and thrower, would be in center field, Robby said. He wanted a left-handed thrower like Stengel in right, he said, because of a theory he had about left-handed vs. right-handed throwers out there. He took Stengel and Riggert out to right field one day during practice to show the sportswriters what he meant. Base hits near the foul line tend to curve toward foul territory, he said, and on such difficult chances a left-handed thrower can handle the ball and throw it to the infield more quickly than a right-handed thrower. He had Stengel and Riggert take turns fielding balls batted out along the foul line, and it was obvious that Stengel was a lot quicker at grabbing the ball and throwing it back in. Whether this was because of the right-lefty difference or just because Stengel was a better ballplayer is not clear, but the theory, which the papers printed, impressed young Casey. Sixty years later, talking about

Roberto Clemente with a sports broadcaster, Casey practically echoed Robinson's words while expressing amazement at the right-handed Clemente's ability to get to a ball along the right-field foul line and throw it quickly to second base.

But in 1913 he resisted the change Robinson wanted to make. He had played center field since his arrival in Brooklyn, and he didn't like being evicted. Robinson, who couldn't help exuding kindliness even when he was bawling out a player ("He sounded like a friendly Newfoundland dog going woof-woof," a sportswriter said), smoothed Stengel's feathers, flattered him, and Casey, grumbling a little, found himself playing right field.

Then Jack Dalton arrived in camp. The momentary hero of 1910 (Brooklyn would never forget the four hits he got off Matty) had been in the minors for three seasons and was in spring training with Newark when Robinson's Robins obtained him on March 24. Stengel had hurt himself sliding and was out for a few days, and Robby needed outfielders. He put Dalton, who was an excellent fielder, in center and shifted Riggert, right-handed thrower or not, to right. Dalton, an impressive-looking man with a deep bass voice, was almost thirty, but he turned out to be a much better ballplayer than he had been four years earlier. He quickly established himself as a full-time regular in center, between Wheat in left and Stengel, after he returned from his injury, in right. Riggert was summarily relegated to the bench. Stengel played all the time, even when the Dodgers (the names Dodgers, Robins and Superbas were all used for the team, sometimes in the same newspaper paragraph) met the minor-league Baltimore Orioles in an exhibition game shortly before the season began and faced the sensational young left-handed pitcher George (Babe) Ruth. Ruth beat the Robins 10 to 6, partly because of a tremendous triple he hit over Stengel's head in the second inning, but Stengel batted well against the left-handed Babe. His double in the sixth drove in Brooklyn's first run, he walked in the seventh, and he hit another double in the ninth to score the Dodgers' last run. Ruth's triple was his only hit, Stengel gathering in the long fly to right that he hit later in the game. So much for Casey's stories about Wagner and Ruth whacking balls over his head even after he played extra-deep against them the second time they batted.

The Dodgers, led by Dalton, who batted

.469 in April, got off to a fairly good start in the regular season, but by mid-May they were flagging. Wheat and Stengel were in terrible slumps, and Robby threatened to bench both of them. When the Robins faced a tough left-hander named Hank Robinson in St. Louis late in May, Robinson put Riggert in for Stengel, although Wheat remained in the lineup. Riggert drove in the winning run, and after that Robby alternated him with Stengel, using Riggert against lefties, Stengel against righties.

The league standings were volatile all season, all eight teams bunched closely most of the year. The depleted Phillies, for example, fell from third place to seventh in three days. Late in May the Giants, going after their fourth straight pennant, moved strongly to take over first place, and the Braves dropped down to last. Brooklyn started going down, too, losing with depressing consistency, and toward the end of June they displaced Boston in the cellar.

Throughout July and August they played fitfully, winning in bursts to climb as high as fifth, then losing again to fall back into last place. Dalton, batting .339, continued to play very well, and Daubert, as usual, was hitting over .300. Wheat and Stengel, on the other hand, were struggling, although the carefree Casey did not let his anemic batting average disturb his penchant for enjoying himself. Before an exhibition game in Bellaire, Ohio, in the middle of July, he came in from the outfield to the infield during practice and began to pantomime fielding ground balls. He was extremely funny doing it, and the crowd began to laugh. Other players joined him and soon the Robins were putting on a phantom infield drill, waiting for mythical grounders, stabbing them, leaping for high throws, firing a nonexistent ball around the bases. They kept it up for ten minutes, and the crowd loved it, showering them with applause when it was over.

In the real world, things were not as good. Riggert, who had started well, slumped terribly, as had the previous Stengel alternates, Callahan and Collins, a year earlier. Riggert was sold to St. Louis and another right-handed outfielder named Hy Myers was brought up from Newark to platoon with Casey. Myers did very well, but then fell and hurt his shoulder and was out for several weeks. Injuries seemed endemic in Brooklyn. Robinson had been using a rookie named Ollie O'Mara at shortstop, who had done a fine job in the field, but early in August O'Mara broke his leg. Daubert injured his foot. Wheat pulled a muscle. Dalton sprained his wrist. Rucker, tormented by bursitis, was able to start only sixteen games all year. Everything was going wrong, and as late as August 23 the Dodgers were still in last place.

And then they began to look like a ball team. Stengel, whose batting average had dipped as low as .225, broke out of his slump and began to hit hard and consistently. Daubert came back from his injury. So did Wheat. So did Myers, who began to play so well that when Dalton's wrist got better Robinson alternated Dalton with Stengel, shifting Myers back and forth between right and center depending on which of the other two was not playing. Best of all, Robby found an impressive young pitcher named Ed Pfeffer to take Rucker's place as ace of the staff. Pfeffer, a big strong right-hander, was nicknamed Jeff after his brother Frank, who had pitched in the National League some years earlier and had been called Big Jeff after Jim Jeffries, the heavyweight boxing champion. His kid brother inherited the name. Pfeffer won twenty-three games and lost only twelve in 1914.

The Robins were beginning to shape up, although no one much noticed because of the extraordinary National League pennant race. The Giants were still in first place, had been since late May, but the Braves, last in the middle of July, had been winning games at a sensational rate and had climbed up through the tangled standings into second place, right behind the Giants, as August ended. On September 2 in Ebbets Field the Robins knocked off the Giants 6–2 to dump them out of first place. McGraw's team rallied to regain the league lead, slipped back again, and a week later in the Polo Grounds lost two in a row to the Dodgers to go tumbling two and a half games behind. The relentless Braves kept on winning, and the Giants collapsed. Three weeks later they were ten and a half games behind, and the Braves had the pennant.

Stengel continued his batting tear to the end of the season, his average climbing over .300 to .316 as the season ended. Dalton finished at .319, and so did Wheat, which meant that the Robins had a .300-hitting outfield, one of the few times in big-league history that's happened. Daubert batted .329 to win his second straight batting title. Except for Pfeffer, the Dodger pitching wasn't much in 1914, but the hitting was remarkable. Four of the five leading batters in the league were from Brooklyn: Daubert, first; Dalton, third; Wheat, fourth; Stengel, fifth. (Myers, who was a regular by the season's end, batted .286.)

The strong hitting lifted the Dodgers into a wild sprint down the home stretch. Still in seventh place on September 11, they won eighteen of their last twenty-six games to finish the season in fifth place, only four games under .500, for their best performance since 1903. The future looked bright. The Federal League was still a threat, still firmly committed to going after players from the old, established teams, but Ebbets and Robinson weren't too concerned. Most of their key players had long-term contracts, and Ebbets moved quickly to sign up the others as soon as the season ended, particularly the stubborn Stengel. It took a little negotiating, and Ebbets had to go higher than he wanted to, because Casey had, after all, batted .316. But on October 21, Ebbets signed him to a two-year contract for about $6,000 a year, or more than six times as much as Charley Stengel had been making when he joined the Dodgers from Montgomery two years earlier.

9 *UNCLE ROBBY:*
WHO DROPPED THE GRAPEFRUIT?

The only important player Ebbets failed to hold on to was Jack Dalton, who jumped to Buffalo of the Federal League for $8,000 in January. That left Robinson with only three outfielders, Wheat in left, the relatively untested Myers in center and the sometimes erratic Stengel in right, but neither he nor Ebbets worried about that. In fact, Robby boasted to reporters, "I batted .500 when I kept Charley Stengel away from the Feds," the implication being that the manager had persuaded Ebbets to go high to sign Stengel, overcoming the club president's reluctance to give in to the impudent, outspoken outfielder. Ebbets, a somewhat self-important man, always had his doubts about Casey, and when Stengel arrived in training camp early in March 1915, the doubts appeared justified. Everyone was shocked by Stengel's appearance. Where was the vigorous, broad-shouldered, thick-chested athlete they had said goodbye to the previous fall? Now he was pale and thin, his face drawn. He was down to 157 pounds, 20 pounds below his playing weight. He was recovering from typhoid fever, had been in a hospital and, he said, had come pretty close to dying. He was better now, but he was still weak. He insisted he'd be ready by opening day, but he was unable to work out and the newspapermen covering the team wrote that the Robins couldn't expect much help from Stengel that season. He didn't put a uniform on for nearly a month.

Stengel's illness has been the subject of some conjecture. The venerable baseball writer Fred Lieb, in *Baseball as I Have Known It*, a quiet, low-key, but refreshing memoir of his life as a chronicler of the game, which he published in 1977 when he was nearly ninety, told a story about Stengel that Lieb had regaled friends with but had never written for publication while Casey was alive. Lieb said the story had been told him by George Underwood, an old-time New York sportswriter who had covered the Dodgers in Daytona Beach that spring of 1915. According to Lieb, Underwood said he had driven from Daytona Beach late one night over to the Western Union office in Daytona to file a story. On his way back over the trestle bridge that crossed the tidal lagoon between Daytona and the beach he saw a lonely figure far out on the trestle, staring down into the deep water. He recognized Stengel, stopped his car, and called out, "Casey, what the hell are you doing out here? If Robby knew you were out this late, he'd slap a fine on you."

"George," said Casey, "I'm trying to get up the guts to jump in."

"What for?" asked the astonished Underwood.

"I'm not hittin'," Stengel said. "Robby don't like me. And I've got the clap."

Underwood got Stengel off the bridge and back to his hotel and said no more about it, except to Lieb. In his book, Lieb went on to write, "Bothered by his VD problem, Stengel let his batting average drop from .316 in 1914 to a puny .237 in 1915."

The implication could be that Stengel came to camp suffering not from the after-effects of typhoid but the present distress of gonorrhea, but that seems a bit too glib. "The clap," while an unpleasant and distressing disease, does not ordinarily cause a precipitate loss of weight or leave its host as palpably weak as Stengel was when he reported to Daytona. Typhoid, on the other hand, does, and typhoid was a recurring menace in the America of the day. That same spring, cases of typhoid broke out in the New York Giants' training camp in Marlin, Texas, and McGraw had the healthy members of his squad inoculated against it. The sportswriters covering the Brooklyn camp wrote about Stengel's typhoid as soon as he reported to the camp. If he had been suffering from gonorrhea it seems unlikely that they would have agreed on such a dramatic and potentially fatal disease as typhoid as a euphemism for VD.

On the other hand, it is entirely possible that Stengel, a bachelor, a party boy who loved to go out nights, did indeed catch a "dose of the clap" in Daytona. The Brooklyn team was scattered among several small hotels and rooming houses, rather than being gathered together in one place, and Robinson had little control over his players' off-field behavior. The symptoms of gonorrhea appear quickly, often within a week of exposure, and the Dodgers were in Daytona Beach for a month. It is then at least possible that when Stengel finally did put on a uniform and begin playing, he had a "dose," wasn't hitting, and the gruff, outspoken Robinson was annoyed. Harold Rosenthal, who covered the Yankees for the *New York Herald-Tribune* during Stengel's tenure as Yankee manager, said he once asked Garry Schumacher, then publicity man for the Giants but for many years a New York baseball writer, why Stengel showed such little interest in the women who always cluster around baseball players — the groupies, both young and middle-aged.

"Well," Schumacher said, "he had a little of that Cupid's Catarrh when he was a young fellow, and it made him a little shy ever since."

In 1917, during another of Stengel's holdouts, Ebbets issued a public rebuke of Casey's charge that the club was cheap, citing Brooklyn's benevolent "treatment of him in 1915, when he was incapacitated through his own fault." Ebbets might have meant that catching typhoid was Casey's own fault, but maybe not.

No matter, Casey was pretty much a convalescent during the first month of spring training, which brings into the discussion another, better-known aspect of the Stengel legend, the story of the infamous grapefruit.

In Daytona Beach that March was Ruth Law, one of the first women aviators. She had a biplane, a fragile-looking thing that seemed to be made mostly of pipes and wires. She had been hired by Daytona Beach entrepreneurs to make daily flights as a publicity gimmick, one day for instance dropping golf balls on the hard sand of the beach to promote a local golf course. Just about every day except when it rained, Miss Law would take off from the beach (so hard that automobile speed records were set on it), fly around for a while, then land and take off again, often bringing tourists aloft with her, one at a time.

The Dodger training field was close to the beach, and the players, as fascinated as everyone else was by the novelty of an airplane, got to know Ruth Law. So did Ebbets, who early in the second week of training announced that on Thursday of that week, the day of the first formal exhibition game of the spring, he would throw the first ball from Miss Law's plane instead of throwing it from his box seat. Then he'd land and return to the field, and the game would begin.

Ebbets' proposed stunt never came off, possibly because of plain old fear of flying, although the official story was that Miss Law had telephoned Ebbets at noontime on Thursday to say that she was so booked up that she couldn't keep her appointment with him. Considering the publicity such a flight would generate, that hardly seems likely. Another version was that Trainer Kelley had put his foot down, declaring that a man of Ebbets' age (he was fifty-five) and ailments, whatever they were, should not go up in an airplane. Kelley may have made the statement, but he himself was an enthusiastic flier, going up with Ruth Law three different times.

The day after Ebbets' aborted flight, eight people from the Brooklyn party took flights in her plane. Kelley was one. Others were Elmer Brown, a pitcher; Otto Miller, the big catcher; Sherry Smith, the left-handed pitcher Stengel had faced in his first big-league game and who was now with the Dodgers; Ed Donalds, a rookie pitcher; Leon Cadore, another rookie pitcher who was making a name for himself in camp with his sleight-of-hand tricks; Billy Zimmerman, a rookie outfielder the optimistic Robinson hoped would be good enough to alternate with Stengel; catcher Mack Wheat, Zack Wheat's kid brother; Tommy McGuinn, another rookie; Frank (Buck) O'Neill, one of the sportswriters; and Mrs. Raleigh Aitchison, whose pitcher husband had won twelve games for the Dodgers in 1914. Mrs. Aitchison went up in the plane after her husband declined to do so, saying that when he died he hoped it would be in a soft bed without a struggle, and not on the hard sand of Daytona after a long drop. Mrs. Aitchison, a lively young woman, called her husband a "scaredy cat," put on a heavy sweater, pulled a cap down over her ears and climbed aboard. She waved and called out, "So long, boys," as the plane started moving, and after she landed said, "It was exhilarating but nothing extraordinary. I had confidence in Miss Law. It felt as though we were skimming along the sand in an automobile, and then without warning the earth just fell away. When I became accustomed to the roar of the motor and the rush of the wind, I looked around. It was a beautiful sight."

Two other players, Dick Egan, a shortstop, and Hy Myers, were urged to fly, but Egan said he had promised his wife that he wouldn't. Myers said sure, he'd go up, but *his* wife, who was with him, said sharply, "You will *not*."

The players took turns flying while the Dodgers were practicing. Robby ran a loose camp, and he had no objection to the players going over to the beach to go up in the plane. The flights didn't take long, and Ruth Law gave each of her passengers a signed certificate attesting that the person mentioned had indeed flown in an airplane. The certificates were proudly shown around, and, naturally, the conversation much of the afternoon and evening was about flying, what it felt like and so on. The bouncing golf balls were mentioned, and the ball that Ebbets had intended to drop. Jack Coombs, the old Philadelphia Athletics pitcher, had caught on with the Dodgers that spring (Robby liked to experiment with old pitchers other teams discarded; he knew they had had the ability to win once, and he was skilled at coaxing another good year or two out of their tired arms). Coombs had considerable knowledge of mathematics and physics, and he tried to figure out just how fast a ball would be going when it reached the ground after being dropped from a plane. Mention was made of the well-publicized achievement of Charles (Gabby) Street, the Washington Senators' catcher who a few years earlier had caught a baseball dropped from the top of the Washington Monument. Some players doubted that a ball dropped from an airplane could be caught.

"Oh, hell," boomed Robinson. "I could catch one." Robinson was three months short of his fifty-second birthday and hadn't caught in competition for a dozen years, but he had been one of the best catchers in the game in the 1890s. (And a pretty good hitter, too.

Boasting about it one day in the Dodger camp, he said, "Christ, I got seven hits in seven at bats in one game back in 1792." "*Seventeen* ninety-two?" one of his listeners asked, "I didn't know you were *that* old." Perplexed, Robby stared at him for a second, then realized his slip. "Oh shit, you know what I mean," he said.)

Robinson was proud of his catching ability, and he repeated his boast. One thing led to another, and it was decided that someone would go up with Ruth Law the next day, Saturday, and drop a ball over the field for Robinson to catch — or try to catch. A game with Birmingham of the Southern Association was scheduled for Saturday, and Robinson didn't want any of his players to be away from the field, so Kelley, the trainer, said he'd go up.

Robinson might have suspected something, for Kelley and Comerford, the clubhouse man, were known as "the comedy twins." You will recall Comerford's delicate humor vis-á-vis the black cab driver two years earlier in Augusta. In Daytona Beach, Comerford and Kelley had noticed a store called the Women's Exchange. The two went into it. A saleswoman looked at them inquiringly, and Comerford asked, "Is this the Women's

Exchange?" She said, "Yes," and Comerford said, "Well, I'd like to exchange two brunettes for a blonde." The saleswoman didn't bat an eye. "I'm sorry," she said, "we're out of blondes." Coming around the counter, she opened the door and said, sweetly, "But we can turn a man into a street." Kelley enjoyed telling that one around camp.

It rained Saturday, on and off, and the game with Birmingham had to be canceled, but Robinson had his players out practicing anyway between showers. Early in the afternoon, Kelley left for the beach, and a few minutes later along came Ruth Law's airplane, heading over the ball park. Robinson put on a catcher's big mitt and stationed himself near the pitcher's mound. The plane, flying forty-five miles per hour, crossed over the field at an altitude of about 500 feet, and Kelley dropped the baseball.

Except, of course, that it wasn't a baseball. In his hurry to get over to the airplane, Kelley had forgotten to take a ball with him. At least, that's the story that was in the newspapers the next day, and that's the story Stengel told in his autobiography half a century later. There wasn't time for Kelley to go back to the ball field to get one. It was spitting rain, and it might start coming down hard. Ruth Law had never flown in rain before, and she was eager to get the flight over and done with. And, if Kelley went back, Robby might abruptly decide to call the whole thing off. Someone near the plane had a grapefruit and handed it to Kelley, suggesting he drop it instead. It's also possible that Kelley was afraid that Robinson could be hurt by the impact of a rapidly accelerating baseball and substituted the grapefruit for safety's sake. It's just as possible that Kelley's bizarre sense of humor was at work. Whatever the reason, it was a grapefruit that he dropped.

Robinson circled under it. Remember the circumstances. He was in his fifties, and he was forty or fifty pounds heavier than his playing weight of twenty years earlier. It was drizzling. The field was wet. When the "ball" came down close to the pitcher's mound, Robinson circled with his head back, the way a catcher does under a high pop fly. Still moving slightly, he got under it, raised his mitt to catch it, and — splat! The grapefruit glanced off the heel of his mitt and split open against the upper part of his chest, near his shoulder. Its force, combined with Robinson's unsteadiness and the slippery condition of the field, sent him flat on his back, his chest and face splattered with grapefruit juice and fragments of fruit. "Jesus, I'm killed!" Robinson cried. "I'm dead! My chest's split open! I'm covered with blood!"

The players, startled at first by the explosion of the "baseball," ran to his side. When they saw what had happened they began laughing, roaring, rolling around the ground helplessly. Robinson sat up, touched his face, tasted the glop, recognized what it was that he had tried to catch, and began swearing, something he was awfully good at. "Who done this, Stengel?" he is supposed to have said, and added another string of obscenities. After a while, he calmed down. That night, listening cheerfully as the story was told and retold, he said, "If it had been a baseball, I'da caught it," although later he admitted, "I was lucky. If that had been a baseball, I probably *would* have been killed."

Presumably, Robinson continued to blame Stengel for putting Kelley up to the trick, although in newspaper reports of the incident the day after it happened Stengel's name was not mentioned, as it surely would have been if he had been involved. Or if anyone even suspected he'd been involved. Nor was he one of the several players who went up in Ruth Law's plane the next day, Sunday, when Kelley took his third flight in seventy-two hours.

In his autobiography, Casey, never one to be modest about such feats, disclaimed having had anything to do with the grapefruit. He said that Robinson was so annoyed with Kelley for substituting the grapefruit that he got rid of him six months later. And, in fact, Kelley was gone from the club the next season.

But never underestimate the vagaries of memory, the selectivity or whimsicality of the aged in recalling the events of their youth. One evening in the 1950s, Stengel was reminiscing during a Yankee road trip through the Midwest, and Harold Rosenthal asked him to tell exactly what had happened in the grapefruit incident.

"Why, sure," said Casey, and told the story in great, colorful detail, including the following: "We fixed it up so that I rode in a kind of kitchen chair on the wing of the plane. I guess they picked me because I had a pretty good arm." And, "We were over the ball park, about in the middle, Ruth Law gave me a wave, and I let the ball go, only it was this small grapefruit."

Rosenthal said, "I can still hear Stengel's laugh after he finished the story. He had a most unusual laugh. He sort of barked, 'Ha!' once, and let it go at that."

Ha, indeed. Rosenthal, an enterprising reporter, tracked down Ruth Law and asked her what had happened. She wrote Rosenthal a long, gracious letter in which she said, first of all, that there was no kitchen chair. "I was considered wild," she said, "but not wild enough to have someone riding on a chair on the wing of my plane. It was tough enough to keep them flying straight without stunts like that."

But she also told Rosenthal that *she* was the one who had forgotten the baseball, and that one of the young fellows in her crew had a grapefruit in his lunchbox and gave that to her to drop. She didn't mention Kelley or any other passenger, and the assumption is that she dropped the fruit herself, which doesn't jibe with the stories written by the reporters on the scene.

For that matter, in one of his versions of the story in which he was not the hero, Casey said that Ruth Law used to say that Raleigh Aitchison was the one who flew with her and dropped the grapefruit. Stengel said Miss Law assumed it was Aitchison because the night before Stengel happened to be dancing with her and told her that's who it would be. But, Casey said, Aitchison's wife wouldn't let him fly, so Kelley went up instead. In view of Mrs. Aitchison's flying record and her husband's reluctance, that seems totally fanciful.

Whatever happened, Stengel got the credit, and still does, for dropping it, probably because over the years he told the story so often and so well, with pantomimes of Robby staggering around and falling on his back and exaggerated bleats of, "I'm dead! I'm covered with blood!"

Casey did a lot to create his own legend.

Casey was in the Robins' opening-day lineup in 1915, but he was still weak and his hitting was terrible. Wheat wasn't doing well either, and the disappointing Dodgers, after bumbling along at a .500 pace for a couple of months, slid down to last place near the end of June. Stengel was bad enough the first month, hitting only .206, but then he got worse and his average went all the way down to the .150s. Robinson kept playing him because he had no one else good enough to alternate with him, the two or three he tried in Casey's place now and then, like young Bill Zimmerman, turning out to be inadequate. And Stengel, despite his woeful batting average, was fielding beautifully. At Ebbets Field he had gotten into the habit of going out to the park early, borrowing three or four beat-up old practice balls from Comerford's ball bag, and going out to right field, where he'd throw ball after ball against the wall, studying the way they bounced off it. He was learning to "play the angles," as Danny Shay had beseeched him to do when he was a rookie with Kansas City in 1910.

He practiced. Satchel Paige, talking to Stephen Banker about his fabulous control as a pitcher, explained that when he first started pitching in the Negro Leagues he was wild. "But it's such a thing as I *practiced* all the time," Paige told Banker. "I just *practiced* control. Anything you practice, you begin to come good at, regardless of what it is, whether it's baseball or not." Stengel practiced, learning how to play right field, and he became good at it. His ability to handle batted balls caroming off the concrete wall in Ebbets Field was uncanny. He became adept too at catching batted balls hit into the sun. Games were played much later in the afternoon then than they are now, and the sun was lower in the sky and therefore much more of a daily problem for outfielders. Casey was one of the earliest outfielders to wear sunglasses. He displayed a flair for making brilliant plays. "Stengel contributed his daily sensational catch" was a typical newspaper comment in the summer of 1915, although Robinson would tell him, "If I keep watchin' you staggerin' around under them fly balls long enough, I'll get a heart attack." But Stengel's fielding in 1915 was the only thing keeping him in the lineup. Robby boasted to reporters, "I made a real good right fielder out of Stengel, and against his wishes."

Robinson liked Stengel, although he was never averse to putting him down when he felt it was called for. One day, with the famous umpire Bill Klem behind the plate, Casey topped a little roller along the firstbase line. It went into foul territory, and Klem called, "Foul ball!" Then the ball hit a pebble or a clump of grass and trickled back into fair territory. The first baseman grabbed it and stepped on the base, and Klem yelled, "You're out!" Casey, outraged by such unfairness, turned on Klem and began shouting and arguing. Robinson hurried out of the dugout to join in the discussion. Klem explained to Robinson what had happened, that the ball had started foul and that he had called it foul, but that it had come back into fair territory and thus under the rules, which were very clear on that point, was a fair ball. Casey kept ranting at Klem, but Robinson just nodded, shoved Stengel away, and said, "If Bill says you're out, you're out. Stop makin' so much noise and get back to the dugout."

Robby enjoyed ragging Casey, although sometimes his intent got ahead of his wit. After a game in which Stengel made a bad play, Robinson got off a couple of casual digs in the clubhouse and then, when Stengel, naked, passed him on his way to the shower, added caustically, "Hell, with legs and an ass like that, you shouldn't be a ballplayer anyway. You should be a . . ."

He paused and Stengel said, "I should be a what?"

"I was just tryin' to think," Robinson said, "but I give up."

Casey also practiced hitting. He was a big swinger who liked to hold the bat down at the end, not at all a common practice in those days of bunts, scratch hits, and low-scoring games. He had a closed stance, with his right foot closer to the plate, his bat cocked well back, his face peering around his right shoulder at the pitcher, the way Stan Musial's did thirty years later. He could hit hard — he was a power hitter, an extra-base hitter — but he could be badly fooled by a change-up. He'd talk to himself at the plate. "Casey, *why* did you swing at that pitch? Come on!"

He struck out a lot, more than anyone else

on the Dodgers as a rule. The pitchers learned that he was weak against balls thrown high and inside, on the fists. He was not a good hitter against left-handers, who would set him up with a succession of curves and then fire a fastball past him. "They said I couldn't hit left-handers," he once complained, "and they'd pull me out as soon as a left-hander appeared. But how was I expected to hit them when I never faced them?" He faced some, of course, and when he was on a hot streak he hit them well. But, all in all, he was a much stronger batter against right-handers.

He had a lot of trouble in his first season or two with the spitball, a then legal pitch which dropped sharply near the plate. "I'd swing down at it like a guy chopping wood," Stengel said. Rucker, whose hard curveball dropped straight down — a sinker, they'd call such a pitch later on — took him out to the park and threw sinker after sinker to him until Casey got so that he could hit them a little, taking a long swing like a golfer instead of his halfhearted chop.

He'd spar with a pitcher when he was at bat, moving around in the batter's box, trying not to let the pitcher control him. He could pull a ball hard to right, but he was also adept at snapping his bat at an outside pitch and punching it to left.

But not in 1915, at least not the first half of the season. The fans were getting on him regularly, although that never seemed to bother Casey. He enjoyed the crowd's reaction, whatever it was. Whenever he lost his temper, which was often, it was almost always with an umpire or another player, not with the crowd. He was amused by the fans. He used to talk later about the ones who sat on fire escapes on buildings beyond the outfield fence and watched the games from there. It cost them only ten cents for a pail of beer to sit up there, and, Casey said, "They didn't get real insulting until the beer began to take effect about the fourth inning." He once said that being in the outfield in Ebbets Field during a ball game was like "playing for Harvard against Yale."

Despite his physically depleted performance and the so-so record of the club, he was enjoying life. He liked being in Brooklyn. He had gotten to know Jim Mulvey, who had married Steve McKeever's daughter, known to everyone as Dearie. The Mulveys would invite various players to their brownstone house in Brooklyn, and they'd have coffee and cake and music. Dearie played the piano and Jim the violin, and everyone would sing and dance. "That's where I really learned to dance," Stengel said.

Finally, in July, during a long home stand in Ebbets Field, the Dodgers began to move. Robinson's patient handling of his patchwork pitching staff was a big factor — Robby worked six different starting pitchers into his pitching rotation, with marked success — and so was the hitting of Hy Myers, who batted safely in twenty-three straight games, was stopped once and then hit safely in eleven more. Brooklyn won four of five from the Giants, swept the Braves, swept the Cubs, won three of four from the Reds. They moved quickly upward through the tightly packed field and by late July were in second place, only a game and a half behind Grover Cleveland Alexander and the league-leading Phils, whose infield, shattered by Federal League raids, had been healed by the arrival of a brilliant rookie shortstop named Dave Bancroft.

Stengel missed a couple of games in mid-July with a slight muscle pull, but after he returned he found his long-missing batting eye and ripped off ten hits in fourteen at bats to raise his dreadful batting average close to .200. On the western trip that followed, he continued to belt the ball, two singles and a double one day, a triple, a double and a single the next. It was important for the Robins that Stengel had begun to hit, because Myers after his great streak slumped badly and Wheat was still in his inexplicable season-long doldrums.

In August when the Dodgers were in Chicago to play the Cubs, Louis Stengel again came over from Kansas City to see his boy. Casey's mother had once come all the way from Kansas City to Brooklyn with her daughter, Louise, to visit Charley, but she went only once to the ball park to watch him play. She was so offended by the casual abuse tossed at her child by the noisy Brooklyn fans that she wouldn't go anymore. In Chicago, Mr. Stengel was slightly apprehensive because of his memory of the trip two years earlier when Charley was benched just as he arrived. Now, though, his son was on a hot streak, and he performed heroically before his parent. In a Sunday doubleheader before a big crowd, Casey was in the lineup in the first game against Jim (Hippo) Vaughn, the Cubs' pitching ace, who was six feet four inches tall, weighed 240 pounds and was the best left-hander in the league. Casey, up with the bases loaded against Vaughn, hit a single that drove in two runs, and later hit a double to drive in two more.

In the second game, however, Casey tried to beat out a grounder to second and pulled a tendon in his right knee as he crossed first base. He couldn't play in the field, and he was unable to play on Monday and Tuesday as Pop Stengel watched from the stands. On Wednesday in the last game of the series in Chicago, the last game of the road trip, the last game Stengel's father would see before he returned to Kansas City, Robinson in a nice gesture sent Stengel up to pinch-hit. Casey belted a single, hobbled to first base and then left the game for a pinch runner.

He sat out for more than a week after that, but renewed his vigorous hitting after he returned. In a game against the Cardinals, Brooklyn hopped off to a good lead, lost all of it, and then came back to win the game when Stengel hit a home run over the center-field fence. He continued to hit hard right to the end of the season, and his final average of .237 meant that he had batted well over .300 through the last half of the season after his terrible start.

Brooklyn stayed close on Philadelphia's heels through August, but in September the Phils picked up the pace and went on to win the pennant easily, while the Robins slacked off and finished third, ten games behind. Nonetheless, it *was* third place, Brooklyn's best finish since Ned Hanlon's day. The team had finished ahead of the Giants for the first time since 1902.

10 THE 1916 PENNANT: CASEY HITS THE BIG ONE

Wilbert Robinson is usually remembered in baseball circles as a benevolent fat man who amused sportswriters and fans while his players did odd things on the field. Perhaps that's what he was later on, but in his early years with the Dodgers, he was a fine manager, a man who knew what players he needed and who worked hard at finding and developing them. He had played for Ned Hanlon and had worked with John McGraw, and he admired what they had done with their teams. In 1916, what he had learned from them paid off.

Robinson *taught* his players, working in spring training, for instance, on making his pitchers learn how to cover first base on ground balls hit to the right side of the infield, a common tactic today but one that was often neglected by pitchers in the good old days. He had his theories on outfield play, as we have seen, and he appreciated the intrinsic value of an unpublicized player like Cutshaw, whose skillful fielding was so important to his pitchers' performance and who was a consistent producer of runs despite a mediocre batting average.

Robinson was particularly fond of pitchers, although no statement like Connie Mack's "Pitching is 75 percent of the game" is credited to him. He particularly liked big pitchers, men who could throw the ball hard; the six starters he depended on in 1916 were 6'4", 6'3", 6'3", 6'1½", 6' and 6'. He liked veteran players, men who had been around and had done well in the past, even though they might seem to be on the way down now.

From the Cubs he got Larry Cheney, a big right-hander who had won twenty games or more for three straight seasons before going bad. He picked up players from McGraw's Giants, who had slid rapidly downhill after their collapse at the end of 1914 and had finished last in 1915. McGraw was cleaning house, and one of the players he got rid of was Rube Marquard, a once-splendid left-handed pitcher who had had a terrible season in 1914 and didn't do much better in 1915. Robinson snapped him up. He picked up another of McGraw's discards in thirty-five-year-old

Chief Meyers, who had caught Marquard and Mathewson and Jeff Tesreau and the other stars of McGraw's powerful pitching staff, and in 1916 he obtained first baseman Fred Merkle from New York. During the 1915 season he picked up Ivy Olson, Stengel's old grammar-school bully, who had been a shortstop for several years in the American League before shifting to Cincinnati and then Brooklyn. He also got Mike Mowrey, a third baseman who had been around the National League for ten years, and Jimmy Johnston, a right-handed-hitting outfielder who had played a little for the Cubs — and who Robby figured could definitely fill in for Stengel against left-handed pitchers.

Johnston had been in the minors in 1915, but he signed a contract with the Federal League for $4,000 after the season. But the Federals went out of business during the winter, and Ebbets signed Johnston — for $3,600, although the player wanted the same $4,000 the Federals were going to pay him. He held out for a time. Ebbets was adamant (resisting Robinson, who was pressing him to sign Johnston) and said $3,600 was as high as he would go. The outfielder eventually gave in. His capitulation was clear indication that with the demise of the Federal League the owners had the upper hand again.

There was some talk that the defector Jack Dalton might return to Brooklyn now that the Feds were gone, but Ebbets pointedly expressed no interest in the outfielder, who eventually signed with Detroit and played only a few games there before leaving the big leagues for good. Ebbets was growing a little sour anyway about ballplayers and salaries. Raleigh Aitchison, whom the Dodgers had released to the minors early in 1915, had signed an ironclad, no-Federal League contract with Brooklyn after the 1914 season, but when he was sent down to the minor leagues his salary at Milwaukee in the American Association was only $1,325, compared to the $4,000 he would have received with the Dodgers. Aitchison went into court, and the court found for him; Ebbets had to make up the $2,675 difference between Aitchison's minor-league pay and the money he'd been guaranteed under his Brooklyn contract. Another former Dodger player, Charley Schmutz, sued Ebbets in a similar case and won.

So Ebbets was grumpy in 1916. Most of his players had high-priced holdover contracts signed during the Federal League war, and like other big-league owners Ebbets could hardly wait for those contracts to expire so that he could cut his payroll down toward the "prewar" level.

The Robins had a good spring in Daytona Beach in 1916, with little of the rain that had hampered practice and grapefruit dropping a year earlier. They came into the season in good shape, and it was evident from the start that they were one of the big teams in the league. They took possession of first place in May and stayed there through June, July and August. Stengel didn't do much to help during the first month, hovering around .200, but after that he was very much in evidence and hit steadily for the rest of the year. Robby alternated him in right field with Johnston, although occasionally when Myers slumped Johnston would take his place in the lineup and both he and Stengel would play, Jimmy in right field and Casey moving over to center.

Whether he was in the lineup or on the bench, Stengel was full of fire and ginger all season long. "He made more noise than a boy with a new drum," one old-timer said. Chief Meyers, the Brooklyn catcher, told Larry Ritter in *The Glory of Their Times*, "I always maintain that Stengel won one more pennant than the record books show. That was in 1916, with Brooklyn. It was Casey who kept us on our toes. He was the life of the party and kept us old-timers pepped up all season."

The Robins were a rambunctious club. Olson, slated to be a reserve, was so competitive a player that he even got angry in practice sessions during spring training; he was so annoyed by an umpire's call in an intrasquad game that he argued furiously, threw sand all over the ump and was ejected. From an intrasquad game. Stengel loved that, although Casey had trouble of his own with bad tempers that season. He had a misunderstanding with Pfeffer because of an outfield play he made when Jeff was pitching. There were men on second and third with no one out and the Robins ahead by one run. A fly ball was hit to Stengel in right field. Casey was thinking in high gear. He decided that the runner on third was too fast for him to catch with a throw to the plate, and that if he threw there not only would that run score but the man on second would get to third, from where *he* could more easily score the run that would put the other team ahead. So after he caught the fly, Stengel ignored the man going home and tried to throw out the man advancing from second to third. His throw got away from the third baseman, and there was no one backing up the base because Pfeffer had gone behind home plate to back up the catcher, expecting Stengel's throw to go there. The second runner scored. Thus, both runners scored on the one fly ball, and the Robins and Pfeffer lost the game. Stengel said, "Pfeffer didn't think that was a very good play, and nobody else thought it was a very good play, and it *wasn't* a very good play." Even though it derived from sound Stengelian reasoning. Pfeffer had some harsh words for Casey, Casey said some harsh words back, and it was a few years before they became friends again.

Another incident didn't end even that peacefully, and it may have contributed to Stengel's eventual departure from the Robins. There was a big young pitcher from Texas named Ed Appleton, whom everyone called Whitey. Appleton had been fairly impressive with the Robins in 1915, but he wasn't doing as well in 1916 and his temper grew short. He didn't like the garrulous Stengel anyway, and when Casey made a bad play behind him one day Appleton told him off. Nothing much happened then, but that night several of the players went down to Coney Island to see the sights and have a few drinks. Appleton and Stengel ran into each other, Appleton renewed his criticism, Stengel replied in kind, and the two went at each other in a big, raging brawl. Both were banged up, the police were called in, and Stengel and Appleton hurriedly made up a story about falling down a flight of stairs. The McKeevers placated the cops, and the two ballplayers were bandaged up by the same doctor. The next day they were called on the carpet by Ebbets, who was on record as having said, "I'll have no hard citizens on my roster." There were jokes in Brooklyn about Ebbets declaring piously, "Lips that touch wine shall never touch mine." He bawled out the players and said their drinking bouts would have to stop.

"We only had four beers," Stengel said innocently, holding up four outstretched fingers.

When Robinson heard that, his big body shook with laughter. "Yeah," he said, "you only had four beers, but each one was as big as a pitcher." The story got around, and for a long while Stengel would be greeted by opposition players holding up four fingers and yelling, "I only had four."

Stengel took a lot of riding. One day when he was picked off second base in a game with the Giants he argued frantically, almost desperately, with umpire Ernie Quigley, trying vainly to convince him that he had been safe.

He circled the umpire, pleading, trying to explain. He bent low over the bag and made circles wth his hand to show how his foot had eluded the tag. The umpire ignored him. Buck Herzog, the Giants' shortstop, laughed at Stengel's complaint and began to mock him, imitating his gestures, bending over himself and making exaggerated circles with his hand. The umpire walked away, laughing, and Stengel followed. He grabbed Quigley's arm and spun him around to command his attention and . . . zip! The umpire threw him out of the game. Herzog and the other players were all laughing, and the frustrated Stengel didn't know what to do. "One thing that helped make Stengel vexed," wrote a newspaperman, "was that nobody was taking him seriously."

Brooklyn was in first place as the pennant race entered September, two and a half games ahead of Boston and five games ahead of Philadelphia, but things were becoming unsettled in Flatbush. Daubert was having a lot of trouble with his legs and missed several games. Merkle, who took over at first base when Jake was out, didn't hit. Johnston couldn't play for a while after he was beaned by a pitch thrown by Three Finger Brown. O'Mara, the shortstop, was batting about

.200. Robby benched him and put the truculent Olson in his place. The catchers, Meyers and Miller, were fielding well, but except for Wheat and Daubert, Stengel, in the .260s, had the highest batting average in the lineup.

On the first day of September the Phillies, then in third place, shocked Brooklyn by beating the Robins in both ends of a doubleheader, one of the games a 3–0 shutout by Grover Cleveland Alexander, and the Phils went on to defeat them three more times to knock the Robins out of first place, Alex winning again 3–1. The Braves were now in the lead, but the Phils beat them three in a row to take over first place themselves. It looked like a repeat of the 1915 season, when Brooklyn faded away to third in the wake of Philadelphia's drive to the pennant.

But the Robins held on. Losing 2–0 to the Giants in the seventh inning, they rallied on successive two-out singles by Johnston, Daubert, Stengel, Wheat and Cutshaw. Stengel drove in one run and scored another that put the Robins in the lead. Later he bunted his way on and scored an insurance run in a 5–2 victory. The next day he had a single and a double as Brooklyn beat the Giants again.

That defeat of the Giants was significant, because it was the last time the Giants were to lose for nearly a month. McGraw had been rebuilding since his last-place finish in 1914, and now his team was ready; it took off, winning twenty-six games in a row, the longest winning streak in major-league history. The Giants were too far behind when they began to finish higher than fourth that year, but their winning streak helped the Robins win the pennant, because when the Phillies took an eight-game winning streak and an apparent firm grasp on first place into the Polo Grounds they ran into the Giant steamroller and lost four games in a row. That let Brooklyn slip back into the league lead. For the next three weeks the two clubs played at almost precisely the same fast pace: The Phils won twelve and lost only four; the Robins won thirteen and lost only five to hold onto their slim lead.

On Thursday, September 28, with less than a week left in the season, the Phils came into Ebbets Field for a final three-game showdown. Alexander, who had already won thirty-one games, coasted to an 8–4 victory on Thursday, and Philadelphia was only half a game out. Stengel had one hit in four at bats against Alexander but was called "Bonehead!" by a fan when he was thrown out at second base trying to advance on a passed ball.

The Friday game was rained out and rescheduled as part of a morning/afternoon doubleheader on Saturday (there was still no Sunday baseball in New York State). The Phils won the morning game behind left-handed Eppa Rixey and moved past the Dodgers into the lead. Stengel didn't play against the left-hander. Brooklyn's hopes for the pennant seemed slim. They had lost seven straight times to Philadelphia, and the redoubtable Alexander was pitching against them in the afternoon game.

Brooklyn was not optimistic, particularly after the Phils took a 1–0 lead in the top of the first inning. One run always seemed huge when Alex was pitching — he had sixteen shutouts that season. But in the bottom of the first, Stengel hit a little squib between the mound and the third-base line and beat Alexander's peg to first base. With Wheat up, Casey broke for second on a hit-and-run play, Zack poked the ball through the hole into right field, and Stengel sped around to third. Wheat then tried to steal second, the catcher's throw bounced away from the second baseman, and Stengel raced in from third base to tie the score.

It remained 1–1 into the fifth inning. Stengel led off that inning for Brooklyn. Alexander's first pitch appeared to be over the plate, but the umpire called it a ball. Alex came back with one right down the middle. Stengel swung at it and lifted it over the right-field wall for a home run. It was stunning, unexpected. It shook the Phillies and it sent the Brooklyn players and fans into ecstatic displays of joy. Casey took his time trotting around the bases, savoring the moment.

It took the heart out of Alexander and the Phils. The Dodgers pecked away, scored again in the sixth, again in the seventh and twice in the eighth. They had beaten Alexander and stopped the Phillies at last, and they were back in first place. After the season Stengel called it his biggest moment of the year, and when he was an old man he recalled that home run with relish.

The Robins still had three games with the blazing Giants before the season ended, but that same Saturday afternoon in Boston the Giants' long winning streak ended. On Monday, Jack Coombs shut them out for the Dodgers while the Phils were splitting a doubleheader with the Braves. The Robins' lead was now a full game. On Tuesday the shattered Phillies had another doubleheader in Boston. The news reached Brooklyn during the afternoon that they had lost the first and were losing the second, and the Robins rallied from a 4–1 deficit to beat the Giants again, 7–5. Casey had a double and a walk and scored two runs. After Brooklyn went ahead in that game, McGraw shouted, "You bunch of quitters!" at his team and stormed off the field. When Wheat caught a fly ball for the last out, the normally undemonstrative Zack tossed the ball exultantly into the stands and raced for the dugout. The official word — that the Phils had lost and the Dodgers had clinched the pennant — came when the players were still in the clubhouse. There was cheering, shouting, joyful pummeling, a snake dance around the room. The players made Robby climb up on a bench and make a speech. "It was quite a night in Flatbush," a newspaper reported.

McGraw, meanwhile, was blasting his own team to the press, saying, "I do not say my players did not try to win, but they refused to obey my orders. They disregarded my signals. It was too much for me, and I lost my patience. Such baseball disgusted me, and I left the bench. I do not like indifferent playing of this kind, and I refused to be connected with it."

When reporters told Robinson that Mc-

Graw had called the Giants quitters, the Brooklyn manager laughed. "That's a lot of shit," he said. "That's a joke. The fact is, we're a better ball club, and McGraw knows it. We outclassed them. We beat the Giants fifteen times in twenty-two games. Tell Mc-Graw to stop pissing on my pennant."

Stengel got a couple more hits in the final game of the season to finish with a batting average of .279, best on the club after Wheat and Daubert. He was third in batting in runs, behind Wheat and Cutshaw, and third in scoring runs, behind Wheat and Daubert. Wheat and Pfeffer, who won twenty-five games, were surely the most valuable players on the Dodgers and after Alexander probably the most valuable in the league, but twenty-six-year-old Charley Stengel had had a pretty good year himself.

The World Series with the Boston Red Sox was a disappointment, the Dodgers losing rather quickly, four games to one. John K. Tener, president of the National League at the time, is supposed to have said that he had never seen a club go into the Series "so willing to settle for the losers' end." If Tener did say that, the judgment was both unfair and inaccurate. The Robins played strongly in their first three games, all of which were decided by one run; they won one of the three games, lost another one 2–1 in the fourteenth inning and came within one brilliant fielding play of winning another. A more obvious trouble with the Dodgers in the 1916 Series appears to have been Robinson, who like so many other good managers outsmarted himself by overmanaging. He decided that it would be shrewd baseball to put right-handers Pfeffer and Cheney, his two winningest pitchers, in the bullpen and start left-handers against the Red Sox. Why he was reluctant to start either of his stars against Boston is hard to understand. Pfeffer had had one of the best earned-run averages in the league, had pitched six shutouts (only Alexander had more), and had worked 329 innings, more than anyone in baseball but Alexander and Walter Johnson. He was by all odds the best bet on the Brooklyn staff for a short series, the kind of strong-armed pitcher who could start two or even three games and do well each time out. Cheney had won eighteen games and had five shutouts, and his earned-run average was almost as good as Pfeffer's. Yet Pfeffer did not start until the last game (although he did pitch two and two-thirds strong innings in relief to save the only game

Brooklyn won), and Cheney appeared only once in the Series, and then for only three innings.

Further, Robinson had little to be afraid of in the Boston batting order. True, Babe Ruth was on the Red Sox, but Ruth had not yet blossomed into the power-hitting superman he was to become. Boston manager Bill Carrigan used him only as a pitcher, although he did have the Babe pinch-hit occasionally. The Red Sox were basically a weak-hitting team that relied on slick fielding and a great pitching staff. They scored fewer runs than all but two teams in the American League and had only one regular who batted higher than .272. Nor was their lineup preponderantly left-handed and thus a potentially difficult one for right-handed pitchers like Pfeffer and Cheney.

Robinson also stayed rigidly with his righty-lefty theory and alternated Stengel and Johnston in the Series. On the surface, it's hard to criticize him for this, since both Stengel and Johnston batted over .300 against Boston, the only Dodgers who did. But Myers batted only .182 and had only one hit in his last sixteen at bats. Stengel had been hitting hard for two months, he had demonstrated a remarkable ability to play well in clutch games (one writer noted that he had batted .500 in the big games against the Phils and the Giants at the end of the season), and he hit with more power than either Myers or Johnston. You go with your hot hand in a short Series, and Stengel was hot.

He was bouncing with energy on the train that took the Robins from New York to Boston for the first two games. He told someone he was going to open a café in Kansas City with his share of the World Series money and told someone else he was going to invest it in his father's street-sprinkling company. He kibitzed Ollie O'Mara, who was playing cards on the train, reminding him that he, O'Mara, had stuck gum on Stengel's hand earlier in the day. O'Mara, concentrating on his cards, said, "I'll stick something else on your chin if you don't get out of here." Stengel swiped a twenty-five-cent piece from O'Mara's pile on the table, and the game was temporarily called while O'Mara chased Stengel through the car to get his money back. Casey grinned, gave him the money and went on into the next car to see what he could do there.

Stengel was in the Brooklyn lineup in the first game, because the Boston pitcher was Ernie Shore, a right-hander. Shore was Carrigan's fourth-best pitcher that season, but he was a man the Red Sox manager trusted. He had started twice for Boston in the World Series a year earlier, and he started twice this time, winning both his games, even though the strongest hitters in the Brooklyn lineup, Wheat, Daubert and Stengel, were all left-handed, and even though Carrigan had three first-rate lefties in Ruth (who won twenty-three games that year), Dutch Leonard, and Rube Foster. So much for rigid adherence to the righty-lefty theory.

Boston scored a run in the third inning (after Dick Hoblitzell, a left-handed batter, tripled off the left-handed Marquard), but in the top of the fourth, Stengel opened with a single and scored on Wheat's triple to tie the game. Boston scored again in the fifth after Harry Hooper, another lefty, hit a double, and then the Red Sox broke the game open with three more runs in the seventh when the Dodger infield made a succession of bad plays.

With the score 5–1 Boston, Robinson brought Pfeffer in to pitch the eighth inning, and the Red Sox scored again when Stengel's throwing error let a run in. Then, in the ninth, losing 6–1; the Dodgers batted around and scored four runs to narrow the score to

6–5. Stengel, second up in the inning, singled, scored one of the runs and was on deck with a bat in his hands waiting to hit again when Jake Daubert made the last out. With the bases loaded, the tying run on third, the possible winning run on second, Daubert slashed a hard grounder toward left field, but Everett Scott, the Boston shortstop, made a fine stop in the hole and a great peg to first base to just nip Daubert, who dove at the bag in an attempt to beat the throw. The game was over, and there was Casey, still on deck with his bat in his hand.

That night when someone on the Robins wondered aloud which Boston pitcher would be going against them in the next game, Stengel said flatly, "Ruth's going to pitch." How did he know? "He's the logical choice," Stengel said. "He's a left-hander, and the best left-hander they got." He went on for several hundred words developing his theme, which reflected the best Wilbert Robinson thinking: The Dodgers' best hitters were left-handed (Casey modestly included himself in the list), and a lefty was the best bet to stop them, and Ruth was the best left-hander on Boston, and on and on.

Ruth did pitch, beating the Dodgers' Sherry Smith in one of the classic World Series games, a fourteen-inning duel which the Red Sox won 2–1. The righty-lefty wisdom kept Stengel out of the game, even though Casey had hit Ruth hard two years earlier in spring training when the Babe was a rookie with the Baltimore Orioles. Robinson stuck with his plan, though, and it looked sound when Myers homered off Ruth in the first inning, an inside-the-park poke that got between the right and center fielders. And Johnston got a single and a walk off Ruth. But after the homer, Myers struck out, grounded out twice and hit into a double play, while Johnston was caught stealing both times he reached base and in the eighth inning, with runners on second and third and two out, tapped weakly back to the box to end the inning. Stengel sat on the bench throughout the game, through all fourteen innings.

Down two games to none, the Dodgers fought back to win the third game 4–3 behind the right-handed Jack Coombs. Stengel played and was in evidence all afternoon. He ended a Red Sox rally in the first inning by throwing a runner out at third base. He sacrificed successfully with men on first and second in the Dodgers' half of the first, although Brooklyn failed to score. In the third he singled to set up the Dodgers' first run. In the sixth, when Daubert was called out at the plate trying to stretch a triple into a home run, Stengel was all over the umpire, leading the Brooklyn argument. In the ninth, after Pfeffer retired eight straight men in relief to save the Dodger victory, the last out of the game was a fly ball to Stengel, who in the clubhouse afterward shouted, "We're under way! We aren't gonna stop! We've got Boston on the run! We'll keep doing what we did this afternoon! We'll forget how to do anything else! I'm going home with the winner's share of that old World Series coin!"

The next day Robby started Marquard again and benched Stengel, since the left-handed Dutch Leonard was on the mound for Boston. He also benched the left-handed Daubert, who had had three hits in four at bats the day before. Brooklyn jumped off to a 2–0 lead in the first ("We're under way!"), but Marquard gave up a three-run homer to the left-handed-hitting Larry Gardner and the Dodgers lost 6–2 to fall behind, three games to one. Robinson used three pinch hitters in the game, all of them right-handed: Pfeffer, the pitcher; O'Mara, who batted .202 during the season; and Gus Getz, who batted .219. He didn't use either Daubert or Stengel, although he did put Casey in the game in the ninth inning — as a pinch runner.

Stengel played the last game and got one of Brooklyn's three hits off Ernie Shore, who beat them 4–1 to give the world championship to Boston. In the Series, Casey had four hits in eleven at bats for a .364 average, the highest on the team. Wheat batted .211, Cutshaw .105, Daubert, whose only hits had come in the third game, .176. Marquard had started twice and lost twice. In the eleven innings he pitched, his earned-run average was 6.55. Pfeffer's ERA was 1.69 for the ten and two-thirds innings he pitched.

Except for the one victory, the most satisfactory moment for Brooklyn fans came in Ebbets Field during the fourth game when Robinson, with the Robins far behind, brought Nap Rucker in to pitch in the eighth inning. Rucker had been able to start only four games all year because of his bursitis, and he had announced that he'd be retiring after the season. This was his first appearance in a World Series and his farewell to baseball. To Brooklyn's great delight, old Nap (he was only thirty-two) pitched two scoreless innings, gave up only one hit, and struck out three men, including the last batter he ever faced.

That was something to remember, even if the Dodgers did lose.

11 MOVING ON DOWN: FAREWELL TO BROOKLYN

Nap Rucker's farewell was the last warm moment in Brooklyn baseball for quite a while. With the World Series over, Ebbets got down to the serious business of chopping salaries, although he waited first for the annual baseball meetings in December to discuss with his fellow owners how they should proceed. Stengel and Wheat went up to New Haven, Connecticut, to play in an exhibition game organized by a young entrepreneur named George Weiss in which the "Ty Cobb All-Stars," including Stengel and Wheat, played the Boston Red Sox. There was a rule against World Series players appearing in exhibition games after the season, a rule designed to prevent players on the two teams from vitiating the importance of the Series by playing a whole sequence of games against one another in the off-season. Each of the Red Sox was fined $100 for playing in the game, and Stengel and Wheat were fined, too, although the two Brooklyn players were docked only $25 each, apparently because they had not been billed as members of the Dodgers.

In December, during the baseball meetings, a sportswriter wrote that "the baseball magnates expect to keep some of the money taken in at the gate next season." Both the National League and the American League voted unanimously to cut salaries across the board, with the Chicago Cubs declaring that they were going to reduce their payroll by nearly 50 percent. In Brooklyn the long-term contracts of most of the players were expiring, and even though they had won the pennant the signs were clear that this was not a year to expect a raise. Ebbets did some off-the-record talking about what he was going to do with some contracts, and it became apparent that Stengel's contract was one of those he had in mind.

In Casey's defense a newspaperman took a dig at Ebbets by writing, "Because of his clowning Stengel is lightly esteemed as a player by many folks who should know better. The truth is that it's doubtful whether there is a man on the Brooklyn ball team who has more baseball instinct than this same comical cuss." Another said, "Casey

Stengel is one of the very few men in the National League with a striking and interesting personality and whose actions are calculated to amuse and divert, apart from his playing. Putting three or four such persons as Stengel in the lineup of every team would go a long way toward increasing gate receipts." And, "Stengel is spectacular, even when doing nothing in particular."

The propaganda fell on deaf ears. Ebbets was going to cut salaries, that's all there was to it, and Stengel, whose raucous behavior had always annoyed the Brooklyn owner, was a prime target. Ebbets liked a clear line of demarcation kept between baseball's upper classes — the owners, the league officials, the managers — and the lower classes — the players. Today, when star players make five or ten times as much money as the manager, it's difficult to appreciate the inferior position players held in the old days. During the Federal League war Grover Alexander was raised to $10,000 a year by the Phils, the highest salary in the National League, and he was cut back to $8,000 when that contract ran out, even though he'd won more than thirty games a season for three straight years. After winning two successive batting championships, when that meant even more than it does today, Daubert got up to only $8,000 and was the highest-paid Dodger player. But Robinson, the manager, was paid $15,000 and probably got a bonus on top of it. Carrigan, in his third season as manager of the Red Sox, earned $23,000 in 1916, including his World Series share. John McGraw earned $30,000. In fact, some thought that McGraw's temper-tantrum walkout in that game with Brooklyn was a calculated maneuver, since his contract with the Giants was expiring and his managerial skills were in great demand. If that was the case it worked, for early in 1917 when player salaries were being slashed McGraw signed a new contract with New York for $50,000 a year.

Ebbets sent out his new 1917 contracts in January, and there were immediate cries of outrage. Miller, the catcher, said he felt "grieved to the point of pain." Chief Meyers was cut $2,800, almost exactly the size of his World Series share. Olson asked for his release so that he could accept a job as player-manager of Vernon in the Pacific Coast League, where he would be better paid. Pfeffer rejected his contract and counterattacked by demanding a raise to $8,000. Wheat, always quiet, said only that he was "wholly dissatisfied" and left the impression that he might quit baseball and work his farm in Missouri.

Stengel's reaction was the most vigorous. "I thought I might receive a little increase," he said, "but when I saw this figure I said nothin' doin'." Ebbets cut him $1,400, from $6,000 down to $4,600. The Dodgers had a man of all work named Red Hanrahan, who helped Comerford with clubhouse chores and kept track of such things as the team's bats. Stengel sent his contract back to Ebbets unsigned, along with a flip note that began "Dear Charlie," a familiarity that affronted Ebbets' sense of propriety, and went on to say that he must have received Red Hanrahan's contract by mistake.

That angered Ebbets, and he grew even angrier when Stengel sounded off to the press. Casey always had the ear of newspapermen, and he made use now of his easy access to the sports pages to argue his case. "If Ebbets had lost money or even had a poor year financially," Stengel said, "I would have thought he was doing this to cover up the deficit. But I can't see any reason in the world why he wants to cut the boys who made it possible for him to collect such a goodly sum of money last year as his spoils of the World Series."

Casey was in high gear, his mouth running

at full speed. "Ebbets charges the highest admission prices in the National League," he went on. "It seems reasonable that if he charges such high prices to see his players perform, he should meet the fans halfway by giving them the opportunity of watching high-priced players." Pausing for effect, he added a final dig: "And then, you could not say that we are receiving exorbitant salaries anyway."

Stengel was enjoying the dispute. He had had a fine year, Brooklyn had won the pennant, and he had almost always been the winner in these holdout squabbles before. But he misread Ebbets completely. Although it cannot be verified, it seems probable that Stengel made a higher salary in 1915 and 1916 than Wheat, a much better ballplayer. Wheat had signed a three-year contract after the 1913 season, when the Federal threat first appeared. Stengel, by signing for only one year then, was able to ask for and receive a much higher stipend a year later, after he batted .316. He may have been the highest-paid Dodger after Daubert, and possibly Rucker, and Ebbets was determined to cut him down to size, a determination made stronger after Stengel's highly publicized rejection of the pay cut. Ebbets was fifty-seven years old,

Stengel twenty-six. Young men didn't act that way toward distinguished members of the community. Ebbets sent Stengel a second contract, this one calling for an even greater cut than the first one had.

The Brooklyn owner also replied to the general criticism he'd been receiving by saying that he and the other owners were only trying to bring salaries back to "normal conditions" — the salary levels before the Federal League war sent them sky-high. "The players must take salary cuts," Ebbets said. "Those high contracts were forced on us by the Federal League." He warned that if the veterans refused to accept the new terms, he'd be forced to use new, young players in their stead.

Slowly, signed contracts began to trickle in until by the time the club was ready to begin spring training, only six men — Pfeffer, Wheat, Stengel, Smith, Mowrey and O'Mara — were still holding out. Smith reported to camp and signed soon after his arrival, and Ebbets solved the disagreements with Mowrey and O'Mara by sending them to the minors (both later returned to the Dodgers). He was not quite so cavalier with Pfeffer, Wheat and Stengel, but he remained stubborn. In Brooklyn, Robinson had mentioned to someone that when he and Ebbets left for the Dodgers' new spring-training camp in Hot Springs, Arkansas — where they would practice near the Red Sox and capitalize on their World Series rivalry by playing a series of exhibition games together — he and Ebbets might stop off in St. Louis between trains to talk with Wheat and Stengel. Ebbets immediately refuted that, saying that while he might meet Pfeffer when the train stopped in Little Rock, Arkansas, he had no plans to talk to the other two. He used the occasion to attack Stengel's holdout, saying, "Stengel received two boosts in salary in the course of the Federal troubles, and they were advances over what he got in 1914. [Ebbets meant that Stengel's World Series share made his 1916 income greater than that of 1915, which in turn was greater than that of 1914; his actual salary was the same in both 1915 and 1916.] As a reward for that boost, he was in miserable condition and almost worthless in 1915 through ill health which baseball had nothing whatever to do with. But he received every cent of his large salary when we would have been justified in suspending him. His contract expired at the end of 1916, and I offered him one that called for $600 more than he received in the normal year of 1914 to play in

1917. He returned that contract with a most impudent letter, after giving out interviews that were published in Kansas City and Brooklyn denouncing the club as thoroughly cheap, despite our treatment of him in 1915 when he was incapacitated through his own fault. That conduct was added to the fact that he got into a disgraceful brawl with Appleton last season, when I had to exercise all my influence to save him from punishment, and also to save him from a terrific roast which one paper intended to give him.

"On February 16 I sent the young man another contract. It calls for the same total as the first, but he will have to show the proper spirit of aggressiveness and earnestness on the field, or $400 of that total will not be paid at the end of the season. I don't want him to sign and then go on the field and sulk and get revenge by indifferent work. The $400 is a gentle reminder that if he pursues such a course he will suffer in his pocketbook. It is up to him to make or lose that sum.

"We have not heard from Stengel since the second contract was sent, but are not worrying."

In short, he had cut Stengel even further but had offered him a bonus arrangement under which Casey could get the second cut re-

212

stored — if Ebbets approved of the way he played. Jack Coombs told Stengel that he'd heard Casey wouldn't get the $400 unless he batted .316 again.

Pfeffer met the Dodger train at Little Rock, but Ebbets put off talking to him until they reached Hot Springs. There, he let Pfeffer languish for a week or so until Robinson, acting as go-between, arranged for the two to meet. A compromise was worked out, and on March 14 Pfeffer signed.

Now only Wheat and Stengel remained outside the fold. Reporters heard Ebbets and Robinson in a loud discussion one night, during which Robby argued that he needed both of them and urged Ebbets to compromise. A day or so later Robinson wired Wheat at his farm in Polo, Missouri, forty miles outside Kansas City, asking him to come down to Hot Springs to talk with Ebbets. Wheat wired back, laconically, "WILL PLAY PROVIDING EBBETS MEETS MY TERMS, WHICH ARE NOT UNREASONABLE. Z. D. WHEAT." He didn't say whether he'd be coming down to Hot Springs or not.

Robinson also said, for all the newspapermen to hear, "Where can we find a man who can play the outfield and grab 'em off that rightfield wall like Stengel? We need that old

213

boy's hitting, too." Exaggerating the facts and by implication contradicting Ebbets, Robby also said, "Stengel played 1915 and a part of 1916 as a sick man, yet he hit .279 last year. We can use him all right."

Taking Robinson's words as a hint, Abe Yager of the *Brooklyn Eagle* got the newspapermen together and on their behalf sent a telegram to Stengel, saying, "THE NEWSPAPER BUNCH WANTS TO SEE YOU GRABBING THEM OFF THE OLD RIGHT FIELD WALL THIS YEAR. CANT YOU COME DOWN AND TALK IT OVER WITH EBBETS. ROBBY WANTS YOU. WE WANT YOU. A. YAGER, CHAIRMAN."

Almost immediately there was a reply. The normally voluble Stengel said only, "MANY THANKS. WILL LEAVE TONIGHT FOR CONFERENCE. C. D. STENGEL."

Ebbets reacted negatively to the news. Perhaps he and Robinson were playing a game, working the old tough cop/nice cop routine on the two holdouts, Ebbets always adamant and threatening, Robinson always friendly and cajoling. The owner expressed displeasure, saying, "I wasn't told about the wires. I have made my final offer to Wheat and Stengel. Having one of them here discussing salary will be bad enough. Having two will be unpleasant." Then, gruffly,

"However, I will talk to them."

All this sent ripples of excitement through the Dodger camp, which increased when Wheat arrived early the next morning, a Sunday, and Stengel that night. Wheat met with Ebbets on Monday morning, but there was no agreement. Ebbets went horseback riding, and Wheat and Stengel worked out with the team. Robinson was asked if Ebbets had given permission for the two holdouts to work out. Robby blustered and said it was the manager's privilege to let holdouts work out. He was reminded that neither Pfeffer nor Smith had worked out before they signed. They didn't want to, was the reply.

Ebbets did not meet with Wheat later on Monday, and Zack announced that if he hadn't reached an agreement by Tuesday he'd have to go back to his farm. Stengel, who had no farm or job to go back to, said he'd hang around a little longer. Ebbets, a shrewd negotiator, said he'd meet with Wheat on Wednesday, and Zack stayed in camp. Finally, on Thursday, March 22, Wheat signed, saying it was for the same salary he had received in 1916. Ebbets said part of the contract included a bonus if Wheat hit .300 again.

Stengel was now the only holdout, his position greatly weakened by Wheat's signing. The bone of contention was simply that $400 bonus clause Ebbets had inserted. Casey had long since given up hope of getting a raise, or the same salary he had received in 1916, or even a smaller pay cut. All he wanted now was the original contract Ebbets. had sent him, the one calling for a $1,400 reduction in pay, the one he had rejected so sarcastically. He argued against the bonus idea, saying, "I'd be playing for me, not the team. I'd be thinking of base hits, not want to bunt, for example."

Ebbets had been ignoring Stengel, but good old Robinson got them together, and on March 27, only two weeks before the season was to begin, Ebbets yielded on the bonus clause and let Casey sign for $4,600, a 23 percent cut in salary.

Now the Brooklyn owner had his club together, practically the same one that had done so well in 1916. He had the same pitching staff, plus young Leon Cadore, who had been in spring training with the Robins in 1915 and 1916 and was now ready to move in as a starting pitcher. He had the same catchers, the same outfield, the same infield (although a newcomer named Bunny Fabrique was tried at shortstop for a while, and another newcomer named Frank O'Rourke shared third base with the reclaimed Mowrey). It was essentially the same club.

But something was wrong. The team was listless, flat. The Robins lost the opening game to Alexander, lost four of their first five, lost fourteen of their first nineteen. They never recovered and finished a terrible, disappointing seventh. There were a lot of injuries, and the players were remarkably slow returning to action after the injuries. Wheat missed forty-two games, and he batted in and scored only about half as many runs as he had in 1916; but he hit .312, exactly what he had batted the previous year. He earned his bonus, if in fact there was one in his contract.

Daubert missed twenty-six games and his extra-base power all but disappeared. Of his 122 hits, 112 were singles. Johnston missed forty-eight games, Myers thirty-one, Olson twelve. Cutshaw, who had missed only one game in the previous three seasons, sat out seventeen games. Pfeffer's win total dropped from twenty-five to eleven, Cheney's from eighteen to eight. Marquard pitched well, and so did Smith and young Cadore, but otherwise Robinson's lovely pitching staff came apart.

The one solid player the Robins had all

year was Stengel, who played in every game but one, batted cleanup, led the team in runs scored and runs batted in and led all outfielders in the league in assists. He carried the club, helping to lift its won-lost record to .500 near the end of August before it sagged again in September.

Yet after the season Stengel was criticized in the *Brooklyn Eagle* for having "slumped badly." His batting average had fallen from .279 to .257. On the other hand, the paper said, Johnston and Myers had "improved" (their batting averages had gone up) and Wheat and Cutshaw were "consistent" (their averages had stayed about the same). Stengel had finished seventh among the regulars in batting average (Wheat, Johnston, Olson, Myers, Daubert and Cutshaw all were higher), but he was first in doubles, first in triples, first in home runs, first in extra-base bits, first in total bases, first in runs scored, first in runs batted in, first in games played. He even stole eighteen bases on his battered legs, second to Cutshaw's twenty-two. And he played well all season long, not going into a deep slump, not bolstering his statistics with one big hitting surge. It was unquestionably his finest season with Brooklyn.

And no one noticed.

Whether Ebbets' wholesale salary slashing was responsible for Brooklyn's depressing performance is conjecture, but Stengel, despite his own fine play, felt that it had a lot to do with it. Years later he said, "The owner says, 'I won't keep you here unless you sign for what I want to pay you. I'll trade you.' Now that's a bad thing. From winning the pennant in 1916 the Brooklyn club dropped to seventh place in 1917. I think one reason was that the owner, Mr. Ebbets, cut some salaries. It's like what the Yankee owners did after we won the world championship in 1958. They did some salary cutting, and then we had our bad year in 1959."

Ebbets' disenchantment with Stengel remained, and it was no secret that in the fall of 1917 he was hoping to trade his rowdy outfielder. You simply did not cross Charles Ebbets. Daubert was a particular favorite of his, but in 1918, when the baseball season was cut short at the end of August because of World War I, Daubert insisted that he be paid for the month of September as well. Ebbets reacted by trading him to Cincinnati.

In 1917 Stengel was so sure that he was going to be traded that he came to New York in December to hang around the baseball meetings to see if he could find out what team he was going to. He was philosophical about the possibility of a trade, although he did say that he'd prefer to end up in New York with the Giants.

"They can send me to Pittsburgh or Chicago or any old place if they want to," he said, "but if I have my choice, give me the Big Town. That's where we all want to end up."

When the trade was made in January 1918, it was Pittsburgh, not New York. Even though the headlines trumpeted it as the biggest trade in years (Stengel and Cutshaw for three Pirate players), it was a hard pill for Casey to swallow. The Pirates had finished last in 1917, the only team to do worse than Brooklyn. It became even more unpleasant when he received his 1918 contract from Barney Dreyfuss, the Pittsburgh owner. It called for the same $4,600 he had been paid in Brooklyn. Stengel wrote Dreyfuss. "I'm in my sixth season as a major-leaguer," he said, "but I'm still making what I was in my second season." He was turned down. Stengel argued that he'd been traded to Pittsburgh as a star and pointed out what he'd done in past seasons. That was before, Dreyfuss said; you haven't done it for me. Stengel tried again, but Dreyfuss said it was a war year, everything was uncertain, no one was getting raises. Wait, he told Stengel. Casey held out almost until the end of March before giving in. It *was* a war year, men were being drafted, there was little sympathy for baseball players holding out for more money. For the second year in a row, his stubbornness had failed him in a holdout.

Stengel batted fourth for the Pirates but didn't play well. His average going into June was in the .250s again, and this time he wasn't batting in many runs. The Pirates were playing better than a year earlier, but not sensationally so. Pittsburgh fans, expecting more, began to get on Stengel. They booed him loudly one day for what they thought was careless, indifferent play on his part. Trying to make a shoestring catch, Casey overran the ball and accidentally kicked it on an angle toward second base. He thought the ball had gone the other way, toward the foul line, and ran in that direction, away from the ball. The crowd jeered him. A few days later when he failed to slide and was tagged out, the crowd hooted as he returned to the dugout. There weren't many people in the stands, and it wasn't hard to hear him when he paused before going into the dugout, looked up at the crowd, and said, "With the salary I get I'm so hollow and starving that if I slide I'm liable to explode like a light bulb."

Dreyfuss heard about that and took it personally. In Brooklyn, Stengel had been called the King of the Grumblers for his constant complaining about low pay, and the title moved to Pittsburgh with him. He was beginning to lose his customary good nature. When the Pirates played in New York early in June he was restless and ready to make a change. World War I was in full swing, and two of the players Pittsburgh had sent to Brooklyn in the Stengel trade had already been affected. One was drafted during spring training, and the other quit to take a draft-proof job in a shipyard. The federal government had issued a "Work or Fight" order that said draft-age men had to be in essential industry or farming or face induction into the armed forces. Baseball players received a temporary exemption from that edict, but it wasn't going to last long.

Back in New York for the first time since he was traded from the Dodgers, Stengel got together with old acquaintances, among them Leon Cadore, the pitcher, who had become a good friend of his on the Dodgers. Cadore had enlisted in the army after the 1917 season, had been commissioned a lieutenant, and was on a ten-day leave from Camp Gordon, Georgia, when Casey arrived in New York with the Pirates. Stengel enjoyed Cadore. He admired Leon's dexterity in doing card tricks ("He could hand you the jack of diamonds," Casey said) as well as in doctoring a baseball. Doctoring a ball, nicking it, scuffing it, made it easier to throw a hard curveball. Cadore was so slick, Casey said, he could scuff a ball with one hand. In Brooklyn, Cadore would glance from the mound out at Stengel in right field, ostensibly checking the outfielder's position but actually to signal him, as though to say, "Watch this." And then, stretching, holding the ball aloft in one hand, he'd scuff the ball with his thumbnail.

Casey loved to watch Cadore do sleight of hand and had been his accomplice a couple of times, notably on one occasion when Cadore had deflated Bill Klem, the umpire. Klem, probably the best umpire who ever officiated a big-league game, prided himself on his ability and his dignity. He was a small man who demanded respect. He had an extraordinarily large mouth and when he was in full cry he bore a resemblance to a catfish, or so the players felt. Occasionally a player would call him Catfish, but not often, for Klem would toss a man out of a game without hesitation if the term was used.

When Klem spent a spring training working with the Dodgers, Cadore decided that he would puncture the little umpire's self-importance. He told Stengel one evening that he was going to "control an umpire" and needed his help. Cadore did his card tricks, and a small crowd gathered around him, including Klem. Cadore began to play to Klem and ultimately did a complicated trick with Klem as the subject, one of those set pieces in which the subject picks a card, the magician puts it back in the deck, and eventually the card shows up in a most improbable place. It was patently impossible for the card Klem had selected to be anywhere but on Cadore's person, somewhere, and when Leon asked where he thought it was Klem made the obvious suggestions. "No, you're wrong, Mr. Klem," Cadore said. No one ever said that Bill Klem was wrong, and the umpire flushed a little. "Look under your collar, Mr. Klem," Cadore suggested, and there was the card, a duplicate which Stengel had slid into place while Klem was concentrating on Cadore. Everybody laughed and applauded, everybody but Klem. Someone else might have been amused, but he was discomfited.

During a game later that season, when Klem was working behind the plate, Cadore began talking aloud after each pitch he threw. "That's a strike," he'd say. "That's a ball. *That's* a strike." He was calling them correctly, but it was too much for Klem to take. Ripping off his mask, he shouted at the pitcher, "Stop calling pitches on me, Cadore! That's *my* job. Keep your damned tricks for after the game!"

Stengel relished Cadore's whimsical nature, and he was happy to see him in New York. They got together with friends at a party in Brooklyn on Saturday night and saw them again on Sunday, when there were no ball games scheduled. On Wednesday Cadore was going to put on a Brooklyn uniform and pitch for the Robins, but on Monday in army uniform he was sitting in a seat behind home plate in the Polo Grounds, watching his friend Stengel play for the Pirates against the Giants.

The Pirates were trying to stay above .500 and needed a win that day to do it. With one out in the first inning, Stengel singled with men on first and second to drive one runner home and send the other around to third. Cutshaw followed with a double-play grounder to the shortstop. Casey was out at second, but he slid hard, hoping to break up the double play so that the man on third could score, and he thought he had succeeded. But the umpire at first base, a relatively inexperienced man named Pete Harrison, called Cutshaw out, and Stengel went half crazy. All the frustrations of the past two years seemed to pour out of him, and he ranted and raved at Harrison. The umpire threw him out of the game. Stengel ripped off his uniform shirt and said, "Here, why don't you play on our side for a change?" He made the long walk to the center-field clubhouse carrying his shirt, his underwear exposed for the world to see. "You in a hurry, Casey?" a fan shouted. "You got a date with a dame in Brooklyn?"

After dressing in his street clothes, Stengel went into the grandstand and watched the rest of the game with Cadore. One assumes that as they sat there watching the game Stengel asked Cadore what it was like in the service, discussed his own situation as a single man facing the Work or Fight order, and explored with Cadore different aspects of military service. Presumably, Cadore had some telling things to say about army camps in Georgia, for Stengel immediately began to think navy. Cadore might also have talked about opportunities for big-name athletes in the service. Certainly, he had had no trouble keeping his pitching arm in shape at Camp Gordon. When he pitched for Brooklyn two days later he threw a shutout.

After the game, while Stengel was beginning to make inquiries about the navy, umpire Harrison sent a report of his run-in with Stengel to league president John Tener, who the next morning wired Casey that he had been fined $25 for his unseemly behavior. When Stengel came to bat in the first inning that Tuesday afternoon he had the yellow telegram from Tener pinned to his right sleeve. Harrison was umpiring behind the plate but said nothing. In the Giants' dugout, George Gibson, a tough old catcher, grunted, "If he tried to pull that in the old days he'd have been tossed out automatically." But Harrison was unsure of himself and he was reluctant to get into another abusive hassle with the loud, glib Stengel. Casey singled to drive in a run, tried to steal second, was called out, didn't argue — and then it was too late for the umpire to make an issue of it. Casey played the rest of the game with the yellow telegram fluttering from his sleeve.

He had another hit against the Giants the next day, while over in Brooklyn Cadore pitched his shutout. On Thursday, June 6, the Pirates went over to Brooklyn to play the Robins, the first time Stengel had been back to Ebbets Field since the big trade. The Brooklyn fans gave him a big hand the first time he batted, and they were generous with their applause for him throughout the series, even though he made only one hit in the four games. He went hitless against Cadore in the second game of a doubleheader on Saturday, and that night and the next day visited with friends again. Cadore, his leave and his short two-game season ended, got ready to return to Camp Gordon, and Stengel made his decision. He went hitless again on Monday, which dropped his batting average to .247, and that was the end of *his* season. When the Pirates left for Boston that night, Stengel wasn't with them.

Three days later he reappeared at Ebbets Field and announced that he had enlisted in the navy, had passed his physical and was about to report for duty at the Brooklyn Navy Yard. "The doctor took a look at me," he said, "and pronounced me a perfect man."

Stengel found navy life congenial. He spent a few weeks doing various menial jobs — he was assigned to the commissary — but he also made good use of his major-league background by becoming a kind of physical-education director, with emphasis on baseball. He was put in charge of the Navy Yard baseball team, which meant that he spent a good part of his duty time doing exactly what he'd been doing in civilian life: hanging around a baseball diamond. One of his players was Dave (Jimmy) Hickman, a Dodger outfielder who had also enlisted, so Casey was even in the company of his peers. He arranged games with teams made up of personnel on navy vessels newly arrived in Brooklyn. "I used to board them ships as soon as they docked," he said, "and try to set up a game for the next day. I wanted to play them before they got rid of their sea legs. We won quite a few games that way."

It was a pleasant way to sit out the war. Casey managed to keep up his acquaintance with Brooklyn friends, including newspapermen covering the ball games, and he still displayed his gift for publicity. Late in August during a practice game at Prospect Park in Brooklyn, he asked a boy to hold his money for him while he was out in the field. A short time later he saw the boy riding away from the field on a bicycle. He yelled and chased after him, to no avail. He reported the loss, $40 or $50, to the police, and the story of the theft of Casey Stengel's money appeared in the New York papers. Casey told that story often in later years, saying, "I can still see that kid riding away with my fifty bucks. The moral of the story is, never trust a boy on a bicycle."

12 AFTER THE WAR:
A SPARROW IN HIS HAT

Five months after Casey enlisted, the war ended, and by the late winter of 1919 he was back in the world of baseball, arguing again with Barney Dreyfuss, the Pittsburgh owner. Dreyfuss still refused to give Stengel the raise he demanded, saying with some justification that Casey had not yet done anything for the Pirates that warranted a raise. Stengel held out for a long time, but for the third straight year capitulated just before the season began. Even his modest salary with the Pirates was more money than he could expect to make working around Kansas City.

This time he played much better ball for Pittsburgh, batting fourth again and keeping his average close to .300. But he was continually griping, complaining about his meager pay, carping at Dreyfuss, who found his loquacious presence as much of an irritant as Ebbets had. In May, Stengel got into another

231

big argument with Pete Harrison, the umpire he had tangled with in the Polo Grounds. Pirate manager Hugo Bezdek joined the discussion, and both he and Stengel were thrown out of the game. Stengel was fined $50 (up from $25 a year earlier, an example of postwar inflation), and Bezdek was suspended for three days. Dreyfuss blamed Stengel for Bezdek's suspension, and the rift between player and owner grew wider.

Anyway, Casey's heart was still in Brooklyn. When the Pirates arrived in Ebbets Field in May for three games with the Robins, Stengel's first appearance there since his enlistment almost a year earlier, he was full of life. He had a perfect day at bat in the first game of the series and a lot of fun exchanging badinage with the fans and the Brooklyn players. The next day he and Ivy Olson got into a boastful argument about hitting and bet a straw hat on who'd get more base hits that afternoon (Olson won, with a double and a triple to Stengel's single).

On Sunday — 1919 was the first year that New York State permitted Sunday baseball — more than 20,000 people turned out, and Casey had a rough afternoon. Sherry Smith, the left-hander, made his first start for Brooklyn since returning from military service and pitched a three-hit shutout to give the Robins a clean sweep of the series with Pittsburgh. The Pirates, who had been in third place when they arrived in Brooklyn, tumbled down to sixth.

Stengel had a lot of trouble at bat against Smith, striking out twice and grounding out to the shortstop, and the crowd got on him each time he came to bat, crying, "One out!" He made a nice catch in right field and lifted his cap mockingly to the crowd after it, but a couple of innings later he ran into trouble. The score was still 0–0 but the Dodgers had two men on base when Hy Myers hit a long hard fly toward the wall in right center. Stengel, trying to prevent any runs from scoring, made a desperate try for the ball but missed it and saw it hit the wall and rebound past him. He chased it into center field while three runs crossed the plate and the crowd cheered raucously. The fans hooted as he came into the bench after that inning.

He had his revenge a short time later. It was the custom throughout Ebbets Field's forty-five years of existence for right fielders of both teams to stop occasionally in the Dodger bullpen, which was in foul territory near the right-field wall, and stay there between innings when it was unlikely that they'd be coming to bat, instead of making the long jog into the dugout and back. Cadore was in the Dodger bullpen that afternoon — he was due to pitch the next day and was throwing a little to loosen up — and Stengel stopped by to visit a couple of times. After the sixth inning he paused at the bullpen on his way to the dugout and noticed that Cadore was holding something. It was a bird, a sparrow ("of the type vulgarly termed 'chippy,'" one paper reported). It had wandered in some confusion into the bullpen, where Cadore, with his deft hands, had captured it.

"Let me have it," Casey said impulsively, the germ of an idea forming in his mind. He covered the sparrow with his cap and carried it into the dugout. Just before he went out to bat he put the bird on his head under his cap. The crowd greeted him with mock applause and a round of good-natured boos. Casey turned toward the stands, bowed and lifted his cap, and there was the sparrow, which immediately fluttered away. The crowd howled, and even the plate umpire, Cy Rigler, joined in the laughter. The *New York Sun* said the next day, "Casey Stengel, the jolly right fielder of the Pirates, has pulled a lot of comedy in his life, but yesterday he got one off in Ebbets Field that wins the brown derby."

And the *Times* said, "Stengel, despairing of getting a hit off Smith, turned magician in the seventh inning. He doffed his cap and from out of the darkness of the headpiece there flew an irate but much relieved sparrow."

Wilbert Robinson grumphed and said, "Hell, he always did have birds in his garret."

About the only one who wasn't amused was Barney Dreyfuss. The Pirates kept on losing after their weak performance in Brooklyn and fell well below .500. Stengel was playing well, leading the team in both hitting and runs batted in, but Dreyfuss longed for the gentlemanly Max Carey, his star center fielder, who had damaged his shoulder early in the year and hadn't played since. He had Carson Bigbee, a steady player, in the outfield, and Billy Southworth, who joined the Pirates in 1918 after Stengel left for the navy and led the league in hitting the rest of the year. Southworth, too, had been injured early in 1919, but he returned to the lineup the day before Casey let the sparrow out of his cap. When Carey returned at the beginning of August, his shoulder better, Dreyfuss had a surfeit of first-string outfielders, and Stengel was still pestering him about raising his salary. Dreyfuss solved both problems on August 9 by trading Casey to the Philadelphia Phillies for

Possum Whitted, an outfielder who could play the infield, whom the Pirates immediately stationed at first base. Whitted hit a splendid .389 the rest of the season for Pittsburgh, but Stengel didn't bat anything at all for Philadelphia. Irritated by the trade, he sent a wire to William Baker, the Phils' owner, demanding an increase in salary before he'd report. Baker, who had sold Grover Alexander to the Cubs after a salary dispute, replied that there wasn't much money in Philadelphia. Stengel said, well, in that case he could be found in Kansas City. He refused to report to the Phillies. He packed his bags and went home — in the middle of August.

In Kansas City he gathered a ragtag team of semipros and ex-minor-leaguers and under the guidance of a promoter named Logan Galbreath took them on a barnstorming tour through oilfield towns in Kansas, Oklahoma and Texas and then on through New Mexico and Arizona to California before returning to Kansas City. One stop was at Fort Huachuca, a military base near Douglas in southern Arizona just above the Mexican border, where they played a team of black soldiers that included a pitcher Stengel recalled as "Grogan" and whom he described as "next to Satchel Paige, the best colored pitcher I ever saw."

"Grogan" was Joe (Bullet) Rogan, a hard-throwing right-hander who became one of the titans of Negro baseball in the 1920s and 1930s, when black players were barred from organized ball. Stengel also admired a black shortstop named Dobie Moore. "They were as good as any major-leaguers," Stengel said. (When he returned to Kansas City the following winter he mentioned the black stars he had seen to James L. Wilkinson, a white man who was organizing a team of black players to be called the Kansas City Monarchs. Wilkinson signed Rogan, Moore and three others.)

In California after the major-league season ended Casey added Emil Meusel and his kid brother Bob to the team. Emil, known as Irish, played left field for the Phillies (Bob was about to join the Yankees and would play for ten years in the same outfield with Babe Ruth), and he helped persuade Casey to work out his differences with Bill Baker. Stengel had made good money on the barnstorming tour, but he knew that no matter how talented and well known a player he was he couldn't earn as decent a living playing exhibitions in tank towns as he could playing outfield in the big leagues, even for a last-place team like the Phillies.

During the winter he agreed to terms with

Baker and in 1920 played right field for Philadelphia. He and the good-natured Meusel became fast friends, going out together, making jokes together about playing ball in Philadelphia. The ball park the Phils used was called Baker Bowl, and it was tiny, with a small outfield area that in right field was bounded by a high fence faced with tin. "Playing right field there was the softest job in baseball," Stengel said. "I had the wall behind me, the second baseman in front of me, the foul line on my left and Cy Williams, the center fielder, on my right. The only time I had a chance to catch the ball was when it was hit right at me."

Meusel had a chronic sore arm and hated to throw, although he led the Philadelphia outfielders in assists in both 1919 and 1920. Stengel's once fleet legs were creaking and his back was bothering him, and he no longer felt the need to chase joyously after every fly ball hit anywhere near him. He and Meusel began to let Williams take all the flies he could reach. They did it so routinely that later on, when Casey and Irish were playing together on the Giants, they'd automatically shout, "Take it, Cy!" on every ball hit to the outfield.

Baker, who did not appreciate the humor

of it, called Stengel "just plain plumb lazy" when he sat out games and let a splendidly named substitute called DeWitt Wiley (Bevo) LeBourveau take over for him. Baker's petulance was fueled by Stengel's loud, persistent criticism of the tight-fisted owner.

Nevertheless, Casey was enjoying baseball again, despite the aches and pains that had become chronic. One day that spring, as the Phils barnstormed home after leaving their training site, the club played a game in Fort Wayne, Indiana. Crowds gathered early before such exhibition games in order to watch the major-leaguers in practice, but one loud-mouthed yokel sitting near the Phils' dugout kept up a noisy harangue, mocking the players' ability and disparaging every ball that was batted. "You can't hit, you city loafers!" he'd cry. "You call that hitting? Anybody could hit better than that."

After a time the Philadelphia players began to answer him back. Finally one of them said, "You've got a pretty big mouth. You think you could do any better?"

"Dang right I could," said the fan, who was wearing overalls and a farmer's straw hat, with a red bandanna around his neck.

"Why don't you come out here and try?"

"All right, I will," said the farmer. He

clumped his way onto the field, picked up a bat and went up to home plate. To the astonishment of the crowd he was good. He whacked out line drives and long flies and even put a couple of balls over the fence. Well, of course, it was Stengel, putting on a show for the crowd.

Another day that spring he put his uniform on backward and wore it that way all through batting practice. The Phils' manager was Gavvy Cravath, their once-great hitter, now in his last season in the majors. Cravath was a strong-jawed, impressive-looking man who later became a justice of the peace in California. He had a bad cold the day Stengel put the uniform on backward and wasn't terribly amused by the joke. "I'm not surprised, though," he told Stengel. "You've done everything else backward down here. You might as well wear your pants that way too."

Casey did a reprise of his sparrow trick in 1920. In Baker Bowl one afternoon before a sparse crowd of 500 or so he saw a bird in the outfield grass, popped his cap over it and put bird and cap on his head. A moment or so later a high fly came in his direction and, with everyone watching, he lifted his cap after he caught the ball and the bird flew away.

Some days he'd get the crowd laughing by

catching easy fly balls behind his back. He enjoyed that kind of obvious fun, but he appreciated the hard, competitive aspects of baseball too. The Phils had a pitcher that season named Lee Meadows, a chunky right-hander who wore glasses and could throw hard, a combination that tended to make batters nervous at the plate. One day, with Meadows pitching, the Phils were leading the St. Louis Cardinals by one run in the ninth, with men on second and third, two out and Rogers Hornsby, the best hitter in the league, at bat. Cravath ordered Meadows to walk Hornsby intentionally and pitch to the next man. Stengel, out in right field, thought that was absolutely the right thing to do, even if there were two out. Hornsby was a devastating hitter.

Meadows thought different. With Hornsby waiting for a walk, Meadows slipped the first pitch over the plate for a strike. Hornsby got ready to swing at the next one, but Meadows threw the ball behind his head, and Hornsby had to hit the dirt. Meadows slipped the next pitch over for strike two, and then, with Hornsby angry and ready, knocked him down again. And then knocked him down a third time. With the count three and two, Meadows threw a hard curve, hoping for strike three, but Hornsby stepped into the pitch and hit what Stengel called "the damnedest line drive I ever saw." It went on a low flat line directly to Meusel in left field, who caught it for the final out. "That was the roughest I ever saw a man pitched to in the major leagues," Stengel recalled, "but the biggest thing was what Hornsby did, after all those fastballs thrown behind his head. Instead of falling away on that last curveball, he stepped in and hit a tremendous line drive."

That was the connoisseur of baseball talking, appreciating an example of rare skill and courage in the game he loved so much.

Casey batted .292 for the Phillies in 1920 but appeared in only 118 games in the outfield, the fewest he had ever played in a full season. Nonetheless, he hit nine home runs and only five players in the league hit more, two of them his fellow outfielders, Williams and Meusel. It had been a satisfactory season.

But 1921 was something else again. His legs were no better, and his back was worse. By the end of June he had been to bat only fifty-eight times. He was hitting over .300, but he wasn't much help to the team. He ached. The multiple injuries he had incurred during his career — the ankle, the knee, the shoulder, the pulled muscles, now the back

— made him feel like an old man. He was going to be thirty-one in a month, and his best years were gone. The family back in Kansas City was getting by, but Casey knew they needed the money he sent them. His father's street-sprinkling business had petered out, and, past sixty now, he had a bad heart that kept him from working.

Casey had done the best he could, but the future seemed bleak. Time had somehow passed him by when he wasn't looking. He wasn't "the fair-haired youth" anymore. He was in his eleventh season as a professional ballplayer, and while his major-league salary was nice it wasn't nearly as much as he might have been making. The distaste that Ebbets and Dreyfuss had felt for him, the exile to Pittsburgh and then to Philadelphia, the negative influence of the war — all those things had turned what should have been the peak of his career, the years from 1917 through 1921, into a kind of slow-motion seriocomic nightmare.

The 1921 season in Philadelphia was nightmarish enough in any case. Cravath had been dropped as manager, even though he had improved the team's won-lost record in 1919 after taking over as manager in midseason and had improved it again in 1920, and Wild Bill

Donovan had been named in his place. Wild Bill, so called because of the many bases on balls he had given up when he was a big-league pitcher, had had some remarkably successful seasons when he was a player (27–14 in 1901, 26–4 in 1907), but he had, literally, a fatal tendency to be in the wrong place at the wrong time. He had been made manager of the Yankees in 1915 after Jacob Ruppert and Cap Huston bought that once tatterdemalion team and started it on its road to glory. But Donovan had become the manager too early, before the team acquired its great players, and after three seasons he was dismissed.

If he was too early for the Yankees, he was too late for the Phils, who had finished first or second four times in five years, not long before Donovan took over from Cravath. Now they were a bad team getting worse, and Donovan didn't even last out the season. He was gone in August. In 1923, by then managing New Haven in the Eastern League, he was riding in a sleeping car through upstate New York on his way to the winter baseball meetings in Chicago with his boss, George Weiss. Weiss, a younger man, let Donovan have the lower berth in their compartment. That night there was a train wreck and Donovan was killed, while Weiss escaped without serious injury.

In June 1921 in Philadelphia, Donovan was not a happy man, and he let his players know it. He was quick to criticize, and his players chafed under his displeasure. The Phils had a portly red-faced catcher named Frank Bruggy, who owned a Stutz Bearcat. Donovan used to cadge rides home with Bruggy after games, which the catcher hated because Donovan would tell him on the way home what Bruggy had done wrong in that day's game. One day when Bruggy was catching, Donovan kept yelling at him from the bench to have the pitcher mix up his pitches. Bruggy had the pitcher throw his fastball, his curve, his change of pace, everything he could think of, but Donovan kept yelling, "Mix 'em up! Mix 'em up!" Bruggy finally called time, took off his mask, stood up, and turning his head so that Donovan could hear him, called out elegantly to the pitcher, "If you have anything else in your repertoire, please deliver it."

That amused the players but did little to cheer up Donovan, who continued to bawl people out. Stengel, whose locker was close to the manager's, finally moved his gear into a little closetlike space off the dressing room to get away from Donovan's post-game tirades, and possibly to gain a little privacy and a semblance of the dignity a man of his years and experience deserved. One rainy Thursday afternoon, the last day of June, after the game the Phillies were scheduled to play that day had been postponed, Jim Hagan, the club secretary, came into the clubhouse. Casey was in another room, having his leg worked on by a trainer. He heard Hagan ask, "Where's Stengel's locker?" Back there, someone said. "Back there?" said Hagan, "Well, he'll be dressing farther away than that pretty soon."

"Uh, oh," Stengel thought, "I'm gone. Donovan's gonna send me to Kalamazoo." Big-league careers ended abruptly in those years.

Hagan came into the trainer's room, saw Stengel, and said, "I've got something for you." He handed him a piece of paper. Casey glanced at it — and everything changed. It said the Phillies had traded Stengel and second baseman Johnny Rawlings to New York.

"Yee-ow!" Stengel yelled. He leaped off the table and began jumping around the room. The trainer stared at him.

"I thought your leg hurt," he said.

"Not anymore," Stengel shouted. "Not anymore. I've been traded to the Giants!"

All the things that had happened to Charley Stengel — the high school championship in Missouri, the batting title in Aurora, breaking in so spectacularly in Brooklyn, hitting that home run off Alexander, winning the pennant, batting .364 in the World Series, all the triumphs, all the fun, all the battles, all the injuries, all the failures — had been little more than a preamble. The most rewarding part of his life was about to begin.

13 THE LITTLE NAPOLEON: McGRAW OF THE GIANTS

John McGraw was Stengel's hero. Casey admired and praised no one else in his life as much as he did the almost legendary manager of the New York Giants. "I learned more from McGraw than anybody," he said. When Stengel joined the Giants on July 1, 1921, McGraw was in his twentieth season as Giant manager, and he was without question the dominant manager in baseball. Indeed, with the possible exception of the newly emergent Babe Ruth he was the dominant figure in baseball. He combined the endearing personal traits of George Steinbrenner and Billy Martin — he was arrogant, combative, aggressive, insolent, cocksure, skillful, quick to take advantage, quick to take offense — and, like Steinbrenner and Martin, he was successful, a winner or close to it year after year.

Beyond winning, McGraw imposed his personality on his team and on the game. He was the best, his team was the best, and he wanted everyone to know it. From 1903 through 1925, McGraw and the Giants were first or second nineteen times. (He continued to manage until 1932 but after 1925 finished as high as second only twice.) He won ten pennants in twenty-one seasons. His closest rival, Connie Mack, had six by then (and would add three more in 1929, 1930 and 1931), but Mack had broken up his sixth championship team after the 1914 season and finished dead last for seven straight years. McGraw, like Mack, finished last in 1915, but he fought his way back to fourth place in 1916 and to another pennant in 1917. He could not have lived finishing last year after year, as Mack did.

McGraw had been born in 1873 in upstate New York, the son of an Irish immigrant. His mother, two brothers and two sisters died in a diphtheria epidemic in 1885 when he was twelve. This massive onslaught of death was traumatic enough, but it was aggravated by his distraught father's subsequent drinking and anger, most of it directed at his young, shattered son. When he was thirteen, McGraw ran away from home and from then on was on his own. He matured early, a short, lean, wiry, tough, unsmiling youth who found satisfaction and accomplishment, and eventually money, playing baseball.

In 1890, just seventeen, he started in minor-league ball along the New York-Pennsylvania border. The following winter he traveled to Cuba and Florida with an "all-star" team playing exhibition games, and in the spring of 1891 was in a minor league in Iowa. By August 1891, still only eighteen, he had moved up to the Baltimore Orioles of the old American Association, then in its last season as a major league. The Association folded the following winter, but Baltimore was taken into an expanded twelve-team National League in 1892. McGraw was a substitute during his first two seasons but in 1893 he was the regular shortstop, and in 1894, after being shifted to third base, became one of the stars of one of the most famous teams in baseball history — the storied "Old Orioles" of McGraw, Willie Keeler, Hughie Jennings, Wilbert Robinson and the rest.

McGraw spent the rest of his life talking about that team, giving himself and Jennings most of the credit for molding the Orioles into the smart, shrewd, scrambling, innovative team they became. He put down roots in Baltimore, married a Baltimore girl and eventually opened a bar and restaurant with his teammate Robinson. But things soured. He caught typhoid fever and played little in 1895 and 1896. In 1899, Ned Hanlon, the Orioles' manager, switched to Brooklyn, taking four of his stars with him. McGraw remained in Baltimore and succeeded Hanlon as manager, but the team wasn't the same. It finished fifth, and the franchise folded after the 1899 season. McGraw's young wife died of a ruptured appendix, and in 1900, no longer a manager but a common player again, he was traded 750 miles west to St. Louis. He was only twenty-eight but was just about finished as a player.

He returned to Baltimore in 1901, married again and became player-manager of a new Baltimore team in the new American League. This team didn't do well either, and McGraw grew increasingly discontent. Belligerent toward umpires and opposing players and league officials, he was under suspension in July 1902 when he jumped the Orioles to switch to the National League and the Giants. The New York club was an absolute mess, a disorganized team that had finished better than seventh only once in seven seasons and would finish eighth that year. McGraw was the club's seventeenth manager in eleven years, but he served notice on Andrew Freedman, the Giants' curmudgeonly owner, that he, McGraw, would be in complete command by summarily telling Freedman that half the men on his team's roster were worthless and had to go. He brought three good players with him from Baltimore (pitcher Joe McGinnity, catcher Roger Bresnahan and first baseman Dan McGann), firmly reestablished young Christy Mathewson as a pitcher (the previous manager had taken to experimenting with Matty as an outfielder and as a first baseman), began making trades, poked some life into his moribund ball club and was off and running.

From then on, it was McGraw, McGraw, McGraw, and his presence in the game rang through Stengel's life. When McGraw first became manager of the Giants, Charley Stengel was a baseball-playing twelve-year-old on the Kansas City sandlots. He was thirteen when McGraw lifted the Giants all the way up to second place in 1903, and he was fourteen when the Giants won eighteen straight games in 1904 on their way to McGraw's first pennant.

He was a hotshot kid pitcher about to enter high school when McGraw's 1905 champions crushed Connie Mack and the Athletics four games to one in the World Series, with Mathewson pitching three shutouts and McGinnity another. And he was the star of his high school team in 1908 when McGraw lost another pennant because of Fred Merkle's famous "boner": On what should have been the gamewinning hit for the Giants with two out in the last half of the ninth inning of a vitally important game with the Cubs, Merkle, the New York runner on first base, followed the careless baseball practice of the day by sprinting directly to the clubhouse without bothering to touch second base before he did; a Chicago player got the ball, or some ball, pushed his way through the crowd of exultant Giant fans running on the field, stepped on second and created a force-out, thus negating the run; the game ended in a tie, and the Giants lost the replay and with it the championship. McGraw was outraged by what he felt was the pedantry of the umpire's decision — he never blamed Merkle — and his thoroughly explicated wrath was part of Stengel's baseball education.

As a professional ballplayer Casey was keenly aware during his first five seasons in the game (1910-14) that McGraw and the Giants won three pennants and finished second twice during those years. In 1915 when Stengel batted .316 for the third-place Robins and in 1916 when he helped Brooklyn win the pennant, part of the marvelous sense of triumph he felt was the idea of finishing ahead of John McGraw. Not many people did. His Giants were the most feared, the most respected, the most admired team in baseball.

He was the Little Napoleon, the five-foot-seven-inch king of all he surveyed. He approached life with a chip on his shoulder, irritable and quick to anger. He disliked criticism, always assumed he was right and carried that assumption to extremes in angry arguments — and fist fights — both on the field and off, even with friends and acquaintances. He insisted on absolute obedience from his players. "You did it his way," said George Kelly, who played for McGraw in the 1920s, "or he got you out of there real quick."

He wanted high performance from his team, and when he was displeased he would flail his charges with sharp, obscene, skin-curling language. His speech was usually highly charged. A newspaperman asked him in the summer of 1921 about rumors that he was going to pay a minor-league owner named Jack Dunn $150,000 for three players. The printed report of McGraw's reaction was: "He said he wouldn't give Dunn $150,000 for his whole emphatically qualified ball club."

He was mean-tempered, sneering, bullying, unpleasant, and at the same time warmhearted, generous, even charming. He made lasting friendships with people of taste and quality (the gentlemanly Mathewson was his closest friend). In baseball he was a genius, a tactician whose sense of the progress of a game was uncanny, a strategist who could see impending strengths and weaknesses in his own and other clubs before anyone else.

"What a great man he was!" Marquard, the old Giant and Dodger pitcher, said to Larry Ritter, and Meyers, the Dartmouth-educated catcher who played for McGraw in the same era, used precisely the same words. Marquard called McGraw "the finest and grandest man I ever met. He loved his players and his players loved him." Yet Rube also said that in 1915, the year the Giants finished last, "McGraw started riding me. After I'd taken as much riding as I could stand, I asked him to trade me."

Fred Snodgrass, for several years the Giants' center fielder, said, "Naturally, McGraw and I didn't always see things alike and sometimes he'd bawl the dickens out of me, as he did everybody else." But, Snodgrass added, "It was an education to play under John J. McGraw." Third baseman Heinie Groh described McGraw's method of teaching him how to field: " 'Get in front of those balls,' he'd say. 'You won't get hurt. That's what you've got a chest for, young man.' "

On the other hand, catcher Bob O'Farrell, who had played for the abrasive Rogers Hornsby, said, "McGraw was rough as a manager, very hard to play for. You couldn't seem to do anything right for him, ever. It was always your fault, not his." Outfielder Edd Roush, who was with the Giants briefly as a rookie, said, "I didn't like New York. Well, it wasn't exactly that . . . it was really McGraw I didn't like. If you made a bad play he'd cuss you out, yell at you, call you all sorts of names." When Roush was traded back to the Giants a decade later, he balked at first. "I was around thirty-four," he said, "and I wasn't about to start taking abuse from McGraw that late in life."

It's fairly standard practice for players to criticize successful managers. McGraw, for instance, while telling story after story about the old Orioles, seldom praised Hanlon, the Baltimore manager. Another old-timer said, "Those old veterans didn't pay any attention to Hanlon. They'd look at him and say, 'For

Christ's sake, just keep quiet and leave us alone. We'll win this ball game if you only shut up.' " McGraw left the same impression, implying, perhaps deliberately, that Hanlon had had little to do with the Orioles' success.

Yet McGraw learned his craft from Hanlon. When Ned became manager of Baltimore early in 1892, McGraw was a nineteen-year-old benchwarmer and the Orioles were a last-place team in a twelve-team league. Two years later they won the pennant. It was Hanlon who made the daring trades and shrewd moves that turned a sow's-ear team into a silk purse. He took the same radical, autocratic approach to the job that McGraw followed when he became manager of the Giants a decade later. Hanlon assumed total command of the Orioles, to the point of discomfiting the Baltimore owner, Harry Vonderhorst, who went along with what his manager wanted but wore a button on his lapel to which he'd point when someone inquired about his team. "Ask Hanlon," the button read. He found his players on the bench, where McGraw was, bought them from the minor leagues, signed other teams' troublemakers, traded for rookies and undeveloped players, acquired veterans other clubs thought were washed up. He knew talent and he wasn't afraid to trade good players or throw substantial amounts of cash into a deal to get what he wanted.

Hanlon also understood that baseball wasn't static, that it changed over the years. When a new rule lengthened the distance between pitcher and batter in 1893, Hanlon realized before most of his contemporaries did how radically different the game was going to be. Pitching was going to lose much of its importance and hitting was going to take over (he was right — the overall batting average of the National League rose 64 points in two seasons). The crux of the game moved from home plate (pitcher vs. batter) to the bases (fielders vs. base runners). Hanlon's Orioles weren't the best hitting team in the league, but they were the best fielders and the best base runners, and they won three straight pennants and were dominant through the 1890s.

McGraw may have been correct when he claimed that he and Jennings were instrumental in adding the refinements that made the Orioles famous, but it was Hanlon who found the right players, put them in the right positions and turned them loose. Why he isn't in the National Baseball Hall of Fame in Cooperstown is a mystery, explained in part by the fact that the baseball writers who hung on McGraw's words for three decades, accepting on faith his version of baseball history, never heard much about him.

If McGraw didn't praise his old manager he nonetheless learned important things about baseball from watching him operate, things Stengel was to learn watching McGraw. One was the obvious fact, often overlooked, that the team with the best players usually wins. Know who the best players are and where they are and grab them when you need them — if you can. McGraw had a network of unofficial scouts, old friends, former ballplayers, sometimes sportswriters, who could tip him off to promising youngsters. He studied players already in the big leagues. When he saw a weakness developing on his team and felt that a player from another club would correct it, he went after him with determination, often dressing up a trade with a name player from the Giants whose value on the field no longer equaled his reputation, more often salting the deal with a substantial amount of cash. McGraw did this so often that he was accused of "buying pennants," as Stengel's Yankees (and Steinbrenner's Yankees) were similarly accused in later years. In his short story "The Three Day Blow"

Ernest Hemingway has this dialogue:

> "*What did the Cards do?*"
> "*Dropped a double header to the Giants.*"
> "*That ought to cinch it for them.*"
> "*It's a gift,*" Bill said. "*As long as Mc-Graw can buy every good ball player in the league there's nothing to it.*"
> "*He can't buy them all,*" Nick said.
> "*He buys all the ones he wants,*" Bill said.

McGraw also learned from Hanlon that you change with circumstances. Most big-league managers operate by rote, following "percentage," doing things by the so-called book, religiously adhering to tradition. Hanlon made his own tradition. So did McGraw. So, later, did Stengel. Hanlon understood what was happening in baseball in the 1890s and altered his team to suit. Ten years later the pendulum swung back and the game became low-scoring again. McGraw therefore built his early Giant teams around pitching, and on offense maneuvered to scratch out the few runs his good pitchers needed. This was "inside baseball," the tight, low-scoring game that Ring Lardner loved and hated to see disappear under the avalanche of home runs that came into the game with Babe

Ruth. But when home runs turned baseball around, McGraw changed again. Stengel said, "McGraw was the best manager I ever saw at adapting from the dead ball to the lively ball." He spiced his lineup with power hitters like George Kelly, Irish Meusel, Bill Terry, Mel Ott and, not incidentally, Stengel, who while never a Ruthian slugger had the reputation of being able to poke a ball a long way now and then.

Awareness of change helped make Hanlon and McGraw and Stengel great managers. Stengel came into baseball when it was a low-scoring, singles-hitting game, was still a player when home runs and high batting averages took over, managed three decades later when it was home runs and *low* batting averages. Watching McGraw, Stengel learned about change and at the same time he learned what was immutable. He learned, for example, that you not only have to have the players, you have to know how to handle them, to keep them motivated. Al Bridwell, the Giant shortstop who hit the "game-winning" ball against the Cubs in 1908 that led to Merkle's boner, said: "The reason McGraw was such a great manager, and he was the greatest, was because he got the most out of each man. It wasn't so much knowing baseball. All of them know that. What makes the difference is knowing each player and how to handle him. At that sort of thing nobody came anywhere close to McGraw."

Hanlon did and Stengel did. When Casey had the players to work with, as he had with the Yankees, he held them to a high level of performance for a dozen years. To keep a team playing that well for that long a time is more than luck.

It's fun to imagine a genealogy of managers. Ned Hanlon's children include not only McGraw but such other pennant-winning managers as Jennings and Robinson (who said, on becoming manager of Brooklyn, "I'm gonna train the men the same way as Hanlon did, and McGraw does") and Kid Gleason and Fielder Jones and Fred Mitchell and Miller Huggins and, for that matter, Connie Mack, who played for Hanlon at Pittsburgh before Ned moved on to Baltimore. McGraw's pennant-winning offspring, aside from Stengel, are Bill McKechnie, Bill Terry, Frank Frisch and Billy Southworth, not to mention Jennings and Robinson, both of whom played under McGraw for a time. Stengel's pennant winners include Al Lopez, Ralph Houk, Yogi Berra, Hank Bauer, Gil Hodges and Billy Martin.

It doesn't seem to be stretching the point too far to say that Ned Hanlon begat John McGraw who begat Casey Stengel who begat Billy Martin . . .

14 THE POLO GROUNDS: WAKE UP, MUSCLES!

Rain was general throughout the Northeast the week that Stengel and Rawlings were traded to the Giants. Games had been postponed in Philadelphia on Tuesday and again on Thursday, although the Phils did manage to play (and lose) on Wednesday, when Casey, failing as a pinch hitter, made his last appearance with them. Donovan told Stengel and Rawlings they could stay over and leave Friday morning to join the Giants, and Rawlings followed that advice. But Stengel didn't wait until the next day. He put on his Phillies uniform, ran out onto the field in the rain and slid into first base. Then he ran down to second and slid there, slid into third and slid into home. Back in the clubhouse he took off the muddy uniform, handed it to the clubhouse man and said, "Here. Tell Baker to have this dry-cleaned." He threw a few things into a bag, arranged to have the rest of his stuff sent along later and left Philadelphia in the rain that evening. He caught a train out of North Philadelphia for New York, transferred to a Boston train (the Giants were in Boston to play the Braves) and reported to McGraw the next day. "I wasn't taking no chances," Stengel said. "I didn't want anybody to change their mind."

The Giants' game with the Braves on Friday was rained out, and so was the game on Saturday. Because local law barred Sunday baseball in Boston, the two clubs entrained for New York to play a doubleheader in the Polo Grounds that day. Legend has it that on the Sunday afternoon when Stengel finally appeared on a ball field in a Giant uniform, he smacked his legs and said, "Wake up, muscles! We're in New York now." Perhaps he did. He had reason to. Since damaging a tendon in the first week or so of the season he had appeared in barely a dozen games, and except for a few pinch-hitting efforts hadn't played at all in three weeks. Yet McGraw, wasting no time in finding out what he had to know about his new acquisitions, put Rawlings in the lineup at second base for the doubleheader and the still-injured Stengel in center field.

There is no doubt that in McGraw's eyes

Rawlings was the more important acquisition of the two, for Rawlings solidified the Giants' infield, a remarkable group that included three future Hall of Famers: George Kelly at first base, Frank Frisch at second and Dave Bancroft at shortstop. But the twenty-two-year-old Frisch was in only his second full season and a year earlier he had played third base, with the veteran Larry Doyle at second. Doyle became ill with what was diagnosed later as tuberculosis and was through as a player after the 1920 season. McGraw switched Frisch to second base at the beginning of 1921 and installed a veteran minor-leaguer named Goldie Rapp at third. Rapp looked fine in spring training but played poorly after the season began and by the end of June was batting only .215. Rawlings, tough and feisty, was a fine-fielding second baseman who had been having a rare good year at bat. By putting him at second and returning Frisch to third, McGraw gained experience at both positions. Rawlings was not a great player nor even a very good one, but he did well for the Giants that year and was the linchpin of the infield. So putting Rawlings at second was a logical move. Putting Stengel in center was another matter entirely.

McGraw tested Casey because he was searching restlessly for someone who could play there. He had an established left fielder in George Burns, a Giant regular for almost ten years, and an established right fielder in Ross Youngs, one of the best players in the league, but in center he had had only a succession of fringe players. McGraw knew Casey had played center field in earlier seasons, and he decided to throw him in there and see how he'd do. Some approved the move. Frank Graham, who would still be writing about Stengel forty years later when he was managing the New York Mets, observed, "Despite his propensity to clown at every opportunity, Stengel is a good player." Others, less sanguine, noted that Casey was pretty old and had been on the bench most of the year nursing various ailments.

Fans at the Polo Grounds had loved to hoot and jeer Casey, who'd grin and wave back, whenever he appeared there with Brooklyn or Pittsburgh or Philadelphia, but they welcomed him with warm applause that Sunday afternoon. Unfortunately, the pessimists were right about his inability to play in top form. Early in the game he had to run far back in the deep Polo Grounds center field to catch a fly ball, and it took something out of him. An inning or so later, with two out and a man on first, another Boston batter hit a little looping fly to short right center. Stengel, slow in getting to it, tried desperately to make a shoestring catch. He missed and the ball shot past him for a triple, driving in the runner from first to give Boston a 1–0 lead. The Giants came back quickly to tie the score, and it remained 1–1 into the seventh. Then, with one out, Stengel singled to left, his first hit as a Giant. McGraw called for a hit-and-run — he was *really* testing Stengel's legs — and Rawlings, batting behind Casey, pushed a single to right. Stengel labored around second and into third but he found the third-base coach waving him on — the right fielder had bobbled Rawlings' hit — and he kept chugging and scored all the way from first with what turned out to be the winning run. McGraw took mercy on him then and put a sub in to finish the game in center.

But he had Casey in center field for the second game, which the Giants also won, although Stengel had little to do with the victory. He vainly chased a long Boston triple to left center, struck out, ran hard to first trying unsuccessfully to beat out a hit after he caromed a line drive off the pitcher. McGraw again sent a replacement in to play center in the late innings, and that was about it for Casey as a Giant in the 1921 season. He didn't get into another game for three months, except for a few scattered pinch-hitting appearances.

As Casey sat on the bench, McGraw kept looking for an outfielder. A few days after Stengel's arrival he bought Bill Cunningham from the Pacific Coast League and alternated Cunningham, a right-handed hitter, with Curt Walker, like Stengel a lefty batter. Casey just sat. Near the end of July, McGraw swung another deal with Philadelphia, sending Walker, a couple of minor-leaguers and a bunch of cash to the Phillies for Stengel's old pal Irish Meusel, who at the time of the trade was batting .355, second in the league. He put Meusel in left field and moved the aging Burns to center, with Cunningham occasionally filling in for him.

Casey was strictly a supernumerary, but if his dream of playing for McGraw had been damaged by the realities of age, ailments and better players, Stengel didn't seem to mind. He loved being in New York, loved being part of McGraw's ball club. He kept things lively in batting practice with his incessant, wisecracking conversation, hustled out to coach at first base whenever someone was needed there (teams at that time ordinarily carried only two coaches, and often one of them would be occupied elsewhere). He jockeyed umpires and rival players from the bench and spent a lot of time listening to and watching McGraw and the way he managed. "He was very alert on when to start the runners," Stengel would recall years later. "He hated to see you walk off sluggishly. He said the first steps off a base might make you safe at third or home." And, "He wanted you to be a fighter at the plate, stand in there, don't back off. Get a piece of the ball, something might happen. He'd get very disturbed if you didn't stand up there and fight the pitcher."

Sitting on the bench listening to McGraw, Stengel began to feel at home on the Giants. It was an exciting team and an exciting time, an exciting season. The Giants were in second place five games behind the Pirates when Casey joined them, and for the next two months they were in pursuit of the Pittsburgh club. They closed the gap to two games, slumped a little, then late in July beat the Pirates three straight times in Pittsburgh to move into a tie. They fell back again, losing frustratingly time and again in August. One such defeat, a 1–0 loss to the Cardinals in St. Louis, was the occasion of Stengel's most notable contribution to the Giants' effort in 1921. A St. Louis batter had been hit in the head with a pitched ball and the angry Cardinals accused the Giant pitcher of throwing a beanball, of deliberately trying to hit the batter. Pickles Dilhoefer, the St. Louis catcher, got into a fight with Pancho Snyder, the New York catcher. The umpires broke up the fight and ordered both players out of the game. As Snyder walked off the field the St. Louis fans behind the Giants' dugout reviled him, calling him a pungent variety of foul names. Stengel jumped up on the parapet of the dugout and punched one of the fans. Police intervened and hurried both Snyder and Stengel off the field to the Giants' clubhouse.

By late August the Giants had fallen seven and a half games behind the Pirates, who were being called "the coming National League champions." But McGraw's team swept five straight games from Pittsburgh in the Polo Grounds and went on to win twenty of twenty-four games while the Pirates were losing seventeen of twenty-five and falling into second place. In mid-September in Pittsburgh the Giants took two more games from the Pirates to make it ten straight victories over their chief rivals, and they locked up the pennant. McGraw made a triumphant long-distance call — a signal event in those more primitive times — from the team hotel in Pittsburgh to Saranac Lake, New York, where his old friend Mathewson was recuperating from tuberculosis. A dozen members of the Giants' party spoke to Matty. Stengel may have been one of them; it's hard to imagine the voluble Casey not getting a word in.

He continued his nonplaying bench-jockeying role in the World Series against the Yankees (the first of more than a dozen "Sub-way Series" that would be played between New York teams), which the Giants won after being shut out in the first two games. After the Giants tied the Series at two games each, Stengel was yelling and shouting in the clubhouse: "We've got 'em tottering now. We'll have 'em on the ropes tomorrow." When Babe Ruth crossed up the Giants in one game by laying down a bunt and barely beating it out, Stengel yammered so loudly against the decision at first base that umpire George Moriarty threw him out of the game.

He was, in other words, a full-fledged Giant, one of McGraw's men, *part* of the team that won the pennant and the World Series

— even though he had done little on the field to help. He received his share of the World Series receipts the same as the other players did ("I made more money sitting with the Giants," he said later, "than I ever made standing with anybody else"). His future with the team was nebulous — he couldn't deny that — but he didn't let that bother him. All in all, it had been a wonderful year.

15 WINNING FOR McGRAW: CASEY COMES THROUGH

After the season McGraw traded the veteran Burns for Heinie Groh, which let him move Frisch back to second and bench Rawlings, whose hitting had tailed off in the latter part of the regular season (although Johnny had played splendidly in the Series). Burns' departure would seem to have assured Stengel that he would be kept on the roster, but McGraw was stockpiling center fielders. He had young Cunningham, and he paid a lot of money for Jimmy O'Connell, another Pacific Coast League star, although he decided to leave the youthful O'Connell in the minors for another year of seasoning. He acquired an impressive young player named Ralph Shinners from the American Association. He bought a big, hard-hitting Southerner named Ike Boone, who, like Stengel, batted left-handed, and acquired another young outfielder named Mahlon Higbee.

In spring training of 1922, Casey was surrounded by outfielders, and the sportswriters covering the Giants' camp in Texas assumed that he would be gone from the squad by the time the season began. Casey arrived at spring training in high spirits and excellent shape — his legs felt fine, the best they had in years — but the gloomy future forecast for him seemed inevitable. When McGraw split the squad and sent a second team of rookies and marginal players off on a separate barnstorming tour under the direction of scout Dick Kinsella and coach Jesse Burkett, he kept Shinners, Cunningham and Boone with the big team and assigned Stengel to the yannigans. It seemed pretty close to the end.

Undaunted — the quaint old word fits him — Stengel didn't give up. He worked hard, functioned as an extra coach and instructor under Kinsella and Burkett and played every day, strengthening his legs, sharpening his batting eye. He hit a home run in one game and tied the score with a ninth-inning base hit in another, and when McGraw trimmed his squad as the season began Casey was kept on the roster along with Shinners, Cunningham and Boone. Perhaps his personality was a factor. Two days before opening day the Giants were invited to play an exhibition game at

West Point by General Douglas MacArthur, then superintendent of the military academy, and Stengel was the star of the show, getting two hits, stealing a base, laying down a sacrifice, scoring two runs and amusing the cadets with his antics on the field.

So Casey remained a Giant, although once the season began he was the forgotten man again. Shinners opened the season in center and was an instant success, a fine fielder, a steady hitter and enormously popular with the New York fans. Cunningham and Boone occasionally got into games as pinch hitters, but Stengel just sat. McGraw soon added yet another outfielder, an ex-Giant hero named Davey Robertson who had just been released by Pittsburgh. "McGraw probably wants Robertson in case Shinners fails in center field," wrote one newspaperman, shunting Stengel even further aside.

When Shinners was hit in the head with a pitched ball in Philadelphia, Cunningham finished the game for him, although Shinners was in the lineup again the next day, apparently none the worse for the beaning. X-rays showed no fracture, and it was assumed he was all right. He went on a batting tear and had nine hits in seventeen at bats over the next four games, and he continued to play ev-

276

ery day for nearly a month afterward. The only time he rested was when the Giants played an exhibition game on an off day; Cunningham, Boone and Robertson were in the lineup for that game, but not Stengel. Casey didn't play an inning until the season was six weeks old, and then he was used only as a pinch runner — and was inelegantly hung up between bases on a ground ball. Two weeks later he was used as a pinch hitter. That was his only time at bat into the beginning of June.

But the beaning Shinners had experienced *was* bothering him, although Ralph had complained to no one. His once admirable batting average kept receding, and his once excellent fielding became erratic. In Cincinnati late in May, McGraw grilled his young star and learned that he had been bothered by severe headaches ever since the beaning and that his vision was frequently blurred. McGraw sent him to a hospital for a series of tests and put Cunningham in his place in center field. Shinners rejoined the club in a few days, apparently okay, but not in shape to play. He never regained the skills he had shown before the beaning; he played only a handful of games for the Giants after that, and he was out of the majors by 1924.

Cunningham was now the regular center fielder, but in Brooklyn on June 4, Cunningham smashed a finger in batting practice, and Stengel started the game in his place. He was cheered by the Brooklyn fans the first time he batted and was heartily booed later when he was awarded first base after making little effort to get out of the way of a pitched ball that nicked him on the arm. He made a fine running catch of a short fly ball hit by his old friend Hy Myers, and in the ninth inning capped a stirring Giant rally by driving in the winning run. He started again the next day and had two hits, one a triple. The next day he stole second and third and scored on a wild pitch. The day after that he batted in two runs against Grover Cleveland Alexander. The day after that he won a game with a home run, and a few days later he hit another game-winning homer.

He had waited a long time to play for Mr. McGraw, really play for him, and now that he had the chance he made the most of it. He was a regular now, playing every day except when the Giants went up against a left-hander like Eppa Jeptha Rixey of the Reds. Then McGraw, recalling what sportswriters called Stengel's "aversion to left-handers," would sit him down. Nonetheless, Casey was the number-one center fielder, playing four times as often as Cunningham. He was hitting hard, fielding beautifully, running well. Judge Kenesaw M. Landis, the Commissioner of Baseball, watching Casey hit a double against the Phillies, remarked, "Did you see him go to second on that two-bagger?"

Casey continued at a furious rate, raising his average over .400 and alternating with Rogers Hornsby for the league lead, although he didn't have nearly as many at bats as Hornsby. In July he was hit on the cheek with a pitched ball and was out of the lineup for ten days with a badly swollen face, but he batted just as well after he returned to the lineup. The Giants meantime were in first place but struggling to hold their lead. They lost four straight games after Casey was beaned and for the next month were in a day-to-day battle with Hornsby and the Cardinals, sometimes falling into second place by a game or so, then moving up again into first place. Stengel's bat began to cool off in August, his average subsiding into the .370s, but he was still impressive. He made an amazing catch to save a game in Pittsburgh. With the Giants ahead 7–6 in the last of the ninth, the bases loaded, two out, a Pirate batter hit a long drive to deep left center that seemed certain to fall in safely for a game-ending hit that would score the tying and winning runs for Pittsburgh. But Stengel, running with his back to the infield, reached across his body at the last moment and "plucked" the ball off his left shoulder for the game-ending out. The next day he hit two triples against Pittsburgh, and a few days later in Cincinnati made a tumbling shoestring catch of a line drive by Edd Roush.

His average continued to drop, but Casey was playing first-rate ball, and so were the Giants. They won thirteen of fifteen games in August, as the Cardinals finally faltered, opened up a big lead and coasted to their second-straight pennant. Casey, having the best season of his career, continued to do things. Against the Cubs he was hit by a pitch, stole second, went to third when the catcher's throw to second went awry and scored the winning run on a subsequent base hit. His batting average perked up again and climbed to .368 for the season, second in the league only to Hornsby (although another part-time outfielder, Reb Russell of Pittsburgh, also batted .368).

Then fate, which hadn't been able to slow him down with the pitched ball in the face in July, turned against him late in September.

Nine days before the World Series was to begin Stengel pulled a muscle in his right leg running in for a fly ball. His legs had been fine for more than a year, but now, only *nine* days before the World Series, a Series in which he'd be playing center field against the Yankees for McGraw, they'd let him down again.

He didn't play another inning in the regular season, although he assured everyone that the leg was fine, that he'd be in there for the Series. McGraw started him in the first game against the Yankees, and Casey had an easy day, getting one undemanding single in four at bats, with no baserunning to speak of, and catching four ordinary fly balls in center field.

The next day was different. In his first at bat, Casey hit a grounder to the shortstop, dug hard all the way to first base and beat it out for a base hit. He felt the muscle going as he crossed the bag but said nothing, hoping that he'd have an easy time around the bases and that the difficulty would clear itself up in an inning or so. The next batter hit a bouncing single to right field on which a healthy base runner would have gone to third base easily. Stengel, limping badly, stopped at second. McGraw sent Cunningham in to run for him, and Casey was out for the rest of the Series.

The game in which he was hurt turned out to be a historic one, a 3–3 tie that was called after ten innings because of "darkness," although there was still light enough to play. The fans were angry, and with memories of the recent Chicago Black Sox scandal still vivid began shouting, "Fix! Fix!" —implying that the game had been called prematurely as a deliberate ploy to add an extra round of gate receipts to the pot. Commissioner Landis hurriedly ordered all receipts to be turned over to charity.

In a sense, the tie, and the fans' reaction to it, was Stengel's fault. At any rate, John McGraw thought so. The Giants won the Series four games to none (plus the tie), and after their third victory McGraw said, "The Series would be over by now but for Stengel's injury in the second game. If he had asked for a runner when he was on first base, we would have won that game and today's victory would have ended the Series." McGraw explained what he meant. The hit to right field with Stengel on first base with no one out in the second inning was the fifth hit off Yankee starting pitcher Bob Shawkey, who had already given up three runs to the Giants in the first inning. After Stengel stopped at second and was taken out for Cunningham, the next Giant batter hit into a double play. Cunningham went to third, but a fly ball ended the inning. Shawkey settled down after his shaky start and pitched shutout ball the rest of the way. The Yankees whittled away at the Giants' lead and tied the game in the eighth. McGraw said, "If Stengel had called for a runner when he was on first base, Cunningham would have gone to third on the hit." Cunningham would then have scored from third on the double play. Or if the Yankee infield had moved in to hold him on third they would not have gotten the double play and Cunningham would have scored on the subsequent fly. Either way, the Giants would have had a fourth run and, to McGraw's thinking, would have won the game.

Stengel was uncharacteristically glum in the clubhouse after that game, answering questions in monosyllables. Not only was he in McGraw's doghouse, he knew he'd be unable to play again in the Series. But a couple of days later he was his old self again, roaming the clubhouse noisily looking for something of his that a teammate had mischievously hidden. "He would stop suddenly," said one onlooker, "and with exaggerated theatrical gestures direct facetious quotations from the classics at nobody in particular and everybody in general." Ye gods and Shakespeare, again.

Pulled muscle or not, he was still a full, unquestioned member of McGraw's Giants, for the second straight year the baseball champions of the world. After the Series he and George Kelly and several other major-leaguers went off on a baseball tour of Japan and the Far East, the highpoint of which came during a banquet given the tour when it paused in the Philippines. Frank (Buck) O'Neill, an American sportswriter accompanying the team, was a public speaker of the old school, and he bored the audience with a long, flowery, tedious speech. After he finished, Stengel was called on to say a few words. Casey arose and in pantomime parodied the sportswriter's address, using the same artificial gestures, lifting his chin impressively, imitating the significant pauses and absolutely delighting his audience, including those Orientals who hadn't understood a word of O'Neill's talk. He was the hit of the occasion, as he usually was whenever he stood before an audience, and he hadn't said a word.

In the spring of 1923 when he reported to

the Giants' training camp he again found himself off to the side while McGraw fell in love with another young center fielder. This time it was O'Connell, now deemed ready for the big leagues. He was a left-handed batter, too, the same as Stengel. McGraw had declared that O'Connell would be the regular center fielder, but O'Connell seemed timid, scared and maybe homesick, and McGraw decided he'd alternate him with the right-handed Cunningham. Stengel, now referred to as "ancient Casey," even though he was only thirty-two, apparently did not figure in McGraw's plans at all. Again he traveled with the second squad when the team began barnstorming homeward. Again he served as an instructor for the young players. But he played a lot, too. He hit a notable home run in Toledo and another in Zanesville, Ohio, rejoined the big club in time for the West Point game (although he played only an inning or so this time) and was on the bench when the season began, watching O'Connell and Cunningham share center field.

But at least McGraw had kept him around, and when opportunity came along on schedule, Casey was ready. The California-bred O'Connell caught a cold in the chill, unfamiliar northeastern spring and couldn't play. In stead of using Cunningham full-time, as he had a year earlier when Shinners couldn't play, McGraw decided to platoon Stengel in O'Connell's place against right-handers. Stengel came through with a hit in his first game, at Ebbets Field, and the next day had three more hits, including a home run over the right-field wall into Bedford Avenue. "Casey enjoyed it tremendously," said an account of the game, "and grinned broadly as he made his way around the bases."

Stengel had two more hits and three runs batted in the next day, off the redoubtable Dazzy Vance, but McGraw put O'Connell back in the lineup as soon as he recovered from his cold. He did use Stengel in left field, filling in for the slightly injured Irish Meusel, and again Casey hit up a storm, lifting his batting average to .379. He was the darling of the fans. "If anybody is more popular than anyone else on the Giants," enthused a sportswriter, "it is Stengel."

Then Casey managed to bench himself. The Giants were playing in Philadelphia, and the bad blood between the Phils and the Giants because of the beaning of Shinners a year earlier was still evident. The Giants scored six runs in the first inning (Stengel drove in one of them with a single) and knocked out the starting pitcher. A left-hander named Phil Weinert came in to pitch for the Phils. Weinert was big and fast and wild. He hit Casey with a pitch in the second inning, and when Stengel came to bat again in the fourth Weinert threw a fastball close to his head. Casey threw his bat angrily at the pitcher and ran toward him. Weinert was four or five inches taller than Stengel, outweighed him by twenty pounds and was more than ten years younger, but when they tangled and fell to the ground Casey was on top, swinging. Art Fletcher, a former Giant shortstop who was managing the Phils, grabbed Casey with a forearm under his chin and dragged him away from Weinert. Stengel struggled to get loose and back into the fight, but several policemen came on the field and two of them took Casey in hand. Still fuming, Stengel reluctantly allowed himself to be taken off the field. Next morning he learned that he had been suspended for ten days by National League president John Heydler.

During Casey's enforced absence O'Connell began playing much better, and Meusel, healthy again, returned to the lineup. When Casey was reinstated he found himself stuck on the bench again. His fight with Weinert occurred on May 7, and after it he didn't get into another game, except to pinch-hit, for more than two months.

But poor O'Connell slumped again (his was a brief and star-crossed career; late in 1924 he was thrown out of baseball for life for asking a rival player if he'd take $500 "not to bear down" against the Giants in important ball games). In July, McGraw took Jimmy out of the lineup and put Casey in his place. Again, Stengel rose to the occasion, hitting safely in twenty of the first twenty-two games he played and firmly reestablishing himself as the Giants' number one center fielder. He batted .345 for the rest of the season and was as noisy and rambunctious as ever, his gravelly voice cutting through the thrum of the crowd to drill its way into the hearing of rival players and umpires alike. "That'll be all, Casey," the usually genial umpire Charley Moran said irritably one day after Stengel had said nothing more than "Fine work, Moran" after the umpire called a Giant out on strikes. Casey had a run-in with the equally genial Charlie Grimm, then playing first base for the Pirates, in Pittsburgh one afternoon when he and Grimm bumped together at first base as Casey tried to beat out an infield hit. The two squared off but there was no fight (in time they became good friends). A pop bottle later arced out of the right-field stands in Casey's direction when he ran toward the fence after a fly ball.

His talent for irritating others came to a head in Cincinnati. The Reds were challenging the Giants, who had been in first place or very close to it almost continually for nearly two years. The New Yorkers broke the back of the challenge by beating the Reds five straight times in Cincinnati (reminiscent of their rout of the Pirates two seasons earlier). In the last humiliating game of that series the Reds were losing 6–2 in the eighth inning when the barbed comments from the Giants' bench jockeys got to Adolfo Luque, the Reds' best pitcher, a highly talented Cuban (he won twenty-seven games that season) with an explosive temper. Luque was on the mound, pitching to Ross Youngs, when he suddenly ran off the mound and across the foul line directly toward the Giants' bench, which was a temporary arrangement set up in front of an area that had been roped off to accommodate the overflow crowd. Stengel saw Luque coming but thought he was after Cunningham, who had just gotten off a particularly choice comment. Luque ignored Cunningham and swung at Stengel, knocking him off the bench. Youngs had chased after the pitcher as soon as he saw him leave the mound, and he grabbed the Cuban and pulled him off Stengel. Two policemen took Luque in tow and escorted him to the Reds' dugout. Meantime, Roush, the Cincinnati center fielder, had come in from his position to renew the quarrel, and fans and players were swirling around. The policeman left Luque in the dugout and ran back across the field to stop further trouble. Luque popped out of the dugout carrying a bat and headed for the Giants' bench. The policeman reversed directions, repossessed Adolfo and this time took him all the way to the Cincinnati clubhouse.

The umpires established peace, formally ejected Luque from the game and told Stengel to leave, too. McGraw objected, pointing out that Roush hadn't been thrown out, but to no avail. After the game McGraw fired off a telegram to league president Heydler, complaining that Stengel had been picked on all around the league, that he was always being abused by opposing players and fans and that he was totally innocent of any wrongdoing. Heydler, who was well aware of Casey's glib tongue and pugnacious nature, must have laughed at that, but in any case Stengel received no further punishment.

McGraw's spirited defense of Stengel was

probably no more than routine support of his team against the general enemy. But McGraw had become genuinely fond of Stengel. He often invited Casey out to his new home in Pelham in the suburbs, where he and Stengel would sit in the kitchen talking baseball to all hours of the night. During those long talk fests in Pelham, Casey would raid the icebox and cook up a mess of scrambled eggs and bacon for the two of them, along with whatever else he could find. According to McGraw's wife, the family cook arriving in the morning would shake her head and say, "I don't know how that Mr. Stengel can eat so many peas." Stengel's verve and personality amused McGraw. Once, when DeWitt Hopper, the vaudeville star whose specialty was reciting "Casey at the Bat," stopped by the Polo Grounds clubhouse after a game to say hello to McGraw, the manager called Stengel in to shake hands. Casey had won the ball game that day with a home run, and McGraw occasionally handed out little cash bonuses to players who had done splendid things like that. "They tell me McGraw wants to see me," Casey recalled years later, "and I go running inside in my jock strap, figuring the old man is going to slip me some money. When I got back to my locker the others said,

'What did you get, Casey?' 'Five fingers, I got,' I told them. McGraw had me shake hands with Hopper, and then I had to stand around in there with the sweat dripping down my butt while he recites 'Casey at the Bat.' "

Most casual observers of the day still considered Stengel to be little more than a baseball joke, a comedian, a jester in the king's court, but McGraw recognized his intelligence and his understanding of the game, and he admired Casey's dedication and drive. He said, in 1923, "I'll tell you: Stengel is an old man in a baseball sense, perhaps, but he's the most vigorous old man I ever saw. And he's about as game a fellow as ever lived." McGraw liked a scrapper, although he fined Stengel for starting the fight with Weinert on the field and getting himself suspended. Fighting *on* the field was stupid. Most of McGraw's fights were off the field.

McGraw used Stengel as a part-time assistant without portfolio, sending him out to coach at first base, having him work with young players in spring training, discussing strategy and tactics with him. Stengel often told stories later on about his bad behavior when he played with the Giants, and how McGraw disciplined him, but his accounts were exaggerated. McGraw had some real hell-raisers on the Giants when Stengel was there — Phil Douglas, a brilliant pitcher who was a helpless alcoholic; Earl Smith, known as "Oil" Smith, a hard-drinking tough-guy catcher who had no fear of McGraw or anyone else ("He's a goddamned anarchist," said McGraw, who repeatedly suspended Smith. "He has no respect for law and order"); Jess Barnes and Hugh McQuillan, a couple of partying pitchers whom McGraw called "Gallagher and Shean" after a famous vaudeville team of the day — but Casey wasn't one of them. Stengel liked to drink and he enjoyed sitting in speakeasies talking baseball with similar-minded friends like Frisch and Meusel, but for all of the colorful anecdotes he wasn't one of McGraw's problem children. One of Casey's stories held that McGraw assigned a detective to shadow Stengel and Meusel on their nightly rounds after the two Philadelphia teammates rejoined forces on the Giants. After a time the detective reported to McGraw that he was now confining his surveillance to Meusel, since he and Stengel were no longer going out together. McGraw called Stengel in to his office to ask what was going on. Why were he and Meusel suddenly at odds? Casey is supposed to have replied, feigning resentment, "I don't want to share a detective with anyone else. I want one of my own."

Actually, McGraw tried to use Stengel as a counterbalance to the hell-raisers, assigning him for a time to room with the happy-go-lucky McQuillan. But Stengel was not about to become a fink, a company spy. When he was a manager and presumably a pillar of probity, he told John Lardner, "I wasn't always so respectable. When I roomed with McQuillan I used to wish I could get out at night and play hide-and-seek with McGraw's detectives. But McQuillan kept me honest, because I had to be in the room at midnight to answer his name on the roll call. McGraw had a system at that time where his chief detective would go around the hotel at midnight, knocking on your door. When he said, 'Stengel?' I would sing out 'Here!' in my baritone voice. Then he would say, 'McQuillan?' and I would say 'Here!' in my tenor voice."

It was a lively life all around for Casey playing for the Giants, the high point of his life in many ways. Among other things, he fell in love during this time. Perhaps he felt that playing for McGraw had somehow legitimized him, had left him an accomplished man, and that he now had a right to settle down with someone. As a handsome, personable bachelor with a ballplayer's fame and a good income, he was used to meeting women, some of them very attractive, but none had meant a great deal to him. Now, suddenly, it was different. In the summer of 1923, Irish Meusel's wife, Van, invited a good friend of hers, a girl named Edna Lawson, to come east on her vacation and visit her in New York. Edna, a tall, slim, smart young woman in her late twenties, had been born in Michigan and had moved to Southern California with her family when she was nineteen. Her father was a successful building contractor who did a lot of work for silent-movie companies, and Edna, graceful and attractive and a good dancer, sometimes worked as an extra in films, although her real talents and interests lay in accounting and business. She had a quick mind and understood financial matters. In time she ran a good part of her father's business, a family operation that included houses and apartments and eventually a bank.

In New York that summer, Van and Irish Meusel introduced her to Stengel. The two couples went out dining and dancing, and Casey and Edna hit it off immediately. In a short time Casey made it clear that he was smitten. Edna was a little more cautious about committing herself, but she was stopping in St. Louis to visit her brother on her way back to the Coast, and she agreed to see Casey when the Giants came to town to play the Cardinals. They had a few days together, and, according to Maury Allen, Stengel asked Edna to marry him barely two weeks after they met. While Edna didn't say yes, she didn't say no, either. But she wanted a little time to think about it.

After she returned to California, she and Casey corresponded, although they apparently did not see each other again until the next summer, which is strange. Stengel was a peripatetic traveler who often went as far as California in the off-season, and it's odd that he didn't go there after the 1923 season to see Edna and meet her family, but he didn't. He went home to Kansas City. In his letters he urged her to come east again in 1924, and he asked for the address of her brother, who was an army officer stationed in Belleville, Illinois, across the Mississippi River from St. Louis. Casey and Edna exchanged Christmas presents, and despite the distance separating them the romance blossomed.

Meantime, the 1923 season drew to a close, with the Giants winning the pennant for a third straight year. Stengel played center field regularly most of the time from early July to the end of the year, except for a brief spell late in August when McGraw sat him down for a rest and again at the end of September after he bruised his heel when he leaped for a fly ball near the fence in Chicago and came down hard on a cement footing. He took it easy after that, appearing in only a couple of games before the World Series with the Yankees began (the third straight year the two teams met in the Series). Unlike the injury he had tried to hide a year earlier, this one was more annoying than serious. He put a little rubber pad in the heel of his shoe as a cushion and had no problems when he appeared in a benefit game in the Polo Grounds a few days before the Series. Babe Ruth and a couple of other Yankee players appeared with the Giants in that game. Stengel and Ruth were not in the lineup at the same time — Babe played in the early innings, Casey in the later ones — but it was the only occasion when the two were on the same team.

16 *THE 1923 WORLD SERIES: STENGEL THE HERO*

The opening game of the 1923 World Series was played in Yankee Stadium, the first World Series game ever played in the stadium, then in the first year of its existence. The glamour of the new ball park and the continuing internecine rivalry between the Giants and the Yankees drew a record crowd of 55,307 to the stadium, at that time the largest ever to see a major-league game. Ordinarily, on such an auspicious occasion, the game itself turns out to be a dud, a mild affair that generates little fire or drama. But not this time. The first World Series game ever played in Yankee Stadium was a thriller from the first inning to the last, and the hero of the piece was Charles Dillon Stengel.

The Yankees got a run in the bottom of the first inning when Ruth scored from first base on a double by Bob Meusel. In the top of the second, Stengel almost tied the game when he hit a long fly toward the right-field bleachers that Ruth ran back to the fence to catch. In the bottom of the second, the Yankees scored two more to go ahead 3–0, but the Giants came back in the top of the third with four runs to take the lead. The Yankees put men on second and third with one out in the fourth, but a sensational double play by the Giants, from pitcher to third base to second base, ended the inning. The Yanks came close to scoring again in the fifth after Ruth tripled, but Frank Frisch, running with his back to home plate, made a great catch of a little looping fly ball, then turned and threw Ruth out at home. In the seventh the Yankees finally did tie the game when Joe Dugan drove in a run with a triple. Ruth followed with a vicious grounder down the right-field line that should have put the Yankees ahead, but George Kelly, the Giant first baseman, made a stunning stop and a great throw to the catcher to nip Dugan at the plate. In the eighth a Yankee base runner was picked off second just before another player hit a single to center that would have scored him.

The game was still tied 4–4 in the top of the ninth when Stengel came to bat with two men out and the bases empty. Casey had walked in the fourth inning and singled in the seventh but each time had been wiped off the bases by a Yankee double play. Joe Bush, the Yankee pitcher, had given up only three singles in the six and a third innings he had pitched since coming on in relief in the four-run Giant third.

The count on Stengel went to three balls and two strikes. The next pitch was a fastball, in the strike zone but high and on the outside corner. Bush said later, "The count was three and two and I threw just as hard as I could. He crashed it good and plenty."

Stengel hit the ball on a hard line to left center field, the vast "Death Valley" of Yankee Stadium. It went between left fielder Bob Meusel and center fielder Whitey Witt and all the way to the outfield fence. As Heywood Broun wrote, "The outfielders turned and ran toward the bleacher wall, the ball sailed and hopped and skipped, and Casey sprinted."

Witt got to the ball first and tossed it to Meusel, who had one of the best arms in the majors. Meusel fired the ball in to shortstop Ernie Johnson, a replacement that inning for the regular Yankee shortstop, Everett Scott, who had been lifted for a pinch hitter. Johnson relayed it toward catcher Wally Schang at home plate, for by this time Stengel, churning his way around the bases, was well past third on his way home. The ball and Casey arrived at the plate at the same time, but the throw was a little bit up the line toward first base. As Stengel deftly slid across home plate the ball skipped past Schang and rolled toward the Giant dugout.

"Casey slid into the plate," reported James Harrison of the *New York Times*, "and up onto one knee in a single motion. Then he waved a hand in a comical gesture that seemed to say, 'Well, there you are,' and the game was as good as over." (It was. The Yankees went down in order in the last of the ninth and the Giants won 5–4.)

The Giants poured across the field toward Stengel, mobbed him and escorted him triumphantly to the dugout. The huge crowd had begun roaring the moment Stengel hit the ball, had roared for the quarter of a minute or so it took him to run the 120 yards around the bases with his inside-the-park homer, and it was still roaring. The excitement of the moment was almost indescribable, but the press tried.

Grantland Rice milked the theme of "Casey at the Bat," who had struck out for the Mudville Nine, saying Casey had gotten his revenge at last. Heywood Broun's story had more facts in it than Rice's, although Broun got caught up in the windstorm of hyperbole swirling through the Yankee Stadium press box, starting his copy with the declaration, "It was the best baseball game ever played," and going on to describe Casey's circuit of the bases this way: "Stengel proceeds furiously in all directions at the same time when he runs. He doesn't point very well and seems to need a center board. The dust flew as Casey tossed one loose foot after another, identified each one and picked it up again. Perhaps he didn't go so fast but he ran determinedly. It would have been a thrilling sight to see him meet an apple cart or a drugstore window."

Joe Vila wrote, "Stengel, eyes bulging and mouth wide open, kept on sprinting as if to save his precious life." Frank Graham wrote, "There was very little breath left in his body and that was hammered out of him by his mates as he staggered to the dugout." Hype Igoe called Stengel "a little old man of baseball, gimpy, crooked-fingered, spavined, halt, squint-eyed and mebbe a grandfather." Walter St. Denis said, "The old boys had their day when 'Old Case' Stengel came through."

And then there was Damon Runyon, whose story in the *New York American* pulled out all the stops. Part of baseball lore now, Runyon's story has been quoted and requoted and misquoted for sixty years and has come to be accepted as the authoritative account of Casey's famous homer. Appearing on the front page under a huge banner headline that read, "STENGEL'S HOMER WINS FOR GIANTS, 5-4," it was the lead story in that day's *American*. Below the big black headlines were subheads that said, "60,000 Frantic Fans Screech as Casey Beats Ball to Plate. Warped Legs, Twisted, Bent in Years of Campaigning, Last Until He Reaches Goal."

Beneath the bold byline, "By Damon Runyon," the copy read:

This is the way old "Casey" Stengel ran yesterday afternoon, running his home run home.

This is the way old "Casey" Stengel ran running his home run home in a Giant victory by a score of 5 to 4 in the first game of the world's series of 1923.

This is the way old "Casey" Stengel ran, running his home run home, when two were out in the ninth inning and the score was tied and the ball was still bounding inside the Yankee yard.

This is the way —

His mouth wide open.

His warped old legs bending beneath him at every stride.

His arms flying back and forth like those of a man swimming with a crawl stroke.

His flanks heaving, his breath whistling, his head far back.

URGES HIMSELF ON

Yankee infielders, passed by old "Casey" Stengel as he was running his home run home, say "Casey" was muttering to himself, adjuring himself to greater speed as a jockey mutters to his horse in a race, that he was saying: "Go on, Casey! Go on!"

People generally laugh when they see old "Casey" Stengel run, but they were not laughing when he was running his home run home yesterday afternoon. People — 60,000 of them, men and women — were standing in the Yankee stands and bleachers up there in the Bronx roaring sympathetically, whether they were for or against the Giants.

"Come on, Casey!"

The warped old legs, twisted and bent by many a year of baseball campaigns, just barely held out under "Casey" Stengel until he reached the plate, running his home run home.

Then they collapsed.

"CASEY" SLIDES

They gave out just as old "Casey" Stengel slid over the plate in his awkward fashion with Wally Schang futily [sic] reaching for him with the ball. "Billy" Evans, the American League umpire, poised over him in a set pose, arms spread wide to indicate that old "Casey" was safe.

Half a dozen Giants rushed forward to help "Casey" to his feet, to hammer him on the back, to bawl congratulations in his ears as he limped unsteadily, still panting furiously, to the bench where John J. McGraw, the chief of the Giants, relaxed his stern features to smile for the man who had won the game.

"Casey" Stengel's warped old legs, one of them broken not so long ago, wouldn't carry him out for the last half of the inning, when the Yankees made a dying effort to undo the damage done by "Casey." His place in center field was taken by "Bill" Cunningham, whose legs are still unwarped, and "Casey" sat on the bench with John McGraw.

And so on. It is florid, exaggerated, mildly inaccurate (where Runyon got the broken leg from, I don't know) and shamelessly over-written, and at the same time it is stirring and unforgettable. Runyon was a gifted writer — his tales about Broadway guys and dolls be-came part of the American scene — and jour-nalists are impressed by the fact that his memorable account of Stengel's homer was written under the gun in time for the morning editions.

The stories about his home run made Sten-gel the most famous man in New York for the moment, and possibly in the country. From the tone of the various reports you could have assumed that Stengel had barely survived the game and might never be able to play again, maybe not even be able to walk without a cane. But he was fine — no muscle pulls, no strained tendons, the bruise on his heel no worse for the experience. The rubber pad had shifted as Stengel rounded second and, he said, "I thought my shoe was coming off." The scrabbly style of running so remarked upon by the press was partly a result of Casey's efforts not to let that happen. Mc-

306

Graw sent Cunningham to the outfield in Casey's place in the last of the ninth because Stengel was all in after the homer. Cunningham started in center field the next afternoon, when the Series shifted across the Harlem River to the Polo Grounds, but only because the outstanding left-hander Herb Pennock was on the mound for the Yankees, and Mc-Graw was playing the righty/lefty percentages. Cunningham went hitless against Pennock; McGraw used a pinch hitter (not Casey) for him late in the game and sent Stengel to center as Cunningham's fielding replacement in the ninth. The Yankees won 4–2.

The teams returned to the stadium, and Stengel played center and had another unforgettable day. It was Columbus Day, and the holiday crowd was even larger than the one at the first game. This one too was a jewel of a contest, not as wildly thrilling but almost impeccably played. Art Nehf of the Giants threw a six-hit shutout, and Sam Jones of the Yankees did even better than Nehf, except for one pitch — to Stengel. Casey had hit the ball hard off Jones the first time he batted in the game, lining a fly ball to Witt in center field. His next time up, in the fifth inning, he worked Jones for a walk but for the third time in the Series was eliminated by a double play.

When Casey faced Jones again in the seventh inning the score was still 0–0; only four Giants had reached base — one on a bunt, one on an error and two on walks. With the count on Stengel two balls and one strike, Jones threw a screwball, trying to get it to break away from Casey on the outside edge of the plate. "It didn't break the way I expected it would," Jones said. "It broke in too close." Stengel jumped on it and lofted a high fly down the right-field line that carried into the bleachers for another game-winning home run.

This time Casey had time to savor his feat. As the ball landed in the seats, Casey glanced over at the Giants' dugout and held up two fingers, as though to say, "That's *two*." Between first and second he looked at the disconsolate Jones and, beyond Jones, at the Yankee dugout beyond the third-base line and merrily thumbed his nose at them. Rounding third he blew a kiss at the Yankees, but he was all business as he crossed home plate in full stride and veered toward the Giant dugout. Nehf held the Yankees scoreless, the Giants won 1–0 and the papers shouted exultantly that Casey had done it again. "Stengel 2, Yankees 1" was the most common gag. Fans on a lower Manhattan street watching the action of the game as it was recreated on a large mechanical scorecard on the side of an office building cheered mightily when Stengel's homer became apparent as a little light made a circuit of the bases. "Casey, you lulu! You darb!" shouted a delighted fan. "Hey, maybe that McGraw don't know how to run a team!" In Kansas City, Lou Stengel went around saying to people, "Did you hear about my boy Charley? My boy Charley hit another home run!"

It was the first time a player had broken up a 0–0 game in the World Series with a home run. It was also the first time a player had won two Series games with homers. And Casey's two home runs were the first World Series homers ever hit in Yankee Stadium. All in all, it was indeed an auspicious occasion.

Through the triumph and adulation and publicity Stengel managed to stay remarkably unaffected. He loved the attention — when he came to bat again in the ninth inning of the 1–0 game and was greeted with wave after wave of cheering he stood at home plate grinning from ear to ear — but he wasn't seduced by it. A young woman named Zoe Buckley interviewed him during the Series in a parlor of the ornate Hotel Ansonia at 72nd Street and Broadway in Manhattan, where many ballplayers (Babe Ruth among them) lived during the season. Casey didn't want to be interviewed. Buckley persisted, and he finally gave in and agreed to talk to her. Her reaction to the Runyonesque accounts of his inside-the-park home run are revealing: "From descriptions we'd read of Casey Stengel's performance in winning the first game we expected to see a large loose person of hayfoot, strawfoot awkwardness. But no. Your modern ballplayer is no roughneck. He is trim and immaculate, wears a $90 suit and a camel's hair overcoat. His skin is clear and rosy, his features well cut, his body lithe, with modest bearing but high-proof masculinity."

She asked him why ballplayers disliked being interviewed. "I guess we're scared of getting swelled heads," he said. "We know the hazards — we're the hero today and the goat tomorrow." She asked him about his home run in the first game, and he said, "It only goes to show you that good luck is as sure to stumble your way as bad luck. You've got to learn how to take both. You have to remember that nothing lasts — neither the good nor the bad." He echoed that existential philosophy nearly four decades later when, after winning ten pennants in twelve years, he summed up his life by saying, "I'm a man that's been up and down."

"Baseball's a business," he told Zoe Buckley. "Some of us are plugging sorts, like bookkeepers, and some are plungers — flying high, doing wonderful things by spurts and then slumping."

"Which are you?" she asked. She described his reaction: "Stengel stroked a neatly shaved chin with a well-groomed hand and considered, closing one blue eye and raking the horizon of the big red-and-gold parlor with the other, as though to catch a reflection of himself in the light of thirteen years of professional ballplaying."

"I wonder," he said finally. "I'm not so doggone sure. I've had a pretty checkered career. They call me superannuated now. I'm thirty-three. I'm no wonderful runner and I wouldn't expect to set the Mississippi River afire with my brains. I guess I'm a bookkeeper that had a lucky day."

Stengel's second homer against the Yankees was the high-water mark for the Giants in the Series (they lost the next three games) and in a sense the high-water mark for McGraw in his managerial career. Since losing the first two games in the 1921 Series his Giants had defeated the Yankees eleven times in thirteen games (not including the tie in 1922) and he was within two victories of achieving his ambition of winning three straight world championships, something no other manager had done. But that was as close as he was to come; he did win a fourth straight pennant the next year but failed again in the Series and never won another pennant after that.

As for Casey, even though the Giants lost the next three games he continued to do well, adding two walks and two singles the next day, before McGraw methodically sent Cunningham in to bat for him in the ninth inning when the left-handed Pennock came in to relieve. At that point Stengel had been to the plate a dozen times in the 1923 Series, had reached first base safely nine times, and two of his three outs had come on hard-hit fly balls. Nonetheless, McGraw stuck with the percentages, and Cunningham struck out.

Casey went hitless in the next game and didn't play in the last game of the Series — Pennock again — until the eighth inning, when Jones relieved Pennock. The Giants were losing by two runs and there were two out when McGraw sent Stengel up to bat for Cunningham, but there was a runner on first base. The Giant fans in the crowd cheered Casey wildly as he approached the plate, hoping that he'd hit another homer and tie the game. But Casey lifted a high foul fly to the third baseman, and that was that. The Giants went down quietly in the ninth inning, and the Series was over.

Defeat is always disappointing, but Stengel had had the satisfaction of performing heroically for McGraw and the Giants in New York before huge crowds and under intense observation by the press. He batted .417, led the Giants in runs batted in and tied for the lead in runs scored. His home runs were the dramatic high spots of the Series. True, his nose-thumbing after the second homer had upset Jacob Ruppert, the Yankee owner, but nothing came of it. Ruppert complained about Stengel to Judge Landis in the lobby of the Hotel Commodore the night after the game, saying rather stuffily, "I don't think Stengel's actions were a credit to baseball." A Ruppert cohort named Billy Fleischman added, "It was an insult to all our fans."

Landis listened but did nothing. Asked later by a reporter if he was going to take action against Stengel, the Commissioner grinned and said, "No, I don't think I will. A fellow who wins two games with home runs has a right to feel a little playful, especially if he's a Stengel." Casey used to say later on that Landis bawled him out for the nose-thumbing and others say he was fined $50, but it wasn't so. Babe Ruth, asked what he thought of Casey's behavior, summed up the general feeling by saying, "I didn't mind it. Casey's a lot of fun."

McGraw had said after the first game of the Series, "There isn't anyone I'd rather have seen make that homer than Casey," but a month later he traded Stengel away, sending him to the seventh-place Boston Braves, who had lost one hundred games that season, along with Cunningham and Dave Bancroft. It was a perplexing trade, because McGraw received relatively little in return: Billy Southworth, an ordinary outfielder, and Joe Oeschger, a fading pitcher. But Christy Mathewson, who had left Saranac Lake, had been made president of the Braves by the Boston owner, Judge Emil Fuchs, and Mc-Graw said publicly that he was trying to help out his old friend. Bancroft was to be Boston's playing manager, and Stengel and Cunningham would be regular outfielders.

As usual, there were subtleties about the deal that McGraw didn't mention. He knew that Bancroft was no longer the superb player he had been and that the Giants had an outstanding young infielder named Travis Jackson ready to take over for Bancroft at shortstop. He knew that Cunningham was never going to cut the mustard as a big-league outfielder, and he knew that Stengel, for all his brilliance in the Series, *was* old and fragile and close to the end of his career. In Southworth he was getting a full-time player who could give the Giants everyday stability in center field, and behind Southworth he had a power-hitting rookie named Hack Wilson, who had played a few games in center for the Giants late in 1923. McGraw was cleaning house, sweeping out players who were no longer needed in the continuing scheme of things. And there was another ramification. Fuchs had put money into the deal, quite a bit of money. This time McGraw and the Giants were on the receiving end of a bunch of cash.

Casey, who had gone home to Kansas City, moaned a little about the trade ("What do you have to do? I suppose if I'd have hit three homers they'd have sent me to the Three-Eye League"), but he kept his equilibrium. He wrote to Edna about the change in his life and suggested she come to Boston on her vacation the following spring. He is also supposed to have commented philosophically on his departure from New York so soon after his World Series exploits by saying, "The paths of glory lead but to the Braves."

17 TO BOSTON AND POINTS WEST: MUD HEN GLORY

The Braves had finished seventh in 1923, and in 1924, even with Stengel, Bancroft and Cunningham, they finished eighth. They started off well enough, with Stengel batting third most of the time, but one of their few good pitchers had an emergency appendectomy in May and Bancroft had the same operation in June, and after that the team wallowed.

It was distinctly different from playing on three successive pennant winners. Casey batted .280, below the league norm of .283. There were more than thirty .300 hitters in the league that season. Casey was in 131 games, the most he'd played since Brooklyn, but he wasn't very impressive either at bat or in the field. It was a drab season in Boston, with the biggest moment for the Braves occurring when manager Bancroft fined Oil Smith and Jess Barnes, who had been traded to Boston from the Giants a year earlier, $500 apiece for throwing a chair out of a Philadelphia hotel window.

But Edna Lawson had come around to saying yes and agreed to come east to St. Louis in August, when she and Casey would be married. Stengel had been to see her brother Larry and arrangements were made for the wedding. Edna was waiting for him when the Braves arrived in St. Louis on Friday, August 15. Casey had permission from Bancroft to take Monday off, but he played right field for the Braves against the Cardinals on Friday, Saturday and Sunday. He had no hits on Friday, a single on Saturday, a double on Sunday — obviously a rising crescendo of passion. On Sunday night the team left for a series of games in Chicago with the Cubs, and on Monday, August 18, 1924, Edna and Casey were married across the Mississippi River in Belleville, Illinois, site of the army camp where Larry was stationed, by Father Louis F. Ell, chaplain of St. Elizabeth's Hospital in Belleville.

The Braves played and lost in Chicago that day and were rained out on Tuesday. On Wednesday, Casey rejoined them in time to play both ends of a doubleheader against the Cubs. It was probably only coincidence, but it turned out to be the finest day of the season for the Braves. They beat the Cubs twice, shutting them out 2–0 and 5–0. Stengel had three hits, including two doubles, and batted in both of Boston's runs in the first game, and in the second game he hit a three-run homer. Thus the new bridegroom drove in five of the Braves' seven runs on his first day back. Whatever fire he brought to the club didn't last, unfortunately, and Boston plodded resolutely on to its lastplace finish.

Edna stayed with Casey, traveling back to Boston with him and the Braves, an odd honeymoon, but something better lay ahead. John McGraw, in the process of winning his fourth straight pennant and going to seven games before losing the World Series to the Washington Senators, had arranged with Charlie Comiskey of the Chicago White Sox for the Giants and the Sox to go on a postseason tour together to Europe. He asked Stengel to come along and play with the Giants. The players' wives were invited, too, which meant that Casey and Edna were to have a proper honeymoon after all.

The troupe left New York the day after the World Series ended and went first to Canada, where the teams played four games, the last one in Quebec on the day they were to sail on the liner *Mont Royal*. The ship had to delay its scheduled departure for three hours so that the teams could finish that day's game.

They spent five days aboard ship, sailing down the St. Lawrence and across the North Atlantic to Liverpool, England. The players did exercises on deck each day and made room for the pitchers to throw. They docked in Liverpool on a Monday, and on Tuesday afternoon played an exhibition on a tiny field that was so small almost every normal fly ball went into the crowd for a ground-rule double. British reporters covering the teams' arrival were impressed by this display of hitting and also by the quiet demeanor of the players off the field. "I expected a gang of huskies, a bunch of toughs with a Bowery accent and an Apache slouch," wrote one Englishman, adding, with broad exaggeration, "Instead I met eighteen clear-eyed American university graduates, shy as a bevy of schoolgirls. Over the martinis, to which like all good prohibitionists they gravitated as if obeying a natural law, we were soon discussing Thomas Hardy, Shakespeare, Mussolini, President Coolidge and Ramsay MacDonald's Russian loan."

The teams moved on to London, where the twenty-eight-year-old Duke of York (later King George VI) came to see them on a misty day at the Stamford Bridge grounds, a larger field where they were able to stage a better exhibition. The crowd applauded the way the outfielders chased after and caught fly balls but, except for the handful of Americans in attendance, watched a triple play in silence. In the seventh inning the Americans stood up to stretch, calling out, "Up! All up!" and the English in the crowd craned their necks to see if the Duke was leaving.

The troupe left London for games scheduled in Dublin, Belfast and Manchester, but the weather was bad and attendance minuscule. They drew a "crowd" of twenty people in Dublin. "It was a Sunday morning," an Irishman explained, "and what the hell, everyone was in church."

Back in London they played again at Stamford Bridge. This time King George V came to see them and went on the field to greet the players, shaking hands with each one. Stengel is supposed to have said, "Nice to meet ya, King," when he shook hands, but the story is apocryphal.

The travelers moved on to Paris, where they played a couple of games, again in dismal weather before meager crowds, and McGraw and Comiskey canceled their plan to take the teams on to Berlin and Rome. They gave the players expense money for a week or so of travel on their own before the party reassembled in Paris for the journey home. Casey and Edna, who spent much of their time with Van and Irish Meusel, went on to Rome and back before rejoining McGraw and the others. They docked in New York on December 2, nearly eight weeks after they had left, spent a few days with the McGraws in Pelham and then left by train for California to be with Edna's family for the holidays. Their biggest Christmas present was a house her father was building for them in Glendale. They moved into it that winter, and it remained their home for the rest of their lives.

Casey reported to the Braves' training camp again in the spring of 1925, but it was becoming increasingly evident that he was through as a big-league player. Bancroft had shaken up his last-place team and had acquired among other things a bevy of new outfielders. Casey was relegated to supernumerary status again. After the season began he played hardly at all, except to pinch-hit, and he was batting a microscopic .077 late in May when his major-league career finally came to an end. Judge Fuchs of the Braves had bought a controlling interest in the Worcester, Massachusetts, club of the Eastern

League, one of the lesser minor leagues, and he decided to install Casey as the team's player-manager.

This was not wholly altruism on Fuchs' part, not just a gesture of kindness toward an aging warrior. In those days a minor-league team could be a good investment. Casey could still hit well enough to shine in the minors, and he was a headline name, certain to draw crowds in Worcester. Also, the Braves were trimming their roster and sent several quondam big-leaguers along with Casey to strengthen the Worcester team. As an added fillip, Fuchs made Stengel president of the club, an impressive title that led to early reports that it was Stengel who was buying the team.

Worcester was in last place with nine wins and fifteen losses when Casey took over. He played in a hundred games, batted .320, hit the ball hard and had his usual vigorous on-field arguments. During one game between Worcester and Albany, frustrated by an umpire's intransigence, he angrily threw a ball into the grandstand and got himself suspended for several days. But the team improved markedly under his leadership, rose slowly from the cellar and after a spirited drive through the stretch finished a gratifying third. He made a lot of friends around the league, most notably George Weiss, the general manager of the New Haven club, whom he had first met in 1916. Weiss was as taciturn as Casey was voluble but used to sit up all night with Stengel talking baseball, as McGraw had.

The assumption was that Casey would manage the Worcester club again the next season — or, rather, the Providence club, since Fuchs decided to shift the franchise to that somewhat larger and potentially more profitable city in neighboring Rhode Island. But wheels were turning again. Hack Wilson, the young outfielder McGraw had used in center field along with Southworth after trading Stengel, had hit very well for a while in 1924 and had played in every game of the World Series that fall, but in 1925 he had slumped badly, and McGraw sent him down to the Toledo Mud Hens of the American Association, with the option of recalling him to the Giants after the season. McGraw and the Giants had a financial interest in the Mud Hens. McGraw's younger brother Jim was Toledo's secretary, and Joseph D. O'Brien, a McGraw man who once had been secretary of the Giants, was its president.

Everyone assumed that the Giants would

recall Wilson at the end of the season, and that was their intention, but someone — no one ever said who — made a mistake and no formal notice of that intent was forwarded to the league office. The Mud Hens finished a poor seventh in 1925, even with Wilson; and their manager, Jimmy Burke, was through after the season. Burke knew that the option on Wilson had not yet been exercised, and he tipped off Joe McCarthy to this interesting fact. McCarthy, who had managed the Louisville Colonels to the American Association pennant, had just been named the new manager of the Chicago Cubs. The Cubs were run by William Veeck, father of the Bill Veeck who became famous a generation later as the proprietor of pennant-winning teams in Cleveland and Chicago. Because the Cubs had finished last that season, they had first call in the upcoming draft of minor-league players, and Veeck asked McCarthy if there were any players he was particularly interested in.

"Yes," said McCarthy. "Why don't you draft Wilson of Toledo?"

"Wilson?" said Veeck. "He belongs to the Giants, doesn't he?"

McCarthy explained the circumstances and said, "Why don't you call his name and see what happens?"

Veeck did and caused quite a stir. Apparently Wilson's name was still on the list of available players. McGraw protested, arguing that it had obviously been the Giants' intent to recall Wilson and that he was being cheated out of a player on a technicality. But the facts were that the player *was* available and the Cubs had drafted him, and McGraw's protest was turned down.

Now Toledo was without both Wilson and a manager (Burke was hired by McCarthy to be a coach with the Cubs). McGraw suggested to O'Brien that he get Stengel. His friend Mathewson had died that fall after two years as president of the Boston club, and McGraw felt no compunctions about plucking Casey away from the Braves. Stengel was all for it when the idea was broached to him, and by the first of December O'Brien was telling newspapermen in Toledo that he had a new manager, "a prominent ex-major-leaguer," although he couldn't reveal his name yet. The reason he couldn't reveal his name was that Stengel was still an active player and his contract belonged to Boston — or to Worcester/Providence, which belonged to Boston — and Toledo didn't want to have to give the Braves money or players for Casey.

On December 9, O'Brien announced that

Toledo had signed Stengel as its new manager. A day or so later there were reports that there might be complications about Casey's switch from Worcester to Toledo. Ten days after that a newspaper story said that earlier that autumn Stengel had gone to Fuchs with a problem. Suppose, he said, a higher club decided to draft him as a player from the Worcester roster? Fuchs, busy with details involved in switching the franchise to Providence, said, "You're the president of the club, aren't you? Why don't you fill out a release form for yourself as a player?" Stengel's player contract would then be terminated; he couldn't be drafted and he could rejoin Worcester (or Providence) at his convenience.

President Stengel sat down and did as Fuchs suggested, releasing himself as a player. He then fired himself as manager and resigned as president, and O'Brien formally engaged him as manager of Toledo. Fuchs protested, saying Stengel still belonged to him. Not anymore, Fuchs was told. The Boston owner, chagrined by the turn of events, let his feelings be known to Commissioner Landis. Despite his affection for Casey, the Commissioner told Fuchs that if he wanted Stengel's arrangement with the Toledo club declared null and void, he'd do it and order Stengel back to the Boston organization. Nowadays, if a Commissioner threatened something like that, there'd be a court case in a minute. But in the 1920s and 1930s, Judge Landis was the absolute czar of baseball. His word was literally law. It is not generally realized that the eight Chicago Black Sox players who were banished from baseball for life because of their alleged "fixing" of the 1919 World Series were banned by Landis *after* they had been acquitted of the charges in a Chicago court. In short, if Landis told Casey to go back to Fuchs, he'd have to go. But Fuchs, who at least had had the satisfaction of knowing he could make Casey stay with him, said, "Never mind. If that's the way Stengel works, let him go. We'll be better off without him."

So Casey went home to Glendale from the winter meetings with a new job, manager of a team in the Class AA American Association, just one step below the majors. After his rapid descent to last place and the lower minors, he was beginning to move up again.

Casey managed Toledo for six years. When he took over the club, the Mud Hens, who had finished seventh the year before, were the only team in the American Association that

328

had never won a league pennant. The club's odd nickname reflected its unglamorous history. While Stengel's teams played in Swayne Field, a park with an impressive double-tiered grandstand, earlier Toledo teams had played on grounds in the northeast end of town near where the Maumee River debouches into the western end of Lake Erie. Nearby were marshes and swamps, and the ball field tended to get damp and muddy. Local fans took to calling the ballplayers Mud Hens after a species of coot or gallinule that was common thereabouts, and the unique nickname took hold and has lasted ever since.

Stengel did well his first year, moving the club up over the .500 mark and finishing a good fourth. He played fairly often himself, batted .328 and went back to California feeling good about his first two years as a professional manager — moving a last-place team to third in Worcester, a seventh-place team to fourth in Toledo. In the spring of 1927 he drove east from California, assembled his Hens for spring training in Tennessee and began an extraordinary season. Partly through the Giants' influence — McGraw's brother Jim was still a club official, although John had sold his interest to local people — the Mud Hens were loaded with ex-major-leaguers, among them Bobby Veach, Irish Meusel, Bullet Joe Bush, Rosy Ryan, Jeff Pfeffer, Everett Scott and Bevo LeBourveau, Stengel's teammate on the Phillies in 1920 and 1921, who was a major-league bust but a minor-league phenomenon. Stengel himself saw little action in 1927 — he appeared in only eighteen games and batted .176 — but he contributed the single most dramatic hit of the Mud Hens' season. With Toledo behind 9–8 in the bottom of the eleventh inning in a key game in midseason, Stengel put himself in as pinch hitter. With the bases loaded and two men out, he hit a three-and-two pitch for a grand slam home run. It was the only home run he ever hit for Toledo, and the last homer of his professional career.

The Mud Hens battled their way into the league lead, tumbled out of it, fought back into it again, faltered and then came on again to win the pennant in the last game of the season. The city went figuratively crazy over its first pennant, celebrating its triumph for two or three days afterward. When Toledo won its last game and the flag, Casey reacted emotionally, according to Robert Daniels' admirable history of that season, *Those Mighty and Marvelous, Mildly Miraculous Mud Hens:* "Stengel leaped from the Toledo dugout as if he had been shot out of a gun. He started to run, changed his mind, stood still and stared at the ground for a moment, wheeled and looked into the Toledo dugout again, started in a half-dozen directions, stood still again in a dazed sort of way, then walked slowly into the dugout while Toledoeans screamed, hugged each other and pawed the air." Edna Stengel clapped her hands so hard she broke a blood vessel in one of her fingers.

Things were not as bright after that marvelous year. Minor-league clubs are volatile, the personnel changing radically season to season. In 1928 the Hens fell to sixth place and in 1929 to eighth. They were much better in 1930, finishing a strong third, but in 1931 they fell to last place again. Stengel's years at Toledo were an odd mixture of fun and disaster. He was frequently in bitter, almost irrational disputes with umpires. Umpire Jocko Conlan, who was an outfielder for Stengel at Toledo in 1930, remembered Casey getting in serious trouble with the league office after a furious argument with umpire Joe Rue, who later umpired in the American League. Conlan had hit an apparent triple off the left-field fence to drive in two runs and tie the score in the last half of the ninth inning, but Rue said the ball had bounced in and out of the stands and was therefore a ground-rule double. That brought one of the scoring base runners back to third base and meant that Toledo was still behind by a run. Stengel raved and ranted, and so did the Toledo crowd. After things finally settled down, the next batter flied out to end the game. The frustrated crowd poured on the field and went after Rue. "I got hit pretty good three or four times and they weren't even after me," said Conlan. "Toledo was a rough town." According to Conlan the league president, Tom Hickey, accused Stengel of behavior designed to incite the crowd and cause a riot, and he wanted him thrown out of baseball. Commissioner Landis held a hearing on Hickey's charges but would not banish Stengel.

Stengel and Hickey had a similar conflict three years earlier during Toledo's pennant-winning year. Stengel and other Mud Hens had had a series of disputes with an umpire named Doll Derr. The Mud Hens lost a doubleheader, the second game ending on a called third strike by umpire Derr. The batter objected vigorously to the call, and Stengel came charging from the dugout to badger the umpire, even though the game was over. Hickey was at the game and suspended both Stengel and the player for three days. Later in the season after a Stengel run-in with another umpire, Hickey suspended him for five days. The climax came in Toledo later in the 1927 pennant race when Doll Derr made two successive bad calls — or what the Toledo crowd and the Toledo players thought were bad calls. The calls stifled a Mud Hen rally and to Toledo's way of thinking cost them the game. Stengel raged at Derr and the crowd booed angrily; when the game ended, fans attacked the umpire. He was punched and kicked before Toledo officials could rescue him and get him off the field, and Hickey suspended Stengel again, this time for inciting a riot.

Conlan and others also recall Stengel's rough playfulness in the Toledo clubhouse. There were wooden boxes filled with sawdust into which tobacco-chewers would spit and others would toss all kinds of debris. Stengel, swinging a bat, would deliver lectures to the players on this or that aspect of the game and punctuate his remarks by whacking the sawdust boxes, sending sawdust and spray and gunk all over the clubhouse. Conlan said Casey would arrive at the clubhouse very early and wander around, talking and lecturing, as he dressed. He had everything on but his uniform pants one day when he started to demonstrate the art of hitting the curveball to a player who had just come into the club-house wearing a brand-new suit. Casey swung the bat, whacked the box and spattered slop all over the player's suit. He yelped in protest, but Casey calmly tossed away the bat and said, "Well, that's the way I hit them." He left, perhaps hurriedly, to go out onto the playing field, picking up a fungo bat to hit flies to the outfielders with and a couple of towels. He forgot he had no pants on. Conlan followed him, saying nothing. As they walked onto the field past the stands there were stares, and a couple of women said in shocked tones, "Oh my!" and "Casey!" Casey waved the fungo bat airily and said to Conlan, "They got some crazy women here in Toledo." They kept on walking and there were more comments. Stengel said, "What are they hollering about?" Then he looked down and said, "Why, I haven't got my pants on." Conlan grinned, and Stengel whacked him across the legs with the fungo bat. "Why didn't you tell me I didn't have my pants on?" he demanded, and hurried back inside. From then on, Conlan said, the fans loved to yell, "Casey, where are your pants?"

During one close game, Stengel said he'd buy a new suit for the man who won the game for him. Conlan hit a triple but hurt his leg badly sliding into third base. He said nothing about it and a moment later tagged up on a fly ball and struggled across home plate with the winning run. He barely made it to the plate and had to be carried off the field. He had a broken ankle. For years after that whenever Stengel saw Conlan, he'd say, "Now there's a boy scored a run for me on a broken leg."

"It was a chipped bone in my ankle," Conlan said, "but with Casey it went from a chipped bone to a broken leg, and I think some days he had a piece of broken bone sticking through the stocking. But that was all right with me, because I never did get that suit from him. When I reminded him, he said, 'Ah, that's the way you're supposed to play for me.' "

Conlan told the story for laughs, but it's likely that one reason Stengel didn't buy him the suit was that neither he nor the club could afford to. Times had changed. The boom of the Roaring Twenties had still been on one day in 1929 when Stengel whacked the sawdust box to grab his last-place team's attention. In his best sarcastic tone he said, "Now, you boys haven't been playing very well, but I know there's been a lot on your minds. I see a lot of you reading about the stock market, and I know you're thinking about it. Now,

I'm gonna do you a favor, since you're so interested in Wall Street. I'm gonna give you a tip on the market." Pause. "Buy Pennsylvania Railroad." Pause. "Because" —*whack*! — "if you don't start playing better ball there's gonna be so many of you riding trains outta here that railroad stocks are a cinch to go up."

By 1930 the Great Depression had arrived and money was beginning to grow scarce. Casey had invested in Wall Street himself, and lost most of his investment after the stock-market crash in the fall of 1929. By 1931 the Depression was stifling the country and the Toledo club had fallen into serious financial trouble. Casey had put money into the club, probably a good deal of it Edna's, but there was little hope of getting much of it back. It was a bad year all around, attendance down, the Mud Hens losing a hundred games for the second time in three years and finishing last again. When word reached Commissioner Landis that Toledo was on the edge of bankruptcy, he conducted an investigation. He wanted to be sure there had been no shenanigans, that neither Casey nor the principal owners had been skimming money off the top while the club was strangling financially.

Stengel and the others convinced the Commissioner that nothing devious had been going on, that they were being hurt, too. "People talk about all the money I've made," Casey would complain in later years, "but they never talk about all the money I've lost." The Mud Hens went into receivership, and after the 1931 season Stengel was dropped as manager.

18 THE 1930s: "IS BROOKLYN STILL IN THE LEAGUE?"

He was out of a job for the first time since he'd signed to play for Kansas City in 1910. Looking for a job was something a lot of Americans found themselves doing in the winter of 1931–32, and finding one was becoming increasingly difficult. Stengel was by no means destitute or desperate. Edna's family's enterprises were still in good shape, despite considerable losses. They had no children to be concerned about (he and Edna never had any children). But he was only forty-one, and he needed work, and the only work he knew was baseball.

Like so many other unemployed baseball people over the years, Stengel went hunting a job at the winter baseball meetings, held that year in New York, and once again the complex machinations of the game turned to his benefit. When Charlie Ebbets of the Brooklyn Dodgers died on April 18, 1925, the presidency of the club automatically passed to his associate, Ed McKeever. Then an odd, typically Brooklyn kind of thing happened. As the funeral party assembled in Greenwood Cemetery in Brooklyn for Ebbets' burial, it was discovered that the grave had not been dug wide enough to accommodate the grandiose casket in which Ebbets had been laid out. Standing around in a cold wet drizzle with the other mourners, waiting for the grave to be widened, the elderly McKeever became chilled and caught a cold, and eleven days later he was dead, too.

Ownership of the club was now shared by Ebbets' daughter, Genevieve (represented by her husband, Joe Gilleaudeau), and McKeever's brother, Steve. Neither side wanted the other to have the presidency of the club, so in what seemed a brilliant compromise they made Wilbert Robinson president as well as manager, and gave him a two-year contract. During the term of that contract Steve McKeever grew increasingly discontent with the loud, boisterous, profane Robinson — whom he saw a great deal of, probably too much of, since at club headquarters in Brooklyn Robinson had to pass through McKeever's office to get to his own. McKeever decided that as soon as the contract expired he'd ease Robby out of the presidency and maybe out of the managerial post, too. The Robins on the field were in a period of stasis; they finished in sixth place seven times in eight years in the 1920s, which led to a memorable admonishment by a writer distressed by the Robins' lackadaisical play one season. "Overconfidence may yet cost Brooklyn sixth place," he warned. This was the team that came to be called the Daffiness Boys for the nutty things that seemed to be happening in Ebbets Field ("Sshh," Robinson warned a player coming noisily into the dugout, "you'll wake Jess." Jess was Jess Petty, an aging pitcher dozing peacefully on the bench). This was the infamous team of cutups like Babe Herman and Dazzy Vance, the team that once managed to land three base runners on the same base (it was third base, and Herman and Vance were two of the three).

McKeever was tired of Uncle Robby, but at contract-renewal time he was sick in bed and in his absence the Gilleaudeaus gave Robinson a new contract as president and manager for *three* seasons, through 1929. This created a serious breach between the two interests, and when Robby's contract came up for renewal again in 1929 there was an impasse. Neither side would budge. McKeever wanted Robinson out. The Gilleaudeaus wanted him in. The contract expired. The club had no president, no manager, and no signs of ever getting one. The National League stepped in and persuaded the partners to work out another compromise: Robinson gave up the presidency but was awarded another two-year contract as manager. But when that one was over at the end of 1931, Uncle Robby, then sixty-eight years old, was dropped and Max Carey, who had starred at Pittsburgh before ending his career with Brooklyn, was named to succeed him.

Stengel had been a teammate of Carey's on the Pirates in 1918 and 1919, and, naturally, he talked to Max about a job with the Dodgers. (With Robinson's departure, "Robins" was dropped as a nickname after eighteen years of use and the club went back to "Dodgers"; sportswriter Tommy Holmes suggested that the team be nicknamed the Canaries, since Carey's real name was Maximilian Carnarius, but he was ignored.) Carey discussed Stengel with management, which felt that the presence of the colorful Casey might ease some of the resentment that had been generated by the departure of the colorful Robinson, and at the end of December 1931, Stengel was hired as a coach.

So he was back in baseball, and back in the majors, although in a secondary role after seven years of running a team by himself. Casey was a good soldier. He worked hard under Carey, did all the things a coach should do and tried not to upstage the colorless, humorless manager. He couldn't help it, though. Ring Lardner told Stengel once that he should never "give" a reporter a story — just talk, Ring said, and the reporter will find it — so Casey did, and the reporters did. Lardner used Stengel as a character in several baseball stories he wrote that year for *The Saturday Evening Post,* new fiction patterned after his classic *You Know Me Al* stories written almost twenty years earlier. Casey appeared in the Lardner stories as himself, described by the semiliterate hero of the pieces as "a kind of asst mgr and coach of the club," an accurate description of Stengel's position under Carey. The hero says, ". . . he kind of took me in toe the 1st day we beggin to work out and now mgr Carey has got him rooming with me so it looks like there taking a special interest in how I get a long as Stengel sets and talks to me by the hr about the fine points of the game that comes up durn practice." The stories were published in book form the following spring, six months before Lardner's death in September 1933.

Things went smoothly on the field for the Dodgers in 1932. Carey managed well, got some good pitching from Vance and Watson Clark and a fireballing rookie named Van Lingle Mungo and brought the Dodgers home third, the club's best showing in eight years. Brooklyn won fifteen of twenty-two games from the sixth-place Giants and finished ahead of the New Yorkers for the first time since 1920. John McGraw resigned as manager of the Giants in June. Carey was given a new two-year contract after the season.

The glow of success soon faded. Despite the club's fine playing, attendance in 1932 was down sharply because of the Depression, which was hurting everything. There was little money in the Dodger treasury, and what was there was of little use in procuring ballplayers because of the continuing rancor among the owners. The club simply had no direction. It floundered on the field in 1933, won only eight of twenty-two from New York as the Giants, under new manager Bill Terry, won the pennant and the World Series. The Dodgers finished sixth, a position that made Brooklyn wince. It was a sour year all round.

Steve McKeever, almost seventy-eight

years old by this time, managed to bring a professional baseball man in to run things. He was John A. (Bob) Quinn, and he was puzzled and then appalled by the listlessness in the Brooklyn front office, a sort of fatalistic attitude that nothing can be done about anything so why try? Quinn liked things to happen. Something did, and he took advantage of it. In January 1934, Terry, the Giants' manager, was talking with a group of reporters about New York's chances of winning the pennant again. He talked about his own club and about other teams he thought might be contenders. Roscoe McGowen, who regularly covered the Dodgers, was looking for a Brooklyn angle he could develop. He asked, "What about Brooklyn, Bill?" Terry grinned and quipped, "Brooklyn? Gee, I haven't heard a peep out of there. Is Brooklyn still in the league?"

It was only a mild joke, but McGowen reported it and Bob Quinn leaped on it. He excoriated Terry, scolding him for putting Brooklyn down like that, charging that his remarks could diminish enthusiasm for baseball in Brooklyn and hurt attendance at Ebbets Field. Terry's remark got wider and wider circulation, and the reaction from Brooklyn was loud and angry.

Carey, still at his winter home in Florida, made no comment about the to-do, which annoyed Quinn, who was trying to pump the publicity for all it was worth. He had words with Max. Carey, a man of dignity and some hauteur, resented Quinn's remarks. One thing led to another and a month later, shortly before the Dodgers were to leave for spring training, Quinn fired Carey, even though there was another year remaining on his contract. Stengel was offered the job. Casey was eager to take it, but he asked, "What about Max?"

"He'll be taken care of."

"I want to talk to him first."

A long-distance call was put through to Carey in Florida. Max was hurt and angry that he had been let out, but, naturally, he urged Stengel to accept the post. On February 23, Casey signed a two-year contract and became a major-league manager for the first time. It's possible that McGraw heard the news, but if he did he was much too ill to comment on it. Two days after Casey was named manager of the Dodgers his mentor died.

At Stengel's first meeting with the press he gratified Quinn by firing a shot back at Terry. "The first thing I want to say is, the

Dodgers are still in the league," he declared. "You can tell that to Mr. Terry. I'll let Mr. Mungo do a lot of the talking for me against the Giants this summer. When he starts heaving that fastball, he won't be easy to contradict."

When Terry came into Ebbets Field with the Giants for the first time that season the Brooklyn crowd hurled abuse at him. Over and over they shouted variations of the question of whether Brooklyn was still in the league. When photographers asked Casey to pose for pictures with the New York manager before the game and Casey affably agreed, the fans yelled at Stengel, "Stay away from the guy, you bum," and threw firecrackers at him. The Brooklyn crowd booed Terry unmercifully all season and for years afterward whenever he appeared on the diamond at Ebbets Field or the Polo Grounds.

Yet as the 1934 season wore on, Terry seemed more right than wrong. The Giants were in the thick of the pennant race, the Dodgers were in the thick of the second division. They did win a few more games for Stengel than they had for Carey a year earlier, but they finished sixth again. There were moments, though. One day in Philadelphia in tiny old Baker Bowl, where Casey had once played right field for the Phillies in front of that high tin fence, the Dodger manager went out to the mound to remove the pitcher, a burly righthander who was then generally known as Walter Beck. Casey felt that the Phils had been hitting Beck pretty hard. Beck didn't agree. In right field for the Dodgers that afternoon was Hack Wilson, who after several years of starring and drinking with the Cubs had been traded in 1932 to Brooklyn, where after one good season he mostly concentrated on drinking. If he had been asked, Wilson would have agreed with Stengel's evaluation of Beck's pitching. Hack was exhausted from chasing baseballs hit by the Phils off the tin fence behind him, and as Casey talked to the pitcher Wilson leaned over with his hands on his knees, his head down, his eyes closed. On the mound Beck argued with Stengel. He didn't want to be taken out. "Give me the ball," said Stengel. "No!" said the pitcher and turned and flung it into right field, over Wilson's head and against the tin wall. The startled Wilson, his head still down, heard it boom against the tin, thought it was another base hit and leaped into action. He raced back, fielded the ball off the wall, turned and threw a perfect strike into second base.

Walter Beck was Boom-Boom Beck after that. And not long after, Wilson was traded to Philadelphia. There were other moments. Robinson died on August 8, and that afternoon Mungo shut out the Giants 2–0, a fitting memorial. Late in the season when the lead that the first-place Giants were trying to protect kept melting away, the second-place Cardinals came into Ebbets Field and whipped Brooklyn in a doubleheader, 13–0 and 3–0. Dizzy Dean pitched the opening shutout, giving up only three hits, but his brother Paul threw a no-hitter at the Dodgers in the second game. ("If I'da known that Paul was gonna throw a no-hitter," Dizzy said, "I'da thrown one too.") Two weeks later, as the season reached its last weekend, the Cardinals had caught the Giants, and the two teams were in a flat tie, each with two games to play, one on Saturday and one on Sunday, the last day of the season. The Cardinals' two games were with the last-place Cincinnati Reds. The Giants' last two were with the Dodgers in the Polo Grounds.

It was like an uprising. Thousands of Brooklyn fans traveled across the East River from Flatbush to Manhattan, some carrying makeshift banners reading, "Is Brooklyn Still in the League?" On Saturday afternoon,

Mungo went against the Giants and bore out Stengel's prophecy not only with his fastball but with his bat, too. He singled in the fifth and scored the first run of the game, and batted in the second run in the sixth. He didn't give up a run until the eighth inning and routed the Giants 5–1. The old black scoreboards hanging from the upper deck in the Polo Grounds showed the Cardinals breezing past the Reds to victory and first place. The subways bubbled going back to Brooklyn after that game.

On Sunday the desperate Giants got off to a 4–0 lead, but the Dodgers scrambled back and tied the score 5–5. Terry sent his pitching ace, Carl Hubbell, in to relieve, but the Dodgers routed him, scored three runs and won 8–5. They had knocked Terry out of the pennant. Few victories in the long history of Brooklyn baseball were as satisfying.

After the game, after most of the players had dressed and gone, Terry and Stengel crossed paths in a corridor outside the Polo Grounds clubhouse. Terry, a decent man, had a surly way of talking.

"If your ball club had played all season the way you did the last two days," he said, "you wouldn't have finished sixth."

He may have meant it as a backhanded compliment, but Stengel took it as a slur.

"No," Casey replied, "and if your fellas had played all season long the way you did the last two, you wouldn't have finished second."

Terry, angry, moved toward Stengel, thought better of it and walked away. Stengel made his way into a crowd of whooping Dodger fans and rode triumphantly home to Brooklyn. Terry was much the bigger man and, as Stengel told Bob Broeg years later, "He could have cleaned my clock. But I have to say I'd have got a piece of him, too."

Despite the triumphant end to the 1934 season, Stengel was still a clown to most people during the years he managed the Dodgers, a humorous throwback hired to lead the latest edition of the Daffiness Boys. He contributed to that attitude, of course, playing the comedian in the coach's box during games. Whenever Nick Tremark, a tiny five-foot-five-inch outfielder, got on base, Casey would make a great show of looking for him through mock binoculars, which always broke up the crowd.

He was there for the laughs — he couldn't shake the reputation. He tried to do a good job managing in Brooklyn, working young players into the lineup to play with seasoned "professionals" like Al Lopez, the gifted catcher, and Tony Cuccinello, the excellent second baseman, but he didn't have enough good players to go around, and the pitching staff, despite the presence of Mungo and one or two others, was woefully thin.

He tried to teach; he was always teaching. "What else are you gonna do when you get a second-division ball club?" he once asked. "You've got a couple of young players on it, you work on them. Who else are you gonna work on? You keep after them. You ask them why they didn't make that throw. You ask them why they played that man there. Then for somebody else they turn out to be good ballplayers, but what of it? You helped to make them good ballplayers, didn't you?" Only a few people had much idea of what he was doing, or what he had done with young players in Worcester or Toledo. "He was very tough on the veterans," said Roy Parmalee, a National League pitcher in the 1930s who had been a rookie under Stengel at Toledo. "He could really get on them. But us rookies — he was like a father to us."

But not all the time. Not every youngster felt the affection and interest that Parmalee spoke of. Sometimes the toughness and biting sarcasm got in the way. Tony Kubek, who was only twenty when he began playing for

Stengel's Yankees, said, "He could be mean." Phil Rizzuto, who lived not far from Ebbets Field, went to a Dodger tryout in 1934 or 1935 when he was sixteen and tiny — he stretched out to his full five feet six inches later on. When Phil was batting during the tryout he was hit in the middle of the back with a pitched ball, and Stengel reacted negatively. After the workout he told Rizzuto not to come back to any more tryouts. "You're too small," he said. "You'll get hurt." Rizzuto protested and Stengel said, "Go on, get outa here. Go get a shoebox."

In 1934 Bill Rosenberg, a slick-fielding young shortstop from New York, went all the way to a Dodger tryout camp in Orlando, Florida, during Casey's first spring as manager. Rosenberg was treated cordially by Lopez and other Dodger regulars but got scant attention from Stengel. Watching the manager hit grounders to an infield of experienced players and feeling that the time he had left to show what he could do was fast running out, Rosenberg blurted, "I can run faster than any of the guys out there." Stengel, annoyed by the interruption, said, "Let's see how fast you can run out of the ball park."

He was impatient. He was trying to apply McGraw's techniques to the game, trying to find players he could use as standard pieces in a complex chess game. But when there's no money, you can't buy them, and it isn't easy to discover and develop players who can execute the plays the way you want them executed. "But he kept trying," said Otto Miller, the old Dodger catcher who was a coach under Casey at Brooklyn. "He reminded me of a guy who has made up his mind to force a pair of deuces to beat four aces, and can't stop trying."

One of the things he kept trying, at least for a while, was something he called his "precision play." It was something to be used in special circumstances, at a point when it was particularly important to keep the other team from scoring a run. There had to be a base runner on third with a right-handed batter up. The pitcher would throw at the batter's head but would yell "Watch out!" as soon as he threw. The idea was that the batter would instinctively fall back out of the way. The base runner would have taken a normal lead but would freeze for an instant when the pitcher shouted and the batter fell down. At that instant the catcher would snare the pitch and have a clear throw down the line to the third baseman, who would trap the runner off the base. Stengel finally abandoned the play.

"The runner would freeze," he'd explain, telling the story, "but so would my man at third, and my left fielder would wear himself out chasing the overthrows."

Tom Meany, who covered the Dodgers in those days, said that Casey "became a desperation manager, like a fellow playing the races with the rent money." He traded Lopez and Cuccinello to Boston for pitching, giving up two solid, dependable players for a commodity he desperately needed, and didn't get enough of.

So he covered his failures with funny stories as the 1935 and 1936 seasons plodded by, the Dodgers moving up to fifth in 1935, down to seventh in 1936, but playing at about the same won-and-lost pace each season. Babe Phelps, a big strong catcher who came to the club in 1935, took over most of the catching after Lopez left, but his strength was in his bat, not his glove. Someone hit a ninth-inning home run off a pitcher named Dutch Leonard to beat the Dodgers. Stengel asked Phelps, "What pitch did you call for?"

"A fastball," Phelps said. Leonard was a renowned knuckleball pitcher.

"Why not his knuckler?"

"His knuckler's tough to catch," Phelps said.

Casey stared at him. "If his knuckler's so tough to catch," he said, "don't you think it might be a little tough to hit, too?" Phelps looked at him blankly.

Some players were all but impossible to teach. Others were a pleasure. Years later someone remarked to Stengel that Lopez, then managing opposite Casey in the American League, was smart. "Sure he's smart," Stengel rasped. "I taught him, didn't I?" Stengel used to say that when Lopez was catching, "Al would run the team from behind the plate and I could sit back and nap."

The laughs were important, however tinged with frustration. One morning after Brooklyn dropped a doubleheader Stengel went into the hotel barber shop for a shave. "Don't cut my throat," he cautioned the barber, "I may want to do that myself later."

He had a lot of fun with a fairly outrageous infielder-outfielder named Stanley Bordagaray, known to everyone as Frenchy. Frenchy was picked off second one day, or at least the umpire called him out, although he seemed to be standing safely on base at the time. Stengel charged from the dugout to protest, but before he could get his argument going Bordagaray said, "No, he's right, Case. I'm out."

"How could you be out?" Stengel roared.

"You were standing on the base."

"I was tapping my foot," Bordagaray exclaimed, "and I guess he got me between taps."

Bordagaray once paused in pursuit of a batted ball in the outfield to pick up his cap, which had fallen off. He stole third base one day even though Stengel, coaching at third, had cautioned him to stay on second, since there were two out and he represented the tying run. Bordagaray slid in safely.

"I ought to fine you for that," Casey said.

"With the lead I had," Bordagaray replied, "you ought to fine yourself for not inviting me over."

One day in batting practice Frenchy accidentally caromed a ball off Stengel's head. The Dodgers had been in a losing streak but that day they won. Bordagaray went to Stengel afterward and said, "Case, I think we can keep on winning if I can just hit you on the head with a ball every day for luck."

Bordagaray created an absolute sensation in that clean-shaven era when he appeared in spring training in 1936 sporting a mustache. Ballplayers hadn't worn mustaches since the turn of the century and wouldn't again until the 1970s. Stengel braced him about it.

"I'm bringing back the good old days," explained Bordagaray. "All the great ballplayers used to wear them. I got to thinking that some great modern ballplayer should bring back the mustache, and here it is."

"Go shave it off," said Stengel, "before someone throws a ball at it and kills you."

Not everything was humorous. Among Stengel's ballplayers on the Dodgers was a left-handed-hitting outfielder named Len Koenecke, who played awhile for the Giants in 1932, went back to the minors and returned to the majors with Brooklyn in Casey's first season as manager. Koenecke was not a young kid — he was twenty-eight — but he seemed a bright bet for the future after batting .320 for the Dodgers in 1934 with seventy-three runs batted in. But Koenecke had serious personality problems, and he drank too much. He slumped to .283 in 1935 and showed very little of the power he had displayed a year earlier. In September, Stengel released him during a Dodger road trip through the Midwest. Koenecke, drinking, made his way to Detroit, where he chartered a two-man plane to fly him to Buffalo. He began to behave irrationally — veteran baseball men say that he made homosexual advances to the pilot and the copilot — and a fight broke out on board the small plane, during which Koenecke was hit on the head with a fire extinguisher and killed. The plane landed in Toronto and the stunning story of the ballplayer's death went out over the wire.

Stengel was having a small party in his hotel suite in St. Louis that night for his wife's brother Larry when someone phoned with the startling news. Stengel said, "I can't believe it. How can it be true?" He seemed to feel personally responsible for Koenecke's death, but he wouldn't answer any questions about the player and refused to talk to any of the newspapermen with the club about the incident. The wire services had been calling for some kind of comment, and a Dodger official — probably Bob Quinn — was worried that Casey and the club might seem callous and indifferent if the manager who had given Koenecke his release on the day of his death said nothing at all about him. He persuaded Roscoe McGowen, who had a deep voice and some acting ability, to phone the Associated Press and pose as Stengel. McGowen did, imitating Stengel's gravelly voice and way of speaking. He said a few obvious things in praise of Koenecke and expressed shock and regret at his death. The AP accepted the voice as Stengel's and included the comments in its coverage of Koenecke's death, and the sad incident was slowly forgotten.

Stengel had been given a three-year contract after the 1934 season, but his position with the Brooklyn management had weakened after two more second-division finishes. Quinn still solidly backed him, but Quinn left Brooklyn after the 1935 season to become president of the Boston Braves. With Quinn gone there was considerable infighting for control of the club, and the Brooklyn Trust Company, which had loaned the Dodgers considerable amounts of money, began to exert its influence. Whatever was happening, Stengel was left out in the cold. Even though he had a year to go on his contract, as Max Carey had, he was dismissed as manager during the World Series between the Giants and the Yankees that fall.

Being let go was a blow to Stengel's pride, but it was assuaged by a huge farewell dinner given him by the sportswriters a few days later. All of baseball was in New York for the Series, and there was an impressive collection of guests. Weiss, his friend from Eastern League days, now director of the Yankees' minor-league farm system, was there. So was Joe McCarthy, who had become manager of the Yankees after being dismissed by the Cubs, and who said to Casey, "Maybe you're getting a break. Maybe you'll be kicked up-stairs, too."

Stengel was not only given the party, he was presented with a large, elaborate clock as a going-away present. The significance of the evening was its indication of the broad popularity Stengel commanded. Stout Steve Owens, the plump, red-faced coach of the football Giants, said, "This must be the first time anyone was given a party for being fired."

19 *DISCHARGED AGAIN: CHEERS FOR A BROKEN LEG*

Among the players Stengel had had in Brooklyn was Randy Moore, a tall, graceful Texan who played outfield in the National League for several years, most of the time with the Boston Braves. He came to the Dodgers in 1936, broke his leg and missed most of the season.

Moore was from Naples, Texas, in the northeastern corner of the state, near the fabulously productive east Texas oilfields that flowed so prodigiously fifty years ago that they gave rise to a lasting American myth: instant riches from bubbling oil. Moore's family was in the oil business, and after he left baseball he went into it full-time. He advised friends of his in baseball, Stengel and Lopez among them, to invest in oil properties he was involved with. Stengel discussed Moore's proposition with the businesslike Edna, who agreed that it sounded like a good thing, and they put up $10,000, a great deal of money in the 1930s. A four-bedroom house in a posh suburb of New York City could be bought for less.

It was a big investment, and it paid off. But Stengel did more than just give Moore the money and run. He went down to Texas with Edna in 1937 and spent time in the area around Naples and Omaha in east Texas, working at oil, learning about it, understanding the investment. A lot of people in baseball assumed that he and Lopez and the others all became millionaires, which wasn't true, but they did make a very nice bundle, and it gave Casey personal security (beyond Edna's money) for the rest of his life. "It's like having an annuity," Stengel once said of his oil money.

He stayed out of baseball throughout 1937, although he was paid regularly by the Dodgers. Some said he was paid more for not managing than his successor, Burleigh Grimes, was for managing. Casey retained at least amiable relations with the Dodgers and was in Ebbets Field, ensconced in a box seat, when his erstwhile charges opened the season's doings with the Giants. It was a typical Ebbets Field day. On the first pitch of the game, Dick Bartell, the Giants' leadoff man, turned to argue with umpire Beans Reardon and was hit in the chest with a ripe tomato. The Dodgers, resplendent in brand-new uniforms, opened a three-run lead but lost the game, 4–3. "Those spiffy new uniforms had me fooled for a while," Stengel said afterward, "but I recognized the boys in the late innings."

He and Edna did some traveling, went back and forth to Texas, visited New York a few times, went to Kansas City for the funerals of Casey's mother and father, who died in 1937, nine months apart. He passed his forty-seventh birthday in July, just another middle-aged man with, apparently, most of his life behind him. But Maury Allen asked Stengel when he was an old man if he had minded being out of baseball that year. "You're damned right I did," Stengel replied. "If it's your work and you ain't doin' it, you miss it, right?"

That fall, slightly more than a year after he had been dismissed by the Dodgers, he was back in the game again. Bob Quinn was trying to revitalize the Braves (in one of his less inspired moves he changed the club's nickname from "Braves" to "Bees" and tried to get everyone to call Braves Field "the Beehive"). Judge Fuchs, Casey's nemesis at

Worcester, had owned the team since 1923 and had tried to upgrade the club with various dramatic, unsuccessful gestures — making Mathewson president, managing the club himself, hiring Babe Ruth for his last hurrah in 1935 — but he was out of the picture now. New people had put money into the ball club, and Quinn was running the show. He needed a new manager, since Bill McKechnie, who had piloted the club for eight seasons, had switched to the Cincinnati Reds. He talked to Stengel. All baseball people dream of owning their own ball club, and Quinn gave Casey the chance to own at least part of one. He (and Edna) invested $43,000 in the Bees. Not coincidentally, Stengel also became manager of the team.

Red Smith, who worked for Philadelphia newspapers for a decade when both the ball clubs then resident in that city finished last year after year, once told an acquaintance, "I did ten years hard in Philadelphia." Stengel did six years hard in Boston. After a respectable fifth-place finish the first year he was there, the Bees were seventh four years in a row, able to finish ahead of only the Phutile Phillies of Red Smith's hard years.

Again, there were moments. Maybe the best came on Memorial Day in 1938, Stengel's first year in Boston, when the Bees shut down Terry's Giants in a doubleheader, 1–0 and 6–0. There were other memorable days, if less welcome. Casey's 1938 club was involved in the front end of one of the unique accomplishments in baseball history when Johnny Vander Meer of the Reds pitched a no-hit, no-run game against the Bees in Cincinnati on June 11. Four days later, Vander Meer pitched a second consecutive no-hitter against Brooklyn. Stengel was on the back end of Vander Meer's feat, too. Four days after his stunning performance in Brooklyn, Vander Meer faced the Bees again, this time in Boston, and held them without a hit through the first three innings. *Three* straight no-hitters? Casey had been coaching at third base, but when the Bees came to bat in the fourth inning he switched over to first base. As he crossed the diamond he deliberately passed in front of Vander Meer, who was throwing his warmup pitches, and without turning his head toward the pitcher said quietly, "John, we're not trying to beat you, we're just trying to get a base hit." That may have made Vander Meer a little self-conscious; he always remembered Casey speaking to him at that moment. With one out in the fourth inning a Boston batter poked a hit through the middle to end the hitless string.

Casey liked being in Boston, despite the downtrodden team he had to manage. He called Boston "a real city" and got to know the place, its feel, its idiosyncrasies. He was aware of the sea breezes that came in from Massachusetts Bay and inhibited batted balls from clearing the outfield fences, and that he called "Old Joe Wind, my fourth outfielder." On the other hand, when his hitters complained about the park, saying it was a tough place for a batter, Stengel would cluck in sarcastic sympathy and say, "Yes, I know. Mr. Hornsby played here one season and hit only .387 into that wind." Frank Frisch, his old Giant teammate, landed a broadcasting job in Boston in 1939 after being fired as manager of the Cardinals, and he and Stengel had a fine year together sampling the seafood and other delicacies at Boston restaurants. Later, when Frisch was managing Pittsburgh, his foot began to act up on him. Stengel visited Frisch in his sickroom, glanced down scornfully and said, "That ain't a foot. That's a claw you got left over from all them lobsters you ate in Boston."

He didn't have a Bordagaray at Boston, but he did have Max West, a rookie outfielder who broke in with the Bees in Stengel's first season. West was a powerful hitter — he won the All-Star Game for the National League in 1940 with a three-run homer off Red Ruffing — and Stengel liked him, but he also liked to kid him. West was a clumsy fielder who couldn't seem to do anything right. When he ran into a wall chasing a fly ball, Casey said sourly, "You got a great pair of hands, Max."

Whether West was the hero of another Stengel-Boston story is not certain. Whoever it was, according to the storytellers, came to bat one day with men on second and third and popped up. He flung his bat away in disgust, jogged down to first while the ball was being caught and then walked back to the dugout, his head down, angry with himself. The first pitch to the next batter was delivered while he was still grumping his way around home plate beyond the catcher and the umpire. It was a wild pitch that bounced past the catcher, and the runner on third broke for the plate. The ball rolled directly to the disconsolate out-maker, who still had his head down. Without thinking, he picked up the ball and flipped it to the catcher, who tagged out the Braves' base runner sliding home. Buddy Hassett, who had advanced from second to third on the play, said to Stengel, coaching at third, "You think they'll give him an assist?" According to Hassett, a few moments later the same player, mortified by his mistake, was walking up and down the dugout berating himself, not only for popping up with men on base but for costing his team a run. He was paying no attention to the action on the field and wasn't looking when a line-drive foul came into the dugout and skulled him. He fell down and everyone rushed toward him, including Stengel, who yelled, "Don't touch him! Leave him lay there. It might drive some sense into the son of a bitch."

One of the few really good players Stengel had in Boston was Ernie Lombardi, the ponderous catcher, who came from the Reds, played one season for the Bees and then was traded on to the Giants. Lombardi was one of the best hitters in the game and also one of its slowest runners. When Lombardi batted, the infielders almost automatically moved back onto the grass because they knew they could still throw him out from that distance. Stengel had great affection for the amiable Lombardi, who was a good athlete despite his almost incredible slowness. One day when Lombardi was on first base, Stengel noticed that nobody on the other team was paying any attention to him as a base runner. The first baseman wasn't holding him on the bag, the pitcher was taking a windup, the shortstop and the second baseman were ignoring him. Suddenly Stengel yelled, "Steal it, Lom!" and Lombardi lumbered off for second. By the time the pitcher got the ball across the plate and the catcher made his throw, Lombardi was sliding into second with a broad grin and a stolen base.

The war years made Stengel's player supply even smaller. Among his shopworn veterans was Paul Waner, who had been a great outfielder with Pittsburgh for fifteen years but now was near the end of the trail. The aging Waner got his 3,000th hit playing for Casey in Boston, and he was supposed to be used sparingly, more as a pinch hitter than anything else. But in the summer of 1942 Stengel found himself short of outfielders, and even though the team was playing a string of doubleheaders he was obliged to use Waner in center field game after game. One day in Pittsburgh, Waner grew so weary chasing balls hit to the far reaches of the big Forbes Field outfield that he fell down running for a fly and was too exhausted to get up. The ball landed only a few feet away and stopped, but Waner just lay there, gasping, while someone else retrieved it. It was that sort of year and that sort of team.

Still, Stengel respected Waner's baseball knowledge and advised a sharp-hitting rookie named Tommy Holmes to talk to him about hitting. "He can teach you six or eight things," Casey said. Waner gave Holmes some of his ideas about hitting, notably that it makes sense to try to hit the ball down the foul lines, pulling to right, pushing to left (both Waner and Holmes were left-handed hitters). "If you miss, it's only a foul ball," said Waner, "but if you get it in, it's a double. If the fielders move over to protect the lines you have more room in left center and right center for hits." Holmes later led the National League in doubles and hit over .300 five times. In 1945 he hit safely in thirty-seven straight games, a National League record that stood until Pete Rose broke it in 1978.

Casey taught what he could to what players he had, and he talked and mugged and joked, but it was a disheartening six years. The new investors in the Braves weren't putting much money into the club. It was always a make-shift operation, a team well larded with slightly tarnished veterans, whereas other clubs seemed to keep coming up with young stars. "Well, they've got another one," he told Bob Broeg, then a Boston writer, late in 1941 after the Bees came back from playing the Cardinals in St. Louis. The Cards had found one sparkling rookie after another for several years; the new one who had caught Casey's eye was an outfielder named Stan Musial. (The Braves did come up with Warren Spahn, who was to win 363 games in his major-league career, but Casey sent him back to the minors in 1942. Spahn pitched for Casey again more than twenty years later, at the end of his career when Stengel was managing the Mets. "I played for Casey before and after he was a genius," Spahn liked to say.)

Stengel was entertaining, but his presence didn't do much to help Boston's won-and-lost record, nor did it do much for attendance, which dropped below 300,000 in his second year and never got that high again during his tenure. Today, a major-league club might talk of a season attendance of 1,800,000 as the "break-even" point. During Casey's six seasons in Boston, the Bees drew a *total* of 1,680,000, an average of 280,000 a year. It was discouraging, particularly after the war began, with players being drafted and the rookies of the future in military service instead of playing on farm teams.

371

The beginning of the end for Stengel in Boston came during spring training in 1943. Lou Perini, one of the new investors, watched an exhibition game and was bothered when one of the Bees bunted into a double play. After the game he asked Stengel what had happened. Perini may have been genuinely curious or, like a typical fan, may have been objecting to Stengel's strategy. He was polite, but he asked about it. Stengel bristled inwardly, as managers do when their baseball wisdom is questioned, but Perini was an owner, so Casey went into one of his convoluted explanations, a wordy smokescreen designed to sound like an answer without imparting much specific information. Perini listened. A logical man, he became confused. Instead of smiling and nodding his head, as so many of Casey's listeners did, he said, "I wonder if you'd go over that again for me." Casey went into another rambling diversion, and when he finished that one, Perini let the matter drop. But it left a bad taste in his mouth. He may not have believed that Stengel was deliberately throwing double-talk at him, but he did think, as he said later on, "This man can't really know much about baseball if he isn't able to explain a simple play."

Not long after that, just before the 1943 season was to begin, Casey was hit by an automobile in Boston as he was crossing a street on a rainy night. He suffered a badly broken leg and was laid up for several weeks. Even an accident as serious as that seemed somehow comical because Stengel was involved. Frisch, managing Pittsburgh, had often mocked Casey about the poor quality of his ball club, and he sent a wire to Stengel at the hospital, addressed in care of the psychiatric ward, that said, "Your attempt at suicide fully understood. Deepest sympathy you didn't succeed." Edna, at home in California taking care of her seriously ill mother, wired when she heard the news and said she'd come east immediately. Casey wired back that it wasn't necessary, saying, "Don't come unless you can set a broken leg."

He didn't rejoin his team until well after the season began, and while the club broke its string of seventh-place finishes and moved up a notch to sixth, it was another drab year. The last blow may have come in a doubleheader with the Reds late in September when Elmer Riddle squashed them 2–0 in the first game and Vander Meer 1–0 in the second.

Perini, who had made a great deal of money in the construction business, decided to revitalize the ball club, and after the season he moved with two of his associates, Guido Rugo and Joe Maney, to gain complete control of it. He was bothered by the club's perennial also-ran mentality and felt that changes should be made. He reinstituted the old name "Braves" and suggested to Quinn that he get a new manager. Quinn protested that Stengel was a first-rate manager. Perini didn't agree. Quinn pointed out that Casey owned stock in the club. "Talk to him," Perini suggested.

Quinn let Stengel know Perini's feelings. Casey was hardly surprised. He told Quinn he didn't want to stay where he wasn't wanted. More to the point he said, "Let them buy me out, and I'll resign." After "the Three Little Shovels," as the new owners were nicknamed by the Boston press, took official possession of the Braves in 1944, they bought his stock, and Casey responded with a formal letter, written perhaps by Edna, that said, "Whenever a new group purchases control of a corporation they have the right to dictate policy. And in order that there be no embarrassment on the part of this group I hereby tender my resignation."

Once again, he was out of baseball. This time there was no surprise, no hurt, just a sort of weariness. Most jobs that might have been available in baseball for the 1944 season had already been filled, although Casey did receive a few feelers. He turned them down. He didn't need the money. His leg was still bothering him, and Edna wanted him to stay home in Glendale and do the exercises he was supposed to do to get it back in shape.

It seemed to be over. Maybe it was time. He was fifty-three years old and he'd been a manager for sixteen seasons. Sixteen seasons of applying what he had absorbed from McGraw and what he had learned for himself, and he'd won only one pennant. After that pennant, in Toledo in 1927, he'd brought a team through a season higher than fifth only once. He had nine years of managing in the major leagues, far more than most men get, and in all nine years he'd finished in the second division.

Maybe it was time. Summing up the season in the *Boston Record,* the acerbic sports columnist Dave Egan had written, "The man who did the most for baseball in Boston in 1943 was the motorist who ran Stengel down two days before the opening game and kept him away from the Braves for two months."

20 COMEBACK: HELPING OUT JOLLY CHOLLY

Stengel went home to Glendale and nursed his wounds through the early months of 1944. Despite his protestations that he just wanted to take it easy for a while, it seems certain that he'd have leaped at another managing job in the big leagues if one had been available. But none was. Casey was the only one of the sixteen major-league managers to be fired after the 1943 season. There were no other jobs open.

Three or four people did approach him about going to work for them as a coach or as a minor-league manager, but Stengel said no. He'd sit in the sun by his swimming pool and nurse his leg.

The 1944 season began with Casey still in Glendale, out of things. But not for long. In Chicago the Cubs won on opening day and then lost nine straight games, distressing their general manager, James Gallagher, and their owner, Philip K. Wrigley. The Cubs had been one of the top teams in baseball in the 1920s and 1930s, had won four pennants, had been a power, but for the past three seasons under manager Jimmy Wilson they had been back in the ruck, and now it looked like more of the same. Gallagher and Wrigley decided Wilson had to go, and they knew just the man they wanted in his place: Charlie Grimm, who had won two of those pennants for the Cubs and was now running the then minor-league Milwaukee Brewers. The Brewers were on the road, playing in Kansas City, when Gallagher got in touch with Grimm and offered him the job.

Grimm was torn. He had managed the Brewers to the American Association pennant the year before, and he had another crack team that had won ten of its first twelve games. But the major leagues were the major leagues, and he wanted the Chicago job badly. However, he had a problem. He owned a substantial interest in the Brewers with young Bill Veeck, whose now dead father used to run the Cubs for Wrigley. Veeck had enlisted in the marines the previous December and was off in the Pacific somewhere. If Grimm left, there'd be nobody at the helm of the Brewers. He couldn't turn the manager's job over to just anyone. A minor-league operation involved a lot more than just running the team on the field. Mickey Heath was Milwaukee's vice-president in charge of office detail, and the manager would have to work closely with Heath, particularly in matters relating to the development and sale of players to big-league teams, which was how a team like the Brewers derived a significant part of its income. Where could Grimm find a man capable enough to do all that, now that the season was under way and all the good men had been hired?

"Bill Veeck and myself have a big investment in the Milwaukee baseball club," Grimm said, "and I intend to protect as well as I can his and my interests. Veeck is gone. I have to make sure that I have the right kind of manager for the Brewers."

Perhaps the solution was obvious, or perhaps it was because Grimm was in Kansas City when Gallagher called him that made them both think of Stengel. Before they approached Casey they tried to reach Veeck to discuss the matter with him, but it was impossible to get in touch with him. Grimm and Gallagher went ahead and talked to Stengel, who was amenable. He was rested, his leg was much better, and with the season under way he found himself bored and restless. He knew and liked Grimm and Gallagher and Heath, and the prospect of running a ball club again appealed to him. He didn't know Veeck, but he told Grimm he'd come east and manage. There was a delay while Grimm tried again to reach Veeck, without success. "I couldn't contact Bill about this change," Grimm told the press, "but I know he wouldn't have stood in my way."

So it was done, without Veeck's knowledge. Grimm moved eighty miles south to Chicago, and Casey came out of his enforced retirement to manage again. He was welcomed reluctantly in Milwaukee, where the ebullient, banjo-playing Grimm was enormously popular. The press did its best to praise the new manager — "Stengel is generally remembered as a baseball buffoon but the mighty Casey for all his crazy capers doesn't miss a thing on the diamond. His smashed hip [sic] is now said to be well enough to permit him to resume his funny caperings on the coaching lines" — but how it hated to see Grimm leave. "There'll never be another Jolly Cholly," wrote one columnist. "As close as the Stengel man comes to it, he'll never be able to pluck a banjo and tell a yarn quite up to the Grimm standard."

That same week in the *Sporting News* a poll of 151 sportswriters rated Casey the funniest of all managers. He had four times as many votes as Jimmy Dykes and six times as many as Grimm. Casey was still king of the clowns.

He arrived in Milwaukee at noon on Saturday, May 6, and that afternoon sat with Grimm in the stands, comparing notes on the team, as the Brewers won again. That Casey knew what he was getting into — taking over a first-place team that had won the pennant the year before from a highly popular manager in a suspicious city — was evident. He realized what most people thought of him. Look at the *Sporting News*. But it didn't shake his confidence in his ability to manage. "To follow Grimm is probably the toughest job I've ever tackled," he said, "but I'm gonna pitch in with everything I have, and I think we'll all get along splendid."

He really didn't seem too worried. After the game Grimm asked one of the reporters, "How many hits did we get?"

"What do you mean, 'Did *we* get?'" interrupted Stengel. "You're a Cub now. Cut out this *we* business."

He made his debut the next day and the Brewers won a doubleheader. They won again the next day and kept right on winning, extending their streak to twelve straight and their record to twenty victories and two defeats while opening up a seven-game lead. Later in the season they ran into one or two slumps, but Stengel kept them in the lead and they won the pennant by six and a half games. When people showered congratulations on him, he said, "I had the horses."

He also had the fans and the newspapermen, most of whom were completely won over. At the end of the season a Milwaukee paper printed a "letter to Bill Veeck" in the form of an editorial cartoon. "Dear Bill," it said, "Casey Stengel came to Milwaukee with two strikes on him — he was an outsider to fans and players alike, and to make it even tougher he was stepping into the shoes of a guy who was considered the indispensable man. But I don't have to tell you how we felt about Grimm. Cholly left the Brewers at the top of the heap and Casey kept them there! He added polish to the team and imparted his years of baseball knowledge to the players. . . . There have been rumors that Case will not be back next year, but as far as we're concerned he has done a helluva job and we'd like to see him back."

Those rumors were not so much rumors as statements from Stengel, who two or three times during the season indicated he would not be coming back in 1945. "I came out of retirement to help Grimm," he said at one point. "I had other offers but I decided to stay out of baseball this year to rest my broken leg. When Grimm asked me to come here I did, but next year will be different."

The reason for Stengel's decision not to remain in Milwaukee lay in a letter that Veeck had written to Grimm and Heath and Jimmy Gallagher early in the season after he finally got word that Charlie was managing Chicago and Stengel had taken his place with the Brewers. Veeck was furious. His letter read:

I learned an hour ago the identity of our new manager. I've waited an hour to write this, hoping to cool off. So far it hasn't been too successful. To say I'm very disappointed is putting it mildly.

I'd like to have a complete explanation of where Stengel came from. Who suggested him? For how much and how long? I don't want anything to do with Stengel, nor do I want him to have anything to do with anything I have a voice in.

I will now proceed to elucidate the above:

First, Stengel has never managed a winner. In my humble opinion, he is a poor manager.

Second, he has been closely connected with Bob Quinn and the operation of the Boston Braves. This in itself is enough to damn him. [Veeck was thinking of all those second-division finishes.]

Third, I don't believe that Stengel is a good judge of ball players so can be of no value in amassing future clubs.

Fourth, from what I know of Stengel he is tight-fisted and this will not prove acceptable.

Fifth, from my observation, Stengel is mentally a second-division major leaguer. That is, he is entirely satisfied with a mediocre ball club as long as Stengel and his alleged wit are appreciated.

Sixth, I have no confidence in his ability and rather than be continuously worried, I'd rather dispose of the whole damn thing.

Seventh, Stengel doesn't fit in at all with the future — and I'm looking, as usual, for the long haul.

If these aren't reasons enough, I don't like him and want no part of him. If Stengel has an iron-clad contract and it will be expensive to break I guess that we'll have to be stuck with him. If not, replace him immediately with Ivy Griffin.

By the time Veeck's letter reached Milwaukee, the Brewers had opened their big lead over the rest of the league. Heath wrote back to Veeck, telling him this and adding that the new manager was fast becoming a favorite with the fans. By the time Veeck got this letter it was obviously too late to get rid of Stengel, and Bill wrote again, reluctantly agreeing that Stengel should be kept on, but only for the season: "I guess I'm over my surprise about Stengel. I'm still of the same opinion as to his ultimate value, but the press seems to have taken to him and with the club doing well he should be okay until the season ends." Even after the Brewers won the pennant Veeck wrote, "I still contend he is a poor manager."

Since Veeck and Stengel later became good friends, it's hard at first to understand the vituperation and the antagonism in the letters. But Veeck was thousands of miles away from baseball, buried for the most part on remote islands and, for a time, in the Panama Canal Zone, hot, certainly lonesome for baseball, a forceful man used to having his own way frustrated by his inability to direct the fortunes of his own ball team. He was badly injured, a recoiling artillery piece having shattered a leg that he had broken earlier in his life. And Casey did have that clownish reputation. No wonder Veeck vented his spleen in his letters.

Stengel became aware of Veeck's attitude toward him and was hurt by it. Beyond his personal resentment he knew that the first-rate job he had done in Milwaukee might be overlooked if Veeck fired him anyway after the season. His chances of getting back to the majors would be a lot stronger if he left the Milwaukee job on his own power. He was careful never to criticize Veeck. "Stengel had no comment on the report that he made up his mind not to come back here when he heard in a roundabout way that he had not been President Bill Veeck's choice to succeed Charlie Grimm," a Milwaukee newspaper said.

"All I have to say," declared Stengel, "is that I decided to help out Grimm and his buddy Bill. I think I did a good job for both of them. Now I can leave with no regrets, and Veeck has a perfectly free hand in selecting my successor. Old Case will be in the game next year, but I am certain it will not be here."

Milwaukee was as reluctant to see him leave as it had been to see him arrive. A reporter with the club noted with some awe that at the team's pennant-clinching party, where the players, who were doing some drinking, could have been excused for poking semi-sober gibes at their manager, instead stood in a cluster around Casey, listening to him, hanging on every word. The reporter asked several of the players their opinion of Stengel as a manager. Tommy Nelson, the second baseman, said, "He taught me more about playing second base than I ever dreamed there was to it." Ed Levy, an outfielder and first baseman, said, "I've played for quite a few managers in my baseball career but never for a smarter, keener one than Stengel." "That goes for me, too," said Bill Norman, a thirty-five-year-old outfielder who a decade later managed the Detroit Tigers. Heinz Becker, who had played in the majors, said, "He's the greatest manager in the game when it comes to keeping his players thinking. I never knew a manager to spend so much time with his players, trying to get smart baseball across to them, trying to prepare them so that when their time comes to go to the big league they'll know what to expect and how to do it."

The paragon of virtue was still the same old Casey, though. For photographers he willingly posed lying on his belly, soulfully contemplating a huge pennant held up by his players. Toward the end of the season the Brewers signed an eighteen-year-old high school star named Dale Long (who twelve years later would set a major-league record by hitting home runs in eight consecutive games). Long was strictly a spectator as the Brewers moved toward the pennant, but one day Stengel beckoned to him. "Come out early tomorrow," he said. Long was excited by the prospect. Stengel was asking *him* to come out early. The manager was probably going to give him a personal workout, the rookie thought, some special advice. What happened, though, was that high school had opened and the two regular clubhouse boys who took care of the players' equipment had to go to school. When Long arrived, eager and early, Stengel motioned to the lockers and said, "Shine those shoes, will ya?"

After winning the pennant the Brewers went into the postseason playoffs and won two of their first three games from Louisville. Then they lost three in a row and were eliminated. That shook Casey. "I can't believe it's over," he said. He went home again to Glendale, without a job. The Milwaukee press hated to see him go, one columnist even calling him "the smartest manager the Brewers have ever had," which was near heresy in Jolly Cholly country.

Veeck returned from the Pacific late in the year to recuperate from his injury (eventually the lower part of his leg had to be amputated) and learned a lot more about what Stengel had done with the team. He was particularly impressed by Casey's ability to bring along players for subsequent sale to the majors. "His biggest job as a minor-league manager," Veeck said once, "was probably developing players to sell somewhere. He got awfully good at it. Mr. Stengel developed and peddled enough athletes to insure winning clubs, healthy gates and a bigger bank balance." During the fall Veeck met with Casey in California and tried to mend fences; he asked Stengel to reconsider and stay on as manager of the Brewers. Casey said he appreciated Veeck's candor and honesty, but he'd made up his mind and he wouldn't change it.

Stengel had hopes that his work at Milwaukee had caught major-league eyes and that he'd be a leading candidate for a big-league managing job. But it was a rare year in the volatile world of baseball: Not one of the six teen managers who began the 1944 season, with the exception of the Cubs' Jimmy Wilson, whom Grimm had replaced, was dismissed. All sixteen who ended the season were returning in 1945. Again, there were no big-league jobs open.

He still didn't have a job of any kind in December, when the winter baseball meetings were held, but he made it clear that he was available, and George Weiss asked him if he'd like to manage the Yankees' American Association farm team in Kansas City in 1945. This was a comedown — World War II had depleted the Yankee farm system of the brilliant young prospects that were usually ripening there — and Casey had seen Kansas City finish last in 1944 when he was leading Milwaukee to the American Association pennant. He'd be dropping from the top echelon of the league to the bottom. Still, a job was a job. It would keep him onstage. He signed with Weiss and did what he could with the Blues, the team he had signed his first contract with in 1910, but he couldn't do much and the team finished a distant seventh.

While he didn't enjoy that season — except for the chance it gave him to visit with old Kansas City friends and relatives — he might have stayed on with the Blues except that late in 1945 the Yankees were sold to a syndicate headed by the high-octane Larry MacPhail. MacPhail ran his own show, and the capable Weiss, Casey's man, was pushed into the shadows. Stengel went home to Glendale, not knowing what he'd be doing in 1946.

The war ended in the summer of 1945, and baseball felt the same sense of rebirth that the rest of the country did as it entered the first postwar year. Attendance promised to be high, and there was a glut of experienced ballplayers, the thousands who had been in service coming home to join those who for one reason or another had been able to play during the war years. Stengel ran into a Californian he knew named Cookie de Vicenzo, who had owned the Oakland Oaks in the Pacific Coast League for years but who sold the club to a highly regarded baseball man named Clarence (Brick) Laws. Laws was looking for a manager. Was Casey interested?

Casey had hopes of getting another big-league job, but again a curious stability reigned in the majors. There had been two managerial changes during the season, but the only club looking for a new manager was the Boston Braves, which let Casey out. Perini, spending money freely now in his efforts to revive the club, lured Billy Southworth away from the Cardinals, where he had been dramatically successful as a manager. The Cardinals, following their practice of promoting from within, replaced Southworth with Eddie Dyer of their Houston farm team. That was it. The other fourteen big-league jobs were occupied.

So Stengel talked to Laws, a skillful operator who was good at supplying a manager with capable players. Oakland was in California, which meant that Casey would be able to get home to Glendale frequently during the season, instead of being far away for months on end. The situation at home had changed. Edna had been taking care of her mother, who had been terribly crippled in an automobile accident in the early 1930s, for more than a decade, but Mrs. Lawson had died in 1944 and Edna's father a year later, and except for the attention she had to pay to family business matters her time was much freer than it had been. It could be a pleasant life, tooling up and down the coast together in the pleasant Pacific weather. He took the job.

Fred Lieb had noted that the three minor-league teams Stengel managed in the 1940s — Milwaukee, Kansas City and Oakland — all became major-league cities later. It was as though Casey, yearning for the bigs, was getting as close as he could to them, one way or the other. The Pacific Coast League in many ways was the minor league closest to the majors in status. Old big-league stars with a fair proportion of their skills intact liked to finish their careers there. Los Angeles and San Francisco were big-time cities. If you couldn't be in the major leagues, the Coast League was the place to be.

21 OAKLAND: IT'S NICE TO HAVE A BRIDGE AROUND

Stengel managed Oakland for three years and had a wonderful time. The war was over and the country was bubbling with joy and relief. Attendance at ball games soared, and Stengel had a rapt audience up and down the West Coast for his rambling conversations. He liked Oakland, he told reporters. He particularly liked it because of the Bay Bridge connecting the city to San Francisco. "I like the idea of bridges," he explained. "Everywhere I go they throw in a bridge as part of the service. Every manager wants to jump off a bridge sooner or later, and it's very nice for an old man to know he doesn't have to walk fifty miles to find one."

Brick Laws supplied the horses and Stengel rode them to a strong second-place finish in 1946, four games behind the pennant-winning San Francisco Seals. It was a long season — the clement climate let the Coast League

393

play a marathon schedule that ran close to 200 games — but Casey shuffled players in and out of the lineup and got 111 victories out of them. Rip Collins, the first baseman of the 1934 Gas House Gang Cardinals, who was in the Coast League after the war, said, "Casey used so many players he drove us all crazy. He had two first basemen one year and both were in 170 games, so you can see how he shuttled them around. I needled him. I said, 'Casey, do you mind if I count the boys on your bench? You're allowed twenty-five but with the changes you make you've got to be carrying more than that.' He just growled and winked. He knew what I meant."

In the postseason playoffs Oakland beat Los Angeles in the first round but lost to pennant-winning San Francisco in the finals. In 1947 the Oaks slacked off a little, finishing fourth, but again won in the first round of the four-team playoffs before losing to Los Angeles in the finals. In 1948 the Oaks went all the way, finishing first in the regular season to give Oakland its first pennant since 1927 and marching through Los Angeles and Seattle in the playoffs.

Casey was a hero in Oakland and a godsend to sportswriters — and to press agents. Harold Conrad, who was doing publicity in Oak land for a new phenomenon, the Roller Derby, persuaded Casey to come out to the rink to pose for pictures. Stengel, the consummate showman, knew that the pictures would promote not only the Roller Derby but the ball club, too, so he went along with the idea. At the rink Conrad asked Casey to put on a pair of roller skates.

"I can't roller-skate, god damn it," Stengel said. "I haven't been on a pair of skates since I was a kid."

"You don't have to skate," Conrad said. "Just stand up on them."

Stengel reluctantly agreed, put on the skates and stood up, a little uncertainly.

"So," said Conrad, telling the story, "I put my hand on his back and gave him a little shove. He went zooming down the rink like this." Conrad mimicked a man with arms outstretched, rigid with apprehension. "Boy, did we get coverage."

Stengel's 1948 club was loaded with veterans, many of them retreads down from the big leagues. Ernie Lombardi, now forty years old, did some of the catching. Nick Etten, who had won the American League home-run championship in 1944, was at first base. Cookie Lavagetto, a hero of the 1947 World Series for the Dodgers, played third base a good deal of the time. Dario Lodigiani, a former American Leaguer, shifted between third and second. Maurice Van Robays, a former Pittsburgh Pirate, was in the outfield. Jim Tobin, who had pitched a no-hitter in the National League in 1944, was on the pitching staff for a while. The Oaks were so long in the tooth that Coast League sportswriters dubbed them "the Nine Old Men," but Stengel kept them young enough to win 114 games, the pennant and the playoff. In the semifinals, after falling behind Los Angeles two games to one, the Oaks beat the Angels in a Sunday doubleheader and won again the next night to take the Series. One of Stengel's veterans said, "If we won a doubleheader Casey would come into the clubhouse and say, 'You fellas did pretty well today and it's up to me to buy you each a three-dollar dinner.' Three dollars meant a pretty good meal then, but he'd come in the next day with a pocketful of bills and give each of us three bucks. After we beat the Angels in that doubleheader in the playoffs — we were getting beat 9–2 in the second game and we came back to win it 23–15, damnedest game you ever saw — Casey came in and said, 'Every man here rates a *ten*-dollar dinner from the old man.' Next day he passed out ten bucks apiece to twenty-seven men —

from his own pocket. No wonder we played our asses off for him."

Not all Stengel's heroes were old veterans. Laws had a working agreement with the Yankees under which Weiss would send promising players to Oakland for further seasoning. Among those that Oakland received in 1946 were Frank Shea, a burly right-hander, and Gene Bearden, a tall left-hander. Shea's season was delayed because of an appendectomy, but he came along to win fifteen while losing five. Bearden did even better, fifteen and four. The Yankees brought Shea up to the majors a year later and by the end of 1947 he was their best pitcher; he started three games in the World Series that year and won two. The Yankees weren't as high on Bearden, who didn't have a major-league fastball. Bearden's father said, "I thought Gene had the stuff and I knew he had the control, but it wasn't until he picked up his knuckleball under Casey Stengel at Oakland that he really arrived." Bearden stayed with the Oaks in 1947 and had a 16–7 record, and then was sold to the Cleveland Indians. Bearden was a sensation with Cleveland in 1948, winning twenty games, including a postseason playoff win over the Red Sox that gave the Indians the pennant, and he was a star of the World Series.

And there was another youngster. In the spring of 1948 when the New York Giants wandered from their Arizona training camp to the West Coast for a few preseason exhibition games, a New York sportswriter named Jim McCulley sat down to chat with Casey, an old friend from the days he had managed in the National League.

"Got any good ballplayers?" McCulley asked.

"I don't know about anybody else," Stengel replied, "but I got one kid I'd bet everything in the world is gonna make it."

The kid was Billy Martin, a local boy who had graduated from Berkeley High School in 1946, tried out with the Oaks and late in the season went off to play with Idaho Falls in the Class D Pioneer League. He was in only a few games there, but in 1947 he put in a full season with Phoenix in the Arizona-Texas League, won the batting championship with a startling .392 average and led the league in RBIs. He was brought up to Oakland at the end of 1947 and in 1948 played third base, shortstop and second base as Stengel needed him. He batted a modest .277 at Oakland (averages were high in the Coast League; Gene Woodling of San Francisco won the batting title with .385) and fielded aggressively rather than deftly, but Stengel admired the drive and determination of "the big-nosed kid," as he called him. Martin did indeed possess a splendid nose at that time, so majestic that photographers got him to pose in 1948 with the patient Lombardi, whose own ample proboscis had earned him the nickname "Schnoz." Stengel helped in the photograph session by pretending to measure each nose with a ruler. Martin didn't like the jokes about his nose and a couple of years later, when he had the money, he underwent plastic surgery and had it abbreviated.

Stengel hit grounder after grounder to Martin, showed him different ways to make the double play, growled at him, laughed at him, bawled him out, praised him, and constantly tried to help the youngster develop into the ballplayer he knew he could become. "Casey always had this special feel for young players," Al Lopez said. "When he got a kid like Billy, a kid with ability, he wanted to see him make it big." Stengel wasn't always thinking of creating a living monument to himself when he worked with talented young ballplayers, but certainly the feeling was deeply imbedded in his mind. The scrawny, scrappy Martin was never going to be a great player, but he was willing and he worked hard and Stengel enjoyed him, even when the hot-tempered Billy would sass him. "He's a fresh kid, ain't he?" Stengel would say admiringly. What he liked more was Martin's ability to do things on the field, play different positions, play a useful role. Billy learned at the knee of the master and went forth and spread the gospel of Stengel's baseball knowledge.

Martin was a kind of guerrilla player for Casey in 1948, moving in here and there as he was needed all season long. He didn't become a full-time Oakland regular until 1949, after Casey had left for the majors. Stengel's skillful work with the Oaks had not gone unnoticed by George Weiss of the Yankees, who had long felt Stengel was a capable manager. Earlier in the 1940s when Joe McCarthy was having trouble with his stomach and occasionally talked of quitting as Yankee manager, Ed Barrow, then the New York general manager, suggested to Weiss, who was his associate, that they start lining up someone for the job in case McCarthy stepped down. Weiss said, "I've got just the man for you. Stengel." Barrow scoffed, "That clown?"

Late in 1946 after Barrow had gone and Larry MacPhail's tempestuous ways had led to the departure of three Yankee managers in the same season — McCarthy, Bill Dickey and Johnny Neun — Weiss suggested to MacPhail that Stengel be brought in to manage New York in 1947. MacPhail dismissed the idea and hired Bucky Harris, who guided the team to a pennant in 1947 and to a near miss in 1948. But MacPhail left the Yankees himself after the 1947 season, selling his interest in the club to his partners, Dan Topping and Del Webb. Topping and Webb named Weiss the general manager. Weiss did not care for Harris as a manager, and as soon as the 1948 season ended, in fact on the day the Cleveland Indians were beating the Boston Red Sox in the American League playoff, he fired him.

Again, Weiss proposed Stengel as manager. Topping didn't go for the idea and offered other suggestions, none of them suitable. Webb, a construction executive whose base was in the West, had some objections to Stengel at first but came around to Weiss' way of thinking and helped convince Topping. "My sole contribution to the Yankees was signing Casey Stengel as manager," Webb used to say. He told Frank Graham, Jr.: "I got to know Casey fairly well in Oakland. I was at a party one night and Casey was among the guests. He was in rare form. He had us standing around with our mouths open, putting on one of the best shows I've ever seen, telling stories, hopping around the room, mimicking other people. I had an important business appointment early the next morning, so I ducked out to catch a couple of hours sleep. When I left, Casey was still holding forth. I got my sleep — not much, but some — and then staggered out and got a cab to take me to my appointment. We went past a vacant lot and there were a bunch of kids with bats and gloves gathered around an old gaffer giving them some instruction. The old gaffer was Casey. I thought to myself then that if he cared that much about baseball he must be a terrific manager."

Weiss was gambling his own future in hiring Stengel, so he did some investigating to reaffirm his opinion. He talked to Brick Laws, who enthusiastically endorsed Casey. He asked Bill Essick and Joe Devine, the Yankee scouts on the West Coast, to give him a report; they said Stengel was the best manager in the league. He talked with Casey, discussing the possibilities. Needless to say, Casey was willing. He didn't hurt his own cause by bringing Oakland home in front. The last two victories in the final playoff with Seattle came in a Sunday doubleheader on

October 10, while the World Series between the Indians and the Braves was being played. The Yankees were committed to Stengel by now, and Weiss was getting impatient. It had been almost a week since Harris had gotten the ax, and there were rumors up and down the West Coast that Stengel was going to replace him. After the Oaks won their championship that Sunday afternoon, Del Webb phoned Casey from Cleveland, where Webb had gone to see the fifth game of the Series, and formally asked him to be manager. Accompanied by Brick Laws, Stengel flew to New York the next day and signed a contract to manage the Yankees in 1949. The news was not released on Monday because the last game of the Series was being played that day and the Yankees didn't want their story to be lost below the Series headlines. But the next day, Tuesday, October 12, exactly twenty-five years to the day after Casey had hit the second of his two game-winning home runs in the 1923 World Series, the Yankees presented their new manager to the public at a press conference at the "21" Club in New York.

At the press conference Stengel was nervous, quiet, subdued. Following Charlie Grimm in Milwaukee might have been the toughest job he'd had before, but that was nothing compared to this. Harris had been popular in New York. In two seasons he had won one pennant and just missed a second (the Yankees finished only two games behind Cleveland and Boston), and his hasty dismissal as soon as the season ended had aroused considerable resentment. The newspapermen liked Stengel well enough ("If you didn't like Casey," said John Drebinger, "you didn't like anybody"), but they didn't welcome him, either. Red Smith said they couldn't reconcile their conception of Stengel, the court jester, with the old Yankee tradition of austere and businesslike efficiency. Most of them were convinced that Stengel's hiring was strictly a public-relations ploy to divert attention from Harris' dismissal and to keep people amused and uncritical while the team was being rebuilt.

Casey was uncharacteristically edgy when it was his turn to say something. He referred to Dan Topping as Bob, which was the name of Topping's playboy brother. When someone asked him a question about Joe DiMaggio, who at the Yankees' request had attended the press conference as a symbol of team support for the new manager, Stengel said he didn't know DiMaggio, and the press buzzed about that. Casey meant that his own background in the majors had been in the National League and that he knew DiMaggio only by reputation. His listeners understood that, but it still sounded awkward. He certainly didn't swing the press around to the club's side that day. He knew it, too. He said later, "I could hear the hum and I knew what they was talking about. They was saying, 'This bum managed nine years and never got into the first division.'"

But he protested that the Yankees knew what they were doing when they hired him, that it was not just a spur-of-the-moment decision or Weiss' desire to hire a friend. A wire-service story out of Oakland commenting on the Yankees' hiring of Stengel stressed his unique talents. "He'll bring a penchant for masterminding from the bench and a revolving door technique of substitutes that works like a charm," it read. "This is a five-million-dollar business," Casey said. "They don't hand out jobs like this because you're a friend."

Sometime later the photographers had him put on a Yankee uniform and a Yankee cap and they posed him behind a backlighted baseball with an exaggerated look of wonder on his face, as though he were gazing into a crystal ball. The photograph was widely circulated and received an impressive response, not all of it to Casey's credit. A member of the Yankee business staff winced when he saw it. "We *have* hired a clown," he wailed.

Up in Boston, Dave Egan got out his typewriter and wrote, "Well, sirs and ladies, the Yankees have now been mathematically eliminated from the 1949 pennant race. They eliminated themselves when they engaged Perfesser Casey Stengel to mismanage them for the next two years, and you may be sure that the perfesser will oblige to the best of his unique ability."

Stengel had spent almost forty years in baseball, and it was as though he had done nothing. He still had to prove himself. He was almost fifty-nine, an age when most men are looking forward to retirement, and he was taking on the biggest challenge of his life.

22 THE 1949 YANKEES: BIGGEST THRILL OF ALL

During spring training in 1949, Stengel's first as manager of the Yankees, Joe DiMaggio was in a quiet corner of the Yankee clubhouse one day talking with Arthur Daley of the *New York Times*.

"What do you think of our new manager?" DiMaggio asked.

"I never saw such a bewildered guy in my life," Daley replied. "He doesn't seem to know what it's all about."

"That's the impression I have," said DiMaggio, "and the rest of the fellows feel the same."

This exchange was quoted in a column Daley wrote some years after the event as he looked back on Stengel's first spring with the Yankees. Daley, an ardent fan of DiMaggio's, apparently didn't stop to think that what he had written reflected on the great Yankee player's attitude. DiMaggio was not just the star of the team, he was the best ball-player in the league and probably in the majors. Only Stan Musial of the National League Cardinals approached him in all-round ability. Ted Williams of the Red Sox, justifiably renowned as a hitter, was inept in the field and on the bases compared to the gifted DiMaggio, and Jackie Robinson of the Dodgers could not hit with DiMaggio's devastating power.

Of all the players on the Yankee squad, DiMaggio was the most important, the one on whom Stengel's success or failure most depended. Yet "early in spring training," according to Daley, DiMaggio was agreeing with a sportswriter that the manager appeared bewildered and didn't seem to know what it was all about and saying that "the rest of the fellows" had the same impression. Phil Rizzuto, some years ago, said, "Joe D and I — we could never figure out why he did this or that. Joe used to say, 'How can this guy win?'"

Such was the precariousness of Stengel's position on the Yankees his first year. Rizzuto has since said that Stengel was in awe of DiMaggio. It seems more likely that he recognized DiMaggio's disdain but knew he had to live with it. DiMaggio was his most important asset, and his presence dominated the Yankees. He was a superb player. He had been a star in the minor leagues with San Francisco for three seasons in the early 1930s (he hit safely in sixty-one straight games in 1933 and batted .398 in 1935) before joining the Yankees in 1936. He was an instant success in New York, helping to fill the void left by the departure of Babe Ruth after the 1934 season, but for a long time he was not a very popular figure. He knew his worth, as Ruth had, and he held out for higher salaries in well-publicized disputes with the Yankee front office; but while holding out never seemed to affect Ruth's popularity, it led to boos for DiMaggio. He hadn't the smiling all-American boy appearance of Lou Gehrig, or any trace of the soaring exuberance of Ruth. He played baseball magnificently, but he did it coolly, calmly, efficiently. Leonard Woolf, Virginia's husband, wrote in his autobiography, "There develops in nearly all arts, and indeed in games like cricket, at various periods after an archaic, vague or inchoate beginning, a classical style which combines great power and freedom and beauty with a kind of self-imposed austerity and restraint." Nothing could describe DiMaggio more perfectly. Classicism, however, does not encourage excited response, and it wasn't until DiMaggio created his major-league record of hitting safely in fifty-six consecutive games in 1941 that he caught the imagination of the crowd and began to acquire the enormous popularity that he retained for the rest of his career and for decades after.

He was regal, the uncrowned king of the old guard, the eight or nine players on Stengel's first Yankee team who had played for Joe McCarthy back in the dignified, pre-MacPhail, pre-Stengel days. Not all of them disliked Stengel, but many of them resented his style, remembering McCarthy's way — quiet, controlled, austere. That was the way a manager should be. Bucky Harris had been more casual than McCarthy, but he didn't break the pattern. Stengel did. For the old guard, he was in the truest meaning of the term a culture shock.

Stengel could not help but be aware of the antagonistic feelings toward him, but he said nothing and went to work. The previous autumn, after Casey had been named manager, Weiss fired the three coaches who had worked under Harris and hired three new ones: Jim Turner, who had pitched for Stengel in Boston; Bill Dickey, the renowned old Yankee catcher who had been for a brief time the team's manager; and Frank Crosetti, longtime Yankee shortstop whose playing career had ended the year before. Stengel was high on Turner, who had managed against him in the Coast League, and Weiss was all for him, too. Turner had pitched three years for the Yankees during the war, knew his way around the Yankee operation and provided Weiss with a backup manager in case something went wrong and Stengel had to be replaced. Weiss' selection of Dickey and Crosetti was shrewd; longtime favorites who had played on Yankee pennant winners as far back as 1928 (Dickey) and 1932 (Crosetti), they provided a strong link to Yankee tradition that Stengel and Turner didn't have.

Casey kept a low profile during the off-season. He went to the winter meetings in Chicago in December but made little stir, even when Weiss swung a major trade by giving the St. Louis Browns $100,000 and a few lesser players for starting pitcher Fred Sanford. While Weiss kept himself busy, releasing this player, acquiring that one, promoting those minor-leaguers, Stengel's name was seldom mentioned. When Casey came east from Glendale at the end of January for the New York baseball writers' annual dinner, he met one day with a few of the writers covering the

Yankees. He was serious, evasive, noncommittal. He made no quips. He said, "I've been hired to win, and I think I will. There is less wrong with the Yankees than with any club I've ever had." He said he'd meet with his coaches about five days before the first day of spring training to discuss plans. When asked about rules of discipline for the team, he avoided a direct answer. "If you have men who make you set rules, then you have rules," he said. "If they don't need rules, then you don't have to make rules."

The Yankee camp opened on March 1 in St. Petersburg. Casey spoke to the squad and then broke it into several groups. Turner took the pitchers. Dickey talked to the catchers. Crosetti had the infielders. Johnny Neun, who had managed the club briefly in 1946 and now functioned as a scout and minor-league manager, worked with the several first basemen in camp (the veteran George McQuinn had been released during the winter, and the Yankees needed a new man at the position). DiMaggio and Tommy Henrich gathered the outfielders together.

Nothing like this had ever been seen in a Yankee camp before, and there was considerable skepticism among the sportswriters and some of the players about the "seminar" type of instruction, not just for rookies but for veterans, too. Stengel defended it. "I don't see how the players can fail to be helped by having the right people teach them," he said. "By God, I would have loved to have had a player of DiMaggio's skill show me how to play ball when I was a youngster. Look at him out there. He's showing them how to get started on a ball. That's wonderful. You can't tell me that's not gonna help."

Stengel instituted two-a-day workouts, not as strenuous as that sounds. The players worked for an hour and a half in the morning, broke for a light lunch in the clubhouse and then put in another hour and a half in the afternoon. But on the second day of training DiMaggio was absent from the morning session. The previous November, Joe had had an operation for a bone spur in his right heel at Johns Hopkins Hospital in Baltimore. He had worn a cast until January, but the heel seemed all right when he arrived in camp. Now, after the first day's workout, DiMaggio was in such pain that it was decided he'd better fly up to Baltimore and have the doctors look the heel over.

He returned in a day or so and remained with the club through March. His heel still pained him, but late in the month he began playing a little, although seldom appearing in two games in succession. Meanwhile, Stengel was studying his squad, learning all he could about it, moving players in and out of the exhibition-game lineups seemingly at random. He told a friend, "I never had so many good players before," and later elaborated this into a gag: "I'm with a lot of real pros. When I think of some of those other teams I had, I was wondering whether I was managing a baseball team or a golf course. You know what I mean — one pro to a club."

He was constantly evaluating, discovering inadequacies, locating strengths. He knew he had a splendid pitching staff. Allie Reynolds, Ed Lopat and Vic Raschi were three superb starters. Behind them were Shea, trying to overcome a sore arm; Sanford, the acquisition from the Browns; Tommy Byrne, a wild fast young left-hander; and Bob Porterfield, the prize of the Yankee farm system, who had joined the club late in 1948. In the bullpen was the redoubtable Joe Page, hero of the Yankees' 1947 pennant drive.

The pitching was very solid, but elsewhere the lineup was shaky, particularly now that DiMaggio was at least temporarily out of the picture. There were some distinguished names on the squad: Charlie Keller, a longtime Yankee hero, in the outfield; George (Snuffy) Stirnweiss, who had won the American League batting title four years earlier, at second base; Rizzuto at shortstop; Henrich, who had played almost fifty games in McQuinn's place at first base the year before, in right field.

The tiny Rizzuto was a tower of strength at shortstop, and Henrich seemed as valuable as ever, both at bat and in the field. But Keller, hampered by injuries, was not the player he used to be, and neither was Stirnweiss. Even so, when the Yankees began playing exhibition games, Stengel, deferring to tradition, had Keller in left field and Stirnweiss at second base.

He had a number of capable outfielders, beyond DiMaggio, Henrich and Keller, but he shied away from making any one of them a "regular" in DiMaggio's absence, even for the time being, as though not wanting to challenge the tradition of the DiMaggio-Henrich-Keller outfield. Instead, he played them irregularly, moving them in and out, testing them in the different outfield positions: Johnny Lindell, a cheerful, playful veteran; Gene Woodling, the 1948 Pacific Coast League batting champion, whom the Yankees had purchased; Hank Bauer, in his first full season with the Yankees, a determined ex-marine with "a face that looked like a clenched fist"; Cliff Mapes, a big young fellow who had joined the team a season earlier. Lindell and Bauer batted right-handed, Woodling and Mapes left-handed. Casey liked that balance. He had it at third base, too, where right-handed-hitting Billy Johnson shared the duty with left-handed-hitting Bobby Brown. "I might do what Bucky Harris did," Stengel said, "and play Johnson against lefties and Brown against righties."

He admired the fielding of a handsome young rookie infielder named Jerry Coleman and used him frequently at second base, although still deferring to Stirnweiss as the regular there. First base and catching were widely recognized as the Yankees' two trouble spots, and there were several players working at each position. Babe Young, a veteran former National Leaguer, was one of the first basemen, but the others were rookies: Dick Kryhoski, Jack Phillips (who had played a few games for the Yankees in 1947 and 1948), Joe Collins, Fenton Mole. Casey had Johnson, the third baseman, play a game or two at first base just to familiarize himself with the position, in case sometime he might be needed there.

There were five catchers in camp: Gus Niarhos, the nominal firststringer, Ralph Houk, Charlie Silvera, Hank Foiles and Yogi Berra. Berra, only twenty-three, had caught seventy-one games the year before, but he had played almost as many games as an outfielder. Berra could hit, that was obvious, but everyone joked about him as a fielder. The exhibition-game lineups seemed to indicate that Niarhos would be the number-one catcher again, but Casey liked the way Berra did things on the field, and he asked Dickey to work closely with him to see whether Yogi could be developed into an acceptable receiver behind the plate.

The first day they worked together, Dickey told Berra four things that he was doing wrong, but was encouraged by Berra's surprising ability and by his willingness to listen and learn. "Yes, he *can* become a catcher," Dickey told Stengel, and he and Berra went to work. "Bill is learning me all his experiences," Berra said cheerfully, and the sportswriters added that to the stream of Yogi-isms, some real ("You can observe a lot by watching"), some manufactured ("Nobody goes there anymore, it's too crowded"), that they fed to their readers over the years. The writers and the older players had already typed the squat, homely Berra as a good-hit, no-field comic figure. The veterans on the team made Berra the butt of much of their broad humor, although Lopat said that some of the ribbing Yogi took was a form of teaching. "Yogi hit a short pop fly to center that dropped in, and he half trotted to first and got a single," Lopat said. "The next man hit a grounder, and Yogi was forced at second. Then there were two fly balls that ended the inning. Charlie Keller said to Yogi, 'You feeling all right?' Yogi said, 'Yeah, why?' Keller said, 'You didn't run on that ball you hit. If you did you could have made it to second, and the ground ball and the fly ball would have scored you.' Henrich and Lindell jumped on him, too. Yogi looked over at DiMaggio, but DiMadge just gave him that icy stare."

Under Dickey's tutelage Berra developed rapidly. He had played more than 120 games in the outfield over the previous two seasons, but Stengel made him a full-time catcher (he didn't play the outfield at all in 1949), and he ripened into a fine one. Frank Graham said that Casey had a tremendous influence on Berra's development. And, Graham wrote, "Casey did more than that for Yogi. Aware, as no one before him had been, that here was a truly sensitive young man who was hurt by many of the quips made about him, yet had the guts to smile through them, Casey acted as a buffer between Berra and those on his own club who poked fun at him. It wasn't long before the slower thinkers among the Yankees gained a realization of what Yogi meant to them." In time, everyone came to recognize Berra's rare skills as a ballplayer (he won the Most Valuable Player award three times) and said nice things about him. "But it is simple justice," Graham wrote, "to point out that Casey said them first."

In April, as the Yankees began a circuitous barnstorming trip home to New York, DiMaggio tried to play every day. He went seven innings in one game, but only two the next day and two the day after that. The Yankees were in Fort Worth, Texas, when he gave up. The pain in his heel was agonizing, and he left the club again to return to Johns Hopkins. This time DiMaggio stayed there, but the heel continued to pain him and there was no indication of when, if ever, he'd be able to return to the lineup.

The Yankees played an exhibition game against the Dodgers in Ebbets Field a couple of days before the regular season began. Grantland Rice, talking with Stengel and a group of sportswriters before the game, laughed and said, "Casey, you're lucky. DiMaggio's injury is a break for you. With DiMaggio healthy, everyone would expect you to win the pennant. With DiMaggio hurt, you can finish fifth and everyone will say what a great job you did." Stengel didn't laugh at Rice's little joke.

DiMaggio's was the big injury, but Casey had other worries. There had been a succession of hurts and ailments all spring. Young Porterfield, who had pitched a no-hitter and a one-hitter in spring training, tore a muscle in his throwing arm in Ebbets Field just before the season began. Then Keller pulled a muscle in his side in batting practice on opening day. Lopat, the opening-day pitcher, showed up with a severe headache but thinking of all the ills the team had endured joked, "This is the first time all spring I've felt normal." In a preseason poll the Red Sox were an overwhelming favorite to win the pennant, with the Yankees third. Red Smith picked them to finish fourth.

Casey was nervous, fidgety and grim before the opening game, but after it he felt a lot better. Lopat beat Washington 3–2 as the Yankees came from behind to win. Berra pinch-hit in the seventh inning (Casey very cautiously started Niarhos behind the plate and Stirnweiss at second and would have started Keller in left if he hadn't been injured), and Yogi drove in two runs to tie the score; Henrich hit a home run in the last of the ninth to win it.

The next day Raschi shut out the Senators 3–0. Henrich hit a homer and a triple. Berra caught. Stirnweiss had hurt his hand bunting in the opening game, and Coleman was at second base. The Yanks won again the next day and were alone in first place. They went up to Boston and beat the Red Sox two out of three, and a few days later beat them two more times in Yankee Stadium.

They kept on winning, Coleman playing regularly, Berra doing most of the catching, Kryhoski and Phillips, the rookie first basemen, sharing that job and each hitting over .300, Johnson and Brown alternating at third base. Henrich was in right field every day, but Stengel moved his other outfielders, Bauer and Lindell, Woodling and Mapes, in and out of the lineup depending on the pitcher. In May (for the first time, as far as I can determine), Harold Rosenthal of the *New York Herald-Tribune* used the term "platooning" to describe what Stengel was doing. The term came from football, where the once rigid rules on player substitutions had been relaxed a few years earlier, allowing coaches to develop "platoons" of defensive and offensive specialists. It came to be called two-platoon football, and Rosenthal wrote that Stengel was "two-platooning" his outfielders.

DiMaggio, meantime, was still *hors de combat.* Late in May he worked out for the first time in almost two months, but the experiment was a failure. The pain was still there. The Yankees were getting good pitching and surprisingly strong hitting and kept winning without DiMaggio, but late in June the hitting surge slackened and so did the team's winning pace. Stengel's young first basemen showed little power, and Casey had Johnson play a few games there before bringing Henrich in from right field to take over. The team was still leading the league, but it was flattening out. The Red Sox finally shook off a perplexing early-season slump and had won twelve of sixteen games when the Yankees went to Boston late in June for three games in Fenway Park, where the Sox were almost unbeatable. (They won sixty-one games and lost only sixteen in Fenway in 1949.)

DiMaggio had begun working out by himself again and reported that his heel felt much better. On Monday night, June 27, in a benefit exhibition game between the Yankees and the Giants in the Polo Grounds, he made his first appearance since spring training and played nine innings in center field. It seemed likely he'd be in the Yankee lineup the next night in Boston for the opening of the three-game series with the Red Sox, but it was by no means certain. How Joe's heel felt would be the key. Go at your own pace, Stengel had told DiMaggio. "Just tell me when you're ready," he said, and to others, "When Joe feels he's ready I'll put him in the lineup."

DiMaggio didn't take the train to Boston with the team but flew up later by himself. Casey still didn't know whether DiMaggio would feel like playing, but Joe was thinking of that left-field wall in Fenway Park. Looking back, he said, "I knew I was going to play. I wasn't going to give that Boston ball park up. We were only going to play there one more time that year."

From the airport he went directly to Fenway, put on his uniform and sat down in the dugout. Casey was sitting on the bench talking with reporters, who were after him for his starting lineup.

"I can't give you the lineup yet," Stengel said. He glanced over at DiMaggio, who was bent over tying his shoes. Joe said nothing, and Casey went on chatting with the reporters, his eyes still fixed on DiMaggio. Finally DiMaggio straightened up and nodded his head.

"*Now* I can give you the lineup," Stengel said, and DiMaggio was in it. It was his first official appearance of the year. He had missed sixty-five regular-season games.

There was an overflow crowd in Fenway that night when DiMaggio came to bat in the second inning. "I just couldn't seem to get around on the ball," he said. "My timing was off. I kept fouling pitches off to right field, but each time I fouled one I got around on the ball a little more. Finally, I hit one over the shortstop's head for a single."

The Yankees didn't score that inning, but they took a 3–0 lead in the third. When DiMaggio came up again an inning later he hit a two-run homer over the left-field wall to make it 5–0. The Red Sox came back with four runs, but DiMaggio's homer was the margin of the Yankees 5–4 victory.

The next afternoon the Red Sox shot ahead and had a 7–1 lead going into the fifth inning. DiMaggio came to bat with two men on and two out and hit a three-run homer. Woodling doubled home three more in the seventh to tie the game, and DiMaggio hit another homer in the eighth to put the Yankees ahead 8–7. They scored once more in the ninth to make the final score 9–7.

In the third and last game of the series, on June 30, the Red Sox scored first. The Yankees tied it 1–1 in the third and made it 3–1 in the fourth. The Red Sox scored a run in the fifth to close it to 3–2 and the score stayed that way until the seventh. Then, with two men on, DiMaggio swung at a three-and-two pitch and hit another homer, a tremendous poke off a light tower above the left-field wall, to break the game open, 6–2. The Red Sox scored what could have been the tying run in the bottom of the inning, but the Yankees won the game 6–3.

DiMaggio had put on an absolutely extraordinary performance. After not playing one inning all season he hit four home runs in three games, batted in nine runs, caught thirteen balls in the outfield, lifted Yankee morale immeasurably and shattered the Red Sox. Boston plunged into an eight-game losing streak, culminating in the loss of a double-header to the Yankees in New York on July 4 that left the Red Sox in fifth place with a record of thirty-five wins and thirty-six losses, twelve games behind the Yankees.

Stengel was four and a half games in front of the field, and even though more than half the season remained the Yankees seemed to have the pennant neatly in hand.

It wasn't that easy. Joe McCarthy, who was managing Boston now, rallied his team and set out after the Yankees again. By the end of July the Sox were eight games behind, by the end of August three games. DiMaggio continued to hit (.346 that season) and the Yankees were winning steadily enough, but the Red Sox were blazing.

Weiss and Stengel agreed that they needed more power in the batting order, and on August 22, Weiss found it. Through the machinations of baseball's complex waiver system he bought the veteran Johnny Mize from the Giants. Mize gave the Yankees an impressive lefthanded home-run hitter to complement DiMaggio's right-handed power, and he filled the hole in the lineup at first base, which let Henrich go back to his natural position in right field. "Pennant insurance," Yankee supporters said smugly. "*Buying* a pennant!" scolded everybody else. When DiMaggio sat out a game with a slightly sprained shoulder, Mize batted fourth in Joe's place and a day or so later hit a two-run homer off Bob Feller to help beat the Indians. With DiMaggio and Mize and Henrich in the middle of the order the Yankees looked unbeatable.

But three days after Mize's homer off Feller the unbeatable team ran into disaster. In the first inning of the first game of a doubleheader in Chicago, Henrich hit an outfield wall chasing a fly ball and fractured two ribs. In the first inning of the second game, Mize fielded a bunt, dived at first base in an effort to beat the runner, tagged it in time but fell heavily and suffered a shoulder separation — six days after joining the team. Both were sidelined indefinitely.

Three weeks later, in mid-September, DiMaggio complained of chills and fever during batting practice and was sent home with viral pneumonia. Despite his painful ribs, Henrich climbed back in uniform and on September 23 played first base in both ends of a doubleheader. Stengel had high regard for Henrich, whose dependable play had earned him the nickname "Old Reliable" and who combined skill and toughness on the field with a mature attitude off it. "He's a fine judge of a fly ball," Casey said. "He fields grounders like an infielder. He never makes a wrong throw. And if he comes back to the hotel at three in the morning and says he's been sitting up with a sick friend, he's been sitting up with a sick friend."

Mize was back in uniform too, but he was unable to throw and Stengel could use him only to pinch-hit. A week before the end of the season, DiMaggio was still at home, too ill to come to the ball park. Yet the Yankees still held a two-game edge when they went to Boston for their last two games of the year in Fenway Park. This time the Red Sox walloped them, beating them on Saturday and again on Sunday to throw the pennant race into a flat tie, the first time since the third day of the season that the Yankees had not held first place by themselves.

The next day, Monday, September 26, the two teams came back to New York to play a makeup game in Yankee Stadium. Still without DiMaggio, the Yankees opened up a 6–3 lead and took it into the eighth inning, with Page pitching in relief. In the top of the eighth the first Red Sox batter singled and the second one walked. Dominic DiMaggio, Joe's brother, hit a line drive directly over Rizzuto's head. Phil leaped and touched the ball but it tipped off the fingers of his glove and rolled into left field. If it had been an inch or two lower Rizzuto might have turned it into a triple play, since both Red Sox runners were well off base. As it was, the man on second scored and the man on first went to third. The score was 6–4, two men on, no one out. Johnny Pesky hit a ground ball to Stirnweiss at second (Mize had batted for Coleman in the fourth inning) that looked like a double-play ball, but Stirnweiss bobbled it. Another run scored, making the score 6–5. There were still two men on base with no one out.

Williams, up next, hit a vicious ground ball to Henrich's right which Tommy tried for and missed, but Stirnweiss, behind him, fielded it cleanly and would have had Williams out at first base except that Page failed to come over from the mound to take the throw. Bases loaded now, still no one out. Vern Stephens hit a long fly to right, scoring the man from third to tie the game and moving Pesky from second to third. McCarthy called for a squeeze. Bobby Doerr, the batter, bunted deep along the first-base line as Pesky raced toward home. Henrich was just a trifle hesitant fielding the ball and his throw to Ralph Houk, who was catching (Berra was on the bench with a damaged thumb), was just slightly to Houk's right. Houk caught the ball, whirled and put the tag on Pesky as he slid across the plate. The umpire, Bill Grieve, cried "Safe!" the Red Sox were ahead, and Houk went into one of the wildest tantrums ever seen on a ball field. His cap and mask off, his blond hair awry, his face beet-red with fury and frustration, he bounced up and down in circles screaming his objections to the call. Stengel came running out of the Yankee dugout. Page flung his glove angrily. The Yankees crowded around the plate as Houk and Stengel raged at Grieve, who stood his ground calmly. Peace slowly returned. Grieve threw neither Houk nor Stengel out of the game, nor Page for violating the peace by throwing his glove. "You don't like to put players out of an important game like this one," Grieve said. The Yankees failed to score in the eighth and ninth; the Red Sox won 7–6 and took sole possession of first place.

After the last out, as Grieve and the other umpires made their way past the Yankee dugout toward their dressing room, Mapes, the big, young outfielder, yelled at Grieve, "How much did you bet on the game, you son of a bitch?" Mapes was fined for the remark and ordered by the American League to apologize publicly or face indefinite suspension. Stengel and Houk were also fined. It was the first time all year that the usually bellicose

Stengel had lost his temper on the field. Grieve said, "I called it right. Houk did not have home plate blocked and Pesky was safe without a question." Pesky said, "Houk was a little slow coming around with the ball, and I slid under him." Cal Hubbard, chief of American League umpires, said scornfully, "How can a team that walks a man, makes an error and fails to cover first base blame the umpires for losing?"

But the adverse call, the furious argument, the fines and the threatened suspension served a purpose. The slipping Yankees, instead of pondering three straight losses to the Red Sox, felt that they had been jobbed. They were angry more than they were upset. The defeats were a mistake. *They* deserved to be in first place. They won their next two games while Boston was splitting two and regained a tie for the lead. DiMaggio, ten pounds lighter, was back in uniform, taking batting practice. Even a defeat on Friday while the Red Sox were winning didn't bother them, though the Red Sox were ahead again, with only two games left in the season.

"Well, that puts it up to us to show if we're a good ball club," Stengel said. He was a game behind, but the last two games were with the Red Sox in Yankee Stadium. He had

Reynolds and Raschi ready, and DiMaggio said he was going to play. If the Yankees won both games they'd win the pennant; if they lost just one, the Red Sox would win.

Reynolds, who started the first game on Saturday, was off form. He gave up a run in the first inning and in the third he walked three men and gave up another run on a single to right. The bases were loaded, there was only one out and the Yankees were already behind 2–0. Stengel couldn't afford to wait to see if Reynolds could pitch his way out of the jam. He took an impressive gamble and called in Page, the relief ace, even though it was only the third inning. Casey's reasoning was that it was a ninth-inning situation. He needed a stopper, right now.

At first the gamble looked terrible. Page walked the first man he faced, forcing in a run, and then walked the next man — on four straight pitches — to force in another run. Some stopper. The Red Sox now led 4–0, still had the bases loaded, still had only one out. But Page was throwing the ball hard, and Casey stayed with him. He was his best bet, really his only bet. Page settled down, got out of the inning and gave up only one hit the rest of the way in six and two-thirds innings of relief.

And the Yankees came back. DiMaggio doubled to start a two-run rally in the fourth and he singled during another two-run rally in the fifth that tied the score 4–4. Now, with Page pitching beautifully, the Yankees felt solid. Stengel had Lindell (a right-handed batter) in the lineup because Mel Parnell (a left-hander) was pitching for the Red Sox, and even after McCarthy replaced Parnell with Joe Dobson (a right-hander), Stengel stayed with Lindell instead of switching to a left-handed hitter. He had Mapes on the bench (Cliff had apologized), but he had to hold Mapes in reserve in case DiMaggio, who was still weak, couldn't finish the game in center. So much for platooning: Lindell hit a homer off Dobson in the eighth to put the Yankees ahead, and when Page closed out the Red Sox in the ninth the Yankees were tied with Boston for first place.

The showdown for the pennant came the next day, Sunday, October 2, the last day of the season. Rizzuto led off the game with a triple and scored to give New York a 1–0 lead, and the score stayed 1–0 through seven and a half innings. Raschi and Boston's Ellis Kinder, who had won twenty-five games that year, both pitched beautifully. In the top of the eighth McCarthy removed Kinder for a pinch hitter, and in the bottom of the eighth Henrich led off the inning with a home run off Parnell, Kinder's replacement. DiMaggio hit into a double play, but the Yankees scored three more runs in the inning to take a 5–0 lead. The Red Sox fought back in the ninth, scoring three runs, two of them on a triple over the struggling DiMaggio's head. Joe called time after that play and slowly jogged to the bench, taking himself out of the game. But Henrich caught a foul fly for the last out, and Casey had his pennant. Bill Dickey leaped up in excitement at the last out and split his head against the concrete roof of the dugout. Red Patterson, the Yankees' publicity man, informed the press that Dickey's injury was the seventy-fourth disability suffered by the Yankees during their injury-ridden season.

In the celebration that followed, Stengel made himself heard long enough to say, "I want to thank all these players for giving me the greatest thrill of my life," and to his death it remained his greatest thrill. McCarthy, who had been part of so many Yankee pennant celebrations, worked his way through the crowd, shook hands with Stengel, and said, "You did a fine job, Casey."

The World Series against the Dodgers was

almost an anticlimax. Reynolds pitched a two-hit 1–0 shutout in the first game, which Henrich won with a home run in the last of the ninth, the first time a 1–0 Series game had been won with a homer since Casey did it in 1923. Raschi lost the second game 1–0, but then the Yankees ran off three straight to win the Series handily, although Page had to pitch five splendid innings of relief in the third game before the Yankees blew it open in the ninth.

Stengel had made his point: a pennant and the World Series in his first season. Back home in California, after the fuss and the fireworks calmed down, he was talking with Babe Herman, the old Dodger outfielder and a good friend.

"Babe," Case said, "I won one. I won one."

23 TAKING COMMAND: IT'S CASEY'S TEAM NOW

Phil Rizzuto said Casey was a changed man after winning the pennant. In 1950 he became loud and sarcastic, took too much credit for the good things the team did, criticized his players when things went wrong, got too chummy with the press. The subdued Stengel who had patched up his underrated 1949 team and held it together to win the pennant was gone and a garrulous, confident know-it-all had taken his place. "We'd have clubhouse meetings that would last an hour, an hour and a half," Rizzuto said, "and he'd talk the whole time. If you listened carefully there'd be something useful for everyone in there, but he confused a lot of players. Especially the younger ones."

And annoyed a lot of the players, especially the older ones. However, what Rizzuto saw as change seems to have been merely a reversion to type. It was in 1949 that Casey had been a changed man. In 1950 he was becoming himself again. Hell, he'd done it, hadn't he? He'd won a pennant. The baseball writers named him the manager of the year. When the 1950 All-Star Game took place in July, Stengel as manager of the American League champions would be the man directing his league's star players. He had shown what he could do. He had been shy, so to speak, in his first year with the Yankees, the new boy on trial, needing to make good. There is no point in conjecturing on what would have happened to him if he had lost one of those two games to the Red Sox at the end of the season and had blown the pennant at the wire after leading the race all season, but considering the old-guard attitude and Casey's lingering reputation as a clown, who knows if he could have held the club together another year? Second-guessing would have run wild. But he *had* won, he had proved what he knew to be the truth, that he was a good manager. Why act shy anymore? He had been feeling his way in 1949, paying proper respect to Yankee tradition, keeping a shopworn Stirnweiss and a damaged Keller in the lineup until their early-season injuries forced them out, deferring to DiMaggio despite Joe's attitude toward him. Now he didn't have to. The Yankees still weren't his team, not yet, but by God there was no question any longer that he was *their* manager. Lopat said, "By the last day of the 1949 season — we all knew by then that he was a marvelous manager." Not quite all. Rizzuto, for one, never came around to that point of view. "You or I," he told Peter Golenbock, "could have managed and gone away for the summer and still won those pennants."

Stengel must have had something to do with the pennant, but he knew as well as Rizzuto did that he won because of the players he had to work with and not because of some occult skill he had. He had finished in the second division too many times to fool himself about that. He made it clear at a dinner early in 1950 when he ran into Billy Meyer, the Pittsburgh manager. Meyer was about Casey's age, had broken into the majors at about the same time and had a distinguished record as a minor-league manager. He took over the last-place Pirates after the 1947 season, brought them home a spirited fourth in 1948, only two games out of second place, and was named manager of the year. But in 1949 the Pirates had slipped to sixth place, and Casey said, "Billy, what I can't understand is how I got smart so fast, and you got so dumb."

He had no illusions. He knew that winning a second pennant could be even more difficult than winning the first and that he had a lot of work to do. The Red Sox had been much the stronger team over the last three months of 1949, and in 1950 the sportswriters' poll again picked Boston to win the pennant. Stengel told his players at the beginning of spring training, "Last year is over. It's history. Forget it. There's no point in looking back. We gotta go out and beat 'em all over again this year."

He was more direct and forceful running the team. Rizzuto didn't like that, but Phil didn't worry Stengel, because Rizzuto was a follower, not a leader. He was a decent man and he always played his best, and Stengel had a sincere respect for his ability. As long as Phil played good ball for him, that was all that mattered. "Rizzuto is the greatest shortstop I ever saw," Stengel said. "He can't hit with Honus Wagner, but I've seen him make plays that old Dutchman couldn't."

Rizzuto was a strong point. Coleman, solidly ensconced at second, was another (Stirnweiss was traded away soon after the 1950 season began). So was the pitching, although there was a problem in the bullpen, where Page was losing much of his effectiveness.

The Johnson-Brown combination at third would do. Casey had Berra behind the plate, and Yogi would catch 148 games in 1950, coming into his own as one of the best players in the game. He had DiMaggio, healthy or reasonably so, in center field, and he had his platoons of outfielders on either side of Di-Maggio, although the cast was changing (Keller and Lindell had also been traded; the old guard was fading away).

The Yankees started slowly, then won several games in a row in May to move into contention. Boston played poorly again in the opening weeks of the season, and in June, McCarthy was out as manager. It became apparent that Detroit was the team Casey had to beat this time. He worried about first base, which was as much of a problem as it had been a year earlier. Mize's arm was still bad, and in May, John agreed to accept a demotion to the Kansas City farm club to work it back into shape. Henrich started the season at first base, but he had hurt his knee and was having so much trouble with it that after a month or so he was able to do little more than pinch-hit. Before the season was over, Henrich had retired, his career over. Stengel used Joe Collins at the position and in June got Mize back from Kansas City. DiMaggio, meanwhile, had been a disappointment, hitting well below .300 and not fielding with the élan of his great years. Casey, his mind roving constantly over lineup possibilities, wondered about playing Joe at first base. He hesitated to approach DiMaggio directly, so spoke to Weiss, who spoke to Topping, who spoke to DiMaggio. Topping had been very considerate of Joe in salary matters, and in appreciation of past favors DiMaggio agreed to try first base. He played only one game there (photographers clustered around to take pictures), felt inept and out of place, was coldly angry with Stengel for causing him such embarrassment and firmly declined to try it again.

If DiMaggio was upset by the experiment, Stengel wasn't. "You're gonna make mistakes," he said. "You can't worry about them second-guessers." He made the thirty-seven-year-old Mize the regular starter at first base and John responded by hitting twenty-five home runs in ninety games. Casey eased the burden on Mize by using the younger Collins as a late-inning replacement in nearly every game Mize played.

To fill the gap left by Page's decline, Weiss traded for Tom Ferrick and Joe Ostrowski, a pair of relief pitchers from St. Louis, and before the next season began Page was gone. Casey didn't miss him. He admired Page's ability but he didn't much like him, despite the fine work Joe had done for him in 1949. Page was a manager's bane, a night person with a cavalier attitude toward authority — except, significantly, the unspoken authority DiMaggio exerted. Page was DiMaggio's aide, so to speak, his personal trouble-shooter (a role that Billy Martin filled for a season after Page left the club). Page's admiration for DiMaggio was as high as his loathing for Stengel was deep. When he was released he blamed Stengel for overusing him in 1949 (although Page had made just about as many relief appearances under Harris in 1947 and 1948) and said angrily, "He's nothing but a clown. He was a clown when he came and he'll be a clown when he goes." Stengel remembered Page's off-field exploits, his failure to cover first base in the crucial game with the Red Sox late in 1949, and other things.

Stirnweiss, Keller, Lindell, Henrich, Page . . . the cast was changing, and Stengel was gaining more and more control. When DiMaggio continued to slump, Stengel dropped him to fifth in the batting order below the booming Mize, a blow to DiMaggio's pride because Casey hadn't consulted him first. Nor did Casey talk things over with Joe before announcing in mid-August that DiMaggio would take several days off "for a rest." It was the first time in his distinguished career that DiMaggio had ever been benched for weak hitting. When he returned to the lineup six days later he was a changed man. Whether he needed the rest or came back to the lineup fired with fury at Stengel for benching him, DiMaggio began hitting again and was his old sensational self through the last weeks of the campaign. He batted over .370 during that period, hitting home runs, winning games, lifting his average above .300 for the season and winning the league's slugging-percentage title. Rizzuto, fielding spectacularly, batted .324 and won the Most Valuable Player award. The Yankees, still pursuing the Tigers, caught them in mid-September and won the pennant by three games.

But DiMaggio's feelings for Stengel, never warm, turned decidedly colder in 1950. Joe was famous even among his good friends for his silences, long periods when he'd hardly speak, defeating all attempts at conversation. He turned this chill on Stengel, barely acknowledging the manager's presence. The sportswriters assumed that DiMaggio had been insulted when Stengel experimented with him at first base and later benched him, and they asked Casey about it. Casey waved it off.

"So what if he doesn't talk to me?" he said. "I'll get by, and so will he. DiMaggio doesn't get paid to talk to me and I don't either. He's getting paid to play ball and I'm getting paid to manage. If what I'm doing is wrong, my bosses will fire me. I've been fired lots of places before."

Stengel never directly criticized DiMaggio and, indeed, always said that Joe was far and away the best player he ever managed. But he saw the deterioration in DiMaggio's skills, and he was strong enough now not to have to pretend to ignore it. Whether he was responsible for DiMaggio's late-season revival or not, he was doing the things he felt he had to do to strengthen his ball club. The departure of the old guard was making room for new young players. One was Martin, who had joined the Yankees that spring. Billy didn't play very much — he was sent down to Kansas City for a while during the season — but he was there, noisy and cocky in the Stengel tradition. In midseason there was another newcomer, a chunky, red-faced, blond-haired left-handed rookie pitcher named Ed

Ford, nicknamed Whitey. Ford did some relief pitching, then started a game and won it, started again and won, and reeled off nine straight victories before incurring his one defeat of the year.

Again, the World Series was anticlimactic. The Philadelphia Phillies had won the National League pennant for the first time in thirty-five years, and the Yankees were expected to overwhelm them — and did, in four straight games. Philadelphia's strong pitching stopped the Yankee hitters, holding the New Yorkers to only six runs in the first three games, but New York's pitching smothered the Philadelphians, who scored only three runs in the entire Series before a Yankee error with two out in the last inning of the last game gave them two more.

Raschi pitched a 1–0 shutout in the first game, Reynolds won the second 2–1 when DiMaggio hit a game-winning home run in the tenth inning, Lopat and Ferrick combined to take the third game 3–2, and young Ford had a 5–0 shutout in the ninth inning of the fourth game when Woodling lost a fly ball in the low autumn sun gleaming over the lip of the Yankee Stadium roof. If Woodling had caught it the game would have been over and Ford would have had his shutout, but two runs came in, and when another base hit brought the tying run to the plate, Casey took the rookie out of the game, to the great displeasure of the crowd, which wanted Ford to stay in and complete the game. They booed Stengel when he went to the mound to replace the youngster with the veteran Reynolds.

As Casey came from the dugout he did a mocking pantomime of Woodling staggering under the fly ball, a curious performance that angered some people as much as it amused others. Woodling resented it and said so, although he and Stengel always got along well enough (the outspoken Woodling wasn't afraid to tell Casey off now and then, and Casey never seemed to mind it too much). But that he could openly criticize one of his own players before a crowd of nearly 70,000 people demonstrated as nothing else had how far Stengel had come in two years in asserting his dominance over the ball club.

24 GROWING YOUR OWN: THE "INSTRUCTUAL SCHOOL"

Stengel's new position of strength and his urge to teach led the Yankees early in 1951 to accede to his request that they establish an instructional school for young players, to run for two or three weeks before spring training proper began. It was something Casey wanted, and Del Webb, not usually active in club affairs, backed him on it. The Yankees were training in Arizona that spring under a one-time-only exchange program with the Giants, who took over the Yankees' St. Petersburg base in Florida. Webb wanted to show off the team to his friends in the West, and he liked the idea of showcasing the Yankees' young prospects as well.

At Phoenix late in the winter the Yankees assembled about forty of their brightest young minor-league players and exposed them to the wisdom and knowledge of Stengel, his coaches and several other instructors,

447

among them Henrich. The "instructual school," as Stengel called it, was something new for the major leagues, an innovation rising out of the seminar training he had introduced at his first Yankee camp in 1949, and it proved to be a gratifying success. Three of the young players (Mickey Mantle, Gil McDougald and Tom Morgan) became Yankees that season, and several others (Tom Sturdivant, Bob Cerv, Bill Skowron, Andy Carey) followed along in later years.

The instructional school became a staple of Yankee spring training. In the mid-1950s Stengel boasted, "Everybody thought old Casey was a joke when the Yankees brought me in, and everybody thought it was a joke when old Case set up the instructual schools. Now everybody else is copying the schools. Only we're three years ahead of them." Mantle was the prize of the school, the nugget. Tom Greenwade, the Yankee scout who had discovered and signed Mantle, told a sportswriter, "I don't quite know how to put it but what I'm trying to tell you is that the first time I saw Mantle I knew how Paul Krichell felt when he first saw Lou Gehrig. He knew that as a scout he'd never have another moment like it. I feel the same way about Mantle."

Mantle was nineteen, a country boy from the northeastern corner of Oklahoma, near the Ozarks, a shortstop who had played two seasons in the low minor leagues and had displayed rare skill and power at bat. In the field, as a shortstop, he had been erratic, making more than a hundred errors in the 184 games he played during those two seasons. By comparison, Rizzuto made only fourteen errors in more than 150 games in 1950.

But Mantle's talents were so extraordinary that nobody worried too much about the errors. He was a switch-hitter who hit with breathtaking power from both sides of the plate, he had a powerful arm, and he ran with a speed that was almost unbelievable. In practice sprints among the players he not only won all the time, he ran away from everyone else.

"My God," Stengel said, "the boy runs faster than Cobb."

Weiss, as aware as Stengel was of Mantle's potential, was planning to send the youngster back to the minor leagues for further seasoning. The boy was only nineteen and there was plenty of time for him to mature, to learn, to develop. But Stengel wanted to keep Mantle with him on the big club. He was thinking of

John McGraw and Mel Ott. McGraw was in his fifties when one of his baseball friends sent Ott to the Giants when Mel was only sixteen. Ott was a prize, and McGraw nurtured him. Every baseball fan learned that McGraw refused to send Ott to the minors for fear that some inept manager down there would ruin the boy's splendid but unorthodox swing (Ott lifted his forward foot well off the ground as he prepared to swing). Ott sat on the bench next to McGraw for a year or two before becoming the National League's home-run king. He played for a dozen years after McGraw's death, and no one ever forgot that he was McGraw's boy.

Stengel wanted somebody like that. He could boast about teaching a Lopez, and a Martin could do all the things Stengel wanted done on a ball field, but Casey had never produced a great player who was his boy, as Ott was McGraw's. Now he had him — a youngster with Cobb's speed and Ruth's power, raw material with the potential to be the greatest player of all time, waiting to be taught by Stengel. Casey said to a friend, "Can you imagine what McGraw would say if he saw this kid?"

The first thing Stengel did was move Mantle from shortstop to the outfield. In later years he would talk about that with just a tinge of regret. Perhaps he was thinking that if Mantle had gone back to the minor leagues in 1951, still a shortstop, he might have developed in a couple of years of ripening into as fine a fielding shortstop as Berra was a catcher. "If I played him at shortstop," Casey would sometimes say, ruminating about radical changes in the Yankee lineup, "he'd be the best there of anyone except Wagner, and I'm going back forty years. You got to remember," he'd tell people, "that he came up as a shortstop and the only reason I switched him to the outfield was because I had Rizzuto and he'd have had to play three or four years in the minors before he could come up as a shortstop."

In 1951 Casey couldn't wait. He didn't need a shortstop. Rizzuto was at his peak, coming off his finest season. But DiMaggio was obviously near the end of the road, and there was plenty of room in the tangled web of Yankee outfielders for this talented kid. Weiss in his role as Yankee farm director had seen dozens of future stars slowly mature in the minors, and he still wanted to send Mantle down. But Stengel argued, and argued. As Weiss said once, "I suppose I have stayed up later and talked longer — or, rather, listened longer — with Casey than anybody else in baseball. He'd talk all night and if you weren't a baseball man you'd think the guy was crazy. But if you were a baseball man, well, by the time you finally got to bed — and the chances were he'd be sitting on the other bed still talking — you discovered you were really learning things. I mean, you'd quit second-guessing him."

Stengel wore him down, and Weiss gave in. Casey kept Mantle, who began surprising people in Arizona not just with his hitting, but, surprisingly, his fielding, too. He had such speed that he could outrun his mistakes, as baseball people say, and he caught up to fly balls other outfielders couldn't get near. And his arm was impressive. After Mantle threw a runner out at home plate Henrich said, "That's the best throw I ever saw."

As always, there were problems. Nine months before Mantle's eye-opening debut in the instructional camp, North Korean military forces had crossed the 38th parallel dividing North and South Korea and precipitated the Korean War. America was drafting men to beef up the peacetime army it had maintained after World War II, and while that draft wasn't the same kind of blanketing conscription that had taken place during the war, when the goal was total mobilization, it was pervasive enough. Ford had been drafted right after the 1950 season and was gone from the Yankees for two full years. Martin was drafted at the same time, although he was released six months later because of financial hardship — he supported his mother and his ailing stepfather. Mantle, too, seemed ripe for the draft, but he had a chronic form of osteomyelitis in his left leg and had been rejected by an Oklahoma draft board as physically unacceptable for military service. There was nothing remarkable in that. The armed forces avoided taking men with physical disabilities that they might have to assume medical responsibility for during the remainder of the man's life, in and out of service.

But this was wartime, and the superpatriots came out in force, demanding to know why Mantle hadn't been drafted. "If he's healthy enough to play baseball," went the argument, "he's healthy enough to carry a gun." One columnist, disparaging reports about Mantle's osteomyelitic leg, said, "What does osteomyelitis have to do with being 4-F? There's no rule that says he has to kick somebody in the war."

The criticism grew so heated that the Yankees asked the Oklahoma authorities to review Mantle's case. Late in spring training in 1951, as the Yankees made their way back to New York, Mantle went home to be reexamined. The doctors looked him over and came to the same decision: He was still 4-F, unsuitable for military service.

Mantle flew from Oklahoma to New York in time to join the Yankees for an exhibition game with the Dodgers in Ebbets Field on the Saturday before the season began. Casey put him in the lineup in right field and before the game walked with him to the outfield to show him the right-field wall, the same concrete barrier Casey had begun playing in front of in 1914, when Ebbets Field opened. He pointed out the cement bevel near the ground that could make a ball rebound oddly and described how a ball hitting the scoreboard above the wall could stop dead and drop straight down. Warming to his task, he said, "Now when I played out here . . ." and Mantle looked at him in astonishment. "*You* played out here?" he asked.

When Casey returned to the dugout he was laughing. "Boy never saw concrete before," he explained to the sportswriters. "I told him not to worry about it, that I never had no trouble with it and I played that wall for six years. He don't believe what I'm telling him.

I guess he thinks I was born sixty years old. They never believe we done anything before they did."

The season began. Again the sportswriters failed to recognize Stengel's club as the best in the league and picked pitching-rich Cleveland to win the pennant. They had good reason-this time for their doubts about the Yankees. DiMaggio wasn't DiMaggio any more. Page was gone and the new relief pitchers weren't worldbeaters. Ford was in the army. First base was still a mess, with Henrich retired and Mize getting on toward forty. There was no solidity in the outfield. Proof of the Yankees' shakiness was in Casey's use of rookies. He had Mantle in right field; he played Jackie Jensen, who had been with the club in 1950, in center whenever DiMaggio wasn't up to playing; he put McDougald at third base; he moved Morgan into the starting rotation. No, the Yankees did not look like a pennant-winning team.

However, Stengel wasn't playing his rookies out of desperation. Al Lopez said once that he thought Stengel's greatest asset was his willingness to gamble on young players.

"He took chances with kids," Lopez said, "and he won with them. McGraw was that way. He'd stick with a young guy and nurse him along. McGraw and Stengel were both very good with young kids. Casey would sit and talk to them by the hour. He never had any children of his own, so he had a lot to give them. Come to think of it, McGraw had no children of his own either. Just thirty years' worth of baseball teams."

Stengel was rebuilding as he was winning, and he wanted young players, and these were good ones. Mantle's talent was obvious. Morgan won nine games and lost only three in 1951. Jensen was a "golden boy" who had played football in the Rose Bowl and had appeared in the 1950 World Series with the Yankees (as a pinch runner), the first athlete to take part in both those sporting extravaganzas. The Yankees traded Jensen a year later, but he was good; he won the American League runs-batted-in title three times.

McDougald, tall, angular, red-faced, with an odd way of cocking his head to one side as though he had a wry neck, was an awkward-looking athlete but the kind of ballplayer Stengel loved. He had been an all-star second baseman in the Texas League the year before, but when Casey asked him in spring training if he could play third base, McDougald said he'd be glad to give it a try. He proved so adept at the position that the Yankees traded away Billy Johnson soon after the season began. McDougald batted .306, was named American League rookie of the year and pleased Stengel particularly because he could "execute." Stengel, in talking about "percentage baseball," said, "Percentage isn't just strategy. It's execution. If a situation calls for a bunt and you have a batter who can't bunt, what's the percentage of bunting?"

He wanted players who could do things, who could execute. McDougald could bunt, hit-and-run, punch the ball on the ground to the right side of the infield in order to advance runners from second and third, hit, hit with power (he had fourteen home runs in his rookie year), run bases, throw well. And he was versatile. He was Stengel's third baseman, second baseman and shortstop in different seasons, and he led the league in making double plays at each position. Of all the players Stengel managed in New York, none better exemplified the kind of team he was trying to develop than the talented, professional McDougald.

The Yankees started the season slowly again and dawdled while other clubs played with the league lead. The Chicago White Sox ran off fourteen straight wins and burst into first place. Chicago was still leading after the

All-Star Game but then folded quietly and finished fourth, seventeen games behind. Boston took over for a while and then gave way to Cleveland, which opened a three-game lead in August.

The Yankees, although they were behind, had been moving steadily along. There had been a few problems. Mantle looked good for a while, but he was too inexperienced to cope with big-league pitching and began to strike out with disheartening regularity — five times in one game. He began to display an explosive temper at his own shortcomings, hurling things around in the dugout, kicking things. In July, Casey gave up and let Weiss send the boy down to Kansas City to ease the pressure on him and bring his batting eye back. Mantle continued in his slump there and thought of quitting baseball and going home to Oklahoma. His father, who was dying of Hodgkin's disease, although Mickey didn't know it at the time, came up to Kansas City and talked to him and straightened him out. Mantle settled down, began to hit and was recalled to New York six weeks later.

Stengel's pitching remained strong in 1951 — he began putting Reynolds in as a relief pitcher in crucial spots as well as using him as a starter — but otherwise Berra and Rizzuto were his only constants. Coleman, who had hit well his first two seasons, slumped badly, and because Stengel felt he had to have more hitting, with DiMaggio no longer the force he had been, he benched Coleman, switched McDougald from third to second and put Brown at third full-time, ignoring for the moment Brown's inadequacy with the glove. "Brown looks like he's been a hitter for twelve years and a fielder for one," Stengel once observed. Sometimes he'd take Brown out late in the game, move McDougald back to third and put Coleman or occasionally Martin in at second.

He manipulated Mize and Collins and Johnny Hopp, a veteran acquired from the National League (more buying of pennants), at first base, although all three batted left-handed. Collins and Hopp could also play the outfield, if needed. When Rizzuto suffered a minor injury and was out for a few games, Coleman filled in at shortstop, and so did Martin, who also played a game at third. It was like a kaleidoscope. DiMaggio, having a depressing season, missed forty games because of one thing or another, yet only Woodling, who appeared in 116 games, played more often in the outfield than Joe.

Casey weaved DiMaggio and Woodling and Bauer and Mantle and Jensen and Mapes and Collins in and out of the outfield, game after game.

This was the season Stengel really began to get his reputation for platooning players, not just substituting because of injuries as he had in 1949 but shifting them in and out of the lineup for tactical and strategic reasons day by day, even inning by inning. Stengel recalled, "People said in 1949 what terrible luck we were having, all those injuries, but that was one of the luckiest breaks I ever got, because I had to use the men. If you've got a number of good men setting around on the bench you'll do yourself a favor playing them, because every time one of my front players got hurt I noticed the fella I stuck in his place would bust out with hits. Then just about the time he slowed down he'd oblige me by stepping in a hole and another fella would take his place and hit. I decided I'd never count on one player taking care of one position for an entire season. If you've got two or three men who can't play anyplace else pretty soon you're gonna run out of room for pitchers, and that's why you've got to have players who can do more than one thing."

This odd, seemingly improvised method of

managing worked, and when the Indians came into Yankee Stadium in the middle of September for two games, Casey's club was only one game behind. DiMaggio was batting 60 points below his career average but he hit a two-run triple as the Yankees beat Bob Feller to move into a tie for first place, and the next day with the score tied 1–1 in the eighth, Joe scored from third base on an electrifying squeeze bunt by Rizzuto, a play that Stengel still talked glowingly about twenty years later. He may not have been friends with DiMaggio and Rizzuto, but he certainly admired the way they played baseball. The run gave the Yankees the game and the lead in the pennant race, and they never relinquished it, winning their third straight championship by five games. They clinched the flag late in September on Allie Reynolds' second no-hit game of the season, the first time a pitcher had thrown two of them in the same year since Vander Meer's back-to-back no-hitters in 1938.

Reynolds almost lost the no-hitter. With two out in the ninth inning, Ted Williams lifted a high foul fly behind the plate that Berra dropped. Berra got behind the bat again, the admirable Reynolds threw another pitch, and Williams hit another foul. This time Berra, fiercely waving everyone else away, grabbed it for the final out, the no-hitter and the pennant.

In the National League the Giants had come from thirteen and a half games back in August to win the championship on Bobby Thomson's memorable home run, and they continued to play good ball in the Series, beating the Yankees handily in the first game, 5–1. That was the first time Stengel's Yankees had lost the opening game of a Series. They beat the Giants the next day, but it was a gloomy occasion for Casey and the Yankees. In the fifth inning Willie Mays, like Mantle a rookie that year, hit a soft fly ball to right center that both DiMaggio and Mantle ran toward. DiMaggio called, "I've got it," and Mantle stopped. But as he did he stepped on a drain hidden in the grass of the outfield and fell as though he'd been shot. DiMaggio ran over to help him after catching the ball, but Mantle was badly hurt. He had torn the tendons in his knee. He was taken to a hospital, where he was operated on, and he played no more that year.

The Giants won again the next afternoon, to put the Yankees behind again, and the way they did it upset Stengel. In the fifth inning with the Giants ahead by one run and Eddie

Stanky on first base, Berra called for a pitch-out and made a perfect throw to Rizzuto at second base in time to get Stanky, who had been running on the pitch. But as Stanky slid in, obviously out, he kicked the ball out of Rizzuto's glove. It rolled away onto the outfield grass and Stanky, safe after all, scooted on to third. Instead of two outs and no one on base, it was one out and a man on third. The Giants went on to score five times in the inning and won the game easily, 6–2. Stengel was now down two games to one, the Giants had a well-rested Sal Maglie, who had won twenty-three games in the regular season, ready for the next game, and Stengel had a tired Reynolds, who had lost the opener of the Series.

But a day of rain gave Reynolds the extra rest he needed and seemed to throw Maglie off form. And Stengel was growling at his players, "You don't have all season to catch these guys, you know. You have to beat them right now." DiMaggio, hitless the first three games, made six hits in twelve at bats in the last three, including a home run, the last one of his career. The Yankees hit Maglie hard and won 6–2, the next day romped to a 13–1 victory after McDougald hit a grand slam home run, and the day after that appeared to be closing out the Series when they went into the ninth inning with a 4–1 lead.

But the Giants filled the bases with no one out and had the winning run at the plate in Monte Irvin, their cleanup hitter and the National League's runs-batted-in leader. And Bobby Thomson was waiting to bat next. That's when Stengel surprised baseball purists by bringing in the left-handed Bob Kuzava to pitch to the right-handed-hitting Irvin. Kuzava had relieved only fifteen times for the Yankees that season, but Irvin, Thomson and pinch hitter Sal Yvars all flied out and the Yankees won.

"We did it! We did it!" shouted the excited Stengel. He knew what he had done, and it was more than just winning a World Series. He had won three pennants and three World Series in a row. If he could win the pennant again in 1952 he would tie McGraw's string of four straight set in the 1920s, which Joe McCarthy had matched a decade later. If he could win one more World Series he would tie McCarthy's record of winning four straight Series. It was no longer a matter of proving that he could manage. He was in fast company now.

25 FIVE FLAGS AND MICKEY: THE ONE DISAPPOINTMENT

Stengel's next two pennants, in 1952 and 1953, gave him all the satisfaction he thought he'd ever want from baseball. DiMaggio retired in December 1951, two months after the World Series, and Casey, in a way, was on his own at last. These were no longer the DiMaggio Yankees. They were *his* team now.

The sportswriters decided the Yankees were much weaker with DiMaggio gone and in 1952 for the fourth straight year picked another team, the Indians again, to win the pennant. Once more, this journalistic pessimism seemed logical. Mantle was still limping from the effects of his knee injury and subsequent operation. Coleman, a flying officer in the marine reserves, was waiting to be called into service in Korea. Brown, a medical student in the off-season, was also anticipating military service. Morgan was about to be drafted. Martin broke his ankle in spring training while demonstrating the proper method of sliding for a film crew making an instructional film. Berra was nursing a lesser injury. So was Collins. Raschi's knee was bothering him.

Most of all, there seemed to be no one ready to take DiMaggio's place. "Who's gonna hit the home runs now that Joe Di-Maggio's gone?" Stengel would intone, perhaps rhetorically, possibly mocking the sportswriters, more likely trying to motivate one of the young players — Mantle, Jensen, Bob Cerv — with the idea that the job was sitting there waiting for someone. No one seemed ready to take it. The sportswriters agreed that this was Casey's worst team with the Yankees.

Once the 1952 season began, though, things shook themselves into place. After Coleman departed, McDougald played second base. When Martin's ankle healed, Billy took over at second, the first time he'd held a regular position on the club, and McDougald moved back to third. Mantle played right field for a while, with Jensen in center, but in June, Jensen was traded to Washington for outfielder Irv Noren, and Mantle moved into center. Woodling usually played left field and Bauer right, with Noren alternating with either as Stengel saw fit. Reynolds had an impressive year on the mound, and Raschi, after missing a few starts, pitched beautifully. Lopat also pitched well, although he was not able to work as often as he had, and Stengel ended up giving starting assignments to fourteen different pitchers during the season.

Everything worked out nicely. Martin wasn't as smooth a fielder as Coleman, but he did a capable job, and his competitive fire — he twice became embroiled in fights with opposition players — kept the team awake. The Yankees moved into first place in June. Mantle didn't immediately blossom into another Ruth-Gehrig-DiMaggio, which disappointed a lot of people, but he played well enough, particularly the last six weeks of the season, and batted .311. His late hitting helped to stop the Indians, who mounted a determined late-season drive. Lopez, managing Cleveland, said he would have his three stars, Bob Lemon, Early Wynn and Mike Garcia, do all of the Indians' pitching — starting and relieving both — through the last weeks of the season in an effort to catch and pass the Yankees. Informed of Lopez's radical plan, Stengel stroked his chin and said, "Well, I always heard it couldn't be done, but sometimes it don't always work." Whatever that meant, it didn't work this time as the Yankees held off the Indians to win the pennant by two games, Casey's fourth in a row, and then beat the Dodgers in the 1952 World Series.

In 1953 the Yankees looked overwhelming — Ford was back, Mantle was well established in center, Martin was experienced at second base — and this time even the sportswriters picked them to win. McGraw had won four straight pennants and so had McCarthy, and so had Stengel. If he could win again in 1953 he'd surpass them both. (McCarthy had also won four straight World Series, and so now had Stengel. He could become top man there, too.)

Casey was confident. At a press luncheon in May 1953 he said, "The reason this club hasn't made a deal is why should we? When you got players good enough to win a pennant on the road and a World Series on the road, which is where they win the majority of their games and against a tremendous club like the Dodgers, which you know is a great ball club because, why, they have played us more games in the World Series than anybody ever since we been in the World Series for four years, then why would you want to change? If the players are good enough to win four years they should be good enough to win five." But he skittered away from any direct comment on the fact that five pennants in a row would be an unprecedented feat for a manager by saying, in his convoluted way, "There comes a time in every man's life at least once, and I've had plenty of them."

He handled his well-balanced club masterfully. As Ed Linn wrote, "With a full squad to work with, Stengel showed that the bench and the bullpen were just as important as the starting lineup. He demonstrated how games could be won by protecting even good hitters from pitchers who could exploit their one weakness, and by choosing the one best spot to exploit a weaker hitter's strength. It was Stengel who showed that your top pinch hitter should be wheeled in at the first opportunity to break the game open, instead of being husbanded until the late innings."

That is, if you get a foot in the door, shove with your shoulder. If the Yankees had a chance to score in the fourth or fifth inning he had no hesitation in sending Mize up to bat for Rizzuto in hopes of breaking the game open. Rizzuto hated that, hated being relegated to the bench in midstream game after game, but Stengel saw only logic in it. The Yankees had picked up Willie Miranda, a brilliant fielding shortstop who couldn't hit, and Stengel used him repeatedly as Rizzuto's backup man after pinch-hitting for Phil.

The Yankees tore the 1953 pennant race wide apart in June by winning eighteen straight games. Stengel was beside himself during the winning streak, haranguing his players, shouting at them, goading them, driving them. With the winning streak putting distance between him and his pursuers he milked the advantage for all it was worth. "Don't let 'em up!" he'd yell at his players. "Don't let 'em up!" And the Yankees opened a ten-game lead before the streak ended.

Casey had something else in mind during the winning streak. He could never forget McGraw, and he knew that McGraw still held the record for consecutive victories — his Giants won twenty-six in a row in 1916. Stengel wanted that record, or at least the American League record of nineteen straight, but the Yankees fell one short of the American League mark and then, as though physically and emotionally exhausted, did an astonishing turnabout and lost nine in a row. During the losing streak Casey grew surly with the press, finally barring reporters from the clubhouse after games, but paradoxically he was quiet and patient with his players. As it turned out, the slump didn't matter much. The Yankees reestablished their big lead and won easily by eight and a half games, Casey's fifth straight pennant, and again beat the Dodgers in the World Series.

The World Series victories over Brooklyn in 1952 and 1953 came a lot harder than Casey's three earlier Series triumphs. Those were the Dodgers of Jackie Robinson, Pee Wee Reese, Roy Campanella, Duke Snider, Carl Furillo, Gil Hodges, Billy Cox, Don Newcombe, Preacher Roe, Carl Erskine and so many other fine players, a mature, accomplished club that expected to win. In 1952 they beat Reynolds in the first game and after losing to Raschi in the second beat Lopat in the third. They were shut out by Reynolds in the fourth game but again came back to take the Series lead by beating the Yankees in eleven innings in one of the most extraordinary World Series games ever played. Erskine, who pitched the entire game for Brooklyn, allowed only one hit, a bunt, in ten of the eleven innings, but in the fifth inning he gave up five runs on a walk and four hits, including a three-run homer by Mize that put the Yankees ahead 5–4. After Mize's homer Erskine didn't allow another Yankee to reach base and won the game 6–5 on Snider's double in the top of the eleventh inning.

Stengel and the Yankees were behind three games to two, and the last two games of the Series were in Ebbets Field, the Dodgers' cozy home park. Stengel, unflustered, started Raschi and used precisely the same batting order he had against Erskine, except for inserting Noren in Bauer's place against Brooklyn's right-handed starter, Billy Loes. Raschi pitched seven and two-thirds innings and left the game in the eighth with a 3–2 lead, the tying run on second and two out. Reynolds, who had pitched his shutout only two days before, relieved Raschi. He stopped the Dodgers in the eighth and held them hitless in the ninth, and the Series was tied again, at three games apiece.

In the seventh game, Stengel used Lopat for three innings and Reynolds for three and with a 4–2 lead brought Raschi in to pitch in the seventh. But Vic was wild and uncertain, and the Dodgers loaded the bases with only one out, Snider coming to bat, Robinson on deck. A base hit would tie the game, a long hit would put Brooklyn ahead. Stengel crabwalked to the mound and waved for a relief pitcher. In came Bob Kuzava, the same inexplicable choice Casey had made a year earlier in a somewhat similar situation. Kuzava had not pitched at all in the 1951 Series against the Giants until the last inning of the last game, and this was his first and only appearance in the 1952 Series. He was left-handed and so was Snider, and Duke popped up for the second out, the bases still loaded. Robinson was right-handed, but the left-handed Kuzava got Jackie to pop up too. On Robinson's pop fly no one in the Yankee infield made a move to catch the ball as it began descending between the mound and first base. It wasn't the pitcher's play, so Kuzava stayed on the mound. Collins, the first baseman, should have handled it, but he had lost the ball in the glare and didn't move. Rizzuto at shortstop and McDougald at third, anticipating that someone else would handle the ball, made no serious move toward it. Berra, the catcher, still had his mask on at home plate. The Dodgers on base were running full tilt with two outs; two of them were already crossing the plate with the possible tying runs and the third was approaching home with the potential winning one.

For a sudden paralyzing moment it appeared that the ball would drop safely and the Dodgers would have the lead and probably the game and the Series, on a simple pop-up.

Then Martin, seeing what was happening, suddenly charged in and, his hat falling off, caught the ball at his knees for the game-saving, Series-saving out. The quiet, usually unobtrusive Kuzava stopped the Dodgers easily in the eighth and ninth, and for the second straight year this odd candidate for heroism walked off the mound with the World Series in his pocket.

The 1953 Series was not as dramatic. The Yankees won the first two games, the Dodgers the next two, the Yankees the final two. Martin had batted only .257 during the season, but in the Series he made two hits in four of the games and three in another, had a double, two triples and two home runs, batted in eight runs, tied the World Series records for hits with twelve and with his last hit drove in the winning run of the Series in the ninth inning of the sixth game. Mantle had two homers and seven runs batted in. McDougald had four RBIs. Berra hit .429. Stengel's team. He'd made his own heroes.

Five straight pennants. Five straight World Series. Now Stengel stood alone, beyond McGraw, beyond McCarthy, beyond everyone. How he savored that and how he wanted to be appreciated. "You know," he'd say, "John McGraw was a great man in New

York and he won a lot of pennants. But Stengel is in town now, and he's won a lot of pennants too."

With five victories in the bank, Stengel boasted in 1954 that the other clubs had better beat him now, because with the kids coming up through the Yankee farm system he might never lose again. And beat him they did, or at least one club did.

It was not that the Yankees played poorly; it was as though the imperative to win had gone. Maybe they missed Martin, who had been called back into the army, the authorities deciding that financial hardship was no longer a factor in his case. Or Rizzuto, who had slowed down badly — he hit only .195 in 1954 — and was being benched more often by Stengel. Or Raschi, who had held out too long and was abruptly sold by Weiss to the Cardinals at the beginning of spring training. The Raschi deal annoyed Casey, who hated to lose a pitcher of such talent, even though the talent was eroding. The volatile Stengel and the phlegmatic Weiss, an odd couple in any case, often disagreed about player transactions, but, as in the Raschi sale, Weiss' wishes prevailed more often than Casey's did.

At Cleveland, Lopez put together a pitching staff of transcendent skill. Maybe it wasn't a matter of imperative or Martin or Rizzuto or Raschi or anything else but simply that Lopez had a better team that year. Stengel derided the Indians, sneering at their infield, which consisted of three hitters and a shortstop and was probably the worst fielding unit ever to play on a pennant-winning team. The shoddy infield shook Stengel's sense of baseball propriety ("Them plumbers," he'd say), but the Indians could hit and they surely could pitch and they won 111 games, an American League record, and beat Casey to the pennant. Stengel tried — he never stopped trying — and the Yankees finished with 103 victories themselves, more than any of his pennant-winning teams had won, but he couldn't catch the Indians.

The fact galled him. He began fussing and fretting early in the season when it became apparent that Cleveland had one of the all-time great pitching staffs. "If I had Raschi I'd win this easy," he'd mutter, blaming Weiss. Or "I wish I had Martin," blaming the army. When he began to realize that the Indians weren't going to give way, as other teams he chased had, he called them names, questioning their courage, disparaging their ability, but he was blowing in the wind. In Baltimore at the end of July at a little party the writers accompanying the club gave in honor of his birthday, Stengel made an impromptu speech, the burden of which was that the Yankees were still going to win. A birthday cake was wheeled in as he was talking, and Casey, waiting to cut it with knife in hand, said, "If I don't win the pennant this year the owners should discharge me. I'm paid by the Yankees to win. If I can't do it they should get someone who can." Then he cut the cake.

"It's up to me," he said later. "This is where the manager comes in."

But the chase was futile. That year, 1954, after five seemingly endless years of Yankee dominance, a Yankee hater named Douglass Wallop wrote a comic fantasy called *The Year the Yankees Lost the Pennant* (on which the musical comedy *Damn Yankees* was later based). The little book became a big seller, particularly in Cleveland. Someone noticed a copy of it on Stengel's desk in the Yankee clubhouse and asked him what he thought of it.

"I ain't read it," he said. "Some guy sent it to me the other day and it's just been laying there ever since. It ain't a true story. It's fiction."

It was awfully hard for Stengel to accept the true story of what was happening around him. In September the Yankees were six and a half games behind, the farthest out of first place a Stengel Yankee team had ever been, but he dismissed that margin as unimportant. A Sunday doubleheader on September 12 was coming up in Cleveland, and on the train taking the Yankees there the night before the doubleheader Casey was still blustering. "We ain't dead yet," he said. "We're only six behind [Casey never bothered with halves]. We beat 'em twice tomorrow in Cleveland and we're only four out. Them plumbers die after that and we take it all."

Barking at the moon. In Cleveland an enormous crowd of 86,563 filled Municipal Stadium. (It's still the major-league record for attendance at a regular-season game. Only the 92,000-plus crowds at the three Dodger-White Sox World Series games in 1959 at the Los Angeles Coliseum were bigger.) The great mob rejoiced as Lemon and Wynn beat the Yankees twice, 4–1 and 3–2. Casey was so upset by the double defeat that he didn't even bother to dry himself off thoroughly after his shower but dressed hurriedly and left for his hotel.

The next morning he said, "I got a shock

when I looked at the standings. We could have been four games out. Instead we're eight. That frightens me." Asked after the season when he knew he had lost the pennant he said, "I never did. Well, after that double-header. We had no more games with them then."

The Yankees gathered in the lobby of the hotel Monday morning to leave for the train station. Several of the New York writers had received instructions from their papers to stay in Cleveland and do stories on the Indians in anticipation of the World Series. The Yankee road secretary saw them standing in the lobby and said, "Come on, you guys, you'll miss the train." One of the writers said, "Don't worry about us. We're staying. We're picking up the Indians."

Such desertion had never happened before to Stengel, who was used to sportswriters from other cities joining him as the Yankees raced toward the Series. He seemed genuinely shocked.

"You mean they ain't coming?" he asked. "Jesus, I'm losing my writers."

For all the anguish of losing, Stengel would not fault his team. "I never saw a club try as hard as this one did," he said a few days after the debacle in Cleveland. "The effort's been there all season." Then, bristling, he went on, "I defy anyone to say this team ain't worth a quarter. I don't want to blow up another club because the race is still going — and we get paid to win, not blow up other clubs — but Cleveland has played tremendous and we been trying to catch them, so how can you say we ain't worth a quarter?

"I ain't conceding," he said, "but they won because they got amazing pitching like I have never seen in six years in the league. And they was well managed. And they won those games from those other clubs, which makes me wonder why some of those other clubs that is always worrying about the Yankees this and the Yankees that don't get the idea and start worrying about themselves.

"I was surprised I lost," he said. "I didn't expect to lose. The fault was carelessness in all parts, including myself."

He *was* bitter about one player, almost irrationally so, and that was Mantle, who had not become the superlative figure Casey wanted him to be. Stengel said, "He's gotta change a lot. He's gotta change his attitude and stop sulking and doing things he's told not to do. He'll have to grow up and become the great player he should be when he reports next spring."

Casey could not accept the fact of Mantle's injuries, that his damaged legs (something was always wrong with them: ligaments, cartilage, muscles) hampered his ability. Stengel was impatient with Mantle's ailments, annoyed that they kept him out of games or slowed him down, as though the injuries were the boy's fault. Mantle had missed more than thirty games in the outfield in 1953 because of knee problems, and his average dropped off to .295 after his .311 season in 1952. After the 1953 season he had an operation on his knee, two operations as a matter of fact, and was supposed to follow a strict program of planned exercise and rest during the winter of 1953-54 to strengthen it. Instead he went hunting and fishing and fooled around on a basketball court, and the knee was still bothering him at the beginning of spring training. Mickey's immobility frustrated a plan Casey had to school him intensively in certain aspects of the game Casey felt he was weak in, although it is doubtful that he'd have had much luck teaching Mantle. Once when Mickey was having trouble with his bunting, Stengel arranged for Frank Crosetti, the coach, who had been a skillful bunter, to work with Mantle each day before practice. Crosetti showed up for the sessions but Mantle didn't. After three fruitless days the lessons were abandoned.

Stengel tried to get Mantle to hit down at the ball instead of always swinging big, trying for the seats. Stengel called that the "butcher boy," chopping down at the ball. Stengel figured that with Mantle's power and speed he'd pick up a lot of extra hits. Mantle kept on swinging big. Casey wanted him to control his swing in order to cut down on his strikeouts. Mickey led the league in striking out five times during the years he played for Stengel. Casey argued that with his strength Mickey could take a shorter swing and still hit as many home runs. Mantle listened but didn't change.

Stengel was frustrated. Here he was, a great teacher of baseball, and here Mantle was, an athlete with more potential than anyone else Casey had ever seen, and he couldn't teach him. "What's the good of telling him what to do?" he'd complain. "No matter what you tell him he does what he wants."

"I never learned anything," Mickey admitted to Bil Gilbert years later. He said it with a kind of amused ruefulness, with a note of affection for Casey and mock despair for his own intransigence.

Because Mantle was his special project,

Stengel's preoccupation with him was intense. But he was never able to understand Mantle's country shyness and stubbornness. With a Billy Martin, he could talk and teach and yell, and if Martin objected to something Billy would yell back and curse and show his rage and resentment. Once when Martin was fuming at something Stengel had done — lift him for a pinch hitter or whatever — Casey ambled along the bench and defused Martin's temper by saying, "Widdle Biwwy mad at me?" That kind of open back-and-forth was impossible with Mantle. Mickey had been devoted to his father, who died after Mantle's first major-league season, and it simply was not in his nature, his background, his breeding, to openly defy the authority figure that Stengel was. The defiance came silently, in not listening, in not paying attention, in not doing, like any intractable teenager.

Stengel was never able to teach Mantle because he was never able to reach him. It was a genuine father-son relationship, but it was an angry father and a stubborn son. Mantle took his temper out in throwing bats and kicking water coolers and in similar petty but annoying displays. One day he slammed something in the dugout after striking out, and Stengel pulled a bat out of the bat rack and handed it to him. "Here," he said, "why don't you bang yourself on the head with this?" Martin has been quoted as saying, "Once I saw the old man grab Mickey by the back of the neck and shake him hard when he did something the old man didn't like. He said, 'Don't let me see you do that again, you little bastard!' Can you imagine him doing that to Mickey?"

In 1954 the disappointment of losing spilled in Mantle's direction. Because of his long recuperation from the knee operation (reason enough in Stengel's mind for irritability), Mickey started off slowly, but he finished the season with twenty-seven home runs, 102 runs batted in and a .300 batting average, an exemplary season for most players. Stengel expected more, much more. He criticized Mantle roundly for not running out a ground ball one day in Chicago. "After all," he said in his best sarcastic growl, "all it means is a player running ninety feet, and if he can't hustle for ninety feet at the salaries they're paid these days something's got to be wrong." During the doomsday doubleheader in Cleveland, Stengel was annoyed because Mickey tried to bunt his way on against Early Wynn with a two-strike count against him; he fouled it off and struck out. The Yankees lost the game by one run. Mantle was a home-run hitter in Stengel's mind, and a home-run hitter doesn't bunt his way on when his team is only one run behind, not with two strikes he doesn't. In 1951 when Mantle was sent down to Kansas City for that month or so in mid-season, he bunted his first time or two at bat. The Kansas City manager, George Selkirk, took him aside and said, "We know you know how to bunt. You're not down here for that. We want you to swing the bat. We want you to get your confidence back." Three years later, against Wynn, he bunted. "You try to tell him something and he acts like you tell him nothing," Casey said.

Mantle was a source of frustration to Stengel not because he didn't become an outstanding player — he won the Triple Crown one year under Casey — but because he didn't become the greatest ballplayer ever. Stengel was getting old and didn't want to wait for Mickey. He wanted him to do it all now. Milton Gross wrote in 1954, "Mantle was to be the monument the old gent wanted to leave behind. Casey wanted his own name written in the record books as manager, but he also wanted a creation that was completely his own on the field every day, doing things no other ballplayer ever did, rewriting all the records."

Stengel's anger toward Mantle subsided with the years, and they got along well enough after Casey accepted the inevitable — that Mantle wasn't going to change. Possibly he came to the realization that even if his protégé hadn't developed into a combination of Ty Cobb and Babe Ruth he was still an exceptional ballplayer. But if he realized that, he never conceded it. When Stengel, after his departure from the Yankees, was asked in the time-honored tradition of baseball to pick his all-time all-star team, he had Berra on it and Rizzuto and DiMaggio, but not Mantle.

26 BECOMING A LEGEND: STENGEL THE PUBLIC FIGURE

Despite Casey's self-disparaging remarks over the birthday cake in July 1954, the Yankees did not "discharge" Stengel but gave him a new contract, which he promptly accepted. "I meant what I said back then and I still feel the same way," he said, "but I'm coming back for three reasons. I want to help rebuild this club, the money is right and the owners want me."

Stengel was in a new period of his life. No longer just a clown, he was becoming a Legend. Baseball had known him for forty years, but now the world was discovering him. He won pennants again in 1955, 1956, 1957 and 1958. He lost a dramatic World Series to Brooklyn in 1955, then beat the Dodgers in the Series of 1956. He lost to the Milwaukee Braves in the World Series of 1957, then came back to beat the Braves in the Series of 1958. With national television covering the

Series (and the annual All-Star Game, at which he seemed always to be one of the managers), he was continually onstage. Anecdotes about him, most of them true, some apocryphal, spilled out of baseball and spread through the country. He became a national figure. *Life* and *Look* and *The Saturday Evening Post*, the dominant American magazines of the 1950s, did stories on him. *Sports Illustrated* came into existence in the middle of the Stengel/Yankees era and spread the gospel. People chuckled over Stengelese, retold the stories about the grapefruit and the sparrow and the manhole cover, smiled at the myriad photographs of him, murmured delightedly when he scurried out of the dugout toward the mound during a ball game.

Stories buzzed. When Casey went to the mound to take a pitcher out, the pitcher said, "I'm not tired," and Stengel replied, "Well, I'm tired of you." Bob Cerv, the big outfielder, was sitting at one end of the empty dugout before a game when Stengel came down the runway from the clubhouse and sat down near him. He looked over at Cerv and said, "Nobody knows this, but one of us has just been traded to Kansas City." Of the clean-living pitcher Bob Turley, when Turley was in a slump: "Look at him. He don't smoke, he don't drink, he don't chase women, and he don't win." Of first baseman Bill Skowron, having similar trouble: "The way he's going I'd be better off if he was hurt." Watching the smooth-swinging Jerry Lumpe cracking out line drives in batting practice, Stengel said, "He looks like the greatest hitter in the world until you play him." He told a writer, "I won't trade my left fielder." "Who's your left fielder?" the writer asked. "I don't know," Casey said, "but if it isn't him, I'll keep him anyway."

Such obscurities fed the legend. Early in the 1950s a reporter phoned him with the news that the Red Sox and the White Sox had completed a trade. The Red Sox had sent Al Zarilla, Joe Dobson and Dick Littlefield to the White Sox for Ray Scarborough and Bill Wight. "What do you think of it, Case?" the reporter asked. "Well, the fella oughta help 'em," Casey replied.

In spring training, to reporters wondering who his third baseman was going to be that year, he said, "Well, the fella I got on there is hitting pretty good and I know he can make that throw, and if he don't make it that other fella I got coming up has shown me a lot, and if he can't I have my guy and I know what he can do. On the other hand, the guy's not around now. And, well, this guy may be able to do it against left-handers if my guy ain't strong enough. I know *one* of my guys is gonna do it." Reporters with the club knew that he was talking about Gil McDougald and Andy Carey and Billy Martin and Bobby Brown, and could sort out the nuances, but out-of-town newspapermen were lost. Sid Ziff, a Los Angeles sports columnist, looked stunned and said, "What the hell did he say?"

A reporter asked him a question, and Casey talked for forty minutes. The reporter said, "Casey, you haven't answered my question." Casey said, "Don't rush me." One writer left the press room in Yankee Stadium to go down to the dugout to talk with Casey late in the afternoon before a night game. An hour later he returned. "Did Casey tell you who he's going to pitch tomorrow?" another reporter asked. "He started to," the first man said, "but he got talking about McGraw and the time he managed in Toledo and the Pacific Coast League and God knows what else. I think tomorrow's starting pitcher is Christy Mathewson."

When he was first with the Yankees, bringing the team north from Florida to New York for opening day, the team stopped in Richmond, Virginia, for an exhibition game. Edna had told him to be sure to phone a convent there and say hello to a relative of hers who was a nun. Stengel dutifully put the call through and explained who he was. "I'm Casey Stengel, Sister, Edna Lawson's husband."

"How nice of you to call, Mr. Stengel," the nun said. "What brings you to Virginia?"

"I'm here with the Yankees," he said.

"The what?" she said. "What are the Yankees?"

"It's a baseball club, Sister."

"Oh," she said, uncomprehendingly. "And what do you do with this baseball club?"

"I'm the manager."

"The what?"

"I'm the fella in charge," said Casey, getting a little desperate. "It's kinda like being the mother superior."

He had odd turns of speech. He called inadequate players "road apples" and would grumble about "them road apples" if a second-rate team defeated him. He'd call his own men road apples sometimes, or plumbers, or dummies. He'd compliment a player by saying "He done splendid" or "He executed good." He'd say "that fella" and "my guy." A batter obviously nervous at the plate had a bad case of "jelly leg." He liked to say,

"You make your own luck." Objecting to an adverse decision by a man he considered an inept umpire he'd say, obscenely, "If I'm gonna be buggered I don't want an amateur handling the Vaseline pot." He said "discharged" instead of "fired" and almost always used the archaic "commence" for "begin." Naiveté was "Ned in the Third Reader," often used in the reverse: "He ain't no Ned in the Third Reader, you know." A playboy was "whisker slick." Ford and Mantle and Martin, who sometimes incurred Stengel's wrath because of their late-night partying, took to calling one another Slick.

Stengel would occasionally look over breakfast checks signed by the players at hotels the Yankees stayed in. "A guy who has orange juice, cereal, bacon and eggs, toast and coffee, something like that, hasn't been fooling around all night," he explained. "It's those guys who have double tomato juice and black coffee who've gone out to mail letters at three in the morning." But he could be tolerant of misbehavior. When Don Larsen banged his automobile into a telephone pole at five in the morning during spring training, before he won lasting fame by pitching a perfect game in the World Series, Stengel made his usual joke about the ballplayer having gone out to mail a letter but aside from making Larsen work a little harder in the team's practice sessions didn't punish him at all.

At team meetings he'd often scold Ford and Mantle and Martin, but Mantle said a lot of that was show. "You couldn't fool Casey," Mickey said, "but he didn't mind too much as long as it didn't show on the ball field. If you played well you'd keep Casey off your back. He was smart. He always pretended he was mad at Whitey and Billy and me even if he wasn't. I think he did it to show the older guys that we young ones weren't getting away with anything. I think he really liked us. He'd lay into us at the meetings, and then on the way out he'd throw us that big wink of his."

Of Ford and Mantle and Martin, Casey said, "Players violated the nights on Mr. Stengel once in a while but the ones that did had the spirit of the ball club. They were trying to win, trying to get to home plate. If you're in a pennant race you can put up with any kind of character, except a man that's lazy. A lazy man is a terrible thing to have on a ball club." Thinking of some who carried their drinking too far, he cautioned, "No ballplayer should get into the habit where he has a few drinks before a ball game, which is what began to happen after night ball came in. When I had one of those boys I said, 'Well, this man is limited. If he don't want to change, why, disappear him.' "

(Joan Didion, in her book *Salvador*, published in 1983, noted that Americans in El Salvador had picked up the Spanish use of "disappear" as a transitive verb, as in "The government disappeared the students." Didion was referring to political kidnapping and murder, Stengel only to dismissal, but he was using the verb the same way twenty years earlier.)

Casey is supposed to have said of wandering players whose nightly carousing had more to do with women than wine, "It ain't getting it that hurts them, it's staying up all night looking for it." And, cynically, "They gotta learn that if you don't get it by midnight, you ain't gonna get it, and if you do it ain't worth it."

His own drinking was steady, and because he would stay up to all hours of the night he gained a reputation as a prodigious imbiber of alcohol. People who knew him best said it was an exaggeration. "Talk is what mattered to Casey, not drinking," Lee MacPhail said. "He could drink, but a lot of times he'd have the same drink in his hand for hours." John

Lardner agreed with that view when he said of Stengel, "He can talk all day and all night, on any kind of track, wet or dry." One night in a bar after Casey and his companions had spent hours drinking and talking, the bartender cleared his throat, pointed to the clock and said, "The bar is closing." "Gentlemen," said Casey, rising to his feet, "there is much more which could be said but my man here in the white coat has said it all. Goodnight."

Clay Felker said he could do more than talk; he could act. His performances would take place anywhere, in a dining car, the dugout, the dressing room, a bar, hotel lobbies. Old sportswriters still talk reverently of the night in Detroit when Casey retold the story of his inside-the-park home run in the World Series and finished it by sliding across the lobby of the Book-Cadillac (now the Sheraton-Cadillac) Hotel. He had many such set pieces, his own versions of the grapefruit, the sparrow, the manhole cover. A particularly choice bit of pantomime was his version of how an old Pittsburgh player slid into third base without breaking a pint of whiskey he had in his hip pocket. George Gobel, the comedian, said, "If he turned pro, he'd put us all out of business."

His greatest audience was the press, the reporters who covered the club day after day. Casey needed the sportswriters, needed their attention, needed their admiration. He knew who the writers were, which papers they worked for, and whether a man wrote for a morning paper or an afternoon paper, an important distinction back when electronic journalism was still in its infancy and people read newspapers to get the news. Reporters for the morning newspapers did game reports, but the afternoon writers needed feature material. Casey helped them get it. "These fellas can't just write the box scores, you know," he'd say.

He protected the regular writers with the club by being reserved and even surly with visitors to his clubhouse or dugout that he didn't know, not trusting them the way he did those journalists he was more intimate with and not wanting to give away stories "my writers" could use. He helped his writers, Roger Kahn said, with "frequent briefings, sly confidences and boundless cordiality."

He knew how to use them, too. Jack Mann, then working for the Long Island newspaper *Newsday,* was fresh to Yankee coverage and didn't think Stengel knew his name, let alone the paper he worked for.

Mann was by himself in the dugout one day watching batting practice when Stengel, sitting some distance away, said in a loud voice, "You know, I got a fella pitching for me don't always signal his infielders when he's gonna throw a slow ball." Mann knew that it was beneficial for infielders to know what a pitcher was going to throw on each pitch but otherwise saw nothing special in Stengel's comment. "I really shouldn't tell you this," Casey went on, "but it's Mr. Ford of Glen Cove." With that, he got up and walked out of the dugout.

Mann, surprised that Stengel knew where Ford lived on Long Island, suddenly realized what Stengel was doing. Players didn't always pay attention when he told them things, but if Ford read Stengel's remark in his local paper, where it would certainly be called to his attention by relatives and friends, he'd be more likely to get the message and correct himself.

Whitey Herzog said, "Casey was the best public-relations man who ever lived. He knew exactly what he was doing all the time." Yet he could be difficult with the press, even with his own writers. After a game in which Martin was ejected by the umpires, reporters gathered around Billy in the clubhouse. Stengel cut the press conference short. "Don't tell 'em nothin'," he said to Martin. Why Stengel imposed that blackout is not clear. Maybe he was only trying to protect the hot-tempered Martin from making an intemperate remark that would get him in trouble with the league office. To Harold Rosenthal, who had offered Stengel his opinion of some baseball move, he said, "You're full of shit, and I'll tell you why." Another time, he was having breakfast with Paul Lapolla, who had come to Casey with a lucrative book idea. "I like you, kid," Stengel said to Lapolla, "and the Yankees want me to do it, and Edna wants me to do it. But I ain't gonna do it and I ain't gonna tell you why. Eat your eggs."

He was unafraid of cameras, but he was not always friendly with those wielding them. In Florida in 1957 he kicked a photographer working in front of his dugout who had obscured his view of first base. The photographer, who was used to Stengel's quirks, made no big fuss about the incident, but his paper did and had the photographer file an assault complaint. The police came to Stengel's hotel in St. Petersburg, arrested him, took him to the stationhouse and booked him, fixing bail at $50. Bob Fishel, the Yankees' public-relations man, put up the bail and a few minutes later Stengel was drinking in the hotel bar, telling people, "For Christ's sake, I just got back from the police station. I been arrested." The incident was quickly settled with an apology.

Later that year in Milwaukee, Stengel had perhaps his most serious run-in with the press. The Braves had moved from Boston to Wisconsin in 1953 and now, only four years later, had created incredible excitement there by winning the National League pennant. Seldom has any city been as caught up in baseball as Milwaukee was that year. Nothing was as important as the Braves. After the first two games of the World Series had been played in New York, the two teams moved west to play three games in Milwaukee. On the morning of the first game the *Milwaukee Journal* put its regular press coverage back on page three, including the astonishing news that the Soviet Union had launched *Sputnik*, the first space satellite ever to circle the earth. Page one was devoted to stories about the upcoming World Series game under a banner headline saying "TODAY WE MAKE HISTORY."

The Yankees went from New York to Milwaukee by train. South of Milwaukee, near Racine, Wisconsin, the train was to pause for a few minutes at a place called Sturtivant.

Wisconsin is a friendly state, and the people of Sturtivant turned out to welcome the Yankees. They had a band, and the mayor was going to make a few remarks. But the Yankee special pushed on brusquely to Milwaukee, with not even a howdy-do to Sturtivant. In Milwaukee there were more official greeters, and again the Yankees were indifferent to the welcome. The team hurried from the train to a bus that would take them to their motel outside the city. A couple of local reporters tried to board the bus to travel along with the club, but a Yankee official — not Stengel — barred them. When the reporters protested the official said, "Come on, stop acting bush. Get off the bus."

"Bush" is the all-purpose baseball noun for second-class, minor-league, petty, unimportant, inconsequential. The reporters wrote about their treatment, emphasizing the word "bush," and Milwaukee was up in arms. "BUSHVILLE," the city rechristened itself in big newspaper headlines. Stengel was accused of using the epithet, and all the popularity he had accumulated thirteen years earlier when he had led the minor-league Brewers to the pennant went down the drain. When he appeared on the field at County Stadium the Milwaukee crowd drowned him in boos. Unperturbed, Casey blew the crowd a kiss. "I been booed before," he said. "I been booed all over the country. I been booed for years."

After the Braves won the Series, Casey was gracious in defeat. He particularly praised Lew Burdette, the Milwaukee pitcher who had defeated the Yankees three times. "He was the big man of the Series," Casey said. "He took care of us all the way. He was just as good in the third game as he was in the second as he was in the first. He made us hit the ball on the ground in nearly every tight spot. He was great."

A year later during Stengel's second World Series with Milwaukee, he had another run-in with a journalist, although this one was in New York after the Yankees had lost the first two games of the Series in Milwaukee, the second by the embarrassing score of 13–5. He and Fred Haney, the Milwaukee manager, were being interviewed for television when the announcer thrust his microphone toward Casey and asked, "Do you think your team is choking?" If "bush" is baseball's all-purpose putdown, "choke" is its ultimate insult, implying that you're too scared to swallow and thereby casting aspersions on your pride, courage, poise, patriotism, love of mother and chances of ever going to heaven. Stengel bristled. He wasn't going to get into a discussion of his team's moral fiber on television. "Do you choke on that fucking microphone?" he said. Then he turned his back on the camera and elaborately scratched the seat of his pants.

Later, having a drink with people at World Series press headquarters, he demonstrated the validity of Whitey Herzog's observation by saying, "When I cursed I knocked out their audio, and when I scratched my ass I ruined their picture."

27 BILLY, PHIL AND ESTES: "I WAS NO DOUBT DISCHARGED"

Stengel's friendship with Billy Martin ended in 1957, during his second skein of pennant-winning years, despite the affection the two had for each other. "I loved that old bastard," Martin said of Stengel. And Stengel said proudly of Martin, "There ain't nothing he don't think he can do. He thinks he knows more about baseball than anybody else, and it wouldn't surprise me if he was right." The only pennant Stengel lost during his first ten years as Yankee manager came when Martin was in military service in 1954.

But George Weiss, conservative in his outlook, always trying to project an image of the typical Yankee player as a model of quiet, efficient professionalism, never liked the raffish Martin. He objected to his temper, his penchant for loud controversial opinion, his combative nature, and he felt that Martin was a bad off-field influence on other young play-

503

ers, particularly Ford and Mantle. In 1957 he got rid of him. In May several Yankee players, with their wives, celebrated Martin's birthday at the Copacabana, a popular nightclub in Manhattan. There was a disagreement at the Copa between another man and some of the Yankee players, and after it the man went to the police and charged Hank Bauer, one of the Yankees at the party, with assault. Later, a grand jury heard the charge, listened to witnesses and decided that there was no basis for indictment. In short, the charge against Bauer — and by extension all the Yankees at the party — was unsubstantiated.

But Weiss was outraged by the incident, which was widely publicized, and so was Topping. All the players who had been at the Copa were fined by the Yankees, although Weiss felt that Martin had probably precipitated the trouble. A month later the Yankees and the White Sox got into a turbulent on-field brawl in which even the sixty-six-year-old Stengel took part. Things were quieting down and the umpires were ordering some of the players off the field when Martin suddenly got into a punching match with one of the Chicago players. Two days later Weiss traded him to Kansas City. Stengel objected, but Weiss was adamant. Young Bobby Richardson had come along beautifully as a second baseman and had taken the job away from Martin anyway, and Weiss felt the Yankees would be better off without him.

Stengel called Martin into his office and said, "Well, you're gone. You were the best little player I ever had. You did everything I ever asked." The emotional Martin, his eyes filled with tears, left the clubhouse charging that Stengel had let him down, and he didn't speak to him again for years. Finally, at a baseball gathering, Billy did what he felt was the magnanimous thing and went over to Stengel and said hello. Stengel, in full conversational flow, switched instantly into a long paean to "this man's" contributions to the Yankees when Billy was Casey's pet there. It was as though nothing had ever changed.

"I loved that old bastard," Martin said, but he never totally understood Stengel. He could not appreciate Casey's pragmatic acceptance of defeat once he realized he couldn't change Weiss' mind about trading Billy away. Martin felt that Casey should have gone to the wall for him. Casey fought for him, but when he saw that the fight had been lost he shrugged his shoulders, spit on his hands and went on to the next battle.

Earlier, in 1955, long after the last out of

the seventh game of the World Series, in which Johnny Podres shut the Yankees out 2–0 to give Brooklyn its first World Series championship, Stengel sat naked in his office, a towel draped casually across his lap, holding a postmortem with one or two lingering sportswriters. All the Yankee players had dressed and gone, except Martin. Dressed in street clothes, his shirt open at the collar, his hair still damp from the shower, he talked about Stengel with Howard Cosell and another man. Martin's eyes welled with tears as he said to Cosell, "A man like that shouldn't have to lose."

Defeat to Martin was destructive, a form of death, and he must have felt that Stengel somehow had been destroyed, or at least badly damaged. What Billy did not understand, and might never understand, was that Stengel was never destroyed by defeat. He wanted to win as badly as Billy did but he was used to adversity. He had lost before. He knew how to ride with trouble, like a smart boxer who has been hit and hurt but knows how to hold on, to keep his poise until things clear and he's able to fight again. He was a man who'd been up and down.

He was at his best in the 1958 World Series, the one during which he had his little tête-á-tête with the announcer with the microphone. Milwaukee had beaten him in the Series a year earlier and in this one took a 3–1 lead in games and apparently had him licked again. The third victory came over Whitey Ford in a shocking game during which Norm Siebern, the Yankee left fielder, lost a succession of fly balls in the sun, letting in runs and ultimately moving even Ford, the imperturbable professional, to turn toward left field with his hands on his hips in an unmistakable gesture of disbelief. The score was 3–0. It was the eighth inning. Warren Spahn was pitching a two-hitter for Milwaukee, and at that moment it seemed probable that another Series was lost. The Yankees looked shell-shocked. Stengel ran up out of the dugout and shouted at his players, rallying them, rolling his forearms in a "Let's go! Let's go!" gesture, shaking them up, reminding them who they were, getting them back on the right track. The Yankees lost the game but they won the next three in a striking comeback to capture the Series. Dr. Norman Vincent Peale, a renowned clergyman of the period, used Stengel's behavior in the face of imminent defeat as the text of a sermon.

More practically, Stengel took on himself the blame for the Siebern debacle, saying he never should have played "a blind sunfielder" in left in Yankee Stadium. Not that he excused Siebern. The next day during pregame practice, watching Siebern chatting and joking around the batting cage, waiting his turn to hit, Stengel muttered, "A man drops two or three fly balls in the sun, you'd think he'd get a glove and go out there and practice a little." Siebern didn't play an inning the rest of the Series and a year later was traded away. His sin was not making mistakes in the field, but not trying to correct them.

Stengel had little patience with men who wouldn't learn how to play the game and, conversely, great admiration for those who did. He got pleasure out of baseball, sheer joy when it was played properly. After a Dodger-Yankee World Series game that matched Lopat and Preacher Roe, two smart pitchers who used guile and control with consummate skill, Stengel said, "Those two fellas certainly make baseball look like a simple game, don't they? It makes you wonder. You pay all that money to great big fellas with a lot of muscles and straight stomachs who go up there and start swinging. And they [Lopat and Roe] give 'em a little of this and a little of that and swindle 'em."

He liked pitchers like that, men who could

"throw ground balls," low pitches that batters tended to hit to infielders who could convert them into double plays. He relished double plays and was always looking for deft second basemen who could "make the pivot." He called the double play the most important play in baseball. "It's two-thirds of an inning!" he'd say. "One ground ball and [slap of the hands] *two!* You're out of the inning." For the same reason, he used the sacrifice bunt sparingly, because when you sacrifice you give away an out, and an out is valuable.

In spring training he and one of his coaches would take young infielders out to second base and show them four different ways to make the pivot — that is, to take the throw from the second baseman or the shortstop (or third baseman or pitcher or first baseman or catcher), step on the base for one out, avoid the sliding base runner, and throw on to first for the second out. They demonstrated the different ways and then said to the youngsters, "If you know another way, show it to us now. If you don't know another way, learn to do it our way."

More and more often, Stengel's philosophical discourses on the game got into print. Red Smith quoted him on protecting young players against tough pitchers: "Maybe they can't hit that real great pitcher. My regulars can't hit that pitcher, either, but maybe they don't worry about it too much. A kid can stop fielding good if he don't get his hits. You can tell him not to worry, but maybe he's out there in the field and he's thinking, 'He fooled me with that pitch. Let's see now, that makes me oh for fifteen and —' Oops, there's a ball hit and it's past him." Clay Felker described Stengel's nights, after the drinking and the talking ended: "Sleep did not come easily, even after a night of conviviality which left lesser men collapsed in stupor. Casey would retire to his room with late editions of the newspapers. There he would pore over box scores and baseball stories, digesting the results in not only the American League but the National League as well. 'Sometimes you have a chance to get a fella from the National League, and suppose you ain't kept account of him, then where are ya? When I get through with the papers I commence going over some of the things we did in the game that day. Maybe there's a way to do 'em better tomorrow. I do that for a while and first thing you know it's getting to be three or four in the morning. Only if we lost a tough one that day I don't always get to sleep then.' "

Stengel wanted execution, and if a player

could not execute satisfactorily Stengel didn't want him. He needed players who could *do* things to make his kind of baseball work. He wanted men who could hit behind the runner, who could bunt on command, who knew how to move on the bases, who knew which base to throw to in a complicated situation. And he didn't like to have to rely on the same eight fielders throughout a game. He understood odds. He disliked playing his infield in to cut off a run, fearing that the defensive gain (a shorter throw to home) was more than offset by the defensive loss (more batted balls could flit between infielders for base hits). "Playing your infield in," he said, "turns a .200 hitter into a .300 hitter." He wanted the best odds he could get, every inning. When you have a weak-hitting, right-handed-hitting second baseman batting against a strong right-handed pitcher with a runner on second base, the odds on getting a hit and moving the base runner around to score are not as good as they would be if you sent in a strong left-handed batter to pinch-hit in the second baseman's place. But if you use the pinch hitter, how badly do you weaken your defense (hurt your odds) the next inning when you send someone else onto the field in the second baseman's place? To solve that dilemma,

Stengel gathered a corps of versatile athletes who could field deftly at different positions, men who were equally at home at second and third, for instance, or at short and second, or at third and short, or sometimes at all three positions. Then if he sent a pinch hitter in for one man he could put another adroit fielder in his place. Sometimes this involved complexities such as pinch-hitting for the second baseman, moving the incumbent third baseman to second and putting a man from the bench at third, but the defense would remain capable *after* the offense had been improved by the insertion of the pinch hitters. It worked with other positions, too. Casey might send a man in to bat for an outfielder and then put the pinch hitter at first base and move the first baseman to the outfield. Or shift a catcher to left field and the left fielder to third base and put a new catcher in who had previously pinch-hit for the third baseman. And so on.

This was the ultimate refinement of platooning, which was not new but which had never been used so extensively before, and never with such proficiency. Stengel *used* his bench ("We're paying twenty-five men," he'd say, "we might as well let them earn their money"). He didn't have substitutes around just for emergencies. The process seems so logical that those familiar with the way Stengel operated feel a vague sense of shock nowadays when they see a major-league team come into the ninth inning a run behind and send up to bat the same weak-hitting shortstop and the same weak-hitting second baseman who have played the entire game. Where are the pinch hitters? Where are the replacement fielders? As a matter of fact, Stengel probably would have hit for them long before the ninth inning. If he was up against a competent pitcher and suddenly saw an opening, he didn't wait for a late inning to pinch-hit. If, say, the leadoff hitter in the fifth inning got to second base on a throwing error by the shortstop, and the weak-hitting end of his batting order was coming up, Stengel would go at once to his pinch hitters, one after another sometimes, probing, pushing, improving the odds of getting that run in from second. Even if he didn't succeed, the pressure he put on the pitcher could turn an easy inning into a tough one and possibly make it easier to get to him the following inning.

The pinch hitters came through, surprisingly often. There'd be a hit, maybe two hits, maybe a stunning home run, and the Yankees would be ahead. Then Stengel would position a new platoon of fielders and be just as strong in the field as he had been, and he'd hold on and win the game. He did this frequently enough to win ten pennants in twelve years. He maneuvered his roster, oblivious to a player's resentment when he was pulled back from the plate for a pinch hitter, sometimes as early as the second inning. He didn't bother being polite. He pushed with all his might at the slightest opening in an effort to break a game open.

In the course of doing everything he could to win he seriously hurt some players' feelings — notably Rizzuto's. Late in August 1956, heading for another World Series with the Dodgers, Weiss and Stengel decided they needed another left-handed-hitting outfielder against Brooklyn's pitching staff, which was almost entirely right-handed. They found they could buy the veteran Enos Slaughter, who had been with the Yankees for a while a year or two earlier. (On that occasion the fiery Slaughter told Stengel he expected to play every day. "My boy," Casey said, "you play when I tell you and you'll stay up here a long time.")

For Slaughter to be eligible for the Series he had to be placed on the Yankee roster before September 1 (after that date extra players can join the team but they can't appear in the Series). Weiss and Stengel went over the Yankee roster to see who was expendable, and they kept coming back to the same name. It was, distressingly, Rizzuto's. Phil was almost thirty-eight, had been in only thirty games that season and had played sparingly the year before. This was almost certainly his last year as an active player anyway. They made their decision. Phil would have to go.

Rizzuto was told Stengel wanted to see him in his office, and, as Phil tells it, "I couldn't imagine what he wanted," an indication of the ego of a great ballplayer. Weiss was with Stengel. They told Rizzuto about the chance they had to get Slaughter but that they had to cut one man to make room for him. They asked Rizzuto to look over the roster and suggest who might be dropped. Phil naively took the roster and went over it, suggesting a spare catcher, a spare pitcher, and listening as Stengel explained why he needed those men.

Slowly it began to dawn on Rizzuto what they were driving at. Stengel made it plain: They wanted to release *him.* Weiss hurriedly assured Phil that they'd keep him on salary and restore him to the roster after September 1, although that meant he would not be eligible for the Series.

And that's how Rizzuto learned that he was no longer of use to the Yankees. Stunned, he said nothing. He walked out of Stengel's office, took off his uniform, got dressed, left the stadium and his career as a player behind him and went home. Slaughter joined the club, batted .289 in twenty-four games before the end of the year and hit .350 in the six games he played against the Dodgers in the Series. The Yankees won but Rizzuto never got over the pain of that day, although the club later hired him as a play-by-play broadcaster and he remained an integral part of the Yankee family.

It was harsh, but it was practical. The Yankees won the Series, and they might not have if Rizzuto had been on the roster instead of Slaughter. Casey was coldly efficient about things like that.

The Stengel legend peaked on July 9, 1958. On that day Casey and a few other baseball people, among them Mantle, appeared in Washington at the invitation of the Senate Subcommittee on Antitrust and Monopoly. Stengel and the others had been in Baltimore for the All-Star Game the day before (Casey's heroes won), and it was a convenient time for them to pop over to Washington to testify be-

516

before the committee. Baseball still had its restrictive reserve clause, which bound a player to his contract for life, and it had been under fire for some time as a monopoly, critics arguing that its methods of doing business violated the historic Sherman Antitrust Act. A bill baseball had been lobbying for had been introduced into the Senate that would legally exempt baseball and other professional sports from antitrust restrictions in certain areas of their operation, such as methods that were used to control competitive playing strength (like the draft), the employment and assignment of players, the rights of teams to exclusive geographical areas, the regulation of radio and television coverage and the "preservation of confidence in the honesty of the contests," which meant a commissioner's authority to function as a supreme authority within the game. The same bill had been passed by the House of Representatives a month earlier.

Senator Estes Kefauver of Tennessee, who had made a name for himself earlier in the 1950s by conducting televised investigations of organized-crime figures, was chairman of the subcommittee whose job it was to study the bill and decide whether it should be sent to the Senate floor for a vote. Although there

517

seemed to be little opposition to it — it was co-sponsored by almost half the Senate — Kefauver didn't feel that such a broad exemption from the antitrust laws should whip through without at least a little discussion first, and he decided to hold hearings on it. Thus, the invitations to Stengel and the others.

Casey, impeccably dressed in a gray suit, white shirt and dark tie, was called on first. Kefauver said, "Mr. Stengel, you are the manager of the New York Yankees. Will you give us very briefly your background and views about this legislation?"

"Well, I started in professional baseball in 1910," Casey said, and he was off and running. "I have been in professional ball, I would say, for forty-eight years. I have been employed by numerous ball clubs in the majors and in the minor leagues. I started in the minor leagues with Kansas City. I played as low as Class D ball, which was at Shelbyville, Kentucky, and also Class C ball and Class A ball and I have also advanced in baseball as a ballplayer. I had many years that I was not so successful as a ballplayer, as it is a game of skill. And then I was no doubt discharged by baseball, in which I had to go back to the minor leagues as a manager. I became a major-league manager in several cities and was discharged. We call it discharged because there is no question that I had to leave."

The three hundred people paying rapt attention in the huge old Senate Caucus Room, where most such hearings were long tedious ordeals, burst into laughter, and laughter continued repeatedly during Casey's testimony, much of which was a classic Stengel monologue, occasionally interrupted and spurred on to greater flights by questions from members of the subcommittee. Kefauver asked, "Mr. Stengel, are you prepared to answer particularly why baseball wants this bill passed?" Stengel replied, "Well, I would have to say at the present time, I think that baseball has advanced in this respect for the player help. That is an amazing statement for me to make because you can retire with an annuity at fifty and what organization in America allows you to retire at fifty and receive money? I want to further state that I am not a ballplayer, that is, put into the pension-fund committee. At my age, and I have been in baseball, well, I will say I am possibly the oldest man who is working in baseball. I would say that when they start an annuity for the ballplayers to better their conditions, it should have been done, and I think it has been done. I think it should be the way they have done it, which is a very good thing. The reason why they possibly did not take the managers at that time was because radio and television or the income to ball clubs was not large enough that you could have put in a pension plan. Now I am not a member of the pension plan. You have young men here who are, who represent the ball clubs, they represent the players. And since I am not a member and don't receive pension from a fund which you think, my goodness, he ought to be declared in that, too, but I would say that is a great thing for the ballplayers. That is one thing I will say for the ballplayers, they have an advanced pension fund. I should think it was gained by radio and television or you could not have enough money to pay anything of that type."

Stengel was obviously trying to say some serious things about the relatively new and quite lucrative pension plan that had recently been established, but which he was not eligible for despite his long service as a player and a manager. He remembered his long arguments for more money when he was a player in Brooklyn and Pittsburgh and Philadelphia, and the absolute control the owners had then over the players' economic futures, but he also recognized the players' glowing economic present. At one point he said, "I have been up and down the ladder. I know there are some things in baseball thirty-five to fifty years ago that are better now than they were in those days," but then he went off on one of his wild stream-of-consciousness diversions: "In those days, my goodness, you could not transfer a ball club in the minor leagues, Class D, Class C ball, Class A ball. How could you transfer a ball club when you did not have a highway? How could you transfer a ball club when the railroad then would take you to a town, you got off and then you had to wait and sit up five hours to go to another ball club?"

The laughter bubbled again. Casey rambled on, talking about owners and travel costs and antagonism toward the Yankees in other cities around the league and the attendance records the Yankees set and even the fact that he no longer owned stock in a ball club as he had fifteen years earlier. . . .

Kefauver said, "Mr. Stengel, I am not sure that I made my question clear."

Much laughter.

"Yes, sir," said Stengel. "Well, that's all right. I'm not sure I'm going to answer yours perfectly either."

When the laughter died down after that, Kefauver said again, "I am asking you, sir, why it is that baseball wants this bill passed."

"I would say I would not know," Stengel replied, "but I would say the reason they want it passed is to keep baseball going as the highest-paid ball sport that has gone into baseball, and from the baseball angle — I am not going to speak of any other sport. I am not in here to argue about these other sports. I am in the baseball business. It has been run cleaner than any business that was ever put out in the one hundred years at the present time. I am not speaking about television or I am not speaking about income that comes into the ball parks. You have to take that off. I don't know too much about it. I say the ballplayers have a better advancement at the present time."

He went on for forty-five minutes, seven thousand words of testimony, and most of what he was trying to say was drowned in laughter and his own prolixity. It was greeted as a great comic performance, and it received tremendous publicity on television and radio and in the press. Excerpts from his testimony were printed and reprinted.

But despite the laughs, he was serious. He was prodding Congress. He was obviously for the status quo in baseball, but he avoided any direct comment on the bill, pro or con, except to say, "I didn't ask for the legislation." He seemed to be encouraging the subcommittee's inquiry into aspects of the game. "I want to let you know," he said, "that as to the legislative end of baseball you men will have to consider what you are here for." In his roundabout way he told the Senators that their deliberations were becoming part of the country's everyday life, even as baseball was. "Forty years ago," he said, "you would not have cameras flying around here every five minutes, but we have got them here, and more of them than around a ball field."

It became accepted truth in baseball that Casey had snowed the Senators, that he had piled up his old double-talk in a successful effort to keep from telling them anything that he didn't want to tell them. In a sense, that was probably so, but the truth seems a bit more complex than that. Stengel had spent almost his entire working life in baseball, and he remembered the hard times as well as the good ones — much of his testimony was about the minor leagues, where there seldom was much money. He had not forgotten the callous way baseball's owners could treat their employees. He recognized the financial gains the players had made, while resenting their failure to include managers and others in the pension plan, but while he conceded that baseball was generally being well run he would not come right out and say the owners should be given carte blanche.

Toward the end of his appearance, heavy-handed political humor plodded onstage when one of the Senators said, probably chuckling to himself, "This is the Anti-Monopoly Subcommittee sitting here. I want to know whether you intend to keep on monopolizing the world's championship in New York City."

Laughter. Stengel was aware, of course, that Milwaukee was the reigning world champion at the moment, but he didn't correct the Senator and instead went off on another spiel about the Yankees and the All-Star Game the day before and Greta Garbo and the twenty-seven cents a visiting team got as its share of each ticket sold at the gate, and so on, all splendidly confusing.

When he finished, Kefauver thanked him for appearing before the committee. Turning to the next witness, he said, "Mr. Mantle, will you come around? . . . Mr. Mantle, do you have any observations with reference to the applicability of the antitrust laws to base-ball?"

To the utter delight of all those in the room Mantle said, "My views are just about the same as Casey's."

The laughter followed Stengel out of the Caucus Room. One of the Senators, tears in his eyes from laughing, said afterward, "The best entertainment we have had around here for a long time."

Everyone was talking about Stengel's performance, but *Sports Illustrated* was one of the few publications to point out that the "hilarious autobiographical fragments, homemade poetry, pungent *non sequiturs*" also included "guarded revelations of lines of inquiry the subcommittee might profitably follow." The magazine called Stengel's testimony "an amazingly frank, cheerful, shrewd, patriotic address that left the Senators stunned, bewildered and delighted."

Still, for most people it was just Stengel at his comic best. And the legend grew.

28 SIGNS OF DISINTEGRATION: THE LONG YANKEE SLUMP

In midsummer of 1958 the Yankees reached a crescendo of performance under Stengel's direction. Everyone was hitting, the pitching was superb, and the club opened a huge lead in the pennant race, assuring Casey of his fourth straight flag, his ninth in ten seasons. By July 26 the Yankees had won sixty-three games, had lost only thirty and were fifteen and a half games ahead of the field. The Indians defeated them twice in a double-header on July 27, but it didn't seem to matter. By August 1 the lead had increased to sixteen and a half games, and every other club in the league was under .500. No one could recall a club's dominating its league that way. *Sports Illustrated* ran a story suggesting that these Yankees might be the greatest team of all time.

Stengel was not as sanguine. "This isn't one of my three best teams," he said, and he was right. The hitting tailed off, the pitching stopped. There was a multitude of injuries, but Yankee teams had suffered injuries before and had shrugged them off. This one didn't. The doubleheader loss to Cleveland late in July wasn't an aberration, a momentary pause in a succession of triumphs, but the beginning of an extraordinary slump that lasted the rest of the season, all through 1959 and through the first two months of 1960. Even though the Yankees lost more games than they won during the remainder of 1958 (twenty-nine wins, thirty-two losses), the enormous lead cushioned their fall. They won the pennant by ten games, Casey's biggest margin ever, and rallied to down Milwaukee in the Series. In 1959, however, they started poorly, fell into last place in May, struggled back into the pennant fight for a while in midseason but played fitfully thereafter and finished a distant third, only four games over .500, their worst performance under Casey's leadership.

Stengel was widely criticized for the team's failure. He passed his sixty-ninth birthday in July, and more and more people were saying, "He's too old. He can't manage anymore." The young players on the team — Mantle among them — bristled under his heavy-handed sarcasm and began turning to Ralph Houk for comfort. Houk had been a reserve catcher on the Yankees for eight seasons without playing more than a handful of games, and after his career ended he became a manager in the Yankee farm system. Young and energetic, he was a great success, and in 1958 Topping moved him up to the Yankees as a coach. Topping was taking an increased interest in the operation of the team (his partner Webb was content to stay in the background), and he was growing tired of Stengel, sharing the popular view that Casey was too old and maybe even a little senile. Topping had hoped that Stengel might retire after the 1958 World Series, but Weiss wanted the manager to stay on and Stengel signed a contract to manage for two more years. Topping did nothing officially, but he decided that these would be Casey's last two seasons. As a gesture toward that finality he ordered the abandonment of the instructional school in 1959, a direct slap at Stengel. Topping was grooming Houk to succeed Casey, and he felt it would be good for him to get some experience with the big team, which is why Houk was made a Yankee coach. Casey didn't care for that decision any more than he did the cancellation of the instructional school. He particularly disliked the idea of Houk's standing in the wings waiting for the old man to get offstage.

As the Yankees kept losing in 1959 the criticism grew more virulent. Jackie Robinson attracted a great deal of attention when he said Yankee players had told him that Stengel dozed off on the bench during ball games. Jackie blamed the slump on Stengel's incompetence and his relentless nagging, which he said was destroying player morale. Robinson had no use for Stengel, whom he had previously called a racist. The most devastating evidence for the charge was a remark Stengel had made four or five years earlier when Elston Howard became the first black to break into the hitherto all-white Yankee lineup, eight long years after Robinson himself had broken the major league's color barrier. Howard was a big, strong, talented athlete, but he was slow afoot, prompting Stengel to say flippantly, "Well, when they finally get me a nigger, I get the only one who can't run." Stengel also at times referred to black ballplayers as "jigs" or "jigaboos" or "jungle bunnies," and he had called Howard "Eightball" when Elston was first with the club.

Stengel disliked Robinson, although not

with the intensity with which Robinson disliked him. Once, after Jackie had run wild on the bases against the Yankees, Casey said sarcastically to his players, "You better look in your lockers and make sure he didn't steal your jockstraps." In 1955, Robinson stole home against the Yankees in the World Series. Stengel, who resented Robinson's outfoxing him with the steal, argued long and loud with the plate umpire, claiming that Berra had tagged Robinson out at the plate. He crowed after Robinson popped up with the bases loaded in the crucial moment in the 1952 Series, when Martin made his last-second catch of the ball. "He came up against a left-hander with the bases loaded," Stengel scoffed, "and he hit a little pop-up." Later, still putting Robinson down, Stengel said, "The only time the Dodgers ever beat us in the Series was when they won the seventh game in 1955 and Robinson didn't play. You can look it up."

Robinson was outspoken in his criticism of the Yankees' slowness to sign black players (a policy that stemmed as much from economic racism, the fear that black players in the Yankee lineup would hurt the sale of tickets to their supposedly upscale audience, as it did from blatant bigotry). After Allie Reynolds, who was part Creek Indian, struck out Robinson three times in the fourth game of the 1952 Series, Stengel said in the clubhouse, "Before that black son of a bitch accuses us of being prejudiced, he should learn how to hit an Indian."

For all of this, it is doubtful that Stengel was a bigot. His distaste for Robinson — or Robi'son, as he always pronounced it — may have been racial at heart (if not overt, then at least latent), but in retrospect it seems to have been caused more by professional jealousy. Robinson was awfully good, precisely the talented all-round player that Stengel admired and would love to have had on his own team. The fact that Robinson was not on his team, that he was the enemy, and an irritating, overbearing enemy, goaded him. Robinson was disputatious (he certainly had the right to be, after all that he'd been through breaking into the all-white baseball establishment), and he was given to outspoken and not always carefully reasoned opinion. Dan Bankhead, a black pitcher from the Negro Leagues who was with the Dodgers in Robinson's first year, said once during an argument, "Robinson, you're not only wrong, you're loud wrong." Casey was loud wrong back, but he was a racist only in the casual, unthinking way that most of his generation of Americans were. Racial and ethnic slurs were characteristic of his era — you called a Swede a squarehead, a Frenchman a frog, an Italian a wop, a Jew a kike, an Irishman a mick, a Spaniard a spic, and so on — and his own sarcastic, parodying nature jumped on a man's obvious features: flop ears, big nose, black skin. But when he played against the black army team at Fort Huachuca, Arizona, during his barnstorming tour in the winter of 1919–20, he admired the skills of the outstanding black players so much that he recommended them to James Wilkinson, who was putting together the Kansas City Monarchs. John Holway says that black players gave Stengel credit for creating the Monarchs.

Casey liked Satchel Paige, against whom he both played and managed. When Paige was working as a relief pitcher for the St. Louis Browns in the 1950s Stengel would admonish the Yankees in the early innings of games with the Browns, "Get your runs now! Father Time is coming!" To Stengel, Paige's most obvious characteristic at that time was his age, not his blackness. In 1954, before the Yankees had ever had a black player in their regular-season lineup, Stengel was asked which opposing player had been best against the Yankees that year.

"Doby," he replied without hesitation, "Doby and Avila. They were the most dangerous against us all season." Larry Doby was the Cleveland Indians' black outfielder, Bobby Avila their Mexican second baseman. Asked to single out the best fielding play, Stengel said, "I never saw a throw like the one Al Smith made in July to catch Slaughter at the plate." Smith was another black Cleveland outfielder.

Howard, the subject of Stengel's racist remark, didn't believe Stengel was a bigot. "I never felt any prejudice around Casey," he said. "He'd scream at Newcombe and Robinson and Campanella during the World Series, but I never heard him scream racial things. He screamed at Reese and Hodges and Snider, too."

Except for the stupid remarks he made when Elston first joined the team, Stengel always displayed a high regard for Howard. "When you see this fella catch," he told people when Howard was a rookie, "you're gonna see one of the finest throwing arms any of us has seen in a long time." Howard could catch, he could throw, he could hit, he could play the outfield, he could play first base, he was intelligent, he took care of himself off the field, he did things right on it. He executed splendid, in other words, and Casey admired him. It was as elementary as that.

He had the same affection for Al Jackson, a small black pitcher he had later on with the Mets. Jackson was one of the few accomplished players that Casey had when he was managing the Mets, a fine pitcher who could field his position skillfully, handle a bat well, run bases intelligently and pitch with guile and courage. "He never treated me with anything but respect," Jackson said.

When Jim Brown, the famous Cleveland Browns running back, was dominating professional football, someone asked Stengel if he thought Brown would make a good baseball player. "Why wouldn't he?" Stengel demanded. "He's big and strong and a good athlete. If he's good in one sport, why wouldn't he be good in another? I tell ya, I'd like to sign that big black —" He stopped abruptly, his racial sensitivities obviously heightened since Howard's rookie days. Some of the people with him laughed. "Well, I'd like to try it," Stengel went on defensively. "I bet he could play. Goddammit, there may be too many of them but give me an All-Star team of them and let me manage."

Whatever Stengel was, Robinson was his

most vocal and visible critic in 1959, although Jackie had his own critics. Red Smith disagreed with his comment that Stengel's bad temper was hurting the team, noting that reporters traveling with the club had said Stengel was calmer and more restrained in this losing season than he had been winning a year earlier. Bill Veeck, whose Chicago White Sox won the 1959 pennant, said, "I know Casey well, and he's no different now from the way he was when he was winning pennants. He just hasn't got the horses. He's had too many injuries, and something has happened to the Yankee farm system. They used to be able to reach down and bring up brilliant players. They're still reaching, but they aren't bringing up anything. Something has gone seriously wrong."

After the season, to bolster the Yankees' sagging fortunes, Weiss pulled off one of his most successful trades. For several years the Yankees had what amounted to a player conduit with the Kansas City Athletics. The Athletics were owned by Arnold Johnson, a friend and business associate of Topping's. Johnson bought the Athletics when they were still in Philadelphia and had moved them to Kansas City for the 1955 season after Topping arranged to shift the Yankee farm team to Denver. For the next several years the Yankees and the Athletics traded players back and forth with abandon, moving cynics to say that Kansas City was still a Yankee farm team. In December 1959, Weiss sent Johnson a package of slightly shopworn players and in return received Roger Maris, a powerful young left-handed-hitting outfielder who had been in the league for three years without particularly distinguishing himself. In 1960 with the Yankees, Maris became the league's Most Valuable Player (and a year later hit 61 home runs to break Babe Ruth's home-run record); he and Mantle gave Stengel a devastating one-two punch in the middle of the batting order.

It took a while for things to come together in 1960, despite Maris' presence. Casey was doing more drinking than usual during spring training, and it was not until his wife came to Florida that he slowed down. Soon after the season began he suffered chest pains that led people to think he was having a heart attack, and in May he went into the hospital in New York for a couple of weeks. "They examined all my organs," he said when he rejoined the team. "Some of them are quite remarkable and others are not so good. A lot of museums are bidding for them."

Houk ran the club in his absence, but when Casey came out of the hospital spry and vigorous he resumed full command. He stopped drinking for the rest of the season, and the Yankees began to click again, after slumping for nearly two years, and moved steadily toward another pennant. Casey had to do card tricks with a pitching staff that had only one man who won fifteen games and only two others who won more than ten games, but he maneuvered it into a league-leading team earned-run average.

Maris led the league in runs batted in and Mantle led in homers, and first baseman Bill Skowron also hit the ball hard. Team morale was much higher — there's nothing like winning to ease tension. In Chicago one night, Stengel and his players mocked Veeck's famous exploding scoreboard (the first to put on an extravagant display when a home-team player hit a home run) by lighting sparklers after a Yankee had hit one over the fence and parading in front of the dugout waving them at the crowd.

The biggest threat the Yankees faced that season came from a young team of Baltimore Orioles who stayed in the race until the end of September and didn't give way until the Yankees won fifteen in a row at the end of the season to take the pennant by eight games. It was Stengel's tenth flag. The only other manager to win that many was John McGraw.

29

THE LAST WORLD SERIES: A SHORTSTOP'S THROAT

Stengel had pushed hard in 1960, eager to finish first again. Ryne Duren, an outstanding relief pitcher for Casey during Stengel's final years with the Yankees, remembers him as "driving, driving all the time. He wanted to win, that man." Stengel was burning to win not only because he wanted to join McGraw at the top of the list but also because he had heard the talk and was well aware that this might well be his last season as manager. He was nursing a vain hope that if he got the Yankees home first again and won the World Series, perhaps Topping would keep him on. But he passed his seventieth birthday in midsummer (noting on that occasion that "most people my age are dead at the present time"), and he was beginning to look awfully old. Jokes were made about the bentover way he scurried from the dugout to the mound ("He walks like a man whose vest is buttoned to his trousers" was one of them). The only other man who had managed a big-league club at the advanced age of seventy was Connie Mack, and Mack owned the team. Few people suspected that Stengel would be fired, but there was continual speculation in the press that he would retire after the season. He didn't enjoy the speculation. He snapped at Doc Greene, the respected columnist of the *Detroit News*, when Greene asked him about it.

"You read that I'm going to retire," Stengel said, "and you're probably running to catch a plane or a train so you can go back home, but you had to come out to ask me if I'm gonna quit, right? Well, you can go catch your plane or your train because I consider this my personal business." He rambled on and Greene tried to say something. "Don't interrupt me," Stengel said, "because whether I quit or not and the first time it was hung on me that I was quitting was nine years ago, and we win a few pennants and flew that big flag on the pole out there since then and it's my personal business anyway. I said I'd talk about it in October and that's when I'll talk about it and not before and when does your train leave?"

Then came the World Series with the Pittsburgh Pirates, a young team that had finished last six times in the 1950s before rising very quickly to the top of the National League. The Yankees were big favorites in the Series, and someone reminded Stengel of his remark in 1954 that he'd quit as manager if he didn't bring the Yankees in first. That wasn't quite accurate — Casey had said he should be fired if he didn't win — but it was close enough to set up the question. Would he quit now if he lost the Series? Stengel confused the issue by saying, "Well, I made up my mind, but I made it up both ways."

He picked Art Ditmar to pitch the opening game in Pittsburgh. Ditmar was a capable but undistinguished right-hander who was one of the many players to come to the Yankees from Kansas City. He had been Casey's most dependable pitcher in 1960. Ford, the ace apparent, had had trouble with his shoulder and won only twelve games. Moreover, Ditmar "threw grounders," a talent Casey always admired. But Ditmar didn't survive the first inning of the first game; he faced only five batters, got only one man out (and that on a line drive to the outfield) and gave up three runs.

The Yankees hit the ball hard but without much luck. They scored a couple of runs early, but double plays took them out of the first two innings, and in the fourth, when Maris and Mantle reached base with no one out and Berra hit a tremendous drive 420 feet to the most remote part of Forbes Field, Pittsburgh center fielder Bill Virdon made a marvelous catch against the outfield wall to keep the Yankees from a big inning. The Yankees made thirteen hits in the game but didn't score again until Howard hit a two-run homer off the Pirates' renowned relief pitcher Roy Face in the ninth inning, too late to do anything but bring the final score to 6–4.

It was a frustrating defeat, but Stengel felt better after the Yankees crushed the Pirates 16–3 and 10–0 in their next two meetings, with Ford pitching a four-hit shutout in Yankee Stadium in the latter game. Stengel thought he was about to take a commanding lead in the Series the next day when the Yankees rallied from a 3–1 deficit in the seventh inning. A double and two singles scored one run, and when Bob Cerv, back with the Yankees after spending a couple of seasons in Kansas City, poked a long one to deep right center it seemed certain that two more runs would score, putting the Yankees ahead with only two innings to play. But again Virdon made an amazing catch, and the Yankees didn't score; Pittsburgh won, and the frustrated New Yorkers found the Series tied at two games apiece.

The Pirates routed Ditmar again the next day to win 5–2, and Stengel had his back to the wall, down three games to two with the Series returning to Pittsburgh's ball park. But Ford pitched another shutout, the Yankee hitters exploded for a 12–0 win, and everything came down to the seventh game — which turned out to be one of the damnedest games, as Stengel's man in Oakland might have said, ever played in the World Series.

Vernon Law, starting his third game in the Series for Pittsburgh (he had won his first two), began strongly, giving up only two singles in the first four innings. The Pirates, meanwhile, scored twice in the first inning and twice in the second to take a quick 4–0 lead. Stengel brought in little Bobby Shantz, a five-foot-six-inch left-hander, to pitch, and Shantz stopped the Pirates for five straight innings — he gave up only one walk and one single through the seventh.

The Yankees scored off Law in the fifth on a bases-empty home run by Skowron, drove him out of the game in the sixth and with Roy Face now pitching against them scored four times to take a 5–4 lead. They scored two more runs off Face in the eighth and had a

7–4 lead with only two more innings to play.

Stengel, showing little confidence in his other relief pitchers, then did an uncharacteristic thing. He abandoned his old open-door policy (if you have an opening, push with all your might) and let Shantz bat for himself in the eighth inning with men on second and third and two out. Here was a chance to blow the Pirates out. Casey had plenty of hitters available, and if the Pirates walked the pinch hitter intentionally to fill the bases he had Bobby Richardson up next, and Richardson was the hottest Yankee hitter in the Series (he had already batted in twelve runs to set a new Series record). Shantz had a reputation for being a good-hitting pitcher, but he had been to bat only ten times all season. And he had already pitched five innings of relief.

Yet Casey decided to stay with Shantz, who flied out, and Bobby was still on the mound when the Pirates batted in the bottom of the eighth. Gino Cimoli, pinch-hitting for Face, opened the inning with a single, but Virdon followed with a double-play hopper to Tony Kubek at shortstop. Stengel used to say that the Pirate infield was as hard as an airport runway; Virdon's grounder hit something, took an odd bounce and struck Kubek in the throat. Instead of a double play, both runners were safe and Kubek, painfully hurt, had to leave the game.

Dick Groat singled to score Cimoli, making the score 7–5, with Virdon stopping at second, and Stengel took Shantz out of the game. He brought in Jim Coates, who had pitched two good innings of relief a few days earlier. Coates secured two quick outs on a sacrifice that moved the runners to second and third and a fly to right that wasn't hit far enough to score the runner from third. He got Roberto Clemente, the Pirates' great right fielder, to hit a slow chopper — Stengel's "butcher boy" kind of hit — to first base for what should have been the third out, but Clemente ran hard and beat it out for a base hit. The man on third scored on the play to bring the score to 7–6, still with two on and two out. Hal Smith, the Pirate catcher, came up and hit a three-run homer, and suddenly, stunningly, Pittsburgh was ahead 9–7. Stengel wearily took Coates out of the game and brought in Ralph Terry, who belatedly got the third out. Instead of going into the last inning with a safe lead, Casey was behind two runs.

Again, the Yankees rallied. Richardson and pinch hitter Dale Long singled to open the inning. Maris fouled out, but Mantle singled one run home, Berra's ground ball to the infield scored another, and the game was tied 9–9 as it moved to the last of the ninth.

Then, abruptly, it was all over. On Terry's second pitch of the inning, Bill Mazeroski, Pittsburgh's magnificent second baseman, hit a home run over the left-field wall. Berra, playing left field, watched it go, put his head down and jogged slowly off the field. The Pittsburgh fans celebrated ecstatically, while under the stands an old man swallowed the most bitter defeat he had ever experienced.

Five days later the Yankees held a press conference in a room called Le Salon Bleu at the Savoy Hilton Hotel in New York. A few minutes after noon Stengel appeared, quiet and nervous, wearing a blue suit, a white shirt and a bold horizontal-striped tie. A gaggle of reporters and photographers swarmed around him, asking him if it was true that he was leaving as manager. Joe Reichler, the principal baseball writer for the Associated Press, had spoken to a Yankee official before the meeting and had reported that Casey was going to resign. Milton Richman, Reichler's counterpart on the United Press, had spoken to Casey and his story said Stengel was being fired. Stengel said little as he turned this way and that for the photographers taking his picture. A Yankee official called out, "Can we start the meeting, please?" and the hubbub slowly quieted. Stengel stood, strangely out of place, in the front row of reporters gathered close around Dan Topping, as the Yankee owner unfolded a sheet of paper and began to read from it.

"Casey Stengel has been — and deservedly — the highest-paid manager in baseball history," Topping said. "He has been — and is — a great manager. Two years ago Casey quite reluctantly signed a new two-year contract . . . with the understanding that after the first year he could retire if he desired to do so." Topping went on, circling the subject, mentioning a profit-sharing plum of $160,000 that the Yankees were paying Casey, suggesting that the five-year waiting period for Hall of Fame eligibility be waived in Casey's case.

"Do you mean he's through?" a reporter yelled. "Has he resigned?"

Topping said nothing, and it was Stengel's turn at the microphone. He was nervous, tightening his tie, straightening his jacket, thrusting his hands into his coat pockets, talking uncertainly at first in a grim, flat tone. Soon he warmed up.

"Mr. Webb and Mr. Topping have started a program for the Yankees," he said. "They want to put in a youth program as an advanced way of keeping the club going. They needed a solution as to when to discharge a man on account of age. They have paid me off in full and told me my services are not desired any longer by this club. I told them if this was their idea not to worry about Mr. Stengel, he can take care of himself."

The reporters took notes as Casey rumbled on, his voice picking up and getting stronger, his hands no longer in his pockets, his arms waving.

"Casey," a reporter shouted. "Were you fired?"

"No, I wasn't fired," Stengel shouted back. "I was paid up in full." Everyone laughed, except Stengel. "Write anything you want," he snapped. "Quit, fired, whatever you please. I don't care."

Reporters were running off to phone in their stories, others were taking their places near Stengel, people were clamoring about. Reichler, the AP man, hurriedly updated his story, and a reporter who had spoken to his own office called out to Stengel, "Casey, an AP bulletin says you've been fired. What do you think about that?"

"What do I care what the AP says?" Stengel said. "Their opinion ain't gonna send me into a faint." Then, almost smiling, demonstrating once again his subtle knowledge of the ways of the press, he asked, "What did the UP say?"

A slender old man who chanced to be in the crowd made his way up to Stengel and stuck out his hand.

"Mr. Casey," he said, "I've lived in New York City seventy-nine years and . . ."

Casey grinned and shook the old man's hand, but one of the reporters yelled, "Go away, go away, we don't want you here," and another said, "Beat it. Call him on the telephone." The old man was pressured away. The television people, who didn't have priority over newspapers then, took Stengel to one side for their interviews. Finally, Casey broke away, heading for the bar. He had stayed pretty much on the wagon all season, doing no more than sipping a drink at the Yankees' pennant celebration two weeks earlier, but now he said, "I'm gonna get a drink. Where's a drink?"

He took a bourbon and soda and sat down with a group of writers, talking with his usual animation about baseball and everything else. "I been hiding out for three days," he said, discussing his departure from the Yankees. "I didn't answer the phone at all." He was pulled away for another camera-and-microphone interview, at which Topping said, "I'm just sorry Casey isn't fifty years old, but all business comes to the point where it's best for the future to make a change." Casey said later, "I'll never make the mistake of being seventy again."

He had another drink, did some more interviews, told stories, looking less concerned than any of the people around him. He went into the hotel dining room to have lunch with Topping and some other Yankee officials, and told them, "I'm taking a jet home, and I'm charging it to the club. A man gets his transportation home even if they don't want him anymore."

After lunch he started to leave but some old friends persuaded him to come back to the bar for another drink. "Well, okay," Casey said. "Just for five minutes. Then I'll get out of town." A waitress came up to him and kissed him on the cheek. "God bless you," she said. "Thank you very much," said Casey.

He stood up at last, taking his leave. "I gotta get home to my parents," he said. Accompanied by Roger Williams and Maury Allen, both young reporters with *Sports Illus-*

trated then, he walked to the corner of Fifth Avenue and 58th Street, a block or so from the Essex House, where Casey and Edna always stayed when they were in New York. He answered a few last questions, then said goodbye and hurried across the street. "Halfway across," Williams said, "he broke into his stooping, scuttling trot. He hopped onto the curb, paused a moment, then disappeared into the crowd."

There was a great deal of comment on his dismissal, much of it critical of the Yankees. The writers hurriedly organized a farewell party the next night at the Waldorf-Astoria, similar to the one given Stengel a quarter century earlier when he was dismissed as manager by the Dodgers. Surely, among baseball's myriad records, there ought to be a line saying, "Most times given a banquet for being fired: Casey Stengel, 2."

There was a distinguished collection of guests, including Topping, who said lamely, "Twelve years ago we were ridiculed when Casey came to us. Now we're being ridiculed as he's leaving us." Weiss spoke, too, his phlegmatic visage dissolving in tears as he spoke emotionally about Stengel. Casey, wearing the suit and tie he'd been fired in, poked momentarily at his own eyes with a handkerchief but then spoke strongly. He told the writers, who had been filling their columns with praise of Stengel and his accomplishments, "I don't know what to say to all of you, but you've been writing better stuff in the last couple of days." At the end of his talk he stuck out his chin and said, "Don't give up. Tomorrow is just another day, and that's myself."

And he was gone.

30 OUT AND IN: GOODBYE YANKEES, HELLO METS

George Weiss was dismissed as general manager of the Yankees two weeks after Casey was fired. Weiss, sixty-five, had worked for the Yankees since 1932, when he was hired by then general manager Ed Barrow to run the Yankee farm system. The minor-league teams Weiss put together for the Yankees were some of the best in history, and the constant flow of talent to the parent club was testimony to his skill in finding and developing players. Weiss had become general manager of the club after the 1947 season and had directed the Yankees through their most successful era. Now he, too, found himself in the way of Topping's move toward younger people. He left the Yankees more quietly than Casey, with a lucrative five-year contract as an "adviser."

Presumably retired from the game, these two old men were soon to join forces again in a revolutionary venture that changed the face of baseball.

After fifty consecutive years of stability, from 1903 through 1952, during which the National League and the American League each had the same eight teams in the same eight cities, major-league baseball began to push its way out of the northeastern quadrant of the country. In 1953 the Braves moved from Boston to Milwaukee. A year later the Browns moved from St. Louis to Baltimore (a retrograde movement geographically but still indicative of the great changes taking place). In 1955 the Athletics moved from Philadelphia to Kansas City. In 1958 the most astonishing change of all took place when the New York Giants and the Brooklyn Dodgers, those vigorous rivals, left New York City together and moved to California.

Stung by the departure of the Giants and Dodgers, people in New York worked for the next two or three years to get another National League team to fill the void. William Shea, a prominent lawyer and behind-the-scenes politician, working with Mayor Robert Wagner's encouragement, talked to teams in other cities, trying to persuade one of them to pull up stakes and switch to New York. He didn't have a very broad field of opportunity.

554

Of the eight National League teams, two were the Dodgers and the Giants, neither of which was about to come back. The Braves were content in Milwaukee, where they had led the league in attendance for four straight years. The Cubs weren't going to leave Chicago. The Phillies and the Cardinals had benefited from the departure of the Athletics and Browns and were enjoying the new one-team monopoly they had in Philadelphia and St. Louis. Only the Reds in Cincinnati and the Pirates in Pittsburgh paid much attention to Shea's blandishments, and while they were tempted they decided to stay where they were.

Shea and New York were momentarily blocked. They couldn't persuade a National League team to come to New York, and the Yankees would not relinquish their territorial monopoly and let another American League team in. Expansion of the existing leagues from eight to ten teams had been discussed casually for decades, but it was too radical a step for either of the old leagues to consider seriously.

Shea then turned to the idea of developing a new major league, a concept that was eagerly embraced by Branch Rickey, eight years Stengel's senior and also retired from baseball after a successful career of running the affairs of the Cardinals, the Dodgers and the Pirates. Rickey, despite his years, was still a man of energy, intelligence and daring, and he and Shea helped create the Continental League, gathering around them wealthy entrepreneurs from several cities who were eager to own a major-league team, or what might pass for one. The Continental League never got off the drawing board, but it had enough clout behind it, which is to say money, to make the existing major leagues nervous. The Continental League wanted access to the same pool of players that the two old leagues had. Wary of antagonizing Congress, which had never passed the bill exempting baseball from the antitrust laws that had prompted Stengel's appearance before the Senate subcommittee, the baseball establishment did not declare war on the upstart league but instead worked out what seemed to be an amicable agreement with it. At the same time it undermined the new organization by deciding to expand after all, adding two new teams to the National and two to the American. Since the obvious place to find owners with enough money and interest to float a new franchise was among the putative owners of the Continental League teams, that's where baseball looked. And found them.

Shea and Rickey, both shrewd, pragmatic men, saw the writing on the wall and by July 1960 had worked out a new agreement with major-league baseball under which the Continental League would dissolve, disappear, go out of the business it had not yet really gotten into, and the existing leagues would absorb four of the Continental League franchises: Minneapolis-St. Paul, Los Angeles, Houston, and, significantly, New York. Shea had accomplished the mission he had begun after the Dodgers and Giants had left; he had brought a major-league team back to New York.

New York City, with the help of New York State, agreed to build a stadium to house the new team. A rather plump, cheerful rich woman named Joan Whitney Payson, wife of Charles Shipman Payson and a member of the fabulously wealthy Whitney family, had been persuaded to be one of the backers of the proposed Continental League club in New York, and when for various reasons the other investors backed out after the Continental idea died she became the principal owner of the team. A corporation was formed called the Metropolitan Baseball Club of New York, and on October 17, 1960, it was officially awarded a franchise in the National

League. It would begin play in 1962.

Shea suggested that Rickey be hired as general manager to run the team, and Mrs. Payson, who had been a knowledgeable and enthusiastic baseball fan since John McGraw's day, was all for the idea — until Rickey laid down his terms. He wanted complete control of the operation of the club and a $5,000,000 budget to work with. Mrs. Payson was rich, but she and her family didn't get that way by giving over control of their money and property to anyone, even a Branch Rickey. A business associate of Mrs. Payson's, a Wall Street broker named M. Donald Grant, also a baseball fan and in fact a one-time member of the board of directors of the New York Giants, was named president of the club, and a veteran baseball man named Charlie Hurth, a former president of the Southern Association, was named general manager.

The day after the National League awarded Mrs. Payson a franchise, the Yankees fired Stengel, and two weeks later they fired Weiss. Grant, who knew a little about baseball because of his relationship with the Giants, had nothing against Charlie Hurth, but he was a minor-leaguer. Weiss was a major-league force. Moreover, he knew New York;

he was used to dealing with people in New York. Grant talked to him about joining the new team.

Weiss was much more amenable than Rickey. He liked the idea and was eager to get back into baseball, but he had a problem. Under the retirement contract he had with the Yankees he could not take a job as general manager of another major-league club for five years.

Grant solved that problem. He kicked himself upstairs and became chairman of the board. Weiss was named president, and Hurth continued as general manager, although it was obvious that Weiss would run the baseball operation. Topping and the Yankees were irritated by this transparent end-run but declined to take any action to prevent it, and on March 12, 1961, Weiss took over the direction of the new Metropolitan Baseball Club, which in May adopted the nickname "Mets." Weiss hired a staff of scouts and competent administrators, and began looking for a manager. He knew exactly who he wanted.

Stengel had turned down several job offers during the winter, notably one to become manager of the Detroit Tigers, who finally accepted Casey's no and picked Bob Scheffing to run the team. Casey spent the fall and winter at home, puttering around, going to football games, attending to the minimal duties required of him as a "vice-president" of the Valley National Bank, Edna's family bank. In January he went from Glendale to Toluca Lake, where Valley National was opening its first branch office, slipped and fell heavily on his back, damaging a few things. That slowed him down for a while, but he got going again and in July went up to San Francisco for the first of two All-Star Games played by the major leagues that year (there were two All-Star Games in 1959, 1960, 1961 and 1962). Weiss was at the All-Star Game too, and he took Casey aside and talked to him about becoming manager of the new New York team. Stengel didn't think it was such a good idea. He'd turned down the Tiger job, Edna wanted him to take it easy, he'd hurt his back. He didn't think so. Weiss was persistent. Stengel said, well, he'd think it over.

Weiss hired a couple of former major-league managers, Cookie Lavagetto and Sollie Hemus, as coaches so as to have someone ready to manage if Casey wouldn't give in, but he kept after him. Just before the end of the season he phoned Casey from New York, again offering him the job. Stengel was wavering. Weiss got the engaging Mrs. Payson to phone Casey, which flattered him. Grant phoned too. Stengel missed baseball, and the idea of working again with Weiss in New York — familiar environment all around — appealed to him. And, always important, "the money was right." He said yes, and on Monday, October 2, two days before the Yankees and the Cincinnati Reds met in the first game of the 1961 World Series, the Mets introduced Stengel as their new manager. They held the press conference in Le Salon Bleu of the Savoy Hilton Hotel, fifty weeks after Casey had been discharged in the same room.

Casey said, "It's a great honor for me to be joining the Knickerbockers," a remarkable slip of the tongue that somehow metamorphosed the Mets through the New York Knicks, the city's pro basketball team, into the historic Knickerbockers, the New York club that in 1845 played the first formal game of baseball in America on grounds called the Elysian Fields, just across the Hudson River in New Jersey. Casey had neatly linked the newest team in town with the oldest.

The day after the World Series ended, the Mets and the Houston Colt .45s, the other

561

new team, took part in the National League expansion draft (the two new American League teams had started a year earlier). The draft was a kind of enforced auction in which the two new teams selected second-rate, washed-up or embryonic players from the eight established teams for extravagant sums of money that were, in effect, initiation fees for joining the league. The Mets' first pick was a catcher named Hobie Landrith, who had been around the National League for a dozen years without establishing himself as a first-string catcher. "You have to have a catcher," Stengel explained, "or you'll have a lot of passed balls."

Weiss spent $1,800,000 of Mrs. Payson's money in the draft and a lot more in the months after it acquiring players. He chose them with a certain practical cynicism. He based the team's future on his staff of scouts, which he felt would discover and sign exemplary prospects who would turn the Mets into a respectable team in five or six years. For the time being, though, he had to attract customers to the ball park. The new stadium New York was building wouldn't be ready until 1964, and the Mets would be playing their first two seasons in the ancient Polo Grounds, right across the river from Yankee

Stadium, where Weiss' old team was still the best in baseball.

Weiss knew there was a great body of National League fans in New York who had not turned to the Yankees after the Giants and Dodgers left town. The Yankees' attendance had actually dropped in 1958, the first year after the other teams had gone. Whereas the Houston club selected young, unknown players of promise, Weiss loaded his roster with familiar baseball names: Gil Hodges, Roger Craig, Gus Bell, Don Zimmer, Frank Thomas, Clem Labine, Richie Ashburn, Charlie Neale, Johnny Antonelli, Billy Loes. Several of these players retired from baseball and never played a game for the Mets, but their names helped in publicizing the new club. Weiss brought Casey back in from California for the annual Thanksgiving Day parade in New York, at which Casey appeared, waving to the crowd. "I may be able to sell tickets with my face," he said. When Topping that winter switched the Yankees' training camp in Florida from St. Petersburg to Fort Lauderdale so that it would be closer to his home on Florida's east coast, Weiss leaped into the void and put the Mets into the old Yankee camp in St. Petersburg. More good publicity, more creation of the feeling that the Mets were an honest-to-God major-league team.

Stengel, with fifty seasons behind him in professional baseball, was on familiar ground when he returned to St. Petersburg in the spring of 1962 after an absence of only one season. People flocked to see him and his new team, and he talked overtime. The New York press, hungry for another source of baseball news after four years with only one club to write about, descended on Stengel in force. As Ed Linn said, they covered him instead of the team. When the Mets met the Yankees in an exhibition game in St. Petersburg, it was built up as the battle of the century. The Yankees took it in stride as a spring-training exhibition, but Stengel played it to win, using his best pitchers, and when the Mets topped the Yankees 4–3 it was big news back in New York.

The Mets won almost as many games as they lost in spring training, although Stengel said, "I ain't fooled. They play different when the other side is trying too." When the season opened — they met the Cardinals in St. Louis — the Mets were terrible. Zimmer, the third baseman, took the first ground ball of the year and threw it wildly over the first baseman's head; Craig, the pitcher, balked a run across home plate; and the Mets were trounced 11–4. In St. Louis several Mets players were trapped in a hotel elevator for an unseemly length of time, which seemed an omen. The team returned to New York, where the city welcomed them with a parade up Broadway. Stengel, given the key to the city, said, "I got a lot of keys to a lot of cities, but this one I'm gonna use to open a new team." But the new team lost and lost again and kept on losing, nine straight times, including two to Houston, their rival expansionists. The Pittsburgh Pirates opened the season with ten straight wins, so that after their first nine games the Mets found themselves nine and a half games behind.

They finally won a game ("Break up the Mets!" became an instant gag) behind the pitching of an engineering student from Northwestern named Jay Hook, but lost three more after that. The big names were becoming less important. Frank Thomas did hit thirty-four homers during the season, but Hodges had a badly damaged knee. Labine was released. Zimmer went hitless in his first thirty-four at bats and was hitting .077 when the Mets traded him to Cincinnati.

But in mid-May a small miracle happened. The Mets won five of six games, all with late-inning rallies, a tremendously exciting turn of affairs for the fans who had been cautiously watching them. In a thirteen-inning night game that didn't end until almost an hour after midnight, the Mets won 6–5 when Landrith was walked with the bases loaded to force in the winning run. They won another extra-inning game by the same score the next day and moved out of last place.

The euphoria didn't last long. The Mets had a terrible road trip, including a delayed all-night flight from Milwaukee to Houston that didn't get them to their hotel until after eight o'clock in the morning. Stengel, staggering to his room for a few hours of sleep, said, "If anybody wants me, tell them I'm being embalmed." The Mets lost seventeen games in a row, and later in the season had losing streaks of eleven straight and thirteen straight. Sandy Koufax no-hit them in June. Roger Craig, presumably their best pitcher, lost twenty-four games. Craig Anderson, another starter, lost sixteen straight and had a 3–17 record.

The Mets' ineptitude was astonishing. "Can't *anybody* play this here game?" Stengel demanded one day, a remark that with its words transposed to "Can't anybody here play this game?" became a widely publicized motto of Met incompetence. When the team got into a brawl on the field in San Francisco, Jack Mann wrote, "The Mets can't fight either." But their incompetence somehow became endearing. Leonard Koppett said the perverse popularity of the Mets stemmed in part from the social revolution that was occurring at that time. John F. Kennedy was the new, youthful President of the country, a symbol of the young taking over from the old; the Beatles, with their shockingly long hair, were revolutionizing popular music; the Twist, a new form of dancing that disconcerted the older generation, was sweeping the country; miniskirts, their hems halfway to the hips, were even more disconcerting. "The times they are a-changin'," sang Bob Dylan, the iconoclastic hero of the young.

The Mets were different, they were counterculture, they were fun. The worse they were, the more fun they were. A big, powerful but not very good first baseman named Marv Throneberry joined the club. Throneberry had been a highly touted Yankee rookie several years earlier but had been a failure in the majors. The year before, playing for Kansas City and Baltimore, he had batted only .226, although he hit eleven home runs. A sportswriter, mocking the Mets' earnest statement that Throneberry's bat might be just the thing the club needed to get moving, dubbed him Marvelous Marv.

Throneberry hit some homers for the Mets, but batted only .238, fielded ineptly and made extravagant mistakes during games. He hit a triple one day but was called out for failing to touch first base. Stengel went out to argue with the first-base umpire. The second-base umpire wandered over and said, "I hate to tell you this, Casey, but he missed second base, too." Stengel glared at him, then looked over to third base, where Throneberry was standing, and said, "Well, I know he touched third base because he's standing on it." With Throneberry out and off the bases, the next Met batter hit a home run. The club lost 8–7, but if Throneberry had remembered to touch the bases the Mets would have tied the score and maybe even won. In another game the Mets picked a man off base but before they could tag him out Throneberry got in his way and the umpires ruled the runner safe because of interference.

All this and more was gleefully recounted in the press. Throneberry's locker was next to that of Richie Ashburn, who had played fourteen splendid seasons with the Phillies before before coming to the Mets for one last year before retiring. (He batted .306 and was voted the Mets' Most Valuable Player, an honor that amused him. "Most Valuable Player on the worst team ever?" he'd ask. "Just how do they mean that?") Ashburn was witty, and Throneberry, who had country humor, could laugh at himself. Reporters began gathering around the two lockers after games, listening to Ashburn poke fun at Throneberry and Throneberry poke fun at himself. They began writing Marvelous Marv stories, and the fans ate it up. Throneberry became a huge favorite with the crowd, the lasting symbol of the hapless but lovable Mets of 1962, as well as a spur to other stories about other players. The Mets obtained a catcher named Harry Chiti from Cleveland in a transaction that required the Mets to send a player to a Cleveland farm team thirty days later. The player they sent was Chiti. The Mets got a pitcher named Bob Miller, and then they got another pitcher named Bob Miller. Robert G. Miller was a lefty, Robert L. Miller a righty. Robert G. won two games and lost two, but that respectable .500 performance didn't win him the Met fans, who greatly preferred Robert L., who made twenty-one starts, completed one and had a 0–12 record before winning his last game of the season. Robert L. fit the Met pattern. He understood things. He was a relief pitcher as well as a starter and was in the bullpen one day when the phone rang. It was Stengel on the phone. "Get Nelson ready," Casey said. The bullpen coach said, "Who?" The Mets didn't have a Nelson. They had a *broadcaster* named Nelson, Lindsay Nelson, but no player by that name. "Nelson," Stengel said. "Get him up." The bullpen coach looked around. "Who's he want?" Miller asked. "Nelson," the coach said. "That's me," Miller said, and got up and began throwing. He was right. He knew Casey called Lindsay Nelson "Miller." Before the Millers became household names for Met fans, they appeared on the TV quiz *To Tell the Truth*, the format of which called for panelists to query three contestants, each claiming to be the same relatively obscure but interestingly employed person, in an attempt to determine which one of them was actually the person he claimed to be. When the announcer asked the ultimate question, "Will the real Bob Miller please stand up?" there was confusion and then delight when *two* of the three contestants turned out to be the real Bob Miller.

The first really big weekend of the season came late in May when the Dodgers and the

Giants rolled into New York for the first time. There was a doubleheader with the Dodgers on Wednesday, Memorial Day, a single game with the Dodgers on Thursday, a single game with the Giants on Friday, a doubleheader with the Giants on Saturday, a single game with the Giants on Sunday. Weiss' understanding of the nostalgic feeling for the National League was borne out when a crowd of more than 55,000 people filled every seat in the Polo Grounds for the Memorial Day doubleheader. There was another good turnout the next day, and the Giants drew more than 40,000 on Friday and nearly that on Saturday and again on Sunday. Huge crowds for a last-place team. That the Mets lost all seven games didn't matter. The fans had a wonderful time, and something was beginning to happen to them. They cheered their old heroes — the few that were still with the Giants and the Dodgers — but they booed them as visitors, too. A group of young men in the upper right-field stands, who still resented the fact that Dodger owner Walter O'Malley had taken their beloved Bums out of Brooklyn, walked down to the railing of the boxes and with admirable coordination unrolled seven window shades on which they had lettered:

OMALLEY
GO HOME

It was a takeoff on anti-American signs then appearing all over Europe that said, "Ami Go Home." The young men were hurriedly chased away and their window shades confiscated, but they had made their point: to hell with the Dodgers, and to hell with the Giants, too.

The crowds began to cheer the Mets vigorously on the rare occasions when they did things well. The counterculture kids began chanting "Let's Go Mets" as a kind of parody, along the lines of "Fight Fiercely, Harvard," and soon everybody took it up. The rhythmic roar "Let's Go Mets! Let's Go Mets!" became a theme that lasted for years. Banners became more and more commonplace, though Weiss deplored them and tried to keep them out of the park. But "Marv" appeared, and "Marvelous Marv" and "Cranberry Strawberry We Love Throneberry." A quintet showed up with placards that spelled out "MARV!" and then reversed positions so that they spelled "VRAM!" The crowd loved it. More and more banners — the messages of the people— appeared during the season, and Weiss, always practical, finally gave in and let the banner people have their way. In the Mets' second season he even staged a special Banner Day in the Polo Grounds at which the fans were allowed to parade on the field with banners before the game. On that occasion, after the fans left the field, the Mets themselves filed out of the clubhouse, each carrying a card held face down. They stopped near second base, faced the stands and held up the cards, which spelled, "To the Met Fans — We Love You Too." Stengel came trotting out of the dugout, went to the end of the line and held up his card. It was an exclamation point.

When the Giants and Dodgers came back to the Polo Grounds again in July 1962, the Mets put on an old-timers' game. The fact that a brand-new team could have an old-timers' game in its first season fit the bizarre image of the Mets that was developing, but Weiss was only being practical. The old-timers were old Giants and Dodgers, and the idea was to stimulate attendance, which it did. The Mets drew more than 900,000 people in 1962, almost 50 percent more than the Giants drew in either of their last two seasons in the Polo Grounds, and the games with the Giants and the Dodgers provided half of it.

Stengel dominated the scene all year long.

He sat in John McGraw's old office, telling stories, talking with reporters, talking with anyone, keeping attention focused on the Mets. "We *sold* this team," he said afterward. "Amazin'," he kept saying, "amazin'," and the word caught on. Soon it was "the Amazin' Mets," like a phrase on a circus billboard. "Come out and see my amazin' Mets," Stengel said. "I been in this game a hundred years but I see new ways to lose I never knew existed before." His putdowns of his team seemed somehow charming. "We're a fraud," he said, and after one more defeat, "The attendance got trimmed again," meaning the crowd.

In St. Louis he got into a cab with several young writers accompanying the club. "Are you fellows players?" the cabdriver asked. "No," said Stengel, "and neither are my players players." He liked Jay Hook, the Northwestern graduate, but he wanted Hook to pitch more aggressively, to loosen up the hitters at the plate in order to be more effective. When Hook didn't, Casey said, "I got the smartest pitcher in the world until he goes to the mound." He called Ken MacKenzie, a Yale graduate, into a game in a tight spot and said, "Now just make believe you're pitching against Harvard."

He had his usual trouble with names. Throneberry was "Thornberry." Chris Cannizzaro, a reserve catcher, was "Canzoneri." Stengel said, "Canzoneri is the only defensive catcher who can't catch." He had a terrible time trying to remember Gus Bell's name before the Mets' first opening day: "And in left field, in left field we have a splendid man, and he knows how to do it. He's been around and he swings the bat there in left field and he knows what to do. He's got a big family [Bell had six children] and he wants to provide for them, and he's a fine outstanding player, the fella in left field. You can be sure he'll be ready when the bell rings — and that's his name, *Bell!*"

He confused Jim Marshall, a left-handed batter who played first base at the beginning of 1962, with John Blanchard, a left-handed-hitting catcher he had had on the Yankees, but he remembered the important thing. "Blanchard!" he called one day as Marshall was about to bat. "Yes, sir," Marshall dutifully responded. "You see them lines?" asked Casey, gesturing toward the foul lines. Marshall nodded. "Do you know what them lines are for?" Marshall waited. "They are there to hit the ball on," Casey said, even as Paul Waner had advised Tommy Holmes twenty years earlier in Boston, "and those other ballplayers are all out there in the middle."

Players came and players went (Marshall was traded early in May, Gus Bell a few weeks later), but the Mets stayed the same. They slogged their way through the season and finished last with a record of 40 wins and 120 defeats, more defeats than any other major-league team had had since 1899. In their last game of the year they hit into a triple play.

31

A WAY TO RETIRE: ONE BROKEN HIP

Nineteen sixty-three was more of the same. The Mets were still in the Polo Grounds, they lost the first eight games of the season (instead of nine), they drew a lot of people (slightly over a million) and finished last again, forty-eight games behind the pennant-winning Dodgers and fifteen games behind ninth-place Houston. But "Let's Go Mets" was chanted even louder and there were more banners than ever. Throneberry, batting .143, was sent to the minors early in the season, his big-league career at an end, but ineptitude remained the hallmark of the team. Craig lost eighteen straight games, tying a National League record set more than fifty years earlier. In August in Pittsburgh the Mets were leading 1–0 in the last of the ninth. There was one out and the Pirates had a man on first base. Manny Mota hit a ground ball that could have been a game-ending double play, but it went past the pitcher, between the shortstop and the second baseman, and into short center field. The Met center fielder charged in to field the ball in order to hold the base runners at first and second, but he missed it and they kept on running. The right fielder, backing up the play, picked up the ball and heaved it halfway between third base and home. The Met pitcher, running over to back up third, tried to reverse direction and fell down. The first runner scored, tying the game 1–1, and Mota, running all the way, rounded third and headed for the plate. The Met pitcher got up, located the ball and threw it to the catcher, who whirled to make the tag and discovered that he was five feet away from the plate in foul territory. Mota scored and the Pirates won 2–1 — on a ground ball past the pitcher. Stengel stood motionless in the dugout for five minutes staring out at the field before slowly making his way to the clubhouse.

The peak of accomplishment came in an exhibition, the Mayor's Trophy game between the Mets and the Yankees in Yankee Stadium on June 20. More than 50,000 people were there, most of them Met fans carrying banners, who were beside themselves with joy when the Mets won 6–2. In the season itself, the Mets won 51 games and lost 111, which may have been terrible but which the optimistic fans pointed out was a great improvement over 1962.

The new ball park was completed during the winter of 1963–64 and named Shea Stadium, after the prime mover in the creation of the Mets. It was located in Queens, out on Long Island, right next door to the New York World's Fair, which was opening in 1964, and strategically located on subway lines that connected it to the city and highways that led to the heavily populated suburbs of Long Island and Westchester County. It was an impressive-looking place, and after the Mets lost their opening game there (a Pittsburgh Pirate rookie named Willie Stargell hit a home run, the first ever at Shea), Stengel was asked what he thought of the new stadium. "Lovely, just lovely," he said. "The park is lovelier than my team."

One of the reporters told him that some Mets had complained that the stadium had a bad hitting background. Stengel said, "My hitters have complained about the bad background here for three years and they've only played here one day." Someone else said the Pirates had done all right against the background. "Yeah," Stengel said, "and you didn't notice no one pulling any shades down for them when they come to bat, did you?"

He had derided the team earlier on a spring-training trip to Mexico City. Asked if the mile-high altitude in Mexico bothered his players, he said, "The altitude bothered my players at the Polo Grounds, and that's below sea level." He told a coach in spring training to take a group of players over to another field to work out. "I want to see if they can play on the road," he said.

The 1964 season began with only four straight losses, which the counter-culture merrily pointed to as concrete evidence of the Met's steady progress: nine straight losses to open the season in 1962, eight straight in 1963, four this year. Late in May in Chicago the Mets achieved a breakthrough of sorts by defeating the Cubs 19–1. A widely circulated story said that a fan had called a newspaper office in Waterbury, Connecticut, during the game to find out the score.

"How are the Mets doing?" he asked.

"They've got nineteen runs."

"Are they ahead or behind?"

Earlier on that road trip the Mets got into a fight with the Braves after Ron Hunt, a lively second baseman they had found some-where, slammed into Ed Bailey, the Milwaukee catcher, even though Hunt was clearly out at the plate. Bailey swung at Hunt, Hunt swung back, and both benches emptied as everyone rushed into the melee, including the seventy-three-year-old Stengel, who grabbed at twenty-three-year-old Denis Menke. Menke, who had been a Big Ten football player, jerked his arms away, and Stengel lost his balance and fell. Tracy Stallard, a Met pitcher, said, "I stepped over somebody, looked down and saw it was the old man. I started laughing so hard I couldn't fight." Casey said later, "Oh, I grabbed him and he just pulled away a little. You would have thought him and me was goin' dancing down Main Street the way I hung on to his arms."

The crowds poured into Shea Stadium, most memorably on May 31, a Sunday, to see the Giants in a doubleheader. There were more than 57,000 people in the stands when the first game began, shortly after one o'clock, but almost 40,000 of them had gone home by the time the second game ended nearly ten and a half hours later. The Giants, who won the first game, had taken an early 6–1 lead in the second but the Mets tied it at 6–6 in the sixth inning, and that's the way the score remained through the next sixteen innings, before the Giants scored twice in the top of the twenty-third inning to win 8–6. As the crowd in Shea diminished and the afternoon and evening wore on, the much larger number of people watching the game on television kept increasing, as word of the marathon contest spread. There was a popular television quiz show called *What's My Line?* that went on the air live every Sunday night. At the beginning of the show there was usually a little casual banter between the master of ceremonies, John Daly, and the regular panelists, one of whom was Bennett Cerf, the publisher. On this Sunday night when Daly greeted him, Cerf said, "Boy, what a baseball game!" Daly said, "Baseball game?" Cerf said, "The Giants and the Mets! I've just been watching it on the TV set outside. They're tied 6–6 in the seventeenth inning!" All over the metropolitan area thousands of viewers hurriedly switched from *What's My Line?* to the ball game. Two weeks later another big crowd turned out on Father's Day and saw Jim Bunning pitch a perfect game against the Mets.

Still, despite such memorable afternoons, it wasn't quite as much fun watching the Mets lose. The act was growing a little tired. The fans were ready now for some improvement in the team's performance, but the Mets were able to win only two games more than they had a year earlier and finished a distant last again, thirteen games behind ninth-place Houston, which in turn finished ten games behind the eighth-place team.

The muttering began. Tim Harkness, who had played first base a good part of 1963, was dropped early in 1964 and complained, "How can you play for a manager who sleeps on the bench?" Jimmy Piersall, who played forty games for the Mets in 1963, said, "He isn't a manager anymore. He's just on display." Jackie Robinson, Stengel's old antagonist, got in his licks by saying, "He's too old to manage. He sleeps on the bench. He should quit." Howard Cosell echoed Robinson's criticism and hammered at Stengel in his broadcasts.

A rumor spread that Alvin Dark, then managing the Giants, would succeed Stengel in 1965, with Casey remaining home in California as president of the Angels. Although Stengel was annoyed by the rumors all he said was, "I'm interested in building this team. That's why I took the job. Whoever manages this club next will have better players. I hate to say this, because you know what can happen, and if they don't make it it's a bad thing, but it looks to me like some of these young pitchers are *gonna* make it."

He worked with the young players in the instructional school. He grilled Dick Selma, who had graduated from high school the year before, asking shrewd questions about his background and his previous pitching experience, and then said, "I don't want to tell you that you have a job or anything like that, but you have a good chance. Now don't go out and eat a fifteen-dollar steak on me and get fat." Selma made it to the majors a year later and was a useful pitcher for the Mets for three seasons after that.

But it was obvious that Casey was discouraged. Even though Weiss had reinstituted the instructional school for him, he groused at the front office for not giving him better players. The Met scouts had uncovered some very promising players, but their best days lay several years in the future, and Stengel was becoming more concerned about *now*.

He was beginning to sour a bit on young players. He was disappointed by his failure to persuade more youngsters to sign with the Mets, the hot prospects just out of high school or college. Stengel felt that a young player ought to be eager to cast his fortune with the Mets, since he'd have a much better chance of moving quickly up the ladder to the major leagues. A lot of the youngsters didn't see it that way. "The youth of America," Casey complained. "You tell them, 'Here is the opportunity.' And the youth of America says, 'Where is the money?' "

Like Mantle before them, they didn't want to learn. "You bring the youth of America in here," he'd say, "and they swing as hard as they can. You tell them to just m-e-e-t the ball, and they look at you." He remembered that look, the one that said, "I'll listen, but I won't pay attention." It was frustrating. He got angry at Ron Swoboda one day, a Met hero in 1969 but only a rookie at the time, when Swoboda after dropping a fly ball stomped on a batting helmet and crushed it. "How would you like it if I stepped on your watch?" Stengel said. He grumbled about the Met bullpen. "What am I supposed to do with the plumbers I got down there?"

But he continued to manage, and at the very end of 1964 there was gratification. The National League had a four-team race sizzling in the last week of the season, after Philadelphia lost ten straight games and an apparent lock on the pennant. The Cardinals were half a game ahead of Cincinnati on the Friday before the season ended, with the Mets coming into St. Louis for three games. The Reds lost

Friday night. If the Cardinals could beat the Mets they'd clinch a tie for the pennant. They sent Bob Gibson, now in the Hall of Fame, out to pitch, and Stengel countered with little, left-handed Al Jackson, whom he admired so much. "Jackson is a *pret-ty* good-looking pitcher," he'd say, which was high praise. (The admiration was mutual. Jackson said years later, "Casey would stand in the dugout and say real loud, 'If I was a left-handed pitcher, here's what I would do right now.' That's when I knew he was talking to me. There were men on first and second, and you knew the other team wanted to bunt them over. Casey would say, 'Here's what I would do. I would let him bunt. I would throw him a little slider, and I would break toward the third-base side, and I would throw his ass out at third." In six years as a Met pitcher, never once did Jackson allow a man to be sacrificed from second to third when he was on the mound. "Casey had the guts to tell you what he'd do in a certain situation *when* it came up on the ball field," Jackson said. "He didn't wait until after it was over and then second-guess. He'd tell you right now, and he'd tell you what the *other* team should do. He's the only man I ever saw do that.")

In St. Louis that Friday night Jackson outpitched Gibson and won 1–0. On Saturday the Reds didn't play; they had one game left, on Sunday. Again, the Cardinals could clinch a tie for the pennant if they could defeat the Mets on Saturday, and again the Mets defeated them. On Sunday the Mets tried a third time — the weakest team in the league, thirty-nine games behind the Cardinals, trying to sweep three straight from a club that was one game from the pennant. It was a little like knocking off Bill Terry's Giants thirty years earlier.

The Cardinals scored, and the Mets tied it. The Cards scored again, the Mets tied it again and then went ahead 3–2. But that was all. Gibson came on in relief, the Cardinals went ahead to stay, won 11–5 and captured the pennant as Cincinnati lost. But, damn, it was a great moment for the Mets. They had been a factor in the pennant race! For the first time they began to feel legitimate, like a genuine major-league ball club.

Just as gratifying were the attendance figures for the season. The Mets, even though they finished last for the third straight year, drew 1,732,597 to Shea. The Yankees, finishing first for the fifth straight year, drew only 1,305,638 to Yankee Stadium.

By this time it was likely that even Weiss

and Grant and Mrs. Payson were hoping Casey might step down. They weren't pushing him, but he was going to be seventy-five in 1965 and it seemed like a good time, with the club a success in Shea and a winning team still several seasons away. But Casey couldn't stop. A reporter said in 1964 that Casey looked as at home on a jet plane as he must have looked riding a sooty, steam-driven locomotive in 1910. This was his world, and he wasn't getting off.

He was there in spring training in 1965, as garrulous and as sarcastic as ever. He signed a new contract and continued as the unquestioned boss of his team. At a team party near the end of training a cocky young outfielder named Duke Carmel made a heavy joke about Casey managing the Yankees. "Anybody could win pennants with that team," Carmel said. "That didn't take talent." Stengel didn't laugh. Carmel came over to him later, put his arm around his shoulders and said, "You knew I was just kidding, didn't you?" Maybe he did, but when Casey cut his squad a short time later Carmel was gone. Duke blamed his departure on his wisecrack, and some of the writers were inclined to agree, even though no other club thought enough of Carmel's talents (he had hit .233 the year before) to give him another shot at the majors. "God damn it," Stengel said when he heard the talk, "do you think I'd fire a man for that if he could play?"

He continued to mock his team. The Mets went to West Point for an exhibition game with the Cadets, more than fifty years after Casey first played there (so many things that happened in his later life seemed tied to events that had occurred decades earlier), and Stengel fell walking down a concrete ramp and broke his wrist. Back at Shea he joked, "I got this broken arm from watching my team. All they gave me last year was a head cold." But he was still a cheerleader. When Danny Napoleon, a young outfielder from Pennsylvania, hit a triple to win a ball game Casey came whooping into the clubhouse yelling, "Vive La France!"

He wasn't able to do much to improve the team's performance. In June the Mets lost twenty of twenty-three games, and in July they lost ten straight. They were just as bad as they had been in 1964, when they were just as bad as they had been in 1963. Enthusiasm for Met ineptitude continued to wane. A season earlier the crowd had laughed at a banner about nineteen-year-old Ed Kranepool, a glittering prospect when he had been signed at the age of seventeen but who hadn't developed as rapidly as the Mets' publicity indicated he would. "Is Ed Kranepool over the hill?" the banner asked. That didn't seem so funny in 1965.

The fans were still coming into Shea, helped by the next-door presence of the New York World's Fair, which was in its second year, as well as by various special promotions the Met management tied in to ball games. On July 25 they would hold their fourth annual old-timers' game, and in conjunction with it they decided to stage an onfield celebration of Stengel's seventy-fifth birthday, which would actually occur five days later, on July 30. The Mets returned from a road trip on Friday, the 23rd, glowing a little. Jackson had pitched a two-hit shutout against the Pirates on Thursday and had a no-hitter through seven innings, and on Friday the Mets beat the Phillies 10–5. On Saturday they lost to Philadelphia 5–1, in a game that is worth noting only because it was the last game Stengel ever managed.

That night there was a party at Toots Shor's restaurant in Manhattan for the old-timers who had come for the Sunday festivities. It was an impressive party, a long evening of eating and drinking and talking.

Sometime after midnight Casey lost his balance, fell and hurt his left hip. Joseph DeGregorio, the Mets' comptroller, felt it would be better for Casey to come home with him instead of going to his suite in the Essex House on 59th Street. Edna was home in California nursing an infected eye, and Casey would be alone at the hotel. Besides, DeGregorio lived in Whitestone, Queens, only a few minutes from Shea Stadium, and it would be a lot easier for Casey to get to the ball park the next day from there than from the Essex House.

Casey drove home with DeGregorio and went to bed, but he had a very uncomfortable night. At eight Sunday morning DeGregorio phoned Gus Mauch, the Mets' trainer, and asked him to come over. Mauch arrived, realized that something was seriously wrong and phoned Dr. Peter LaMotte, the club physician, at his home in Connecticut. "I'd never seen Casey in such pain," Mauch said. LaMotte drove down at once to DeGregorio's, examined Stengel and phoned for an ambulance to take him to Roosevelt Hospital in Manhattan. X-rays confirmed that the hip was broken. Someone phoned Edna in California, and she flew to New York that night. Sunday afternoon at the ball park a message from Casey was read over the public address system: "I know I can't make it to the stadium today. I do feel sorry for all those people who went to all that trouble for my birthday."

Various muddled stories tried to explain what had happened. Casey had twisted his hip getting out of DeGregorio's car. He had stumbled over the curb. He had had a muscle spasm in bed and had hurt his hip that way. He had hurt himself at Shor's and then aggravated the injury getting out of the car on Long Island. No, it was after he arrived there. At first the injury was a twisted hip. Then a badly bruised hip. Finally a broken hip.

That an old man who had had a lot to drink had fallen down seemed too hard a thing for anyone to say, particularly since this old man frequently had a lot to drink without falling down, and without showing much wear and tear the next day. However he hurt himself, he was operated on at Roosevelt Hospital on Monday and an artificial hip joint was installed in place of the damaged one. He was on his feet in a surprisingly short time, walking up and down behind a walker. He and Edna celebrated his seventy-fifth birthday in the hospital.

On August 7, wearing a bright-yellow kimono, he held an audience for several of the writers at the hospital. He showed them how he could get around with the walker, said he'd be leaving the hospital soon, wasn't sure that he'd return to active managing that season and grew irritable when he was asked if he'd manage again next year. "I always sign a one-year contract," he said. "When the season is over I'll go in and talk with Mr. Weiss."

Asked if the club had talked with him before sending Danny Napoleon to the minors several days earlier, he said shortly, "They've talked to me ever since I've been in this job. I'm still manager of this club."

Three weeks later, out of the hospital and staying at the Essex House with Edna, he changed his mind. Edna wanted him to give up managing and take it easy. The club, quite obviously, did too. Dr. LaMotte explained how long his recuperation would take, and how restricted his mobility would be for a long time to come. A press conference was arranged on August 30 at the Essex House, where Casey, walking with an oddly shaped black metal cane, told the assembled reporters that he was stepping down.

"If I can't run out there and take a pitcher out," he said, "I'm not capable of continuing as manager." Wes Westrum, a Met coach who had been serving as "interim manager," was named his successor.

A few days later, on September 2, he was driven out to Shea, where, gaunt and pale in a dark business suit, he walked slowly out to the pitcher's mound for an odd ceremony at which his uniform was "officially retired." It was several hours before game time and the stadium was empty. He posed for pictures, spoke to the team, listened in return to a jumbled thank-you speech from one of the players ("He seems to have picked up a little Stengelese," Casey said) and slowly walked off again.

His uniform shirt was put on display in a glass case in the stadium's Diamond Club, although Casey said before leaving the ball park, "I'd like to see them give that number 37 to some young player so it can go on and do some good for the Mets. I hope they don't put a mummy in the glass case."

He and Edna returned to the Essex House, packed and went home to California, pausing on the way in Kansas City so that he could visit his seventy-eight-year-old sister, Louise, who had just broken her hip, too.

32 DO NOT GO GENTLE: TALKING, TALKING, TALKING

Stengel lived for ten years after his retirement from the Mets — ten years and a month, to be exact. He was out of baseball. The Mets made him a vice-president, gave him a nebulous assignment as overseer of scouting in California, invited him to spring training and to club affairs and continued to pay him, but after fifty-six years it was finally over. He was no longer a factor in the game.

He kept as close to it as he could. He went to the World Series in Los Angeles in 1965, barely two months after his operation, looking natty in a yellow shirt and a blue tie, "just in case they want me on television." He flew back to New York in midwinter for the baseball writers' dinner, and in the spring of 1966 he showed up with Edna at St. Petersburg to watch the Mets in training.

Dressed in a red-checked sport jacket and a red tie and swinging his crooked black cane, he talked in St. Petersburg about the Mets and many other things and joked about the cane. "I don't really need this," he said, "but I have to limp or I can't get into the Hall of Fame." There is a rule that says a man must be out of baseball for at least five years before he is eligible for election to the Hall of Fame. It's a foolish provision, put into effect because baseball is afraid of its own sentimentality; it worries that it might elect someone impulsively who really doesn't belong, disregarding the fact that there is a bullpenful of men who were elected to Cooperstown *after* the waiting period who don't belong there, either. After his retirement from the Mets the seventy-five-year-old Stengel faced five years of waiting before he could even be considered for election. However, the Baseball Writers Association of America, which conducts the Hall of Fame elections, consulted feverishly but secretly and agreed to waive the rule in Stengel's case. An unpublicized ballot was taken and Casey was voted in, not long before he reached St. Petersburg that spring, although he didn't know about it yet.

On March 8, a few days after he had arrived in Florida, the Mets asked Casey to come out to the spring training field to take part in a ceremony. The sportswriters were giving a plaque to George Weiss, he was told, and they wanted Casey to make the presention. They told him to bring Edna along, too. It was a coldish morning for Florida, with a little of what Jimmy Cannon called "New York" in the wind. Stengel, wielding his cane, limped onto the field and walked with surprising quickness toward the clubhouse. He had on street clothes but wore a Mets baseball cap. As he reached the clubhouse he was surrounded by writers and photographers, and he saw TV cameras, and he began to suspect something. The Commissioner of Baseball, General William Eckert, was on the field, and so was Ford Frick, Eckert's predecessor and a member of the Hall of Fame committee.

Casey looked around, wondering. Someone gave Edna a bouquet of flowers and someone else guided Casey toward a microphone where Frick stood, waiting to speak. Casey leaned over to Edna and said, "I gotta find out what I'm doing here."

The Met players stopped practicing and gathered around. The small crowd of spectators who had come to watch practice crowded closer to the chain-link fence that kept them off the field. Frick began to speak. He explained the eligibility rule and the fact that it had been waived and said a special vote had been held and Stengel had been elected to Cooperstown.

Casey, holding his cap in his hand, bowed his head quickly, then waved his cap, and everyone applauded. Edna kissed him. Casey was grinning, his wrinkled face beaming, looking, as Cannon wrote, very young. He stepped to the microphone.

"Edna," he said, "I appreciate that kiss."

He spoke for a few minutes, saying, among other things, "It's a terrific thing to get in it while you're still alive." After the little ceremony ended he went over to the fence beyond third base to talk to the spectators gathered there, most of them elderly.

"They just put me in the Hall of Fame," he said. He mentioned a formal breakfast he had been to that morning, saying, "I got one leg and a cane and I thought they was giving me a doughnut at the breakfast, which is pretty good because they get fifteen, twenty cents for a doughnut now, but they give me the full course, very good. I walked over thirty feet without the cane on a carpet to make the speech at the breakfast. But a coach walks ninety feet and there ain't no carpet, so I can't be a coach." The crowd laughed and applauded, and Casey acknowledged the applause by bending over halfway to the ground in a long, low bow, sweeping his cap across the ground.

A Met official asked him if he could walk over and talk to the spectators in the little grandstand beyond home plate. "I can't make the same speech," he said, but he limped over and spoke for a while there and then sat down on the team bench, still holding his black cane. He said, "Being in the Hall of Fame is an amazing thing. I didn't expect it to be so quick." He paused, then said, "It's bigger than I thought it was. This Hall of Fame thing is bigger than anything I ever saw."

For the rest of his life, whenever Stengel signed an autograph, he'd add the Hall of Fame to his signature. Even his letters were signed that way. When Ira Berkow wrote Casey outlining a book they might do together, Casey replied: "Dear Ira: Your conversation's; and the fact you were the working writer were inthused with the Ideas was great but frankly do not care for the great amount of work for myself. Sorry but am not interested. Have to many proposition's otherwise for the coming season. Fact cannot disclose my Future affair's. Good luck. Casey Stengel, N.Y. Mets & Hall of Famer."

That summer he and Edna went to Cooperstown for his formal induction to the Hall of

Fame. Ted Williams had been elected at the same time as Casey, and the two were honored together. Williams, often an arrogant and difficult man when he was playing, made one of the best speeches ever heard at Cooperstown, a sensitive, intelligent expression of what baseball meant to him, what it had done for him and what it could still do for others.

Stengel followed, and while for once in his life he was unable to top another speaker, he was fine, too. He said, "I want to thank everybody. I want to thank some of the owners who were amazing to me, and those big presidents of the leagues who were so kind to me when I was obnoxious." He thanked his parents and he thanked George Weiss, "who would find out whenever I was discharged and would reemploy me." Casting back over his half century in baseball, he encapsulated his career in one brief sentence: "I chased the balls that Babe Ruth hit."

Stengel returned to Cooperstown faithfully every year after that for the Hall of Fame ceremonies, a pilgrimage that took considerable effort for an old man: from Glendale through Los Angeles to the airport; a flight across the country to New York City; another flight on a smaller airline to an airport in central New York state; a forty-mile drive from the airport over country roads to the little village of Cooperstown. He'd almost always arrive a couple of days early so that he could move around town, visiting and talking with people, savoring the atmosphere of baseball, his hawklike walk and garrulous face, as Kevin Cunningham called it, recognized everywhere.

His energy and drive remained high, even into his eighties. He and Edna would fly east each spring to the Mets' training camp in Florida. He'd return to New York every summer for the Mets' old-timers' day. He'd attend Dodger games in Chavez Ravine and Angel games in Anaheim. He dedicated a baseball field in Glendale that was named for him and said, "I feel greatly honored to have a ball park named after me, especially since I've been thrown out of so many."

He'd go to the World Series. He'd fly to New York in January for the baseball writers' dinner there, and he'd go to other cities for dinners, luncheons, gatherings of almost any sort. He spoke at all of them. At them, before them and after them. He never flagged. At one dinner after talking glowingly about the Mets he grabbed a broom that chanced to be near the speakers' table and marched off the dais chanting, "Metsies! Metsies! Metsies!" Asked not long before he died who was the best manager he ever saw, he said, "*I* was the best manager I ever saw, and I tell people that to shut 'em up and also because I believe it."

Early in 1973, a month or so after Roberto Clemente of the Pirates was killed in a plane crash off Puerto Rico, Stengel went all the way to Manchester, New Hampshire, for a sports dinner. He spoke at the dinner, as did Curt Gowdy, the broadcaster, who delivered an eloquent tribute to Clemente. After the dinner, broadcaster Ken Meyer of WBZ in Boston took Casey aside for a taped interview. It turned out to be a classic Stengel performance.

What follows is a nearly exact transcription of that half-hour interview, with bracketed annotations here and there that try to explain some of the things Stengel was talking about. He was eighty-two years old, he was 3,000 miles from home, he had attended several banquets and luncheons on his journey, and on this day he had been talking, almost without stopping, for hours. He talked over breakfast, talked through lunch, talked with small groups of friends and admirers over predinner drinks. During the banquet he talked with the people sitting on either side of him on the dais. He had made his customary rambling speech in his heavy, growling voice, seemingly without taking a breath, charming and confusing his listeners, most of whom laughed automatically, not really knowing what they were laughing at.

Now, late at night, the banquet over, the long day done, he sits in a small room and talks on. Rather, he flows on, a Mississippi of words, overwhelming, unceasing. Meyer begins the interview by asking Stengel about Clemente and about the 1960 World Series when Clemente and the Pirates defeated Stengel and the Yankees.

"What," asks Meyer, "do you remember about that Series and Clemente?"

That's the petcock that opens the flow. Stengel starts talking, his voice hurrying, one sentence running into the next without pause:

"Well, I tell ya, it's an amazing Series. I thought I was going to win the Series easy when I went to Pittsburgh and I was very, uh, uh — I blame myself on the whole Series. I mean for the Yankees losing. Now here's the reason why I make that statement was because I thought Ford was so good, and I thought that my pitching staff was a little better than what they had in, uh, Pittsburgh, and they had — the idea was I never pitch Ford in the first game in the World Series and that's why I'm blamin' myself in the Series in

603

the long run. When Ford did pitch the second game [*actually the third game*] he was never scored on. He wasn't scored on in the second game he pitched so the blunder I made not stopping, *starting* him in the first game was because in the last of the World Series I went to pitch Ford and Ford says, 'Why, I can't loosen up my arm.' Now if I'da pitched him in the first game he'da been in better shape to go in the last game when I blow the Series [*if Ford had started the first game, he probably would have pitched the fifth game instead of the sixth, which would have given him sufficient rest to come back as a relief pitcher in the seventh game*].

"Therefore was on carelessness, and as good as the club was [*Pittsburgh*] I didn't think that they was gonna have much of a chance. But I found out the longer I played in that Series, Clemente commenced being alive again. In other words, I mean he was a right fielder and a right fielder — he's like Kaline. He plays right field and a man that's a right fielder — uh, I was played many outfield positions. [*This preoccupation with right field and right fielders is caused by the slip Casey makes when he says Clemente "commenced being alive again." He is talking about Clemente in the 1960 World Series, but the player's recent death*

604

intrudes and Casey is momentarily flustered. He gets back on the track by taking a fix on right field: Clemente was a right fielder; so was Al Kaline; so too was Stengel for part of his career.] He has to throw to second base. You run a ball out and you run hard, and he's facin' throwin' to second, he's facin' throwin' to first, and there, facin' there, but when you get to first base and you go to third [*on a ball hit to right*] just thinkin' a man that hits the ball down the right-field line the right fielder *has to turn around to throw to third.* He's out of position, where a left-handed man on the foul line is *in* position to throw to second, to throw to third on the hit-and-run plays from first to third. [*A right-handed-throwing right fielder fielding a ball near the foul line has to turn his body in order to throw to second or third base, whereas a left-hander does not.]* And in his *hitting* [*Stengel suddenly recalls Clemente's hitting, mentions it, and then drops it*]. In turning around, a left-handed man, you'd think he'd be better out in right field, but he [*Clemente*] displayed, he and Kaline, that it's an amazing thing how a right-handed thrower could be that great as they were in the outfield.

"So then — Clemente then got *better* [*better than what? It's not clear, but it's a compliment*]. Now when it comes to hitting, you'd — he's so *quick* with the *wrists* and, you know, with the bat. Every time we went to pitch different to him, we were supposed to throw at him, back of him, you know, or move him back from home plate, and then when we'd pitch the ball over the plate, why he could hit down on the ball and he rubbed the balls out [*hyperbole: Clemente wore the imprint off the ball*], which they said the effort he put into his work is like Gowdy said [*at the banquet*]. The effort he puts into his work all through the Series showed up, and it showed up there that he beat out three of those balls on me in the infield and if he hadn't I woulda finally won the last Series. Except that I, uh, pitchin' Ford the second game insteada the first game I never got to pitch Ford in the third game [*a third time*] of the Series and he wasn't scored on in two games. Now he's an outstanding player [*Clemente again*], he can do everything and it's like Kaline did and I studied outfielding so much I can't understand how a man where I can play the best or in center field why a man what's right-handed shouldn't be in left field because a left-handed man in left field and he's out of position so half the time himself, yessir?" [*Stengelese at its most undecipherable. I don't know what he means by, "where I can play the*

606

best or in center field," although I suspect DiMaggio and Mantle are stirring in his subconscious. The inanity of the passage seems suddenly to weigh upon him, and he returns the lead to the interviewer with an abrupt "Yessir?"]

Meyer says, "All right, you mentioned Ford and it seems a logical question: Why did you choose to pitch Art Ditmar in the first game instead of Ford? What caused the change?"

"Well," Stengel says, "I told ya because they pitched their best pitcher. Who was their best pitcher? It's the man that lived out in Idaho and he was, uh, was that, uh, wonderful pitcher. [*Vernon Law. Casey can't remember his name but he remembers that Law was from Idaho*]. He pitched in the spots [*was used in the tough games*]. He's been a coach and so on and so forth [*Law became a coach after his playing career ended*]. He was a terrific pitcher, and I figured why pitch Ford against him? I know Ford is good and I thought I was gonna beat 'em the Series anyway, and we did, we had fourteen to nothing and sixteen to two [*the Yankees won three games overwhelmingly, 12–0, 10–0 and 16–3; the Pirates won their four games by margins of one, one, two, and three runs*], but they commenced then. They had Virdon in center field he commenced makin' good catches, and then I had Shantz that had a crippled arm and when the ball went through and hit Kubek in the jaw, see? [*Casey is talking now about the seventh game of the 1960 World Series, the loss of which still galls him more than ten years later*.] The main thing about that was there was just a double play and my pitcher had to go out on the next thing, because we had a secret on the bench and he said, 'I am gonna pitch for ya but my arm is sore.' So every time he warmed up he'd give me a signal to go without changin'. I'd warm a man up every inning [*Ralph Terry said Casey had him warm up five times during that game*] but he pitched five innings until that play that happened to Kubek, in which he missed the ball on the double play. Then he told me, he says, 'I can't pitch any more, my arm is sore.' I mean, he said it was hurting *more*. Each inning I made him go out and warm up. The pitcher. So he was — Shantz was all right while he was in there. [*Sore-armed Bobby Shantz pitched five innings of excellent relief in the seventh game of the 1960 Series until that potential double-play ball took a bad bounce and hit Tony Kubek in the throat, but each inning as he warmed up he'd glance at Casey on the bench and signal whether or not he could go on. Fin-*

nally, after the abortive double play, Stengel took him out.] Then I took him out and there wasn't anybody that I picked was right [*Jim Coates gave up a three-run home run, and Terry the game-winning homer*]. And then I asked Ford to go in and Ford said, 'Well, I said I can't loosen up.' And that's true 'cause he pitched the day before, and I shoulda pitched him the first game and I'da had him to relieve in the last game."

Meyer abandons the question of why Stengel picked Ditmar to start and says, "Another guy that was paid tribute to and who was lost during 1972 was a guy you also played in World Series competition with five or six times: Jackie Robinson [*who had died a few months before, in October 1972*]. What reflections and memories do you have about a great athlete like this?"

"Well," says Stengel, "I think he was a great athlete. I think he was one of the best football men that ever played. So was other men out there, like Tipton [*Eric Tipton, a Duke University football star who was a major-league outfielder from 1939 to 1945*]. Both of them were amazing in the same things in the same league in the Pacific Coast. [*Tipton played against Southern California in the 1939 Rose Bowl, and Robinson was a halfback for*

UCLA at the same time, so Casey seems at least mildly justified in lumping them in the same league. On the other hand, he may also be thinking of Kenny Washington, a great black running back who played football with Robinson at UCLA.] And Robi'son at first was great. But as I ask ya now, ya have Satchel Paige here [*Paige was another guest at the banquet*] and I think later he might say a few words for ya. Because I watched Satchel Paige play twelve years before Robi'son started. And when Robi'son played against us and when he hit the ball as he did to the infield it was because no left-hander had ever completed a game in the Dodger stadium at Ebbets Field and when I put in the relief pitcher that I put in, why, that's when they popped the ball up the — to the — catcher because a relief pitcher did not start a game he just relieved. Which the relief for me was left-handed as it made Robi'son pop the ball up like he did [*the popup Robinson hit in the 1952 World Series off left-hander Bob Kuzava; Stengel starts to gloat a little but thinks better of it and switches to compliments*]. Robi'son was a very good base runner and stealer. He was sensational stealing. [*But he cannot go on praising this man he disliked so.*] And, aaah, he was not the greatest fielder in my position [*he means "opinion" and he gets flustered again*]. I know four or five men and where everybody said he was, he was in for the Brooklyn club at that time, but when they played with the Monarchs in Kansas City — that was one of the many colored teams I ever saw — I thought that they had four or five men that were outstanding in their play." [*He gets off the subject by ending the last sentence with an abrupt downward intonation and waits for the next question.*]

Meyer says, "All right. After ten pennants in twelve seasons, et cetera, you came back [*to the majors*] with the Mets. What induced you to come back and start over with an expansion ball club?"

"Well," Stengel says, "I, uh, I was turned loose by the Boston club one year and I said, 'Why not lay out in the, uh, and see if you wanna go back into baseball?' [*Casey gets a little mixed up here between 1937, the year after he was fired by Brooklyn, and 1944, the year after he was fired by Boston.*] And at that time I was offered an opportunity to go to two clubs [*that was 1944*] and while I went out I was in the oil business [*that was 1937*]. I looked up and I was given a chance to go with the Boston Braves [*after 1937*]. So I said, 'Well, I laid out one year [*1937*] and got a job, so this time [*1961, after being fired by the Yankees*] I laid out another year and that statement of yours [*earlier, off microphone, Meyer had asked him about the job offer he had received from the Detroit Tigers*], that's true. Mr. Fetzer [*John Fetzer, the Detroit owner*] came to see me himself and two of the — well, I guess they had two of the men who run the higher office [*the Detroit front office*] also called on me and asked if I would consider allowing my name to be used after, I think, they got rid of — Scheffling, wasn't it? *No!* They *hired* Scheffling [*Bob Scheffling, who became the Detroit manager in 1961*] when I told them Scheffling, uh, would be hired [*Casey recommended Scheffling*] and they said Scheffling instead of hiring three or four men that they had in view. I did. [*Recommended Scheffling, apparently.*] I still laid out a year. And then they [*the Continental League?*] offered me the opportunity so that Branch Rickey came and offered me a chance to go, uh, uh, if I would go, uh, in with the college team before they decided on expansion [*I think Casey means "Continental," not "college"*], which two teams not to use, or what teams to use. Why, he gave me a chance that I coulda gone with a club if he got in charge of it for an expansion, see? I mean, I coulda gone with him [*Rickey? Fetzer?*] but insteada that I had, uh, had, uh, Mrs. Payshon [*Joan Whitney Payson*] and, uh, Mr. Grant [*M. Donald Grant*] called me on the phone out on the coast twice and offered me a chance if I would go, and I said, no, I was gonna maybe lay out for the rest of the year. But insteada doin' that Mr. Weiss was down at a race-track, or in the winter he was in New Orlins, and he was also down in Florida, and he talked to him [*Grant talked to Weiss*] and he says [*Weiss says*], 'I myself will take a position over here with the Mets.' So they made him president of the Mets at that time and allowed him to get in touch with me, and then he convinced me after a period that I would go. Well, I was known in Brooklyn and I played with the Giants in '21, '22 and '23, when we played against Ruth and the Yankees, and I had a feeling out there that everybody knew me, see? More so than I would say to pick some other team. And when they decided they would start in the expansion league out in New York that's why I accepted the task. When Weiss took the job he convinced me that I could go there and do the best I could and they've been very nice to me up there. Of course, we were what you could call a complete flop." [*Voice lifting gently at the end*.]

Meyer says, "But in 1949 you were not a complete flop. Your first year with the Yankees, seventy-four injuries, and you still won yourself a pennant. You were like a magical wizard. How did you do it?"

"Well," says Stengel, "I believe it was platooning like the latest thing they asked me [*at the banquet*] and I never talked about it tonight [*pause, as though wondering why he* hadn't *talked about it*] was why is it now that I hope for you to have pinch hitters. I was a platoon manager, and McGraw platooned me, so if he platooned me I found out he was right, because he win three pennants [*during the three years Casey was with the Giants*]. And I felt when I started in baseball that they were not the same [*the two players being platooned?*]. They got twenty-four clubs [*there were twenty-four big-league teams in 1973*] and they can't fill the rosters. And I say right now with twenty-four clubs, as good as their training and their schools are to educate players, they're not whatcha want [*said almost sadly*]. In other words there still is too many holes to fill or some man gets sick or gets injured on ya and, uh, uh, it's, uh, it — [*he's forgotten the question and can't find his way back to it*]. To me they *have* to have platooning, and that gives an old man a job. Or if you owned a ball club for fourteen million or twelve million or ten million, how would you like to go along and say, 'I won't pinch-hit'? [*Stengel is objecting to players who object to platooning, who don't want to sit on the bench to be used as pinch hitters.*] Now, like I would say, 'The National League and you wouldn't pinch-hit?' Well, let me give you a good tip about it. What if you're in last place and you got new pinch hitters there and you turned them loose? Or what do ya, what if, how many men can hit good that are *pitchers?* Like today they honored Wood out there. [*Joe Wood, the famous old Boston Red Sox pitcher, who was honored at the banquet, was an excellent hitter, but Casey doesn't dwell on that and goes off on a tangent.*] I saw that man play, Wood. He's eighty-four years old and I'm eighty-two, and I watched him and I saw him today, you know, talked to him. I went out with my father to see him [*Wood was a Kansas City boy*], now think of that, though it's true. I, when I was seventeen years old and he was nineteen, and he was pitching when he was seventeen, so I was fifteen when I went out and saw him. I said, 'Oh my goodness.' I'm thinkin' then of maybe going in semipro ball. Later I worked up in the big league and, uh, so on and so forth [*Casey is trying to recall something*] and it's like — Waite Hoyt! Waite Hoyt come out [*to Ebbets Field for a tryout as a pitcher when Stengel was a player*] with, his mother made his trousers. And he pitched battin' practice when I was in a slump in the big league, and I got mad. Waite Hoyt is — I'm eighty-two, Waite Hoyt now must be seventy-one years of age, and when I saw him out there, fourteen or fifteen, I was mad that the ball club made me — give me him for batting practice, a young kid in town [*Hoyt was a schoolboy sensation*] that the pitcher brought up. But now that he's seventy and he been into Europe, been in a World Series. He shut out — in '21 he pitched for the Yankees and shut us out, twice, when I was with the Yankee ball — I mean the Giant ball club. Later on in life, just think, I went over to Europe and Asia with him, China, so forth. And he was an outstanding pitcher then [*when he was fourteen*] but he didn't *look* that way then, see? Now, now I'm seventy [*a slip of the tongue*] and I saw him in two of these meetings in the Hall of Fame and he's, uh, just think, he's seventy years old! Retired. I'm eighty-two [*correcting himself*]. But when I was twenty-four and that guy was only fourteen years old — now when they brought him out to the park I thought I'd *kill* him, you know, when he was just —

threw the ball up to the plate and the pitcher brought him out. We didn't have many men, and I was disappointed [*that I had to bat against a kid*]. But then in '21 in the World Series I saw what he could do. Then he got better different times. He was a fellow that took care of himself, changed his methods of living. [*Hoyt, a heavy drinker, stopped and became a success in Cincinnati as a play-by-play announcer.*] He was a young, wonderful kid, and a terrific kid, and a handsome kid. And he always went on the air and he worked for, always, somebody that was on radio. And he was such a handsome kid he ought to a been working on *television* when he started because he was, uh, uh, had, had beautiful looks and there's, uh, and he, uh, without going on very far, important to the team and a very good speaker. [*Stengel is trying to remember what he was talking about before he got off on the subject of Waite Hoyt. He can't regain the thread and so he finishes talking about Hoyt in a confidential tone.*] He laughs when he tells the jokes but they say you shouldn't do it, but he enjoys his own jokes and I guess [*chuckles*] that's why he laughs at them."

Meyer, going back to the topic Casey forgot, asks firmly, "How about your '49 club?"

"It was a very *good* club," Stengel says,

welcoming the topic back, "and I had the best man on the club was, who? Joe DiMaggio. He's worked up to be. When I took over the ball club they commenced losing some of their best players. Now I commenced then and I had Rizzuto at shortstop, and that's terrific. Now at second base we had four or five men, that I would say during the year which one would you play? I like Coleman for a double play [*Jerry Coleman*]. Beautiful, wonderful fellow, great. Could throw straight overhand and if it was an ordinary first baseman he [*Coleman*] never threw bad because he threw overhanded. If he threw sidearm the ball would sink and sink into the ground. So he became a good double-play man. And I had Rizzuto, who was perfect there [*at shortstop*]. Then later on I had, uh, naturally I had Martin that I brought up [*Billy Martin, who joined the Yankees in Casey's second year as manager*]. And they had to fight it out [*Martin and Coleman were both second basemen*]. Each one went away to the war and save me [*from picking one over the other*]. Like when Martin went into the service for a year, why I had McDougald to play for me [*Gil McDougald,*] and a very awkward man, a wonderful man. And now he's coaching now, I guess it's — is it Fordham he's coaching, or New York University? *Fordham*, yeah, and he's gonna be, I bet he'll be a splendid coach. 'Cause his wife writes me very good letters. Every Christmas she writes they have four or five kids and she writes what the four or five kids do almost every day of the year. And that's a terrific thing. We don't have any children. And I liked him and I liked her. We went to Europe [*he means a trip the Yankees made to the Orient after the 1955 season*] and she quit halfway over. I mean the Orient. She quit halfway on the trip because she was too excited and not having those children at home without her, see? So she left the club and went back there after a short trip over in the Orient. [*Mrs. McDougald went as far as Japan and then returned home.*] Then he became better than he looked [*not after his wife left; Casey means McDougald looked awkward when he arrived in the majors but proved to be a far better player than he appeared to be*]. And he always hit. And they used to say to me, 'Why do you play that man with that silly stance?' [*McDougald had an odd batter's stance.*] And I said, 'Al Simmons did it that way,' and Al Simmons [*now in the Hall of Fame*] did put his foot in the bucket, or bent over, you know? And this boy here [*McDougald*] with men on base was a terrific hitter, and he hurt his back the last

619

year he played for me and he didn't tell me, or they shoulda told me [*the doctors?*]. And I played him then at third again [*McDougald was a third baseman, later became a second baseman and then a shortstop before ending up on third again*], but if he'da been better — with a bad back you can't play third base because you gotta dip too quick, see? And when you're playin' shortstop even —. Amazing after Rizzuto went into television, he was amazing playing shortstop. [*McDougald, before he hurt his back, took over at shortstop when Rizzuto was released. Actually, he became the regular shortstop when Rizzuto was still with the team.*]

"And then he could, and I put him in there [*at shortstop*] without buying another shortstop [*to replace Rizzuto*] because for this reason: He said I could play it if I played a month. But he had a wonderful way of studying. He could *surmise* you're gonna hit it to your right or to your left when he played short. And he played deep and got rid of the ball quick. So he did an outstanding job where I could have blown, with the ball club being weak at short.

"I was so successful [*self-directed sarcasm*] after I found DiMaggio played for me. To think: There's a man played in a ball park that wasn't fitted for him. He played in a park that wasn't built for him. [*Yankee Stadium with its enormous left field works against right-handed batters like DiMaggio.*] Williams [*Ted*] played in a park where he hit to right field [*Fenway Park with its long right field, where the left-handed Williams had a problem similar to DiMaggio's in Yankee Stadium*] and — he should have — a right-hand man hits to left field and it looks like a bandbox [*Fenway, with its short left field*]. I used to say, well, uh, there with, uh [*a vague thought has distracted him; it's that Joe's brother, Dominic, a fine player and a right-handed batter, played for the Red Sox in Fenway without becoming a great hitter, and Stengel doesn't want to criticize him, especially to a Boston broadcaster*]. I had to say with DiMadge that if DiMadge had played in Boston — I don't mean that his brother wasn't great — but he should have played for us [*Williams, that is, not Dominic*] and somebody should've had DiMaggio there [*Fenway*] for years and he musta — he would've had an *outstanding* career, I imagine, of just tapping that ball and playing with it against that fence and — but he was terrific on my ball club. When I came up to the big leagues he was so good that I found out I never had to watch the outfield [*that is, signal the outfielders where to play*] because DiMaggio, wherever he went — if he went to the left center ya didn't have to yell at the right fielder or the left fielder. They shifted automatically. They were positive his judgment was right, and it was, too, and it saved me, too. Many a tight place where the ball was hit where this man was lodged out there in the proper position.

"Casey —" Meyer begins.

"I'd like," Stengel says, "the best pitchers. I'd like ya to ask about them sometime."

"Go ahead," Meyer says.

"Well, I tell ya why I liked the best pitchers. I — I never — the first pitcher I got there then I got stuck on was Reynolds [*Allie Reynolds, who with Vic Raschi and Ed Lopat formed the big three of Stengel's pitching staff through his early pennant-winning years*]. Because I put him in and he could strike out [*opposing batters*] and then I put him in one game to relieve and, my goodness, he got 'em out, and [*chuckles*] I had six pitchers back there. And the best part about pitching in that pitching staff was this. He [*Reynolds*] could start and he could relieve, and when I had the Quiz Kids — we were playing them. [*The young Philadelphia Phillies, whom the Yankees played in the 1950 World Series, were nicknamed the Whiz Kids, but Casey got that*] *name mixed up with the name of a popular radio quiz show of the late 1930s and early 1940s that featured precocious youngsters called the Quiz Kids.*] I had Ford pitch [*in the World Series against the Phils*] and people that never knew how to write a World Series with both ball clubs came from all over the United States just to get in on free tickets and write and never had sports editors. [*Casey sweepingly indicts the sportswriters who criticized his strategy in the 1950 Series.*] *They* wondered why I took Ford out in the seventh inning [*it was the ninth*] and it was true they hit some balls hard off Reynolds [*who relieved Ford*] and I know that he [*Ford*] always said, 'Well, that old man knows,' that I'm hired by the club when he [*Ford*] was in the Eastern League. Now the trouble with that [*the press criticism*] was this. That I went and put in Reynolds — when Reynolds went in there, they [*the Phillies*] put in a couple of their boys, sure they hit him, and they just *got* to make a *b-e-e-g* foul, you know? And *foul* and *foul*, and they were out. [*Casey has confused Reynolds' relief of Ford in the last game of the 1950 World Series — when he came in with two out in the ninth and struck out pinch hitter Stan Lopata, a power hitter who did hit a hard foul — with Reynolds' relief of Raschi in the last game of the*

1953 World Series, when he took over after the seventh inning, was hit hard but won the game and, as in 1950, the Series.]

"So," Casey goes on, "when I went in [*the clubhouse*] they quizzed me and said, 'Why'd you take that Quiz Kid out?' [*Meaning Ford, who was only twenty-one*.] And they'd been writing the Quiz Kwids [*sic*] with the Philadelphia players, but that was *wrong*. The Quiz Kid was *Reynolds*, and he was the oldest fella I had on the club [*delivered in an ingenuous Mark Twain "There you are" tone*].

"So he became a two-way man. Reynolds. Berra was catchin' good too then and we had a terrific thing with, uh, with, uh, I'd say Raschi. He was, uh, he was, I thought Raschi was the best pitcher I had on the team for nine innings [*meaning as a starting pitcher, in contrast to Reynolds, who could start and relieve*]. Now I tell ya why. Every time he pitched in the seventh, eighth and ninth he'd almost *die* out there, tryin' to throw a ball hard. He knew that he *tried* to put more on that ball now. If I'm *tired* [*great emphasis on "die" and "tried" and "tired," so that you hear the effort, hear the weariness*] my arm will have too many baseballs being called balls. That guy in the eighth and ninth inning he'd give me, he'd give me, I mean he was almost a sure bet and Berra admits that now, too. Boy, he was the best on the club in the eighth or ninth inning. But if I relieved with him, you'd be surprised. I was shocked. He couldn't do it.

"Now, Joe Page. Joe Page was what you'd call, well, they called him the fireman. Go up to Boston and they'd say, they got 'em now, they got the Yankees done. And I'd just call him in from the bullpen and when he went around there they'd start in fainting in the stands. They'd say, 'Oh my God, putting in that fireman.' And he did a tremendous job. He had guts. I believe in platooning pitchers now, too. And now they want to know why you can't pitch nine innings. Like Satchel Paige. I watched him pitch, but he had to pitch every day where he went. And I watched him when he had to rub it [*his arm, not the baseball*]. And you take now how scientifically they can hurt your arm, you know, at the elbow, or guys that work —. Well, we used to have to drive automobiles with a clutch. You'd get sore joints. [*From shifting gears?*] Like a hinge bad on a door, you can't close it. Nowadays the best thing that I saw in the great Case's opinion was, I think, is a — everybody has a doctor [*every team*]. Now the doctor don't mean very much — they do it for spring training [*the doctor comes to Florida for a vacation*]. And here every club now has an outstanding doctor. It's wonderful, but they just do —. I guess when they go and say —. [*Casey decides not to go on criticizing doctors*.] Well, with my experience, football, baseball, basketball, they got ways of handling fellas."

"Casey," says Meyer, ending the interview, "I'm going to use another word from your own vocabulary and that's 'amazing.' That's what you've been for these last twenty-five minutes. Thanks so very, very much."

"Yes, it's very good," Casey says, not ending the interview. "I wanted just to ask you another question about some of the players that I had I told you about when I changed to those other clubs. I had people come around and say, 'Well why don't ya?' [?] I used to have an interest in minor leagues and each time I had an interest was — it was to take young fellas and start 'em out. I believe in young fellas. I believe right now in young fellas. I believe right now that it's almost impossible to have some of the men not fail with the rapid thing of seeing a man's weakness. It used to be they [*young players*] didn't believe ya when you're watchin' the ball come across the plate. They [*the coaches*] would say, 'I'm tellin' ya this and you stand there. Do this, see? Look right at home plate. *Now* if you don't hit the ball you understand?' All right. Say, 'Well, you leaned in.' They say, 'Naw, I didn't.' Then if you show them that quick replay now do they get it? 'Well, uh,' they say, 'I swore I did not.' [*A strong protesting "Naw, I didn't," a meek embarrassed "I swore I did not."*]

"Well," says Casey, "the pitcher watches the ball and that's the reason why you lose what any other teacher would tell ya. And that's why if you lean in, there's six guys like Paige and he's watchin' ya, and if you lean in he goes around once more and he throw in here. How can you lean in and pull back and the distance is sixty feet? And that's why he [*Paige*] became great. I saw him when he could throw like lightning, and I asked him myself. Men interview him at times, you know. And semipro games. And he was great. And you know what he used to do? He used to go in under the hot shower and put the hot shower on him, you know? And this was his rub, because they never had the trainer. And then he'd pitch the next day because he was so well known in the small towns. Yeah, he did a big job.

"All right! [*Now he's finishing the inter-*

view]. It was very nice to do it. Nice to see ya here. I hope sometimes I can meetcha around. Very much enjoyed it, and I think I'll do better next time.

"If you wanta know this here year and know what I'm doin' at any time, I've had five or six offers to do this and that, you call me in Glendale, California, and I'll give you all the answers. And that's what I do now with the Mets. And they ask me. Well, I'm workin' for a woman [*Mrs. Payson*] and they ask me, 'Well, what do you do for 'em?' And I said, 'Well, I'm very careful now that I don't disturb 'em as they're doin' well without me.' I tell you what, I saw rapid advancement, rapid advancement. If you've got somebody and he says, 'Well, he's stupid, and he's laid up.' Half of the men that we used to get, they came in there and they —. I mean they were good enough but they *slowed* up for you. They had injury in their lives. Maybe trouble with — eye trouble. Maybe they'd say, 'I cannot see with one eye.' Maybe they had to say, 'Well, I tell you what, I can't pitch anymore but I can pitch three innings.' But Satchel Paige even said tonight he was going to spring training. He wouldn't pitch Friday and Saturday too. He never was a relief pitcher [*not in the Negro Leagues, but*

Paige was a relief pitcher in the American League]."

"Casey," says Meyer, "thanks again."

"You bet." Casey snaps it off vigorously. "I'll, uh, I'll go, uh, I'll have you in mind and anytime something comes up, ask me what. I told you about the pinch hitter and about the old man. The old man gets to play now, and if he plays —. If you own the ball club and you get the receipts, most of it, you better do well at home. You play half your games at home, and if you don't have a pinch hitter at home and your club is green, why you better have to play those home games in —. The older man gets to play two or three years longer in baseball where the young man in pinch hitting doesn't do great, *but* if the pitcher knew, I'm gonna throw the ball over the plate, the young man goes up, says, 'I'm gonna kill that pitcher.' And then he hits at bad pitches. But the old fella gets hit with the ball or makes you nibble on it.

"Thank you very much. I'm glad you give me that interview, and someday if you're in a pinch call me up and I'll have a better answer."

And that did end the interview.

33 *CODA:*
THE END OF A MAN

Casey didn't slow down until the last year, when the ravages of time began to tear him apart. Edna had a series of small strokes that left her mentally and physically incompetent. Stengel went alone to spring training in 1974, telling people about Edna. "She's no good from here up," he said, motioning from the neck. "She went crazy on me overnight." And, "I miss her."

She was confined to a nursing home in Glendale. Every day when he was home he'd visit her and sit by her bed, holding her hand and talking. She didn't respond. Old friends like Joseph Durso recalled the tremendous affection they had for one another, the amusement they derived from each other. Nat Holman, the old basketball player and coach, who was a bit of a blowhard, told Edna once that he had had a dream in which she and Casey arrive at Cooperstown in style, riding in a Rolls-Royce. Casey loved it when Edna said, "That's nice. Who pays for the Rolls-Royce?"

Edna had a clear eye for money, and together she and Casey made a great deal of it, although her end of their fortune was considerably larger than his, in good part because of her participation in Lawson family enterprises. When he died he left an estate of $807,000 (and supposedly $30,000 or so in cash that he had hidden around the house in Glendale). When she died two and a half years after he did, the entire estate, including real estate, was worth close to $3,000,000.

She enjoyed his lines, too. They were standing together at some affair or other when he turned to her and said conversationally, "They tell me your cream pie is very good." In one of his last seasons with the Mets, he popped out of the dugout before a game to talk to a Met official sitting in a box seat. To his surprise Edna was sitting there, too. Before he returned to the dugout he pointed a finger at her and said, "And you want to see me when the season's over, right?"

"Right," Edna said, smiling.

He continued to live in their big house in Glendale, helped now by a pleasant, middle-aged woman named June Bowlin, who acted as housekeeper, nurse, secretary and general factotum. His health began to go. At the 1974 World Series he ran into Maury Allen, who asked him how he felt. "Splendid, splendid," Stengel replied, "but I can't get my body going." Early in 1975 he caught the flu and was very sick for several weeks. He missed the New York baseball writers' dinner and there were rumors that he was dying, but when Allen called him from New York he said, "I didn't die. I just lost my voice."

Late in June he was in New York for the Mets' old-timers' game, looking unexpectedly old and frail, his head somehow tucked down between his shoulders. But he mugged for the photographers and otherwise was in top form. The Mets had arranged for various old-time heroes to make special entrances from center field. Ralph Kiner, the home-run hitter, rode in across the outfield in an old-fashioned surrey with a fringe on top. Joe DiMaggio and Willie Mays, the masterful center fielders, walked together through center field. And then the gates opened and Stengel entered, riding in a Roman chariot, waving a Ben Hur-style whip. He was wearing his old uniform with the familiar 37 across the back, and when his driver, wearing a Roman costume, stopped the chariot near the dugout Stengel hopped down and waved his whip at the crowd.

Afterward, though, when he spoke at the party the club held for the old-timers and the press, he appeared confused. His rambling speech was almost completely incoherent, but he kept going on and on, unable to stop. There was no humor, and no one was laughing. It was an awkward, embarrassing moment. Finally someone moved toward the microphone and signaled to the piano player, who began, "For He's a Jolly Good Fellow." Everyone joined in the singing and, as Harold Rosenthal said, "Stengel was laughed away from the mike, still rambling, his clenched fists punctuating the air. He flopped down at an empty table and stared at a disarray of used coffee cup. In retrospect, I should have punched the piano player right in the mouth."

He made one more appearance in Dodger Stadium in Los Angeles but after that spent most of his time at home. He didn't make the trip to Cooperstown. Few people in baseball realized how ill he was, but he had developed a form of lymphatic cancer. In September he went into Glendale Memorial Hospital, ostensibly for a checkup, but he was terminally ill.

He lay in bed watching baseball on television. There is a touching story about him in the hospital that I hope is true. Listening to the national anthem being played on television before a game he muttered, "I might as well do this one last time." He swung his legs over the side of the bed, got to his feet and stood at attention with his right hand over his heart, like a Kansas City schoolboy. On Monday, September 29, the day after the 1975 baseball season ended, he died. He was eighty-five.

His funeral did not take place until the following Monday. It was delayed that long because Monday was an off day during the pennant playoffs then under way in each league, and baseball people traveling west to the American League playoff in Oakland would be able to attend. Stengel might have enjoyed the humor in that: Funeral postponed because of game.

Dr. Kenneth A. Carlson, a Methodist minister, conducted the services at the Church of the Recessional at Forest Lawn Cemetery in Glendale. There were eulogies, heartfelt efforts to crystallize what Stengel meant to all those who had known him, but the best tribute was unintentional. As the congregation waited for the service to begin there were little whispers of conversation here and there, and then a low chuckle, a muffled laugh, a giggle. They were talking about Stengel, remembering him, telling stories about him, and the bubbles of laughter kept rising all through the church — "as though," Rosenthal said, "the mourners had completely forgotten the current condition of the guest of honor and the reason they were all there."

Richie Ashburn said, "Don't shed any tears for Casey. He wouldn't want you to. He loved life and he loved laughter. He loved people and above all he loved baseball. He was the happiest man I've ever seen."

AUTHOR'S NOTE

More than twenty-five years ago in a preface to his own book on Stengel, Frank Graham, Jr., wrote, "The biography of Casey Stengel is a persistent serial which grows day by day in the pages of America's newspapers and magazines. His real biographers are the sportswriters who have recorded his accomplishments and preserved the hundreds of anecdotes which have given Casey his unique place in the game of baseball."

I don't know how to improve on that except to add books, radio-television interviews and just plain old-fashioned storytelling to Graham's newspapers and magazines. Stengel's life is not a twice-told tale but a hundred-times-told tale. The same anecdotes appear over and over again in one form or another, and new ones keep cropping up. I have tried to verify and amplify them, and while I am not innocent enough to believe I have completely succeeded, I hope that I have tied many of the wild and cheerful and occasionally unpleasant stories to their proper place in the chronology of Casey's days and nights.

I wish I could list all those who have contributed to the "persistent serial," but it's not feasible. Sportswriters began focusing on Stengel the first day he played in the major leagues and they didn't stop until his death sixty-three years later — if they stopped then. There have been so many newspaper stories, so many articles, so many books, so many tapes, so many stories told over drinks or lunch or in passing.

I have mentioned many of my sources in the text, but I hope that everyone from whom I have derived knowledge of Stengel will accept as partly theirs the thanks I here extend to Ed Linn, Ken Meyer and Harold Rosenthal, who helped me the most, although I must mention at least a few of the others who have been particularly generous with their assistance and encouragement: Charlie Einstein, Roger Kahn, Bil Gilbert, Bob Broeg, Jack Mann, Don Honig, Cliff Kachline, John Thorn, John Holway, Roy Blount, Jr., Doug Bender, Kitchie Sanders, Kitty Hutchings, Charles Stinson, Bob Fishel, Jocko Conlan, Langston Rogers, Jim Creamer, John Creamer.

I also thank Peter Schwed, for suggesting the book, Herman Gollob, for his perceptive editing, and Dan Green, whose patience and understanding and advice have meant more to me than I can properly express.